Social Work and the Law

SOCIAL WORK AND THE LAW

Third edition

Stuart Vernon, JP, MA, LL B
Principal Lecturer in Law,
University of East London

Butterworths
London, Edinburgh, Dublin
1998

United Kingdom	Butterworths, a Division of Reed Elsevier (UK) Ltd, Halsbury House, 35 Chancery Lane, LONDON WC2A 1EL and 4 Hill Street, EDINBURGH EH2 3JZ
Australia	Butterworths, a Division of Reed International Books Australia Pty Ltd, CHATSWOOD, New South Wales
Canada	Butterworths Canada Ltd, MARKHAM, Ontario
Hong Kong	Butterworths Asia (Hong Kong), HONG KONG
India	Butterworths India, NEW DELHI
Ireland	Butterworth (Ireland) Ltd, DUBLIN
Malaysia	Malayan Law Journal Sdn Bhd, KUALA LUMPUR
New Zealand	Butterworths of New Zealand Ltd, WELLINGTON
Singapore	Butterworths Asia, SINGAPORE
South Africa	Butterworths Publishers (Pty) Ltd, DURBAN
USA	Lexis Law Publishing, CHARLOTTESVILLE, Virginia

A CIP Catalogue record for this book is available from the British Library.

ISBN 0 406 89427 2

Printed by Redwood Books, Trowbridge, Wiltshire

Visit us at our website: http://www.butterworths.co.uk

Acknowledgments

Thanks are due to a number of people. My interest in this field has been encouraged and sustained over a considerable period of time by Michael Preston-Shoot and Gwyneth Roberts, my two colleagues in the Social Work Law Research Group. In addition both have read, commented on, and corrected drafts and I am delighted to say that our work together and our friendship continues. Another long-time colleague and friend, Suzy Braye, has commented on individual chapters and provided me with valuable insights into professional practice. Colleagues from the University of East London have also been happy to comment on draft chapters and to help me with the technicalities of the law. I am delighted to record my thanks to Fiona Fairweather, Jane Pickford, Steve Gilmore and Paul Thompson. A special thanks goes to Mary Holmes who has written the chapter on Housing Rights. Her willingness to take on this work saved me from trying to up-date my sketchy knowledge of a complex area of law. Readers of the book will benefit considerably from this arrangement. All these people and many more, have supported me with their time and expertise. Errors in the text are my responsibility.

The acknowledgments to the previous two editions have commented on other types of help. This time I wish to acknowledge the sustaining help of Koblers Bakery, the Turks Head and the Finer Fare Expresso Bar. The ageing Amstrad word processor has now been retired, to be replaced by a PC that has performed almost faultlessly. I have also discovered the significant benefits of laser printers.

One word of reflection and advice! Writing law books during the first six months of a new government is a mistake; they are far too energetic. Consultation Papers, Green Papers, White Papers and Bills have all appeared during the last three months; it is an exciting and challenging time in social work law!

Once again my family have supported and encouraged me during the writing of this third edition. For this, and for many other things, I want to dedicate this to Sue, Kate and Laura with many thanks and much love.

St. Margarets.
December 1997.

Contents

Acknowledgments   v
Table of statutes   xv
List of cases   xxi
Using the book   xxiii
Introduction   xxvii

CHAPTER 1   SOCIAL WORK(ERS) AND LAW(YERS)   1

1   Social work practice within English law and the
    legal system   1
2   Working together – social workers and lawyers   5

CHAPTER 2   THE LEGAL SYSTEM   10

1   Introduction   10
    1.2   Content   10
2   The law and the legal system   11
    2.1   Where does the law come from and how does
          it change?   11
    2.2   Criminal law   17
    2.3   The civil law   19
    2.4   The House of Lords and the Court of Appeal   21
    2.5   Tribunals   21
    2.6   Legal services and legal aid   22
3   The law, the legal system and social work: some issues
    for discussion   25
    3.1   Legal services for service users   25
4   Activities   26
5   Addresses   27
6   Materials   28

CHAPTER 3   CHILD CARE LAW – THE CHILDREN
ACT 1989   29

1   Introduction   29
    1.1   Child care practice   29
    1.2   The emergence of the Children Act   31
    1.3   The Act   32
2   The law   33
    2.1   The principles of the new Act   34
    2.2   The court(s)   36
    2.3   Local authority services for children   37
    2.4   Secure accommodation   43
    2.5   The orders that can be made in family proceedings
          (other than care and supervision orders)   44
    2.6   Care and supervision orders   48
    2.7   Investigations ordered by the courts   54
    2.8   Protecting children at risk   55
3   The Children Act and social work: some issues
    for discussion   60
    3.1   Consulting and working in partnership with children
          and families   60
    3.2   Child protection   61
    3.3   Applications under the Children Act   63
    3.4   Representing the child – the role of the guardian
          ad litem   64
    3.5   The court welfare officer   66
    3.6   The tension between the courts and local authorities
          concerning children in care   66
    3.7   Social work in and for the family proceedings court   69
4   Case studies   70
5   Activities   73
6   Addresses   75
7   Materials   76

CHAPTER 4   CHILDREN WITH DISABILITY   79

1   Introduction   79
    1.1   Principles for practice   80
2   The law   81
    2.1   The Children Act 1989   82
    2.2   The Chronically Sick and Disabled Persons
          Act 1970   85
    2.3   The Disabled Persons (Services, Consultation and
          Representation) Act 1986   87

2.4   Education Act 1996   88
2.5   Housing and homelessness   91
2.6   Mental health services   92
2.7   Health care   93
2.8   Social security benefits   94
3   **Disabled children and social work: some issues for discussion   97**
3.1   Rights to services?   98
3.2   The quality of service delivery   104
4   **Case studies   105**
5   **Activities   106**
6   **Addresses   107**
7   **Materials   108**

CHAPTER 5   FAMILY BREAKDOWN   110

1   **Introduction   110**
1.1   Content   111
2   **The law   112**
2.1   Divorce   112
2.2   The matrimonial jurisdiction of the magistrates' courts   117
2.3   The work of probation officers in the Court Welfare Service   119
2.4   The implications of the Children Act 1989   120
2.5   Domestic violence   122
3   **Family breakdown and social work: some issues for discussion   128**
3.1   Reforming the law of divorce and separation   128
3.2   Mediation   129
3.3   Domestic violence, the law and social work practice   132
4   **Case studies   133**
5   **Activities   135**
6   **Addresses   136**
7   **Materials   138**

CHAPTER 6   COMMUNITY CARE LAW   140

Section 1   Community care law   140
1   **Introduction   140**
1.1   Community care: organisation and reform   141
1.2   Legal structure   143

2   The law   145
    2.1   The legislative structure of community care law (in
          chronological order)   145
    2.2   A wider community care law context   151
3   Complaints and other remedies for service users   156
    3.1   Complaints   156
    3.2   Default powers   157
    3.3   Complaint to the local authority monitoring officer   158
    3.4   Complaint to the local government ombudsman   158
    3.5   Applications for judicial review   159
    3.6   Breach of statutory duty   161
4   Community care, the law and social work practice: some
    issues for discussion   162
    4.1   Assessment, needs and resources   162
    4.2   Enforcing rights to community care services   165
    4.3   Residential care   167

Section 2   Vulnerable service users   170
1   Introduction   170
2   The law for work with vulnerable service users   172
    2.1   Community care law   172
    2.2   Personal welfare   173
    2.3   Elder abuse   175
    2.4   Mental health law   176
3   Reforming the law   177
4   Case studies   179
5   Activities   182
6   Addresses   183
7   Materials   185

CHAPTER 7   MENTAL HEALTH   187

Section 1   Mental disorder   187
1   Introduction   187
2   The law   189
    2.1   The Mental Health Act 1983   189
    2.2   Voluntary patients   191
    2.3   The work of the approved social worker   191
    2.4   Guardianship   196
    2.5   Emergency powers   197
    2.6   People with a mental disorder and the criminal justice
          system   197
    2.7   Patients' civil rights   200

2.8 Treatment 201
2.9 Discharge from hospital 203
2.10 The Mental Health Act Commission 205
2.11 The Court of Protection 205
2.12 Care in the community 206
3 Mental health law and social work: some issues for discussion 211
    3.1 Black and minority ethnic patients 211
    3.2 Care in the community 212
    3.3 Reform of the law and the organisation of psychiatric and social services for people with a mental disorder 215

Section 2 Mental incapacity 218
1 Introduction 218
2 The law 218
    2.1 Definitions 218
    2.2 The current legal structure 220
    2.3 Reform of the law 225
    2.4 Conclusion 229
3 Case studies 230
4 Activities 235
5 Addresses 236
6 Materials 237

CHAPTER 8 THE CRIMINAL JUSTICE SYSTEM 239

1 Introduction 239
    1.1 Social work involvement in the criminal justice system 239
    1.2 Reform of the system 239
    1.3 Principles of criminal justice and criminal law 240
2 The law 241
    2.1 The categories of criminal offences 241
    2.2 Bail 242
    2.3 Pre-trial procedure 244
    2.4 The criminal trial 244
    2.5 Sentencing in the adult criminal courts 246
    2.6 Sentences available in the adult court 249
    2.7 The criminal justicce work of the probation service 255
    2.8 The preparation of pre-sentence reports by the probation service 260

3 Criminal justice and social work: some issues for
    discussion 262
    3.1 Reform of the criminal justice system 262
    3.2 Race and criminal justice 265
    3.3 Racial violence 267
4 Case studies 268
5 Activities 270
6 Addresses 271
7 Materials 272

CHAPTER 9 YOUTH JUSTICE 274

1 Introduction 274
    1.1 Social work involvement in youth justice 274
    1.2 The politics of youth justice 275
    1.3 A model for youth justice? 275
    1.4 The principles of the Criminal Justice Act 1991 277
2 The law 277
    2.1 The child and young person as suspect 278
    2.2 The jurisdiction of the youth court 282
    2.3 The youth court 283
    2.4 Court proceedings 283
    2.5 Pre-sentence reports 284
    2.6 Sentencing youth offenders 285
    2.7 The range of sentences 288
    2.8 Appeals 296
3 Youth justice and social work: some issues for discussion 296
    3.1 The cautioning of youth offenders 296
    3.2 The youth court 299
    3.3 Reforming the youth justice system 301
4 Case studies 309
5 Activities 311
6 Addresses 313
7 Materials 314

CHAPTER 10 SOCIAL SECURITY BENEFITS 316

1 Introduction 316
    1.1 Social work and the social security system 316
    1.2 Materials 318
2 The law 318
    2.1 Contributory and non-contributory benefits 318

2.2   Means-tested and non-means-tested benefits   319
2.3   Benefits which act as passports to other benefits   319
2.4   Industrial and non-industrial benefits   319
2.5   Social security law   319
2.6   The adjudication procedure   320
2.7   Time limits for claims   320
2.8   The benefits   320
3   **Social work and social work: some issues for discussion**   335
3.1   Social work and the social fund   335
3.2   Enforcing social security rights   338
4   **Case studies**   339
5   **Activities**   341
6   **Addresses**   343
7   **Materials**   344

CHAPTER 11   DISCRIMINATION   345

1   **Introduction**   345
2   **The law**   348
2.1   Structure   348
3   **Discrimination law and social work: some issues for discussion**   354
3.1   The limits and enforcement of discrimination law   354
3.2   Racial violence and harassment   358
4   **Case studies**   359
5   **Activities**   362
6   **Addresses**   362
7   **Materials**   364

CHAPTER 12   HOUSING RIGHTS   366

1   **Introduction**   366
1.1   Allocation of local authority housing   366
1.2   Homelessness   367
1.3   Security of tenure and preventing harassment and unlawful evictions   367
1.4   Repairs   367
1.5   Housing benefit   368
1.6   The social work role   368
2   **The law**   368
2.1   Allocation   368

2.2 Homelessness   371
2.3 Security of tenure   378
2.4 Protection from eviction   382
2.5 Licensees   383
2.6 Squatters   383
2.7 Anti-social behaviour and noise   384
2.8 Housing repairs   384
2.9 Housing benefit   389
2.10 Council tax benefit390
3   **Housing law and social work: some issues for discussion   391**
3.1 Other aspects of housing for particular service users   391
3.2 Enforcing 'housing rights'   392
4   **Case studies   393**
5   **Activities   394**
6   **Addresses   395**
7   **Materials   396**

Index   399

Table of statutes

References printed in **bold** type indicate where the section of an Act is set out in part or in full

PAGE

Access to Personal Files Act 1987 14
Adoption Act 1976 125
Bail Act 1976 .... 243, 280
Bail (Amendment) Act 1993 243
Carers (Recognition and Services) Act
   1995 .... 13, 80, 81, 84,
                141, 151, 185
  s 1(1) **150**
    (2) **83**
Child Care Act 1980 79
Child Support Act 1991 .... 112, 114,
                   118, 328
Child Support Act 1995 .... 112, 118
Children Act 1989 .... 3, 11, 12, 13,
          19, 23, 29, 54, 60, 70,
        72, 76, 77, 79, 80, 81,
        91, 98, 99, 100, 103,
      105, 109, 110, 120, 125,
     133, 134, 138, 167, 176,
     177, 215, 228, 276, 278,
      290, 299, 300, 354
  Pt I (ss 1–7), II (ss 8–16) 32, 37, 47,
              130, 131, 132
  Pt III (ss 17–30) 32, 37, 39, 42, 62,
           67, 82, 83, 87, 130,
        210, 367, 374, 392
  Pt IV (ss 31–42) 32, 35, 37, 47,
         48, 65, 130, 131
  Pt V (ss 43–52) 16, 32, 37, 55,
         65, 130, 131
  Pt VI–IX (ss 53–70) 32
  Pt X (ss 71–78), XI (ss 80–84) 33
  Pt XII (ss 85–108) 33
  s 1 .... 2, 7, **31**, 34, 45, 48,
         50, 51, 66, 73, 112,
           114, 119
    (1) **35**
      (a) 67
    (2) **35**

PAGE

Children Act 1989–*contd*
  s 1(3) 35, 45, 48, 50, 66, 116, 345
    (5) **35**
    2(1), (2) **44**
    3(1) **36**
    4 .... 66, 131
      (1)(a) 44
      (3) 36
    7 .... 66, 111
    8 .... 35, 37, 45, 47, 51, 66,
          111, 114, 116, 118,
          121, 131
    11(4) 46
    12 45
      (2) 46
    16 .... 48, 111
    17 .... 39, 82, 92
      (1) **34**, 37, 84
      (3), (5) 84
      (6) 38, 84
      (10) 37, 82, **209**
      (11) **82, 209**
    18 39
    20 85
      (1) **39**
        (c) 85, 92
      (4)–(9), (11) 40
    22(3) **41,** 67
        (a) 85
      (4) 41, 61
      (5) 41
        (c) 347
    23(2), (5) 41
      (6) 42, 61
      (8) 85
    25(1) **43**
    26 102
      (3)–(6), (8) 42
      (7) **43**

PAGE

Children Act 1989–*contd*
s 27 62
  31 .... 45, 66
    (2) 7, **49**, 51, **117**
    (9) 50
  31(10) **50**
  33(3) **52**
  34 .... 52, 61, 68
    (1) 41, 52, 68
    (6) 52
  35(1) 53
  36 .... 4, 54
    (4) **54**
  37 .... 111, 114, 123
    (1) 54
  38 59
    (1), (4), (6) 51
  38A 127
  39 54
  41 64
  42(1) 65
  43 123
    (1) **56**
  44 .... 45, 59, 123
    (1) **57**
  44A 127
  46 59
  47 63
    (1) **55**
  48(9) 58
  100 66
    (3), (4) 67
  Sch 2 .... 37, 39, 83, 84, 210,
                            274, 367, 392
  Pt I 38
    para 1, 2 .... **82**
      3 83
      4, 5 .... **82**
      7(c) 33
      8 .... **83**
      15 42
  Sch 3
    Pt I, II 53
    Pt III 54
Children and Young Persons Act
  1933 278
  s 34A 283
  44 .... **276,** 277, 300
    (1) 286
  53 .... 282, 295, 306
Children and Young Persons Act 1969 ... 49,
                                   285, 296
  s 12(2)(a) **290**

PAGE

Children and Young Persons Act 1969–
  contd
  s 12(b) **289**
    12A(3)(a) **289, 290**
      (b), (c) **289**
    12AA **290**
    12B, 12C, 12D **290**
    15(3)(a) 290
    23 280
      (5) **281**
Chronically Sick and Disabled Persons
  Act 1970 .... 15, 79, 80, 81, 83,
                      100, 141,
                      172, 210
  s 1 .... 85, 146
  2 .... 86, 87, 98, 146, 147,
                      148, 150, 160, 162, 164,
                      206, 208, 392
    (1) 87, 161, 164,
    165, 166
      (e) **391**
Community Care (Direct Payments)
  Act 1996 .... 141, 151, 185
Courts and Legal Services Act 1990 21
Crime (Sentences) Act 1997 .... 19, 240,
                                246, 247
Criminal Justice Act 1991 .... 2, 4, 12,
                                33, 240, 246, 247, 250,
                                257, 259, 260, 262, 277,
                                286, 299, 300, 306
  s 1(2) **254, 294**
    (3) **254, 295**
  3 254
    (1) 285
  4 255
  6(1) **289**
    (2) 248, 289
  7 285
  8(1) 251
  11 252
    (2) **293**
  12, 13 252
  18 .... 249, 288
  28 287
    (1) 248
  29 .... 249, 287
    (1) 287
  31(2) **254**
  58(2), (3) 287
  95 .... 265, 266, 267, 347,
                          353, 354
  Sch 2 253
Criminal Justice Act 1993 .... 240, 247

PAGE

Criminal Justice and Public Order
    Act 1994 .... 11, 240, 241,
        242, 243, 247, 253, 285,
           294, 298, 300
s 1(5) **296**
  34, 35 284
Criminal Procedure and Investigations
    Act 1996
s 49 241
Criminal Procedure (Insanity and
    Unfitness to Plead) Act 1991 .. 200
Defective Premises Act 1972
s 4 385
Disability Discrimination Act 1995 ... 345,
        347, 350, 355, 356,
           357, 362
Pt II (ss 4–18) 349
s 1(1) **349**
Disabled Persons (Services, Consul-
    tation and Representation) Act
    1986 .... 79, 80, 81, 83,
        100, 141, 142
s 1–3 12
  4 .... 87, 148, 162
  5, 6 87
  7 .... 12, 208
  8 .... 87, 149
Domestic Proceedings and Magistrates'
    Courts Act 1978 ...... 117, 119, 121
s 8 118
Domestic Violence and Matrimonial
    Proceedings Act 1976 123
Education Act 1981 .... 88, 91
Education Act 1993 .... 90, 91
Education Act 1996 .... 81, 83, 87, 91
s 312 .... **88**
  321, 323, 324 89
  325, 326 90
  333–336 90
Enduring Powers of Attorney Act
    1985 .... 153, 223
Environmental Protection Act 1990
s 79 386
  80, 82 .... 386, 388
Family Law Act 1996 .... 110, 126, 127,
    132, 134, 136, 138, 176
Pt I (s 1) 128
Pt II (ss 2–25) 112, 120, 128
Pt IV (ss 30–63) 121, 123, 125,
        131, 139
s 13 129
  (1) **130**
  26 130

PAGE

Family Law Act 1996–*contd*
s 42(5) 123
  45(2) **124**
  47 125
  52 59
  60 125
  62 124
  Sch 6 59
Family Law Reform Act 1969 93
Health Services and Public Health
    Act 1968
s 45 .... 146, 149, 170
Housing Act 1985 .... 386, 387
s 190 388
  264 388
Housing Act 1988 .... 379, 380
Housing Act 1996 .... 133, 209, 366,
        367, 379
Pt VI (ss 159–174) 368
Pt VII (ss 175–218) 371, 378
s 152–158 384
  167(2) 369
  175–177 372
  179 .... 371, 377
  184 377
  185, 189 373
  191 375
  193 .... 370, 376
  (2) 92
  194 .... 370, 376
  195(2) 370
  197 376
  198 375
  213 374
Housing Grants, Construction and
    Regeneration Act 1996 155,
        389, 391
s 24(3) 92, 156
Housing (Homeless Persons) Act 1977: 371
Land Compensation Act 1973
s 39 388
Landlord and Tenant Act 1985 388
s 11 385
Legal Aid Act 1988 .... 22, 23, 130
s 15(3)F 131
  G 131
Local Authority Social Services Act
    1970 100
s 7 .... 13, 33, 61, 89, 169
  (1) **13, 144**, 160, 161
  7A(1) 12, 144
  7B 99, 156
  7D 157

PAGE

Local Government Act 1972
 s 111 84
Local Government and Housing Act
   1989 158
Matrimonial and Family Proceedings
   Act 1984 115
Matrimonial Causes Act 1973 .... 112, 121
 s 25 115
   25A 115
   41 114
Matrimonial Homes Act 1983 121
Mental Health Act 1959 ..... 188, 201, 215
Mental Health Act 1983 ...... 92, 153, 176,
         177, 188, 210, 215, 221,
         231, 232, 235, 238, 354
 Pt II (ss 2–34) 193
 Pt IV (ss 56–64) 201, 202
 Pt VII (ss 93–113) 205
 s 1(2) 175, **189,** 219
   (3) 190
   2 .... 195, 199, 203, 211, 219
   (2) 194
   3 .... 148, 151, 193, 194, 195,
         199, 206, 211, 219,
         233, 234
   4 .... 193, 211, 219
   5 191
   7 .... 151, 196
   8–10 151
   12(2) 193, 195
   13 .... 191, 192
   (2), (4) 192
   23, 25 203
   26 192
   29 195
   35, 36 198
   37 .... 148, 199, 206
   41 .... 199, 204, 206
   47, 48 .... 148, 199, 206
   57, 58 .... 201, 202, 205
   63 202
   66 203
   (1)(g) 204
   72(1) **204**
   95 .... **223**
   114(2) 187
   117 .... 93, 148, 149, 161, 166,
         170, 206, 207, 208,
         212, 213, 216
   (2) 148
   132 200
   135 .... 192, 197, 211, 219
   (1) **174, 224**

PAGE

Mental Health Act 1983–*contd*
 s 136 .... 197, 211, 219
   (1) **175, 225**
   139 200
Mental Health (Amendment) Act
   1982 188
Mental Health (Patients in the Community) Act 1995 ..... 93, 141, 150,
         189, 210, 214, 216
National Assistance Act 1948 ..... 4, 79, 82
 Pt III (ss 21–36) 149, 170, 175,
         225, 391
 s 21 .... **145**, 146, 170, **173**, 377,
         391, 392
   26 146
   29 .... 145, 146, 147, 162, 170,
         172, 206, 391, 392
   (1) **145**
   31 143
   47 .... **173,** 176
National Assistance (Amendment)
   Act 1951 174
National Health Service Act 1977: 82, 206
 s 3 170
   21 149
 Sch 8 .... 79, 149, 170
   para 1 147
   2 147
   (1) 84
   3 .... 84, 147
National Health Service and Community
   Care Act 1990 .... 11, 82, 141,
         150, 208, 209,
         336, 391, 392
 Pt III (ss 42–50) 143
 s 21 170
   46(3) 149
   47 .... 163, 173
   (1) **149,**162, 164, **172**
   (2) 149
   50 156
Noise Act 1996 384
Offences Against the Person Act
   1861 359
Police and Criminal Evidence Act
   1984 24
 s 17(1)(e) 59
   38(6) 280
   47(1A) 279
   58(1) 278
Powers of Criminal Courts Act 1973 ... 250
 s 2 .... **251,** 257
   (1) 257, **292**

PAGE

Powers of Criminal Courts Act 1973–
    contd
  s 3 .... **257**
  22 255
Probation of Offenders Act 1907 255
Probation Service Act 1993 255
Protection from Eviction Act 1977 382,
                                   383
Protection from Harassment Act
    1997 .... 240, 262, 265, 268,
                            359, 384
  s 2 353
  3(3) 127
  4 353
  5 127
Public Order Act 1986 .... 268, 348, 359
  s 4 .... **352**
  4A **352**, 353
  5 .... 352, **353**
  17 351
  18, 19 .... 350, **351**

PAGE

Race Relations Act 1976 .... 345, 346,
                            348, 355
  s 71 .... 347, **350**
Registered Homes Act 1984 169
  s 5(3) 168
  11 168
Registered Homes (Amendment) Act
    1991 .... 168, 169
Rent Act 1977 379
Sex Discrimination Act 1975 345,
                            347, 348
Sexual Offences Act 1956
  s 14 282
Social Security Act 1986 .... 12, 329
Social Security Administration Act
    1992 325
Social Security Contributions and
    Benefits Act 1992 .... 325, 329,
                                 389
Welsh Language Act 1993 355

List of cases

PAGE

A

A v Liverpool City Council (1982), HL 66

B

B (minors) (termination of contract: paramount consideration), Re (1993), CA 68
B v Croydon Health Authority (1995), CA 202

C

C (a minor) (care proceedings), Re (1992) 67
C (adult: refusal of treatment), Re (1994) 202, 219
C (a minor) (interim care order: residential assessment), Re (1997), HL 51
C (a minor) (medical treatment: court's jurisdiction), Re (1997) ... 93, 94

D

D (a minor) (contact: mother's hostility), Re (1993), CA 46

F

F (mental patient: sterilisation), Re (1990), HL 220, 227
F (minors) (denial of contact), Re (1993), CA 46
F v West Berkshire Health Authority (1989) 14

G

G (a minor) (parental responsibility order), Re (1994), CA 45
Gillick v West Norfolk and Wisbech Area Health Authority (1986), HL 30, 93

PAGE

H

H (minors) (local authority: parental rights) (No 3), Re (1991), CA .. 45
H (minors) (access), Re (1992), CA 46
H and R (minors) (sexual abuse: standard of proof), Re (1996), HL 50
Humberside County Council v B (1993) 50

K

KDT (a minor), Re (1994), CA 67
King v South Northamptonshire District Council (1992), CA ... 386

M

M (a minor) (care order: threshold conditions), Re (1994), HL 49
Marshall v Southampton and South West Hampshire Area Health Authority (Teaching): 152/84 (1986), ECJ 357

N

Northamptonshire County Council v S (1993) 49

P

P (terminating parental responsibility), Re (1995) 45

R

R (minors) (care proceedings: care plan), Re (1994) 67
R v Avon County Council, ex p M (1994) 160
R v Birmingham City Council, ex p A (1997) 102
R v Devon County Council, ex p Baker (1995), CA 160

PAGE

R v Duggan (1995), CA 353, 359

R v Durham County Council, ex p
Curtis and Broxson (1995), CA .. 160

R v Ealing District Health Authority,
ex p Fox (1993) 148, 161, 208

R v Gloucestershire County Council,
ex p Barry (1997), HL 8, 14,
15, 86, 98, 161,
163, 165

R v Gloucestershire County Council,
ex p Mahfood (1995) 160

R v Islington London Borough
Council, ex p Rixon (1997) 13,
144

R v Managers of South Western
Hospital, ex p M (1994) 204

R v Meredith (1994), CA 285

R v Norfolk County Council Social
Services Department, ex p M
(1989) 62

R v North Yorkshire County
Council, ex p Hargreaves
(1994) 100, 157, 160

PAGE

R v Northavon District Council, ex
p Smith (1994), HL 92, 374

R v Ribbans (1995), CA 353, 359

R v Ridley (1995), CA 353, 359

R v Sefton Metropolitan Borough
Council, ex p Help the Aged
(1997), CA 165

R v Tower Hamlets London
Borough Council, ex p Bradford
(1997) 92

S

S (J) (a minor), Re (1993) 53

S (a minor) (parental responsibility),
Re (1995), CA 45

Sharpe v Manchester Metropolitan
District Council (1977) 385

South Glamorgan County Council v
W and B (1993) 51

W

W (a minor) (medical treatment), Re
(1993), CA 93

Using the book

This book is written as a basic text for the law components of the Diploma in Social Work; the qualifying course taken by social work students. It is also expected that it will be of use to those in practice, particularly in the years immediately after qualification, and to a wider audience within the legal profession and those working within the general field of social welfare and social welfare law.

The subject matter included ranges from the law that is relevant to the major areas of practice, such as child care, child protection, youth justice and work with people who have a physical disability or learning disablement, to areas of law which are relevant across the full spectrum of practice and service users such as social security benefits, housing rights and discrimination. Every attempt has been made to place the discussion of law within the context of practice and to identify the dynamics of the relationship between law and social work practice.

Since the publication of the first edition of this book the statutory framework of social work has undergone a number of significant changes. The Children Act 1989 was implemented in October 1991, the Criminal Justice Act 1991 in October 1992 and the National Health Service and Community Care Act 1990 in April 1993. If anything, the changes in social work law have increased in number and speed since the publication of the second edition in 1993. The complexity of community care law has been increased by the implementation of the Carers (Recognition and Services) Act 1995, the Mental Health (Patients in the Community) Act 1995 and the Community Care (Direct Payments) Act 1995. Criminal justice has seen the Criminal Justice and Public Order Act 1994, and the youth justice system is about to be radically reformed by the Crime and Disorder Bill 1997. In the field of mental incapacity, the Lord Chancellor's department has issued a Green Paper to consult on reforming the law as proposed by the Law Commission in its 1995 report, *Mental Incapacity*.

An attempt has been made to make each chapter self-contained in the sense that each provides a discussion which can stand on its own without the need for frequent cross references to other chapters. This allows readers to dip in and out of the book when and where necessary. This has meant that there are some inevitable overlaps, particularly in the chapters on the criminal justice system and youth justice, in the three chapters on the Children Act 1989, family breakdown, and children with disability, and between the chapters on community care law, children with disability and mental health.

THE STRUCTURE OF THE BOOK

The chapters in this third edition have been re-ordered to better reflect the organisation of diploma courses and the legal context of practice. The Introduction and chapters 1 and 2 consider the development of the subject area, the relationship between social workers and lawyers, and the legal system and the courts as a site for social work. Chapters 3, 4 and 5 cover the law as it relates to work with children and families. Chapters 6 and 7 discuss the law for adult services and broadly covers community care law and mental health. Chapters 8 and 9 are concerned with the law as it relates to social work practice within the criminal justice system and the youth justice system. Chapters 10, 11 and 12 deal with particular aspects of social welfare law, social security benefits, discrimination and housing rights, and the context they provide for practice.

Each chapter of the book, except for the chapters on the legal system and on social workers, lawyers and the courts, follows the same format. It is hoped that once readers become familiar with the structure they will be able to use those parts of each chapter which are appropriate to their course or to their particular needs.

An INTRODUCTION seeks to set the scene by establishing the relationship between the particular aspect of the law considered in the chapter and social work practice. Some information on chapter content may also be provided.

The section on THE LAW provides information on the relevant law and legal processes, placing such information in the context of practice wherever possible.

The discussion section of each chapter deals with issues concerning the relationship between law and social work that are of significance or contemporary interest. The section is entitled to reflect the subject matter of the chapter, eg 'THE CHILDREN ACT AND SOCIAL WORK: issues for discussion'. Often this section will look at the debate or agenda for reform.

As part of a desire to allow the book to be used within a model of interactive teaching and learning each chapter provides a number of CASE STUDIES which can be used as a basis for consolidating an understanding of the area of law, for discussing how the law relates to practice and for identifying models of legally competent practice. There are no right answers to these case studies, they are merely vehicles for teaching and learning, to be used where they might be of some benefit.

The ACTIVITIES section is included to encourage an active participation in learning which goes beyond the classroom and the agency placement. Some of the suggested activities can be used to consolidate work done in college or on placement, others are specifically designed to enable students to build up collections of materials and to keep up to date with contemporary developments in both the law and practice.

A selection of ADDRESSES and telephone numbers are included to enable students to contact pressure groups, publishers and other interests. Again, this information is included as part of the objective of making the book participative and of studying law in the context of social work practice.

No attempt has been made to provide a definitive list of relevant groups and addresses. The more use is made of the ACTIVITIES and ADDRESSES sections the more names and addresses will be identified. There is an enormous amount of good quality materials available to those who are interested, and a surprising amount is available free of charge.

Suggested MATERIALS have been identified in the final section of each chapter. Again, this is not intended to be definitive, but merely to give some indication of materials which will be useful to social work practitioners.

STUDYING SOCIAL WORK LAW

The need continually to up date information and build up a set of materials on the law as it relates to social work practice complements the desire to make the teaching and learning of law on social work courses a participative exercise. There are, of course, a number of ways of achieving this objective and examples are to be found in the activities section of each chapter. Students can also be encouraged to keep a 'scrap book' of newspaper cuttings; the quality press coverage of relevant issues is considerable and is a good source of comment and information. Video collections can be established by groups of students and small study groups can share information and materials collected whilst on placement. Bulletin boards can be created and continually up-dated to the benefit of the whole course group. Web sites on the internet can be accessed to extend and update materials, and courses could even create their own web sites as a means of disseminating information and materials. Involvement in creating course materials and using such materials to extend the basis for discussion can only enhance the quality of a course and of student commitment to it.

Teachers and tutors will have developed their own individual courses and methods over a period of time and there is no intention to supplant tried and successful methods and materials. This book is intended to be used as a vehicle for teaching and learning and it can be used in a number of different ways. Nonetheless it is hoped that it will be found useful, and that it will help in consolidating 'social work and the law', or 'social work law', as a major element of social work training courses and an enjoyable and stimulating discourse within social work.

Introduction

The two previous editions of this book, published in 1990 and 1993, made frequent reference to the rapid pace of change in the law as it relates to the professional practice of social work. This third edition confirms and reflects the continuing pace and substance of change in what we might now call 'social work law'.

The implementation of the Children Act in October 1991, the Criminal Justice Act 1991 in October 1992, and the community care aspects of the National Health Service and Community Care Act 1991 in April 1993 established a significant element of the statutory framework for social work practice within a relatively short space of time. However the period since this legislative 'spree' has seen no reduction in the pace and substance of change in social work law. The 1993 Criminal Justice Act amended the 1991 Act, and the Criminal Justice and Public Order Act 1994 is now in force. In the community care field both the Carers (Recognition and Services) Act 1995 and the Community Care (Direct Payments) Act 1996 have been implemented, and in the related field of mental health care the Mental Health (Patients in the Community) Act 1995 has introduced compulsory care in the community for those patients discharged from hospital subject to a supervised discharge order. In addition to changes in the statutory base of social work, case law is increasingly having a significant impact on professional practice. The body of case law under the Children Act is considerable and cases such *Re H and R (child sexual abuse: standard of proof)* [1996] 1 FLR 80, which considered the threshold criteria for care orders, have an inevitable impact on practice. The field of community care law has featured regularly in the courts since the community care aspects of the National Health Service and Community Care Act were implemented in 1993, and the vexed issue of resources and their impact on assessment has now been considered by the House of Lords in *R v Gloucestershire County Council, ex p Barry* [1997] 2 WLR 459.

It is becoming increasingly clear that community care law is in urgent need of consolidation into one piece of legislation which could then have the same impact as the Children Act has had for practice with children and families. Reform of the Mental Health Act has long been promised and the recent publication, by the Lord Chancellor's Department, of a Green Paper on reforming the law on mental incapacity suggests that major changes are to be expected in this important area of law. The labour government has moved quickly to reform the youth justice system. A White Paper, *No More Excuses – A New Approach To Tackling Youth Crime in England and Wales*, CM 3809, was published in November 1997 and the Crime and Disorder Bill, which contains many of the reform provisions, was itself published in December 1997. It seems that social work law will continue to change; the necessity for practitioners to be informed of current law and to be conscious of the agenda for reform remains as important as ever.

SOCIAL WORK AND THE LAW

The law sets the statutory framework for social work in a number of settings and with particular groups of service users and their carers. This aspect of the relationship between law and social work practice is sometimes identified by the phrase 'the professional law of social work'. Recent writing has suggested a new designation which distinguishes between 'social work law' and 'social welfare law'.[1]

The areas of practice which are constituted by the legal mandate include child care, mental health, work with people who are vulnerable because of a chronic illness, physical disability or learning disablement, youth justice and probation work. Within these areas of work the statutory mandate is marked out by a number of powers and duties enacted by Parliament. Examples include the power of a local authority to take care proceedings under section 31 of the Children Act 1989 and the duty of a local authority under section 47 of the same Act to investigate any situation where they have information suggesting that there may be grounds for bringing care proceedings in respect of a child or young person in their area. In such areas of practice the statutory responsibility is placed on a local

---

1   Preston-Shoot, M, Roberts, G and Vernon, S, *Social Work Law: From Interaction to Integration*, Journal of Social Welfare and Family Law [1998] Vol 20, No 1, 65-80.

authority who discharge their duties or powers through day to day delegation to practitioners. Other powers and duties are designated by statute to individual social workers rather than local authorities; an example is the power of an approved social worker to apply for the admission of a patient to psychiatric hospital under the provisions of the Mental Health Act 1983.

An explanation of the concepts of a 'power' and a 'duty' is necessary. A 'power' is an enabling concept, it allows a local authority or social worker to decide whether to do something. In statute the word 'may' is most often used to establish a power. A 'duty' imposes a statutory obligation on an authority or social worker to do something, to perform or discharge the duty. In statute the word 'shall' is used to establish a duty. Powers and duties are important concepts in the professional law of social work and it is necessary to understand when a power is provided by Parliament and when a duty is imposed.

'Powers' and 'duties' are often joined with the concept of a 'right'. This concept is less easy to define and it is usually used to describe an entitlement to something as in 'welfare rights'. The notion of a right should be widely understood and can encompass eg housing rights and the right of everyone, including social workers and service users, not to be discriminated against on the basis of race, gender or disablement. These are legal rights in the sense that they may be enforced through the law. Other rights are more nebulous eg the right of an elderly person to be treated with dignity and the right of patients to self determination.

It is clear therefore that the relationship between law and social work extends beyond the statutory framework of powers and duties covered by social work law to encompass other areas of law such as housing law, social security law and discrimination law where service users and their carers have legal 'rights'. These areas of law are properly thought of as elements of social welfare law.

The ability to enforce entitlement to social work law rights and to social welfare law rights is also important, so that an understanding of the legal system and of legal services is also necessary to enable service users and their carers to gain access to the law. The notion of social welfare law incorporates these matters and extends the legal framework for social work practice to include quasi-legal processes such as community care complaints procedures and referrals to the local ombudsman.

PUBLIC CONCERN OVER SOCIAL WORK AND THE LAW

That the law is these days publicly acknowledged as one of the principal contexts of social work practice is due to a number of factors. The published reports of child abuse inquiries in the late 1980s received enormous media comment; in turn so did later reports on the experience of children whilst in the care of local authorities in different parts of the country and more recently by enquiries into the care of children who were being looked after under the control of local authorities. Similar concerns have been expressed upon the publication of reports into the care of vulnerable people in residential homes.

The high profile implementation of the Children Act 1989 took place at the same time as the public debate concerning policies associated with community care provisions of the National Health Service and Community Care Act. Publicity surrounding the sentencing provisions of the Criminal Justice Act 1991 was significant, as was concern about the provision of secure training orders in the Criminal Justice and Public Order Act 1994. Indeed the youth justice system and juvenile crime continues to attract considerable public interest. The result is that issues concerning the legal context surrounding social work now 'enjoy' a high public profile at the same time as professional interest is centred on the further development of good practice under the Children Act, the Criminal Justice Act 1991, and the complex canopy of community care legislation.

THE POSITION OF LAW IN SOCIAL WORK TRAINING

In social work education the importance of the legal context has been recognised for some considerable time. In 1974 the Central Council for Education and Training in Social Work (CCETSW) published Paper 4 'Legal Studies in Social Work Education'. The group concerned in preparing the report had received a number of criticisms about the state of social workers' knowledge of law. These criticisms centred on a perceived lack of knowledge and understanding of the specific law relating to the professional practice of social work and of the administration of the law and the legal system. Concern was also expressed that social workers lacked knowledge of their clients' general legal rights. The report advocated an increased recognition of the importance of law teaching in social work education and offered a quite detailed framework for the necessary development. However, new research undertaken in 1987, and published by

CCETSW in 1988 as Paper 4.1 'The Law Report, Teaching and Assessment of Law in Social Work Education', found that on many courses law teaching was still very much a marginal activity and that there were huge variations in the quality of law teaching, the content of law courses and of commitment to it as a major area of study for social work students. In the more than ten years since Paper 4 had been published it seemed that little had changed.

The publication of the Law Report came in the same era as the publication of the reports of a number of major child abuse inquiries. They drew specific attention to the legal aspects of child care practice and of child protection work. Indeed Louis Blom-Cooper in 'A Child in Trust: The Report of the Panel of Inquiry into the Circumstances Surrounding the Death of Jasmine Beckford' paid particular attention to social work training and to the place of law teaching in it. Dissatisfaction with the situation exposed by the inquiry is reflected in the report's comment that 'Training in legal studies must not be allowed to remain any longer the Cinderella of social work training.'

The Social Work and Law Group which undertook the research that formed the basis of the Law Report continued their work after its publication and with a research grant from CCETSW undertook a further investigation in 1989 which was able to identify an increased interest in, and commitment to, law teaching and assessment on social work courses. [2]

Reforms in social work education in the early 1990s resulted in the establishment of the Diploma in Social Work subject to the 'Rules and Requirements for the Diploma in Social Work' (CCETSW 1991, Paper 30). In 1990 CCETSW initiated a Law Improvements Project to inform the law elements of the new Diploma.

The aims of the project were to improve the quality and effectiveness of the teaching and learning of law and of the assessment of legal competence on social work qualifying courses. More particularly the project was charged with identifying the core competencies (knowledge, skills and values) in law required of all social workers; with working towards the effective integration of college and placement based law teaching and learning; and in developing teaching methods and models of good practice for achieving these.

---

2 *Towards Social Work Law: Legally Competent Social Work Practice*, published by CCETSW in 1990 as Paper 4.2.

The project was completed in 1991 and its report was published by CCETSW in October of that year under the title 'Teaching, Learning and Assessing Social Work Law'. Paper 30 has now been superseded by 'Assuring Quality for the Diploma in Social Work – 1: Rules and Requirements for the DipSW', published by CCETSW in 1995, and a new report, again written by the Social Work Law Research Group, 'Law for Social Workers in England and Wales', and published by CCETSW in 1995 now provides updated guidance to courses for meeting the DipSW rules and requirements concerning law. The report provides a model social work core law curriculum for Diploma students which acknowledges the three elements of knowledge, skills and values. In consequence the opportunity is taken here to quote at length from this 'law guidance'.

Knowledge:

Students need to understand:

(i) that the law gives social workers their mandate to practice:

   (a) as employees of statutory bodies (when, for example, employed as a local authority social worker); or as officers of the court (when employed, for example as a probation officer);

   (b) by defining the various groups of people in respect of whom social workers have duties and powers;

   (c) by defining a social worker's legal functions in relation to each client group;

(ii) that legally accountable powers, when appropriately used, can promote and encourage good social work practice: e.g. by emphasising the importance of prevention and rehabilitation; by setting out the conditions upon which compulsory intervention is permissible; by ensuring that compulsory intervention with a person's rights takes place in accordance with proper legal safeguards, such as due process of law and adherence to principles of natural justice;

(iii) that the exercise of legal powers may be oppressive or discriminatory if not used in ways that avoid discrimination and respect client's rights; and that social and legal institutions and processes, such as the court system, to which social workers' practice most often relate, are frequently identified as discriminatory and racist in operation and practice.

Students need to know:

(i) the substantive law which is relevant to social work practice, and its nature and sources;

(ii) the relationship between local authority and probation policy and the law;

(iii) the structures and processes of the relevant court and tribunal systems.

Values:

Students need to have commitment to:

(i) equality, and anti-oppressive practice;

(ii) the right of individuals to receive care/treatment and control in the context of:

- the least restrictive alternative;

- normalisation/non-stigmatisation;

- ethnic/cultural/language needs,

with access to appeal and choice, as far as it is possible;

(iii) social order: eg the right of society to protection from significant risk, danger or harm; the recognition of the rights of significant others eg victims.

Issues of oppression discrimination and civil rights are intrinsic to these values/aims, and social work law courses will need to consider them regularly and routinely as they affect social work practice and social services provision.

Skills:

These should include:

(i) cognitive, interpersonal, decision-making and administrative skills, eg ability to assess, to plan, to communicate, to provide support for clients, their families and carers;

(ii) ability to use correct and appropriate knowledge and values in the interest of the client, the agency, the courts and society;

(iii) ability to conduct him/herself appropriately in adult and youth criminal courts, and in family proceedings courts. Ability to prepare and present evidence.

(iv) development of appropriate report-writing techniques;

(v) ability to work in a multi-disciplinary setting e.g. with lawyers, doctors and health visitors;

(vi) ability to use legal processes, including emergency procedures appropriately in relation to all client groups with whom they work in their assessed practice experiences.

From this prospectus for the legal aspect of social work training it is clear that this area of teaching and learning is both considerable and complex in its inter-relationship between the knowledge, skills and values of social work law. Nonetheless it is now recognised as having an identity which marks it out as an essential element of training courses and of competent qualifying social workers.

The Foreword to the 1995 revision of the Rules and Requirements reflects the increased emphasis on law in social work training:

> In recognition of the central importance of knowledge and under-standing of the statutory responsibilities of social service/work agencies in both the public and independent sectors, Council also required all DipSW programmes to review their law teaching for the September 1995 intakes and, where possible and necessary, to revise their assessment schedules to meet the new requirement for assess-ment of law. This new requirement states that all DipSW students must demonstrate through written formal assessment their under-standing and application of the legislation relating to social work in the country in which they train.

Students are also required to demonstrate their ability to apply and extend their understanding of 'legislation' within practice settings. Consequently the placement experience should provide oppor-tunities for law teaching and learning. Indeed the revised Rules and Requirements provides that all programmes are required to assess a student's competence to work 'in accordance with statutory and legal requirements'.[3]

---

3 'Assuring Quality in the Diploma' in *Social Work – 1, Rules and Requirements for the DipSW*, (1995) CCETSW.

CCETSW's guidance on assuring quality in practice teaching requires that programmes for accrediting practice teachers address their ability to provide appropriate 'law' learning opportunities for social work students on placement. [4] Research recently completed by the Social Work Law Research Group throws doubt on the extent to which these objectives are being achieved:

> Placement experiences will be highly variable. Some practice teachers recognise the central importance of knowledge and skills in social work law in social work training, take personal responsibility for updating themselves, have access to documents for specific guidance, and provide materials to help students. Some agencies have introduced training courses for practice teachers in current aspects of social work law and take this forward through support groups. However, this was true of only a minority of our respondents. Most practice teachers felt inadequate, either generally or outside their usual work experience, exposed by insufficient resources and employer indifference, and doubtful of their ability to make the necessary connections for students. It is questionable, therefore, whether, in the practice setting, students become competent in the law of the country in which they train. [5]

FROM 'LAW FOR SOCIAL WORKERS' TO 'SOCIAL WORK LAW'

It is noteworthy that the 1995 DipSW uses the phrase 'social work law' and the same phrase is used in the research referred to immediately above, both in its methodology and in its reporting. The Social Work Law Research Group, who carried out the research, and whose own name has changed from the Social Work and Law Group, have argued that it is now possible to claim the status of a discipline for 'social work law':

> However, what are the signifiers of a discipline and can social work law make such a claim? Disciplines have traditionally been difficult to characterise with any certainty, but may be identified through their control or monopoly over a subject or practice area, and a distinct and exclusive knowledge base. In arguing that social work law should

4   *Assuring Quality in Practice Teaching*, (1995) CCETSW.
5   'We work in isolation often and in ignorance occasionally', *On the experience of practice teachers teaching and assessing social work law*, Preston-Shoot, M, Roberts, G and Vernon, S, Social Work Education [1997] Vol 16, No 4, 4-43.

be viewed as a subject discipline, the intention is not necessarily to suggest that social work should be accorded professional status. Rather, the intention is to promote a degree of theoretical and practice security and certainty by providing a framework which offers signposts for teachers, managers and practitioners amidst the complexity. Moreover, the argument runs that social work law provides a recognised body of knowledge that can be transmitted and certified; operates in a defined and legitimate area of activity (rather than in an indeterminate zone); and, through social work values and principles of administrative law (such as rules of natural justice), has a code of ethical, legal and humane practice.[6]

Such a claim has added justification when it is viewed in the light of CCETSW's unique placing of law in the Rules and Requirements for the DipSW and in the now well established library of texts dealing with the place and significance of law in social work training and social work practice. Social work law can now be defined in terms of a conceptual framework and theoretical base:

> The subject area of social work law is composed of three distinct but inter-related strands. First, legal powers and duties, set out in a number of statutory provisions and further defined by a number of judicial decisions, provide social workers with a mandate to practise. Secondly, social workers practice also on a basis of certain ethical and professional values, many of which are incorporated into relevant statutory provisions. Thirdly, since most social work practice in Britain today is located within corporate organisations which are subject, ultimately, to the jurisdiction and control of the courts, as well as to scrutiny by non-judicial authorities, such as the Local Commission for Administration, a third essential strand in social work law comprises certain aspects of administrative law, such as judicial review.[7]

Strand 1 – the legal mandate

The legal mandate is identified as setting out the social work functions of prevention and protection, and specifying the groups of service users who may be the recipients of services provided under the provisions of the legal mandate; these include:

---

6 Preston-Shoot, M, Roberts, G and Vernon, S, *Social Work Law: From Interaction to Integration*, Journal of Social Welfare and Family Law [1998] Vol 20, No 1, 65-80.
7 Ibid.

- children in need

- people with mental disorder, including learning disablement

- people with chronic illness

- people with sensory impairment

- people with physical disability

- vulnerable older people

- offenders

Strand 2 – social work values and knowledge

The second strand of social work law is described as comprising social work values and knowledge. The Social Work Law Research Group specify these as including:

- equal opportunities and anti-discriminatory practice

- partnership

- the right of individuals to receive care, treatment and control in the context of:

  - the least restrictive alternative

  - normalisation/non-stigmatisation

  - ethnic, cultural and language needs

- social order: for example, the right of society to protection from significant risk, danger or harm; the recognition of the rights of significant others, for instance victims and carers

- self-determination

It is further argued that these values are reflected in aspects of the legal mandate, for example:

- equal opportunities – Criminal Justice Act 1991 (s 95)

- partnership – Carers (Recognition and Services) Act 1995

- normalisation – Chronically Sick and Disabled Persons Act 1970 (s 2)

- cultural needs – Children Act 1989 (s 1(3))

- balancing care and control – Children Act 1989 (s 17)

- social order – Criminal Justice Act 1991

- self determination – Community Care (Direct Payments) Act 1996

A knowledge and theoretical base is also needed to inform both the above value base and the legal mandate. This theoretical and knowledge base is necessary to practice social work; it includes knowledge of:

- values

- law

- organisational context

- applied social sciences

- user groups

- social work tasks

It is argued that social work law defines a zone of practice, and the values and knowledge to work confidently within it.

Strand 3 – administrative law

The third strand of social work law is provided by aspects of administrative law. For example, local authorities are public (law) bodies; as such they are creatures of and subject to the rules and principles of administrative law. Judicial review, the Commission for Local Administration (the local ombudsman) and Complaints Procedures provide an important avenue of accountability for local authority organisation and the provision of social work services. Mention should also be made of the influence of Directions and policy guidance issued under section 7A of the Local Authority Social Services Act 1970.

The identification and definition of these three strands is central to an understanding of social work law and to the claim that it should now be understood as an emerging academic and practice discipline which has critical implications for justice and people's welfare. The publication of this third edition is another phase in this process.

CHAPTER 1

Social work(ers) and law(yers)

This book is concerned with social work law and with elements of social welfare law which impinge upon social work practice. Inevitably the way in which social workers understand the nature of English law and the way in which they work within the legal system, are important contexts for social work practice. This chapter will begin an examination of these interrelated issues by considering the way in which the nature of law and the legal system impacts upon the social work profession and its practice, and by examining the relationship between lawyers and social workers in a variety of encounters on a continuum of social work law practice.

1 SOCIAL WORK PRACTICE WITHIN ENGLISH LAW AND THE LEGAL SYSTEM

The courts are often perceived by social workers as a frightening and even hostile environment. Lawyers are seen as coming from a distinct professional position which may not be sympathetic to the concerns and interests of social work and service users; magistrates and judges wield considerable decision making powers, the exercise of which may support the aims and values of social work, but equally may frustrate them. Important aspects of social work are subject to specification by statutory provisions and to scrutiny and control through judicial and quasi-judicial decision making; indeed these external references are crucial to the place of social work in our society and constitute an important medium through which the profession is accountable for its actions.[1]

Social workers who are frequent players in the courts, or who work closely with the law, have a professional understanding and even

---

1 These comments refer to the use of Complaints Procedures, complaints to the local ombudsman, applications for judicial review, and referrals to independent enquiries.

familiarity with its provisions and practice. A professional 'ease' with the law becomes part of their competency as a social worker. Though other social workers may never attain this position, an understanding of the circumstances in which a social worker must deal with courts of law and with lawyers may help to reduce the anxiety and unease which often accompanies this aspect of practice.

Lawyers in England and Wales are common lawyers; they have been educated and socialised into a particular way of thinking about the problems that clients bring to them. The common law has historically been developed through case law in the sense that disputes have come before the courts for resolution and the judges have developed legal rules to decide the cases before them. In this sense the common law is said to have a practical basis, a pragmatic character that distinguishes it from systems of law which derive their rules from general principles set out in codes of law as is most often the case in continental Europe.

The influence of this historical legacy still has an impact on the way in which lawyers go about their work. Cases are about 'solving problems', 'finding a way out of this' or 'how do we achieve this?'. Being a lawyer is often about working creatively with the law, using the rules where possible to promote the interests and wishes of a client.

Principles that underpin the law in England and Wales are frequently stated in very general terms, be they expressed in an Act of Parliament or in a precedent decision of the House of Lords or the Court of Appeal. This generality facilitates creative work by judges and lawyers and should also encourage social workers not to view the law as a rigid set of rules that necessarily control or frustrate their practice. For example, section 1 of the Children Act 1989, which identifies the welfare of the child as the paramount con-sideration for the court when it is considering the upbringing of the child, is a general principle within which constructive social work practice can take place. The principle of the Criminal Justice Act 1991 which requires a community sentence to reflect the seriousness of the offence and to be appropriate for the offender in the sense that it addresses his or her offending behaviour and reduces the risk of further offending by the offender, can be understood as a principle which facilitates creative thinking by the social worker or probation officer preparing a pre-sentence report and planning for work with the offender. The flexibility of legal principle as a sight for constructive practice is a feature of English law which applies to the practice of both law and social work.

The relationship between lawyer and client and that between social worker and service user are often characterised as being very different. It is possible to argue that because lawyers take instructions from clients their relationship is characterised by the autonomy or self determination of the client. The relationship between social worker and service user might be characterised as being different, at least to the extent that service users do not give 'instructions' and that, in some situations, social workers can trigger the use of compulsory powers in the best interests of service users, eg a compulsory admission to hospital of a person suffering from a mental disorder. Closer analysis of the two relationships suggests that the differences are often much less than this comment suggests.

The ability of a client to instruct his or her lawyer is mediated through a number of factors of which the professional expertise of the lawyer is one and the relative intellectual and material resources of the client is another. Any observer of proceedings in the magistrates' court will be able to provide evidence that the majority of people who appear there do what their lawyers tell them. The essence of the lawyer/client relationship is the request for professional advice; in reality that advice is accepted. In turn the relationship between social worker and service user is subject to a number of principles that underpin social work practice. The self esteem, independence, dignity, individuality and self determination of the service user are important objectives for practice.

Differences between the two relationships are most obviously identified in the breadth and depth of the relationship. Clients see lawyers in respect of fairly narrowly defined concerns; for example, when defending a criminal prosecution, or applying for a contact order under the Children Act. The lawyer's interest starts and ends, and is restricted in its scope, by the specific task. The relationship between a social worker and service user is far broader and often encompasses much more than the issue which triggered the relationship. This distinction can be seen in the detachment which characterises the relationship between lawyer and client. This detachment is often valued in the sense that it facilitates the taking of an objective view of the circumstances of a client. There are circumstances in which detachment and objectivity are necessary in social work practice but there are also many situations where a practitioner must become involved with the experience of a service user and respect their subjective definitions of that experience.

Social workers are not just observers of the legal system; many are important participants; some occasionally, others on a regular basis. Appearances in court are one aspect of this and some indication of the variety of circumstances in which a social work practitioner will be involved in court based work is given below:

i)   guardians ad litem are charged by the legal system with representing and safeguarding the interests of children involved in a variety of family proceedings. The panels from which courts make appointments are comprised of experienced social workers.

ii)   local authority social workers and probation officers are often asked by the youth court to provide pre-sentence reports under the Criminal Justice Act 1991 so that youth offenders can be appropriately sentenced. If a supervision order is made by the court either the social services department, or the probation service for older offenders, will be required to supervise the order. The probation service provides the same service in the Crown Court and adult magistrates' court.

iii)   in a hearing to decide an application for a care order under the Children Act 1989 the court will require a number of welfare reports to assist in the proceedings. It is likely that most will be written by a social worker.

iv)   social workers apply to the family proceedings court for an emergency protection order under the Children Act 1989 and for warrants so that police officers can enter and search premises for children who need protection.

v)   social workers can apply to the magistrates' court for an order to compulsorily remove a person who is unable to care for themselves from their own home under the provisions of the National Assistance Act 1948.

vi)   an education welfare officer may apply to the family proceedings court for an education supervision order under section 36 of the Children Act 1989.

Despite these, and other, opportunities for exposure to the law, the legal system and to lawyers, there are inevitable tensions between social work values and practice, and legal values and practice. A number of examples of this tension can be provided:

i)   the values and practice of social work may seem to be at odds with the adversarial and partisan history and culture of the legal system and lawyers;

ii)   the individualisation of legal decisions cannot reconcile or embrace the interests of the single litigant with those of other litigants with established needs, let alone with the unknown needs of potential service claimants. This difficulty is particularly acute when the issue concerns the allocation of finite resources;

iii) the inability of law to balance competing and legitimate claims to justice and rights;

iv)   the concern of social work to empower service users will often conflict with legal decision making which is individualised;

v)   the legal or quasi-legal enforcement of service user rights against social work authorities conflicts with their commitment to the principles of partnership and co-operation with service users.

2 WORKING TOGETHER – SOCIAL WORKERS AND LAWYERS [2]

Social work law, and particularly the statutory legal mandate for social work, defines the circumstances in which social workers and lawyers may or must work together. Social welfare law, for instance in welfare rights, housing, and immigration, also provides a variety of sites where the two professions will work together:

> These territories may be mapped by means of reference points on a continuum. At one end of the continuum we can identify interactions which are dominated by the language, methodology and values of the law, such as a plea in mitigation in the criminal courts after the

2   See *Working Together in Social Work Law*, Preston-Shoot, M, Roberts, G and Vernon, S, [1988] Journal of Social Welfare and Family Law, Vol 20, No 2.

presentation of a pre-sentence report The middle ground of the continuum is represented by an application for a care order by a local authority lawyer. At the opposite end of the continuum, the language, methodology and values of social work prevail, and lawyers are rarely involved. Community care assessments and care management are examples of this.[3]

The varied nature of the relationship between lawyers and social workers is best understood by reference to different sites on the continuum. At the law end of the continuum the relationship between lawyers and social workers is dominated by the constructs of the law; it reflects legal rules, procedures, language and values. An example is the situation where a young person is arrested and questioned by the police in the investigation of an offence. In such circumstances the young person is entitled to a series of protections specified in the Police and Criminal Evidence Act 1984 and in the Codes attached to it, particularly by Code C, The Detention, Treatment and Questioning of Persons by Police Officers. There is a right to free legal advice and a requirement for the attendance of an appropriate adult. The former is provided by a lawyer and the latter service is often provided by a social worker. The tasks are very different, the lawyer gives legal advice and the appropriate adult is required to assert and protect the other (non-legal) interests of the young person and to facilitate communication between the young person and the police. Interaction between the lawyer and the social worker in this circumstance will reflect a number of factors, including their different statutory responsibilities, and the fact that lawyers are likely to feel more at ease in the environment of the police station than social workers. Police station duty solicitors do this more often than social workers so that may also be more competent than a social worker acting occasionally as an appropriate adult. The police may take a different view of lawyers and social workers in which the latter are viewed less favourably. This example of social work law work is dominated by the procedures of law and by two of the principal actors of the criminal justice system, the police and lawyers. Social work and its practitioners will be occasional bit players. Though this is a generalisation, the model will prevail unless, for example, it can be influenced by an experienced and highly competent social worker acting as the appropriate adult, or conversely by an inexperienced and incompetent legal adviser.

3   Ibid.

An example taken more from the centre of the continuum will illustrate an interaction between lawyers and social workers which is predominantly the construct of social work. Local authority-employed lawyers working in the field of child care law appear to be working within an environment that reflects the language and values of social work, though the imperatives and concerns of 'law' may well play a central role in local authority child care decisions, at least those that 'approach' the courts.

The initial decision to seek a care order is made within the context of social work with a particular child and family. Once the 'practice' decision has been made, the local authority lawyer is called upon to construct and present the case for the authority in much the same way that a client will instruct a lawyer in private practice. The nature of the professional relationship between the social workers concerned with the child and the family and the local authority lawyer will reflect many factors, including the professional independence of the lawyer and the objectivity of the advice that is given by him or her to the local authority and the social workers involved. It is the task of the lawyer to determine whether there is sufficient evidence to support the application, since the evidence presented by the authority must satisfy the criteria for a care order specified in section 31(2) of the Children Act. If the evidence is deficient the lawyer is expected to resist the call for an application for the care order, even against the view of the social workers that the care order would satisfy the welfare criteria of section 1 of the Act.

The fact that this interaction, and many others in the child care law field, are located on this part of the continuum, is due to the fact that the Children Act 1989 reflects the concerns of social work:

> ... for example, that the welfare of the child is paramount, that children should have rights, and that partnership with parents is more likely to result in effective outcomes. The procedures and practice of the Family Proceedings Court also reflect and support these concerns: for example, in the appointment of Guardians ad Litem and the importance attached to their reports, and in the increased use of expert witnesses, such as child psychologists and paediatricians. The challenge for legal practitioners in this context is to translate the dominant issues and concerns of the social work practitioner, into the language and the rules of the law and the accepted procedures of the Family Proceedings Court.[4]

---

4   Ibid.

Unsurprisingly, the 'social work end' of the continuum reflects the values and concerns of social work practice and is conspicuous by the absence or very rare appearance of lawyers. Despite the plethora and complexity of legislation, community care practice is dominated by the values and concerns of social work: the assessment of need and decisions concerning care plans and service provision. The provision of services is determined primarily by definitions of need, though these are mediated through available resources and eligibility criteria. All this is firmly within the boundaries of social work even though the decision making processes are determined by the relevant form of social work law – statutory duties, guidance and case law. As a site on the continuum, community care practice is different from youth justice or child care work in the sense that courts and lawyers are not normally part of the service being provided or of the decision-making processes employed to resolve a problem.

It should be acknowledged that, in relation to community care law at least, this 'social work end' of the continuum is subject to an increasing legalism. Some service users, subject to reductions in their services caused by decreasing resources are resorting to litigation, through applications for judicial review, as a means of personally resolving the impossible equation of needs and resources. Consequently the assessment of needs and decisions concerning the provision of services to meet needs are increasingly subject to rules of law determined in the courts. [5]

It is clear from this discussion that the continuum of social work law provides a number of sites for social work practice. The law that characterises those sites may reflect and be instrumental in promoting and re-enforcing the values of social work, equally it may be neutral as to those values, and at other times the value base of social work law may actually be in tension with the value base of practice. It is also possible that the culture and structures of the legal system may themselves work against the achievement of social work objectives. Social workers and the lawyers they sometimes work with, have to mediate these tensions and conflicts:

> The emergence of social work law requires both lawyers and social workers to reappraise their own and each other's contribution to health, welfare, equality and rights in contemporary society. A

---

5   See *R v Gloucestershire County Council, ex p Barry* [1997] AC 584.

critical, analytical reflection, coupled with open communication, will make their disciplines accessible to each other and, potentially, enable the exercise of influence over the objectives of welfare policy and the means by which they are to be realised. If professional groups retain the ability and willingness to question, and seek to reconstruct their relationship towards greater integration, they are more likely to be perceived by service users as relevant and to retain the empathy and skills with which to counter inequality, alienation and exclusion. [6]

---

6 Preston-Shoot, M, Roberts, G and Vernon, S, op cit.

CHAPTER 2

The legal system

1 INTRODUCTION

Social work courses cannot, nor should they, attempt to turn out professional social workers who are also quasi-lawyers or para-legals. Nonetheless it is important for social workers to have an understanding of the legal system and of the nature of English law. A number of social work practitioners, particularly local authority employees, approved social workers and probation officers, have an established statutory role in relation to particular aspects of the law and the legal system and other social workers may come into contact with the law through their professional practice with service users. An understanding of the legal system should therefore be an essential element of professional competency within social work. Indeed, the interests of many service users will include the need for preliminary informed advice about the law and the legal system that can only be provided by a social worker who is familiar with the nature of English law and the operation of the legal system.

1.1 CONTENT

The chapter will begin by identifying how legal principles and rules are made and developed by Parliament and the courts. This will allow some brief discussion of the nature of English law and of the power and influence of the judges.

A distinction will be made between the criminal law and the civil law; this will be followed by a brief description of the court system, the character of which owes something to this distinction.

Some time will be spent on identifying the availability of legal services in the belief that such information is important for service users and social workers. The enforcement of service user rights is often only possible through the courts and tribunals of the legal system. In these circumstances access to the legal system is crucial and will only be possible through the legal aid system.

2 THE LAW AND THE LEGAL SYSTEM

2.1 WHERE DOES THE LAW COME FROM AND HOW DOES IT CHANGE?

2.1.1 Parliament's legislative procedures

Within the framework of the British Constitution Parliament is the supreme law making body.[1] The majority of legislative proposals are introduced into Parliament as a Bill by the government of the day. Bills go through a complicated procedure in the House of Commons and the House of Lords which includes debates in both houses and more detailed scrutiny by committee; if they successfully complete this stage they go to the monarch for the royal assent, at which stage they become an Act of Parliament (otherwise known as a statute).

The link between politics, policy and law is often lost and it is important to understand that many statutes have a considerable political or policy history. For example, the Children Act 1989 should be understood as the culmination of a child care law reform process which included the inter-departmental report 'Review of Child Care Law' published by the DHSS, a review by the Law Commission, the child abuse inquiries of the late 1980s and the government's White Paper 'The Law in Child Care and Family Services'. It is also clear that much recent criminal justice legislation, including the Criminal Justice and Public Order Act 1994, reflects a heightened and populist political debate on crime in general and youth justice in particular. An understanding of the policy background to statutes which concern social work practice helps to make more sense of legislation when it becomes law.

Though all Acts go onto the statute book when they receive the royal assent, the date of implementation may be delayed until some time later. Such was the case with the National Health Service and Community Care Act 1990 which was not implemented (in the main)

---

1   It will be interesting to see whether the incorporation of the European Convention on Human Rights into domestic English law will erode or alter this position in any way.

until April 1993. Similarly the Criminal Justice Act 1991 was not implemented until October 1992. Sections 1, 2, 3 and 7 of the Disabled Persons (Services, Consultation and Representation) Act 1986 have never been implemented. The practice of implementing Acts in stages, or even of non-implementation, can cause considerable confusion and it is important for social workers to know what sections of relevant statutes are in force and from what date.

2.1.2   Secondary legislation

Acts of Parliament often contain provisions which allow Ministers to make law themselves; the power to make 'delegated legislation'. This power, which is increasingly important, is most frequently used by the making of regulations which are contained in statutory instruments. As an example, the Social Security Act 1986 introduced the broad principles of income support and family credit and gave the Secretary of State the power to make regulations which detail both benefits. A number of regulations have been made under the Children Act 1989, eg the Children's Homes Regulations which provide, among other things, detailed legal provisions concerning the conduct and administration of children's homes and issues of control and discipline within them. Social workers must therefore take account of both primary legislation (Acts of Parliament) and secondary legislation (regulations in statutory instruments); both constitute the law.

2.1.3   Directions and Guidance

Directions

Section 7A(1) of the Local Authority Social Services Act 1970 provides that local authorities must exercise their social services functions 'in accordance with such directions as may be given to them under this section by the Secretary of State'. An example of these mandatory directions is the Complaints Procedure Directions 1990 which outline the structure of complaints procedures which must be set up by local authorities to investigate complaints concerning the exercise of their social services functions.

Guidance

Section 7(1) of the 1970 Act provides that

Local authorities shall, in the exercise of their social services functions, including the exercise of any discretion conferred by any relevant enactment, act under the general guidance of the Secretary of State.

It is important to distinguish between policy or formal guidance and practice or general guidance. The former is issued under section 7(1) and has a status above that of the latter, though it is not law. In the case of *R v Islington London Borough Council, ex p Rixon* (1996)[2] Sedley J held that:

Parliament in enacting section 7(1) did not intend local authorities to whom ministerial guidance was given to be free, having considered it, to take it or leave it. A local authority was required to follow the path charted by the Secretary of State's guidance, with liberty to deviate from it where the local authority judged on admissible grounds that there was a good reason to do so, but without freedom to take a substantially different course.

The policy guidance issued to support the Carers (Recognition and Services) Act 1995 makes the distinction between policy guidance and practice guidance in terms of setting out the Government's view of what local authorities should be doing to implement the Act – policy guidance issued under section 7(1), and advice on how the Act might be implemented – practice guidance not issued under section 7(1). The policy guidance is issued by the Department of Health and the practice guidance is issued by the Social Services Inspectorate.

The Children Act 1989 is supported by substantial guidance described in the volume concerning residential care in the following terms:

The guidance in this volume is issued under section 7 of the Local Authority Social Services Act 1970 which requires local authorities in the exercise of their social services functions to act under the general guidance of the Secretary of State. It is the fourth volume in a series designed to bring managers and practitioners an understanding of the principles of the Children Act and associated regulations, to identify areas of change and to assist discussion of the implications

2   [1997] ELR 66.
3   Preface to The Children Act 1989, Guidance and Regulations 'Residential Care', (1991) Volume 4, HMSO.

for policies, procedures and practice. [3]

Guidance may also be issued by Circular and this is the normal method adopted by the Home Office for guidance that relates to the criminal justice system. An example is Home Office Circular 18/1994 on the Cautioning of Offenders which was addressed to Chief Officers of Police. Another example is the guidance concerning access to manually kept social work records. The circular, issued by the Department of Health, and identified as LAC(89)2, provides guidance to local authorities concerning their position under the Access to Personal Files Act 1987 and the Access to Personal Files (Social Services) Regulations 1989.

Codes of Guidance or Practice provide detailed advice from government departments on how statutory provisions should be interpreted and acted upon. An example is the Code of Practice on the Mental Health Act 1983 issued by the Department of Health and the Welsh Office.

2.1.4   Judicial law making

Statutes (Acts of Parliament) provide the majority of legal rules by which the courts determine criminal prosecutions and civil disputes which come before them. This task often requires the judges to interpret the meaning of specific provisions contained in Acts of Parliament. Authoritative interpretations of statute by the senior appeal courts constitute legal rules in themselves. In addition a number of areas of law have been developed by the judges and are not subject to statutory provision. In such areas judicial rulings constitute the law and may influence or control social work practice. An example is the House of Lords decision in the case of *F v West Berkshire Health Authority* [1989] 2 All ER 545. The case concerned the difficult issue of the sterilisation of adult women who are incapable of themselves consenting to the operation because of their learning disability. The judgments of the House of Lords judges set out the circumstances in which such operations can take place and provide a procedure through which the doctors involved in such cases can apply to the courts for a declaration that such an operation would not be unlawful. The case also established an important principle of law which is a precedent for similar cases; described simply, it is that medical treatment can be administered to a person who is unable to consent to that treatment so long as the treatment is in the patient's best interests.

A more recent example of important case law is the majority judgment of the House of Lords in the case of *R v Gloucestershire County Council and the Secretary of State for Health, ex p Barry* [1997] AC 584. The majority held that local authorities are entitled to take the state of their own financial resources into account when assessing the needs of people with disabilities for services available under section 2 of the Chronically Sick and Disabled Persons Act 1970.

2.1.5 The influence of the judiciary

The English legal system accords considerable importance and influence to its judges and in particular to the senior judiciary who sit in the House of Lords and the Court of Appeal. This characteristic of the legal system is firmly located in legal history and is derived from the development of legal rules by judges in the everyday hearing of disputes. As a result the English 'common law' is said to be characterised by a pragmatism and detail which distinguishes it from the 'civil law' of continental Europe which is based on legal codes containing statements of principle from which detailed legal rules can be derived. Such distinctions are of course simplifications, but the position and power of the judiciary in the English legal system, and consequently of their decisions, should not be underestimated.

The incorporation of the European Convention on Human Rights into domestic English law is likely to have a significant impact on both the nature of English law and the role and influence of the senior judiciary. The Convention sets out a number of legal human rights principles and these will have to be interpreted when they are utilised by litigants seeking to enforce their human rights through the English courts. Consequently the senior judiciary, who will be responsible for interpreting these principles will inevitably become involved, through this task of interpretation, in issues that involve fundamental human rights and also have considerable political significance.

Though Parliament is the source of virtually all new law the judges retain their law making power through their ability to interpret the meaning of statutes and to develop legal rules through the doctrine of precedent. The system of binding precedent is based on a hierarchy of courts and on the rule that the decisions of the superior courts constitute precedents which are binding on inferior courts. The House of Lords is the senior court of the hierarchy and together with the Court of Appeal they formulate the legal rules which must be followed by the other courts in the system, ie the High Court, the Crown Courts, the county courts, and the magistrates' courts.

Because precedents are made by the senior courts in their everyday work of hearing appeals new rules of law can be made very quickly and what may be lawful one day can be rendered unlawful the next. Whilst such radical changes in the law are rarely made by the judges the character of judicial law making requires those who are affected by particular laws to keep abreast of their development. Legal rules in the English legal system are not static, rather they are subject to development, interpretation and change by the senior judiciary. This feature provides the flexibility and dynamism of the legal system.

2.1.6 How does social work deal with the law and official guidance?

It should be understood that the law impacts upon social work agencies and individual social workers in a number of ways. Acts and Regulations constitute law, Directions are mandatory, and Codes of Guidance and Circulars contain advice and recommendations which constitute an official definition of good practice. Case law may interpret each and all of these. Agencies and individual workers should ideally be aware of each of these sources of law and official advice.

For many individual social workers their knowledge and understanding of the law that circumscribes their practice is received, in the everyday sense, not through the law but through agency statements of practice and procedure. As an example, the law on 'child protection' is contained in Part V of the Children Act. The sections in this part of the Act contain a number of powers and duties which are to be exercised largely by local authority social workers who have been delegated these powers and duties by their employing authority. However, in practice social workers in child protection teams will be working to a very closely defined procedure which has been worked out and prescribed by reference to the Act and to the detailed guidance in 'Working Together', a guide to arrangements for inter-agency co-operation for the protection of children from abuse, published jointly by the Home Office, the Department of Health, the Department of Education and Science and the Welsh Office in 1991. Child protection work will also have to take into account the perceived meaning and impact of case law and of the working relationships established by a particular social services department with other agencies working in the same field and area. It is of course important that in such a sensitive and difficult area of practice individual social workers should be clear about what is good and necessary practice, however, an understanding of the statutory responsibilities must not be lost within the detail of practice procedures.

2.2 CRIMINAL LAW

2.2.1 Crime and the criminal justice system

The criminal law is concerned to protect the social order. Through history the state, primarily by statute but also by judicial law making, has defined behaviour which is seen as threatening the social order, as a crime.

2.2.2 The language and the actors of the criminal justice system

The police are responsible for ensuring that the everyday social order is upheld, for investigating breaches of the criminal law and for the apprehension of those who are alleged to have committed a crime. Criminal prosecutions are brought by the Crown Prosecution Service in the magistrates' courts and the Crown Courts. Defendants plead guilty or not guilty to specific charges and the prosecution is required, in a criminal trial, to prove the allegation contained in the charge beyond a reasonable doubt. Defendants who plead guilty, or are found guilty after a criminal trial, become offenders and are subject to sentence.

It may be useful to see the criminal justice system as being administered by and through a number of agencies and key actors. These include the police, the Crown Prosecution Service, the magistracy, the judges, the criminal courts service (court clerks etc.), juries and the Probation Service.

Most criminal offences are defined by Act of Parliament and for the majority of offences a successful prosecution will need to establish that the criminal act was committed (the actus reus) and that the defendant had the necessary criminal intent (the mens rea).

2.2.3 The criminal courts

CRIMINAL PROSECUTIONS/ADULTS -COURT STRUCTURE

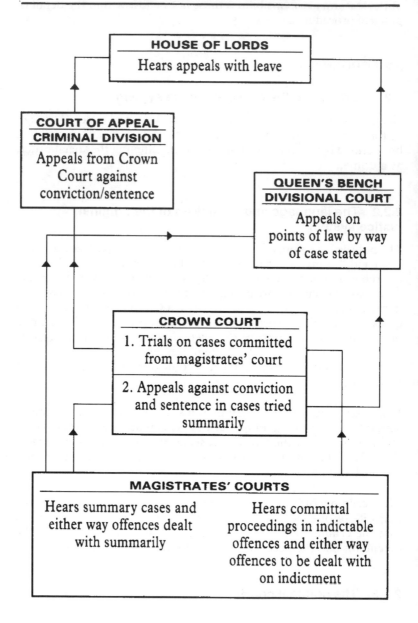

HOUSE OF LORDS

Hears appeals with leave

COURT OF APPEAL CRIMINAL DIVISION

Appeals from Crown Court against conviction/sentence

QUEEN'S BENCH DIVISIONAL COURT

Appeals on points of law by way of case stated

CROWN COURT

1. Trials on cases committed from magistrates' court

2. Appeals against conviction and sentence in cases tried summarily

MAGISTRATES' COURTS

Hears summary cases and either way offences dealt with summarily

Hears committal proceedings in indictable offences and either way offences to be dealt with on indictment

Criminal prosecutions are brought in the magistrates' courts and the Crown Courts. All offences are categorised as either indictable, either-way or summary offences. Magistrates' courts hear and decide all summary offences, whilst the Crown Courts deal with all indictable offences. Either-way offences may be heard in the Crown Court or in the magistrates' courts.

In the Crown Court defendants are tried by a judge and jury; the judge being responsible for matters of law and for sentencing, whilst the jury determines guilt or innocence. Cases in the magistrates' courts are heard by benches of lay magistrates or by a single stipendiary magistrate.

The maximum sentencing powers of the criminal courts are set out in statute by Parliament. Currently both judges and magistrates have considerable discretion in fixing sentences but the implementation of the Crime (Sentences) Act 1997 has reduced this discretion by determining a number of minimum sentences.

2.3   THE CIVIL LAW

2.3.1   Civil disputes

Disputes involving individuals, companies, public bodies and local and central government may have to be resolved by the civil courts. Examples of such disputes include alleged breaches of contract, actions for damages arising from negligence, divorce actions, landlord and tenant disputes and family proceedings under the Children Act 1989. Such disputes do not generally constitute a threat to the social order and therefore do not involve breaches of the criminal law. The interest of the state is therefore limited to defining, by statute and judicial precedent, legal principles to govern the multitude of everyday relationships involving the individuals and other bodies identified above, and to determine the disputes that arise when such relationships break down. The state also provides the courts and tribunals which are available to hear and determine these disputes.

2.3.2   The language of the civil justice system

The parties in civil disputes are generally known as plaintiffs and defendants though in divorce proceedings they are petitioners and

CIVIL PROCEEDINGS
-COURT STRUCTURE

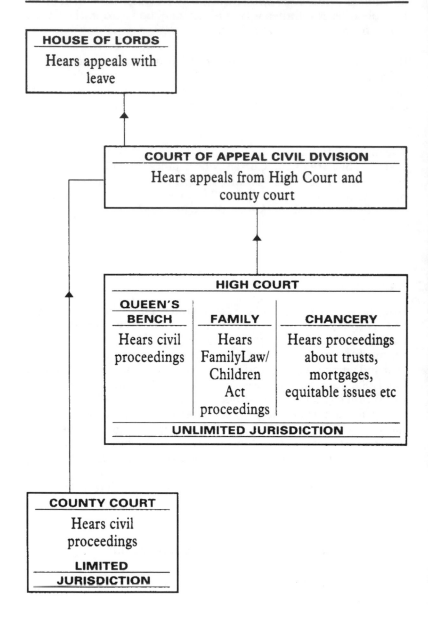

HOUSE OF LORDS

Hears appeals with leave

COURT OF APPEAL CIVIL DIVISION

Hears appeals from High Court and county court

HIGH COURT

QUEEN'S BENCH	FAMILY	CHANCERY
Hears civil proceedings	Hears FamilyLaw/ Children Act proceedings	Hears proceedings about trusts, mortgages, equitable issues etc

UNLIMITED JURISDICTION

COUNTY COURT

Hears civil proceedings

LIMITED JURISDICTION

respondents. Civil actions are taken to secure appropriate remedies or orders. These include awards of damages as compensation for loss suffered, injunctions designed to prevent or stop unlawful activities and possession orders in landlord and tenant disputes. The number of orders available in civil actions is considerable and each is designed to provide the relief or order appropriate to the dispute. The burden of proof in civil actions is on the plaintiff who is required to establish their case on the balance of probabilities.

2.3.3 The civil courts

Major civil disputes are heard in the High Court by a High Court judge. There are three divisions of the High Court, the Queen's Bench Division, the Family Division and the Chancery Division; each has its own specialist jurisdiction. Less serious civil disputes are heard in the county courts by a circuit judge or by a district judge. The jurisdiction of the county courts is defined and limited by statute though recent reforms to the civil justice system, introduced by the Courts and Legal Services Act 1990, have significantly increased their jurisdiction.

2.4 THE HOUSE OF LORDS AND THE COURT OF APPEAL

The House of Lords is the senior appeal court of the legal system and hears both civil and criminal appeals. Its decisions act precedents which bind all other courts in the system.

The Court of Appeal has a criminal division and a civil division. Whilst it is bound by the precedent decisions of the House of Lords the large number of cases heard by the Court of Appeal means that its influence is considerable; its decisions are binding on all other courts below it in the hierarchy. The Master of the Rolls heads the civil division and is said to be responsible for the development of the civil law whilst the Lord Chief Justice, who heads the criminal division, is, in the same way, responsible for the development of the criminal law.

2.5 TRIBUNALS

A large number of disputes, mainly concerning the operation of some state benefit or public service, are not heard in courts but are dealt with by one of the many tribunals that are a feature of the legal system. Tribunals are an important and distinct system for adjudication which is largely separate from the court system. Individual tribunals, such as social security appeal tribunals and mental health review tribunals, are of particular interest to social workers and service users.

2.6 LEGAL SERVICES AND LEGAL AID

The vast majority of legal services are provided by a private legal profession on a fee paying basis and court costs in the civil justice system are also charged to the users of the system. Access to the legal system is therefore dependent on the ability to pay and many people would not be able to take or defend a civil action or defend a criminal prosecution without some form of financial help. Such help is provided through the legal aid scheme which has four main elements: legal advice and assistance, assistance by way of representation (ABWOR), civil legal aid and criminal legal aid. The scheme is administered under the provisions of the Legal Aid Act 1988.

The Legal Aid Board administers legal advice and assistance, ABWOR and civil legal aid. This administration takes place through a number of local area committees or through an increasingly important franchise scheme within which individual firms of solicitors administer legal aid for particular areas of work.

2.6.1 Legal advice and assistance (the green form scheme)

The green form scheme provides preliminary advice and assistance on any matter of English law but its availability to individuals is dependent on a means test. Green form advice and assistance from a solicitor can cover almost any legal matter including writing letters and negotiating, but excluding conveyancing and wills. The amount of advice and assistance that can be given under the green form scheme is a maximum of two hours' worth of work or three hours' work in matrimonial cases. Extensions can be sought from the Legal Aid Board.

Green form advice is free but is only available to those on the basic means-tested benefits, and those whose net income is not more than £75 per week (1997/98) and whose capital (apart from their home) is not more than £1,000. These limits are extended when the applicant has dependants. The means test is administered by the solicitor giving the advice.

2.6.2   Assistance by way of representation (ABWOR)

Assistance by way of representation (ABWOR) provides for the cost of a solicitor to prepare a case and represent the client before the family proceedings panel in the magistrates' courts. Such cases include separation, applications under the Children Act for residence and contact orders and matters concerning paternity. ABWOR is also available to patients appearing before a Mental Health Review Tribunal, for prisoners to be represented before the Parole Board (Discretionary Lifer Panel), and for some prison disciplinary hearings. It is available subject to a means test and a possible contribution.

2.6.3   Civil legal aid

Civil legal aid is available for representation and the other costs of a civil action subject to the applicant satisfying a means test and a 'merits' test. The means test is based on disposable income and capital and the applicant is often required to make a contribution to the costs of the action. The 'merits' test, which is administered by local Legal Aid Board area offices, requires anyone applying for civil legal aid to show that they have reasonable grounds for taking or defending the court action and that it is reasonable to grant legal aid in the circumstances of the applicant's case. The proceeds of a successful legally aided civil action are available to reimburse the legal aid fund for its expenditure on the case.

2.6.4   Criminal legal aid

Representation and the other legal costs of the defence in criminal proceedings can be paid for by the criminal legal aid scheme. Applications are made to the criminal courts, almost always to the magistrates' court where they are decided by the Clerk to the Justices. Applicants must satisfy a means test and, subject to their resources, may be required to pay a contribution. The award of criminal legal aid is subject to the criterion that its grant is required in the interests of justice. The Legal Aid Act 1988 sets out the criteria for deciding whether this test is met:

• the charge is a grave one in the sense that the accused is in real jeopardy of losing their liberty, livelihood or suffering serious damage to their reputation;

- the charge raises a substantial question of law;

- the accused is unable to follow the proceedings and state their own case because of their inadequate knowledge of English, mental illness or other mental or physical disability;

- the nature of the defence involves the tracing and interviewing of witnesses or expert cross examination of a prosecution witness;

- legal representation is desirable in the interests of someone other than the accused.

2.6.5 Duty solicitor schemes

Those who are questioned by the police are entitled, by the provisions of the Police and Criminal Evidence Act 1984, to free legal advice available through a duty solicitor scheme. A similar scheme will provide free advice or representation for those appearing unrepresented at the magistrates' courts for the first time and charged with an imprisonable offence.

2.6.6 Law centres

The law centre movement, which began in Britain in the late 1960s and early 1970s, is an important initiative in the provision of legal services to those who might otherwise suffer an 'unmet legal need'. Law centres provide expert and usually free legal services in those areas of law which have a particular impact on the poor and disadvantaged sections of the community. In many respects they serve the same categories of the population as social work by providing legal skills and knowledge to those with housing and social security problems, people who are elderly and vulnerable, people from the ethnic communities, and in the fields of youth justice and domestic violence.

Law centres use different models of legal practice ranging from individual case work to community work but all adopt a deliberately partisan approach to their work. This has often led individual centres into conflict with local authorities over, for example, housing standards and repairs on council estates. Such conflicts can be particularly difficult where the local authority is also funding the law centre. Financing the law centre movement is a continuing problem and the provision of funds by local authorities, the Lord Chancellor's Department and other sources has never been sufficient or permanent enough to establish the movement in the mainstream of legal services provision.

3 THE LAW, THE LEGAL SYSTEM AND SOCIAL WORK: some issues for discussion

3.1 LEGAL SERVICES FOR SERVICE USERS

Many service users will need the services of a lawyer either to enforce a right or to defend their property, person or other interests. For many their only access to the legal system will be through legal aid; equally their ability to adequately defend a criminal prosecution will depend on legal representation. In such circumstances it is incumbent upon social workers to have an adequate knowledge of the structure of legal services and some 'local knowledge' so that service users can be directed to appropriate help.

The Law Society publishes a series of Solicitors' Regional Directories which list solicitors who do legal aid work and also include the particular areas of work that individual firms will undertake. Unfortunately, this list is no real guarantee of a particular expertise so that service users referred to a firm of solicitors on the basis of the Directory may not receive the expert help they need. Social workers who are able to refer a service user to a lawyer who has specialist skills and knowledge are performing an important professional service. Understanding who can provide appropriate legal services in a particular locality is a valuable skill and such knowledge should also extend to the availability of other advice and support agencies, eg money advice centres, community relations councils, welfare rights advice centres and housing aid centres.

Legal services under the legal aid scheme may, however, not be available to support the interests of service users. For example, the legal aid scheme will not pay for someone to be legally represented before a social security appeal tribunal. An appeal to such a tribunal from the decision of an adjudication officer can often involve difficult points of law and many appellants, including service users, will encounter the greatest difficulty in making their appeal adequately. Referral to a law centre, a tribunal representation unit or other advice agency which can represent their interests is an important and valuable professional task. In the absence of representation a service user with access to expert advice is in a better position than one who does not, and referral to an advice agency may help the chances of a successful appeal.

A wide variety of legal and quasi-legal services are available and service users are frequently in positions where they require such services. An important aspect of social work practice is the ability to put service users in touch with the appropriate legal service. This is likely to be more difficult if cuts in civil legal aid proposed by the Lord Chancellor in October 1997 are implemented. These proposals, which follow the Review of Civil Justice and Legal Aid by Sir Peter Middleton (1997), are radical and centre upon two major changes to civil legal aid: the extension of conditional fee agreements to cover all civil proceedings except family proceedings; and the withdrawal of civil legal aid from all claims for money or damages. The assumption is that conditional fees, in which lawyers will take on a case on a 'no win no fee' basis, will finance those cases which were subject to legal aid. The proposals look forward to a legal aid system which will fund those remaining cases through a system of fixed price contracts between the Legal Aid Board and the providers of legal services. These contracting proposals cover both civil and criminal law. The Lord Chancellor has also proposed the establishment of a Community Legal Service to direct referrals to appropriate legal or other advice agencies and to fund these services through the re-direction of legal aid.

4 ACTIVITIES

1. There is no substitute for seeing a court at work. Access to the youth court may be possible through placements with social services departments or the probation service. Those who cannot secure access to the youth court will nonetheless benefit from observing the adult magistrates' court.

2. Get hold of available leaflets about the legal aid system. These should be available from citizens' advice bureaux, the magistrates' courts, the Crown Courts, and possibly also from the county courts.

3. Construct a directory of advice agencies in your area which are able to provide legal and quasi-legal advice and assistance for service users. Which agency would be able to represent a service user before

a social security appeal tribunal; before other tribunals?

4. Which solicitors will do work under the legal aid scheme in your area? Are there any franchised firms? What are their areas of expertise? Are they sensitive to the problems faced by service users?

5. Do service users have access to a law centre in your area? What sort of work does the centre do?

6. Generally become familiar with the agencies of the legal system in your area. Where are the courts (magistrates', county, Crown), the police stations? Where are the providers of legal services: the law centre, legal aid solicitors, advice centres, CABx, tribunal repres-entation units? It is particularly useful to know someone you can contact or refer a service user to.

7. There are a number of journals which provide information and comment on some of the issues covered in this chapter. Have a look at any of the following:

Childright;
Community Care;
Journal of Social Welfare and Family Law,
Legal Action;
New Law Journal.

5 ADDRESSES

The Children's Legal Centre
University of Essex
Wivenhoe Park
Colchester
Essex CO4 3SQ.
Phone Advice Line: 01206 873820
Fax: 01206 874026
E-mail: CLC@essex.ac.uk
Admin phone number: 01206 872466

Law Centres Federation
Duchess House
18–19 Warren Street

London W1P 5DB.
Phone: 0171 387 8570
Fax: 0171 387 8368

Legal Aid Board
5th and 6th Floors
29–37 Red Lion Street
London WC1R 4PP.
Phone: 0171 813 5300

Liberty
21 Tabard Street
London SE1 4LA.
Phone: 0171 403 3888
Fax: 0171 407 5354
e-mail: liberty@GN.atc.org

Lord Chancellor's Department
Selbourne House
54-60 Victoria Street
London SW1E 6QW.
Web site: www.open.gov.uk/lcd

National Association for the Care and Resettlement of Offenders
(NACRO)
169 Clapham Road
London SW9 0PU.
Phone: 0171 582 6500.
Fax: 0171 735 4666

6. MATERIALS

Berlins, M and Dyer, C, *The Law Machine*, (1994) Penguin.

Ingman, T, *The English Legal Process*, (1996) Blackstone.

Legal aid leaflets, published by the Legal Aid Board, 1997.

Lord Chancellor announces cuts to legal aid. Legal Action, November 1997.

NACRO Factsheets (National Association for the Care and Resettlement of Offenders).

CHAPTER 3

Child care law – the Children Act 1989

1 INTRODUCTION

Child care work is one of the areas of practice that today dominates public discussion of social work. This level of concern reflects the continuing publicity surrounding child abuse inquiries and the treatment of children in care. Social work with children and their families takes place largely within the provisions and principles of the Children Act 1989, though the Act, which was implemented in October 1991, extends beyond child care law to encompass private legal proceedings which may arise from the breakdown of domestic relationships involving children, or from disputes concerning the upbringing or welfare of children.[1]

1.1 CHILD CARE PRACTICE

Child care work involves social work intervention into family life motivated by objectives of support for families with children in need, preventing children suffering significant harm or to protect them from the immediate threat of such harm. Such intervention may well evidence a tension that exists between the autonomy and privacy of the family and the responsibility of the state to protect and control the lives of children when and where necessary. Within the dynamics of this tension lie some of the central dilemmas of social work practice. Social work intervention into the private domain of family

---

1 Discussion of this area of law uses a distinction between public child (care) law and private child (care) law. Public child (care) law refers to legal proceedings which involve local authorities, eg applications for care and supervision orders, and for an emergency protection order. Private child (care) law encompasses legal proceedings which do not involve the local authority and often involve disputes between a child's parents concerning the upbringing of the child.

life is frequently seen and experienced as a form of state control of that family though the motivation for such intervention is essentially supportive of families with children in need; an expression of the principle of partnership in which local authority services are made available to help parents care for their children within the family. Despite the motivation for intervention and the principle of partnership which should inform any such intervention, the involvement of social work within the family can have a very different impact and may carry with it class, gender and racial stereotypes of good and appropriate parenting, and ultimately lead to the compulsory removal of children into care.

Failure to intervene in family life to protect children can have, literally, fatal consequences and the social work profession has been the subject of considerable criticism when it gets such decisions or their timing wrong. The child abuse inquiries of the late 1980s exposed the enormous difficulties inherent in this aspect of child care practice and in many ways they provided conflicting messages for the profession. The Jasmine Beckford inquiry[2] carried the message that social work intervention was needed at an earlier stage to protect children in the face of abuse; in contrast the Cleveland inquiry[3] was critical of the social workers involved on the grounds that the removal of a number of children from their families was precipitate and unwarranted, and of the doctors' diagnostic role. The removals evidenced a failure to make a wider assessment before taking action, and a failure among the social workers involved to reappraise their practice and consider their priorities.

These, and other dilemmas of child care work, reflect the tension that exists between the state, whose power is exercised by and through social work, and the relative autonomy or privacy of family life. This tension is itself overlaid with others: that between parents' rights and children's rights, and that between children's rights and children's welfare.

The 1980s saw an increased understanding of the nature of children's rights and a willingness of the courts to recognise specific examples of such rights. The Gillick case,[4] in which the House of Lords upheld

---

2 A Child in Trust, (1995) London Borough of Brent.
3 Report of Inquiry into Child Abuse in Cleveland, Cm 412, (1988) HMSO.
4 Gillick v West Norfolk and Wisbech Area Health Authority [1986] AC 112.

the legality of providing contraceptive advice to children under 16 without parental consent, was brought by a mother who argued that her rights as a parent over her children extended to the ability to consent to or forbid the provision of such advice. The Children Act reflects an articulation and recognition of the rights and interests of children and though it may be understood as a child centred piece of legislation its various provisions can also be seen to promote the interests of parents and local authorities. Indeed this complexity is to be expected of legislation which seeks to redraw the balance between the interests and rights of children, their parents and the state.

Section 1 of the Act endorses another principle, that of child welfare:

> When a court determines any question with respect to the upbringing of a child or the administration of a child's property or the application of any income arising from it, the child's welfare shall be the court's paramount consideration.

It is argued that the Children Act attempts to reconcile the possible tensions between children's rights and children's welfare:

> The British tandem system, in which children may be represented in public law proceedings by both a guardian ad litem (GAL), presenting a view to the court about the child's welfare, and a children's panel solicitor, acting as an advocate for the child and presenting a view about his rights or the justice of his case, is one which provides a unique balance between children's rights and children's welfare, which establishes a framework of decision making between children and adults, which respects both the rights of one and the responsibilities of the other.[5]

1.2   THE EMERGENCE OF THE CHILDREN ACT

Concern about the legal framework of child care was expressed in a number of official reports in the 1980s including the second report of the Social Services Committee 'Children in Care' (March 1984), the inter-departmental working party report 'Review of Child Care Law' published by the DHSS in September 1985, and the review of

---

5   The Tension Between Welfare and Justice, Judith Timms, January [1997] Family Law, at page 41.

'private' child law published by the Law Commission in 1988. In January 1987 the government published its White Paper 'The Law on Child Care and Family Services'. Concern in these reports and in the White Paper centred on the complexity of child care law, the number of overlapping jurisdictions exercised in respect of children and the use of wardship by local authorities as a backup jurisdiction to provide powers not available under the existing statutory provisions. The continuing debate about the possibility of a 'family court' was also part of the context of reform of child care law. These, and a number of other concerns raised by the child abuse inquiries, were addressed by the Children Act 1989 which was implemented in October 1991.

'The Introduction to The Children Act 1989', published by HMSO, describes the Act in the following terms:

> ... the most comprehensive piece of legislation which Parliament has ever enacted about children. It draws together and simplifies existing legislation to produce a more practical and consistent code. It integrates the law relating to private individuals with the responsibilities of public authorities, in particular local authority social services departments, towards children. In so doing the Act strikes a new balance between family autonomy and the protection of children.

Given this description and even a cursory glance at the statute itself, there is no doubt that the provisions of the Act provide a legislative framework for a substantial part of social work practice with families and children.

1.3 THE ACT

1.3.1 Structure of the Act

The Act is arranged into 12 parts and 15 schedules. *Part I* provides a number of general principles which underpin the operation of the Act and the work of those who have statutory powers and duties under it. *Part II* specifies a number of orders which can be made in 'family proceedings' including the 'section 8' orders; financial orders for children and the family assistance order. *Part III* is entitled 'Local Authority Support for Children and Families' and provides for the work of local authorities in respect of children 'in need'. *Part IV* provides for care and supervision orders and identifies the functions and work of guardians ad litem. *Part V* deals with the protection of children at risk including emergency protection orders and child assessment orders. *Parts VI to IX* deal with the welfare of children living away from home.

Part X is concerned with child minding and day care for young children. *Part XI* details the position of the Secretary of State and *Part XII* includes a number of miscellaneous provisions.

Guidance and regulations

A significant amount of secondary legislation has been made under the Children Act. These regulations, which are contained in statutory instruments, cover a number of areas concerning child care law and practice including residential care, private fostering and child protection.

The Department of Health has also published detailed guidance on the exercise of powers and duties under the Act. Such guidance, if it is issued under section 7 of the Local Authority Social Services Act 1970, requires local authorities, in the exercise of social services functions, to act under the general guidance of the Secretary of State.

1.3.2 Youth justice

The Act does not substantially affect the youth justice system, though it does provide for the inclusion of a residence requirement in a supervision order made by the youth court in criminal proceedings against a child or young person. Criminal prosecutions are taken in the youth court established by the Criminal Justice Act 1991 which was implemented in October 1992.

Schedule 2, para 7(c) requires local authorities to take reasonable steps designed to encourage children living in their area not to commit criminal offences.

1.3.3 Adoption

The Act has no substantial impact on the law of adoption.

2 THE LAW

This section is necessarily detailed but an attempt has been made where possible to structure information within contexts that are familiar to social workers.

The principles of the Act will be identified first and then consideration will be given to the duties of local authorities to children and families. Discussion of the orders that are available in relation to children in 'family proceedings' will be followed by a look at the provisions concerning care and supervision orders. The framework for protection of children at risk will conclude this analysis of the Act.

The Act is a complex piece of legislation and this chapter cannot provide a comprehensive review of its provisions. The emphasis will be on the impact of the law for social work practice and it seeks only to provide an introduction for qualifying social workers. More detailed discussion of the law is provided in 'An Introduction to The Children Act 1989', by the volumes of guidance, both published by HMSO, and by any one of the detailed texts available as guides to the law.

2.1   THE PRINCIPLES OF THE NEW ACT

The Introduction identifies a belief that underpins the Act:

> ... that children are generally best looked after within the family with both parents playing a full part and without resort to legal proceedings.

Local authorities have a general duty under section 17(1):

a)   to safeguard and promote the welfare of children within their area who are in need; and

b)   so far as is consistent with that duty, to promote the upbringing of such children by their families.

Implicit within these principles and general duties is the notion of *partnership* between social services departments and families. This partnership extends to situations where children in need are living with their families and also when such children are being looked after by the local authority.

2.1.1   The welfare principle(s)

Basic principles concerning the welfare of children are set out in section 1 of the Act:

1(1) When a court determines any question with respect to –

a) the upbringing of a child; or

b) the administration of a child's property or the application of any income arising from it,

the child's welfare shall be the court's paramount consideration.

Section 1(2) identifies the general principle that *delay in proceedings to determine the upbringing of a child is likely to prejudice the welfare of the child.*

Section 1(5) tells the court that in deciding whether to make an order under the Act *it shall not make the order or any of the orders unless it considers that doing so would be better for the child than making no order at all.*

2.1.2 The welfare checklist

Section 1(3) provides a checklist for the court to consider when it is deciding upon the making, variation and discharge of contested section 8 orders, and orders under Part IV of the Act, that is care and supervision orders. This *welfare checklist* requires the court to have regard to:

- the ascertainable wishes and feelings of the child (in the light of the child's age and understanding);

- the child's physical, emotional and educational needs;

- the likely effect on the child of any change in their circumstances;

- the child's age, sex, background and any characteristics of his which the court considers to be relevant;

- any harm which the child has suffered or is at risk of suffering;

- how capable each of his parents, and any other relevant person, is of meeting the child's needs;

- the range of powers available to the court under this Act in the proceedings in question.

These general principles, which the court is required to consider, will also clearly have an impact on practice and on the preparation of welfare reports for the court. Any recommendations contained in such reports should obviously address the welfare principle, the checklist, where appropriate, and the principle of no order unless the welfare of the child requires the court to make one.

2.1.3 Parental responsibility

The Act marks a shift from the notion of parental rights to a concept parental responsibility. The emphasis is on the parent's duty to care for the child as the only justification for the authority that a parent has in relation to their child.

Section 3(1):

> 'Parental responsibility' means all the rights, duties, powers, responsibilities and authority which by law a parent of a child has in relation to the child and his property.

Parental responsibility can be shared, eg by parents with the local authority where a child is in care. It provides a right of independent action, subject to limitation by a local authority where the child is in care and by a person with a residence order, so that any person with parental responsibility can exercise their responsibility independently of any other person with parental responsibility. It cannot be surrendered or transferred, but it may be delegated. Parental responsibility can also be lost by court order, e.g. in an adoption or where the court revokes a parental responsibility order under section 4(3).

The importance of parental responsibility is emphasised by the fact that people with it have a status in respect of their children even if they are not currently involved with the child, and that significant people for the child may not have the same status because they do not have parental responsibility for the child.

2.2 THE COURT(S)

Child care jurisdictions have always reflected the division between what are known as private law proceedings between parents concerning their children (and between other people with a close relationship with the child), and public law proceedings, such as care proceedings, brought by local authorities. The Act moves beyond such a distinction by establishing what are called *'family proceedings'* which encompass both private law and public law applications under Parts I, II, IV and V of the Act and therefore include applications for care and supervision orders, and for applications for orders under section 8 to decide disputes and other issues concerning a child's upbringing. The Act also brings a number of other 'private law' matters, such as divorce, domestic violence, occupation of the matrimonial home, and applications for financial relief between spouses, within the definition of family proceedings. The consequence of making such matters family proceedings is that the orders provided in Part II of the Act, ie section 8 orders, financial orders and family assistance orders, can be made in respect of the children of the parties involved in such proceedings. The High Court, county courts and magistrates' courts have concurrent jurisdiction to hear family proceedings. In the magistrates' courts jurisdiction under the Act is exercised by family panels. There are provisions for transferring family proceedings between courts.

2.3 LOCAL AUTHORITY SERVICES FOR CHILDREN AND FAMILIES

Part III of the Act, together with Schedule 2, provides a framework for the support of children in need and their families. The emphasis is on voluntary support based on a partnership between parent(s) and the local authority. Detailed guidance to local authorities concerning Part III of the Act is contained in 'Family Support, Day Care and Educational Provision for Young Children' published as Volume 2 'The Children Act 1989, Guidance and Regulations'.

Section 17(1) establishes the general duty of local authorities to promote the welfare of children in need within the family where possible by providing a range of services appropriate to those children's needs.

Section 17(10) defines a child in need:

... a child shall be taken to be in need if –

a) he is unlikely to achieve or maintain, or to have the opportunity of achieving or maintaining, a reasonable standard of health or development without the provision for him of services by a local authority under this Part;

b) his health or development is likely to be significantly impaired, or further impaired, without the provision for him of such services; or

c) he is disabled.

From the social work point of view it is important to note that the duty extends to children who are disabled, mentally or physically.[6]

Services may be provided by local authorities, or arranged by them, for children and/or families so long as they are directed to safeguarding and promoting the welfare of the child. Section 17(6) defines services to include 'assistance in kind or, in exceptional circumstances, in cash'.

Part I of Schedule 2 identifies specific duties for local authorities in relation to the services established in section 17. They include:

• the identification of children in need and the provision of information;

• the maintenance of a register of disabled children;

• the assessment of children's needs;

• the prevention of abuse and neglect;

• the provision of accommodation in order to protect a child;

• provision for disabled children;

• provision to reduce the need for care proceedings and criminal proceedings;

• provision for children living with their families (family support);

6   For a detailed discussion on the law concerning disabled children see chapter 4 'Disabled Children'.

- the provision of family centres;

- steps to encourage children not to commit criminal offences.

Section 18 imposes duties on local authorities to provide day care for pre-school children and after hours care for school age children.

The Guidance contained in Volume 2 gives an indication of the rationale behind these provisions:

> 2.1 Section 17 of Part III gives local authorities a general duty to safeguard and promote the welfare of children in need and to promote the upbringing of such children by their families, so far as this is consistent with their welfare duty to the child, by providing an appropriate range and level of services. Schedule 2 contains further provisions designed to help children in need continue to live with their families and generally to prevent the breakdown of family relationships. Partnership with parents and consultation with children on the basis of careful joint planning and agreement is the guiding principle for the provision of services within the family home and where children are provided with accommodation under voluntary arrangements. Such arrangements are intended to assist the parent and enhance, not undermine, the parent's authority and control. This new approach should also be developed when a child is in care, provided that it does not jeopardise his welfare.

Clearly therefore, service provision should be directed to supporting children in need and to achieving their upbringing within their own family wherever possible. These principles are central to the philosophy of the Act and should constitute a powerful influence on the allocation of resources and the development of practice.

2.3.1   Accommodation provided by the local authority

As part of the Part III package of services to families with children in need, local authorities are able to provide accommodation for children. In the circumstances of section 20(1) they must do so:

> 20(1) Every local authority shall provide accommodation for any child in need within their area who appears to them to require accommodation as a result of –
>
> a)   there being no person who has parental responsibility for him;
>
> b)   his being lost or having been abandoned; or

    c) the person who has been caring for him being prevented (whether or not permanently, and for whatever reason) from providing him with suitable accommodation or care.

In addition subsections 20(4) and (5) enable local authorities to provide accommodation for children under 16 and for young persons under 21 on the basis that to do so would safeguard or promote their welfare.

The Act requires local authorities to consult with the child it is proposing to accommodate so far as this is reasonably practicable and consistent with the child's welfare (section 20(6)).

When a child is being accommodated by a local authority under the Act parental responsibility does not, in law, pass to the authority. The concept of delegation best expresses the situation in which those with parental rights in respect of a child delegate those powers necessary for the upbringing of a child to a local authority. The philosophy of the Act seeks to encourage agreements between those with parental rights and local authorities who do the 'accommodating' so that there is a shared responsibility for the child based on partnership and agreement wherever possible. As the child gets older, and particularly in the 16-18 age range, this partnership will also have to accommodate the growing maturity and autonomy of the child.

2.3.2 Objections to and removal from local authority accommodation

The voluntary basis of accommodation by a local authority is emphasised by section 20(7) which prevents local authorities from accommodating children in the face of an objection from a person who has parental responsibility for the child and is willing and able to provide or arrange accommodation for the child.

Section 20(8) provides that any person with parental responsibility for the child may remove the child from accommodation provided by the local authority at any time. This right is subject to section 20(9) which specifies that sections 20(7) and (8) do not apply while anyone in whose favour a residence order is in force agrees to the child being looked after by the local authority. Section 20(11) specifies that section 20(7) and (8) does not apply where a child of 16 and over agrees to be accommodated.

2.3.3   Duties owed by local authorities in respect of children being looked after by them

Within the language of the Act children who are being accommodated by the local authority and children who are in the care of the local authority are being *looked after* by the authority. Section 22(3) imposes a number of duties on authorities in respect of all children being looked after by them:

(3) It shall be the duty of a local authority looking after any child –

a) to safeguard and promote his welfare; and

b) to make such use of services available for children cared for by their own parents as appears to the authority reasonable in his case.

The principles of partnership and consultation are underlined by section 22(4) which requires a local authority before making any decision in respect of a child they are looking after, to consult the child, the parents, those with parental responsibility and others if appropriate, and to give due and appropriate consideration to the child's wishes and to those of others consulted.

In addition section 22(5) requires that decisions concerning children being looked after take into account the child's religion, racial origin and their cultural and linguistic background.

Children being looked after by a local authority, whether in care or not, may, by section 23(2), be placed in a variety of forms of accommodation, and in accordance with regulations made under section 23(5) there are limited powers to allow a child in care to live at home subject to Regulation.[7]

2.3.4   Contact and rehabilitation between children and their families

Section 34(1) requires local authorities to facilitate reasonable contact between a child being looked after by the authority and the parents, relatives, friends and others connected with the child so long as this is reasonably practicable and consistent with the child's welfare.

7   See the Placement of Children with Parents Regulations 1991.

Schedule 2, para 15, requires local authorities to endeavour to promote contact between children they are looking after and their families so long as this is consistent with the child's welfare. Section 23(6) requires that where a child is being looked after by a local authority arrangements are made for the child to live with his or her family unless this is not reasonably practicable or consistent with the child's welfare.

2.3.5 Children Act complaints procedure

Section 26(3)–(8) requires local authorities to establish a complaints procedure to investigate complaints concerning the provision of support for children and their families under Part III of the Act. The procedure must consider complaints made by:

- any child being looked after by the authority, or any child who is in need but is not being looked after by the authority;

- that child's parents;

- any local authority foster parent;

- such other person who the authority considers has sufficient interest in the child's welfare to warrant their representations being considered.

The detailed operation of the procedure is determined by the Representations Procedure (Children) Regulations 1991.[8] A staged process requires a response from the authority within 28 days of a representation or complaint being received. The Act requires an independent person to be involved at this stage of investigation. If the complainant is not satisfied with this response then the authority is required to appoint a panel to investigate the representations. This panel must contain an independent person, though this does not have to be the same person involved at the earlier stage. The panel may consider both oral and written representations, and the person making the complaint/representations may be accompanied by another person who may speak on their behalf.

---

8 In practice local authorities have a 'first stage' process of lower level problem solving as a precursor to the formal investigative stage.

When a complaint or representation has been considered the Act (section 26(7)) requires the authority to:

(a) have due regard to the findings of those considering the representation; and

(b) take such steps as are reasonably practicable to notify (in writing)–

   (i) the person making the representation;

   (ii) the child (if the authority considers he has sufficient understanding); and

   (iii) such other persons (if any) as appear to the authority to be likely to be affected,

of the authority's decision in the matter and their reasons for taking that decision and of any action which they have taken, or propose to take.

2.4 SECURE ACCOMMODATION

Section 25 deals with the issue of secure accommodation. Subsection (1) sets out the limited circumstances in which accommodation may be used for restricting a child's liberty.

25(1) Subject to the following provisions of this section, a child who is being looked after by a local authority may not be placed, and, if placed, may not be kept in accommodation provided for the purpose of restricting liberty ('secure accommodation') unless it appears –

a) that:

   i) he has a history of absconding and is likely to abscond from any other description of accommodation; and

   ii) if he absconds, he is likely to suffer significant harm; or

b) that if he is kept in any other description of accommodation he is likely to injure himself or other persons.

The Secretary of State has power to make regulations to specify the maximum period of time that a child may be kept in secure accommodation before court authorisation is needed. This period is currently 72 hours.

Where a child who is being accommodated by a local authority is placed in secure accommodation, a person with parental responsibility for the child may remove the child from the accommodation whenever they wish and without notice.

The welfare checklist does not apply to any court hearing concerning secure accommodation.

2.5 THE ORDERS THAT CAN BE MADE IN FAMILY PROCEEDINGS (other than care and supervision orders)

2.5.1 Parental responsibility

The Act sets out the ways in which parental responsibility is allocated and acquired.

Section 2(1):

> Where a child's father and mother were married to each other at the time of his birth, they shall each have parental responsibility for the child.

Section 2(2):

> Where a child's mother and father were not married to each other at the time of his birth –
>
> (a) the mother shall have parental responsibility for the child;
>
> (b) the father shall not have parental responsibility for the child unless he acquires it in accordance with the provisions of this Act.

A father may acquire parental responsibility by the court making a parental responsibility order (section 4(1)(a)) or by a formal parental responsibility agreement with the child's mother. When the court is considering a father's application for such an order it will consider, among other things: the degree of commitment of the father toward the child; the degree of attachment between father and child; and the father's reasons for making the application.[9] In *Re S (parental responsibility)* [1995] 2 FLR 648, Ward LJ stressed that the essence of a parental responsibility order was in the grant of status, and that it was wrong to concentrate on the 'rights' which it confers.

Where a father has acquired parental responsibility through an agreement with the mother, the court has the power to revoke the order in circumstances where the welfare principle indicates such a revocation.[10]

Parental responsibility may also be vested in other people in addition to natural parents. Others may acquire parental responsibility by obtaining a residence order (sections 8 and 12) or an emergency protection order (section 44). Local authorities will obtain parental responsibility by obtaining a care order (section 31). (see below).

Parental responsibility is a continuing responsibility so it is unaffected for example, by divorce, but it may be limited by court order and cannot be exercised in conflict with a court order. It is shared by parents and it can be shared by parents with others so that when a child is in care parental responsibility is shared between parents and the local authority.

2.5.2 Section 8 orders

These orders can be made by the court upon application, in other family proceedings, or on its own motion; they allow the court to resolve questions and disputes about the upbringing of children. The welfare principles in section 1 apply to the hearings to determine such applications; where an application for a section 8 order is contested the welfare checklist in section 1(3) must be considered.

Contact order

Such an order requires a person with whom a child is living to allow a child to have contact with or visit or stay with a named person. Orders can be as wide or narrow as appropriate and can provide for contact by letter or telephone etc. The basic legal principle is that

---

9 *Re H (minors)(local authority: parental rights)* [1991] 2 All ER 185 and *Re G (a minor)(parental responsibility order)* [1994] 1 FLR 504.
10 *Re P (terminating parental responsibility)* [1995] 1 FLR 1048.

a child has a right of contact with his or her parent(s) and that no child should be deprived of this contact unless the court is satisfied that it is in the child's interests that there should be no contact.[11] It is clear from case law that there will be occasions where the courts will deny contact in furtherance of the child's interests.[12]

Residence order

This is an order which determines with whom a child is to live. If a residence order is made in favour of a non-parent then by section 12(2) that person will also have parental responsibility in respect of the child whilst the order remains in force. If a father is granted a residence order he must also be granted a parental responsibility order which would continue if the residence order were later to be discharged.

The concepts of residence and parental responsibility are different so that where, upon divorce, residence is ordered for one parent, both parents will nonetheless retain parental responsibility. A parent without a residence order has a diminished form of parental responsibility in the sense that they do not have the same day to day authority that goes with the relationship of residence.

It is possible under the provisions of section 11(4) for a residence order made in favour of people who do not live together to specify periods of residence in different households.

The grant of a residence order will discharge a care order.

A prohibited steps order

This order prevents a person with parental responsibility, or any other person, from taking a step specified in the order without the consent of the court. This order is by nature a 'single issues' order concerning aspects of parental responsibility, and is used where contact and residence orders cannot provide for the necessary control over a child's upbringing. These orders cannot be used when a child is in the care of a local authority.

11   *Re H (minors)(access)* [1992] 1 FLR 148.
12   See, for instance, *Re F (minors)(denial of contact)* [1993] 2 FLR 677 involving a transsexual father, and *Re D (a minor) (contact: mother's hostility)* [1993] 2 FLR 1.

A specific issue order

The order provides directions for settling an issue concerning the upbringing of a child. Again such an order can only be used where the main orders concerning contact and residence are not sufficient. Such orders cannot be used where the child is in the care of a local authority.

2.5.3   The availability of section 8 orders

Section 8 orders are available in family proceedings which include:

— wardship;

— proceedings under Parts I, II and IV of the Children Act;

— divorce and judicial separation;

— domestic violence;

— magistrates' courts' matrimonial jurisdiction; and

— adoption.

The orders, together with parental responsibility orders, can be made in any family proceedings so, for example, they are available, subject to specific statutory restrictions, to courts dealing with cases involving domestic violence and in applications by local authorities for care orders.

Some people are able to apply for a section 8 order as of right and they therefore do not require the leave (permission) of the court; other applicants require the leave of the court. Generally parents, guardians and those in whose favour a residence order has been made, may apply without leave.

It is intended that anyone with an interest in the child should be able to get access to the courts to seek a section 8 order; this is provided for in the Act subject to leave being granted by the court. Children under 16 may apply for leave to seek a section 8 order in respect of themselves. Where a child has reached 16 the court may not make a section 8 order other than to discharge or vary an existing order.

Where a child is legally in the care of a local authority no order, other than a residence order, may be made. If a residence order is made in respect of a child in care it has the effect of discharging the care order. Local authorities are not allowed to apply for a residence or contact order in respect of any child.

The Act does not set any specific criteria for the grant, variation or discharge of these orders. As a consequence courts hearing such applications are required to consider them in the light of the principles set out in section 1, and, in contested applications, to apply the welfare checklist set out in section 1(3) of the Act. The child's welfare is therefore the paramount consideration for the court and there is a presumption that no order will be made unless the court considers that it would be better for the child to make an order than not to do so. The general principle that delay in determining the application is likely to prejudice the child must be taken into account.

2.5.4 Family assistance orders

The objective of the order is to provide short term assistance, on a consensual basis, to families or individuals going through or coming to terms with the breakdown of their relationship. As such it is different from a supervision order but its availability supplements the powers of the courts where it is thought that the more powerful supervision order is not necessary.

These orders, available under section 16, can be made in family proceedings. Under such orders a probation officer or local authority social worker will advise, assist and befriend the person(s) named in the order. The persons in whose favour an order may be made are parents, the child, or any person with whom the child is living or anyone in whose favour a contact order is made. The child is not required to consent to the order being made though the consent of others named in the order is necessary. The order may be made for a maximum of six months.

2.6 CARE AND SUPERVISION ORDERS

Part IV of the Act deals with care and supervision orders available under the Act and as such it is of primary importance for social work practice. (These orders should be distinguished from supervision orders as a sentence of the criminal courts; these are available in the youth court under the Children and Young Persons Act 1969.)

2.6.1 Who may apply?

Only local authorities and authorised persons, currently the NSPCC, may apply for a care or supervision order under the Children Act. The Secretary of State has the power to authorise other applicants.

2.6.2 The grounds for the grant of care and supervision orders

These are set out in section 31(2):

> (2) A court may only make a care order or supervision order if it is satisfied –
>
> a) that the child concerned is suffering, or is likely to suffer, significant harm; and
>
> b) that the harm, or likelihood of harm, is attributable to –
>
> i) the care given to the child, or likely to be given to him if the order were not made, not being what it would be reasonable to expect a parent to give to him; or
>
> ii) the child's being beyond parental control.

The grounds in section 31(2) are the only grounds on which a care order or supervision order can be made. The burden of proof is on the applicant for the order, and the court must be satisfied that evidence establishes the grounds in section 31(2) on the balance of probabilities. These grounds are known as the 'threshold criteria'.

Where the court has to decide whether a child 'is suffering' significant harm the court has to consider the position immediately prior to the process of protection being put into motion by an emergency protection order, an interim care order, or by the child being accommodated by the local authority.[13]

---

13 *Northamptonshire County Council v S* [1993] Fam 136, and *Re M (a minor) (care order: threshold conditions)* [1994] 2 AC 424, HL.

Where the application is based on an assertion that a child is likely to suffer significant harm, the court must be satisfied that there is a real possibility of harm. The more serious the allegation the more cogent the evidence required by the court.[14]

Section 31(9) defines 'harm' as ill-treatment or the impairment of health or development. These concepts are further defined:

- 'development': means physical, intellectual, emotional, social or behavioural development;

- 'health': means physical or mental health;

- 'ill-treatment': includes sexual abuse and forms of ill-treatment which are not physical.

Section 31(10) gives a definition of 'significant':

> Where the question of whether harm suffered by a child is significant turns on the child's health or development, his health or development shall be compared with that which could reasonably be expected of a similar child.

The court is faced with what is essentially a two stage task.[15] The first stage is to satisfy itself that the threshold criteria are established by evidence. The second stage is to decide whether to make a care order or not.[16] In the second stage, when the court is deciding whether to make the care or supervision order, it is required to consider the section 1 welfare principles. Consequently the child's welfare is the paramount consideration, delay is likely to prejudice the welfare of the child and the court should not make a care or supervision order unless it considers that doing so would be better for the child than making no order at all. The court is also obliged to consider the welfare checklist set out in section 1(3). It is quite possible for the court to find that the threshold criteria have been established and then to decline to make a care or supervision order on the basis that such an order would conflict with (one of) the welfare principles.

---

14 *Re H and R (child sexual abuse: standard of proof)* [1996] 1 FLR 80.
15 *Humberside County Council v B* [1993] 1 FLR 257.
16 As an alternative the court could make any other order that is available under the 1989 Act though it should be remembered that the threshold criteria only apply to applications for care and supervision orders.

2.6.3 Interim orders

Interim care and supervision orders may be made under section 38(1) and because applications for the full orders are 'family proceedings' the court may make a section 8 order in addition or as an alternative to an interim order. Interim orders are made on the basis that the court is satisfied that there are reasonable grounds for believing that the circumstances of the child fall within the conditions in section 31(2) – the threshold criteria, and the welfare principles would be satisfied by the making of the order.

By powers in section 38(6) directions may be attached to an interim order by the court to allow assessment and examination of the child. A minor with appropriate maturity and capacity may refuse to be examined or assessed.[17] The power in this section has led to a number of cases which have had to deal with conflicts between the directions of the courts and the discretionary powers of local authorities. In *Re C (interim care order: residential assessment)* [1997] 1 FLR 1, the House of Lords held that the court had the power to order a residential assessment so that it could decide whether to make a care order even in circumstances where the local authority had decided against such an assessment, or to pay for it:

> Although an interim care order placed decision making in the hands of the local authority, the court could override the local authority where it was necessary to enable the court to decide whether to make a care order.

> When deciding whether to make a direction under s 38(6), the court should take into account the financial information supplied by the local authority.[18]

Time limits on interim orders are imposed by section 38(4). The initial order may be for up to eight weeks with further orders of up to four weeks. There is no statutory limit on the number of interim orders the court can make but section 1 sets out the general principle that delay is likely to prejudice the welfare of the child concerned. It should be appreciated that an interim care order may satisfy the welfare

---

17   But see *South Glamorgan County Council v W and B* [1993] 1 FLR 574 where the court held that, in the exercise of its inherent jurisdiction, it had the power to override a refusal to consent to a psychiatric assessment and treatment.
18   *Recent developments in children's law*, Nicola Wyld and Lindsey Mendoza, Legal Action, April 1997.

principle even where it may delay the final decision on an application for a care order; an example would be the need for the results of an assessment so that the welfare of the child could be determined.

2.6.4   What is the legal effect of a care order?

Section 33(3) details the legal significance of a care order:

> While a care order is in force with respect to a child, the local authority designated by the order shall –
>
> a) have parental responsibility for the child; and
>
> b) have the power (subject to the following provisions of this section) to determine the extent to which a parent or guardian of the child may meet his parental responsibility for him.

It should be noted that though the local authority has parental responsibility in respect of the child in its care so also do the parents or guardian. Parental responsibility is thus shared so that parents have a voice in the upbringing of their child even though s/he is in the care of the local authority. However, the authority has the power to limit the exercise of parental responsibility by parents or guardian; such a power must not be used unless the authority is satisfied that to do so is necessary to safeguard or promote the interests of the child.

2.6.5   Contact for the child in care

Section 34 includes a requirement that the local authority provides for reasonable contact between a child in its care and the child's parents or guardian and any person in whose favour a residence order was in force or who had the care of a ward of court prior to the making of the care order.

If the authority wishes to deny contact then it must get authorisation from the court. The authority has a short term power (maximum of seven days) to deny contact under section 34(6).

The court has power to make a contact order where disputes arise concerning the fulfilment of the presumption of reasonable contact contained in section 34(1).

The court is also required, on making a care order, to consider the arrangements which the authority has made or is proposing to make concerning contact for the child and to invite comment on them from the parties. The court has the power to make a contact order when it makes a care order and this power is to be used if no satisfactory arrangements have been made or agreement reached. The emphasis is on voluntary agreement between the authority and parents over the issue of contact.[19]

2.6.6   The supervision order

The grounds for making a supervision order are the same as those for a care order. Supervision orders are to be made for one year initially and this may be extended by the court for a period of up to three years.

By section 35(1) the supervisor is under a statutory duty to advise, assist and befriend the child who is the subject of the order and additionally to take the necessary steps to give effect to the order and to consider whether to apply to have the order varied or discharged. The additional duties are directed toward making sure that supervision orders are kept under review and are not left to 'drift'.

Other details concerning the administration of supervision orders are contained in Parts I and II of Schedule 3 to the Act. Included in these provisions is the power of the supervisor to give directions to the supervised child including where to live and the requirement to partici- pate in specified activities. The supervisor may also impose obligations on any 'responsible person', such as the person with parental res- ponsibility for the child, who must consent to this. The objective is to encourage participation by parents in, for example, mother and baby groups and child care classes. Supervision orders under the Act may include, with the consent of the 'competent' child, requirements in relation to medical and psychiatric examination and treatment.

The Final Report of the Children Act Advisory Committee asserts that a supervision order is really only suitable where co-operation is reasonably to be anticipated on all sides.[20]

19   See also Contact with Children Regulations 1991.
20   Final Report. Children Act Advisory Committee. Lord Chancellor's Department. 1997. See *Re S (J)* [1993] 2 FLR 919 for a discussion of the circumstances which should have an impact on the decision whether to grant a care order or a supervision order.

2.6.7 The discharge of care and supervision orders

Care and supervision orders expire when the child reaches the age of 18. Under section 39 both orders may be discharged by the court on the application of the person with parental responsibility for the child, the child or the local authority in whose favour the order was made.

No grounds for the discharge of the orders are specified by section 39 so that the court is bound by the principles set out in section 1, principally that 'the child's welfare shall be the court's paramount consideration'.

2.6.8 Education supervision orders

Section 36 provides for an education supervision order. Such orders may be made by the court on the application of the local education authority on the grounds that the child is of compulsory school age and is not being properly educated.

Being properly educated is defined by section 36(4) as:

> ... receiving efficient full time education suitable to his age, ability and aptitude and any special educational needs he may have.

If a child is not being properly educated then he may be placed under the supervision of the education authority who are required to advise, assist and befriend the child and to give directions to the child and parents that will secure the child's proper education. The wishes of the child and parents are to be taken into account but parents are required to comply with directions. Failure to do so, without an appropriate defence (listed in Part III of Schedule 3 to the Act) is a criminal offence.

Part III of Schedule 3 to the Act specifies the details of education supervision orders.

2.7 INVESTIGATIONS ORDERED BY THE COURTS

Issues concerning the welfare of children may arise in any family proceedings, eg divorce, domestic violence. Section 37(1) gives the court the power to direct local authorities to investigate the circumstances of a child where it appears that a care or supervision order may be necessary. As part of this investigation the local authority must consider whether to apply for a care or supervision order; whether to provide services and assistance for the family, or whether to take any other action. If the authority decides not to apply for a care or supervision order it is required to provide reasons to the court and also to inform the court of any other assistance provided for the family and/or child. The authority is also required to consider whether the case should be reviewed at a later date.

2.8 PROTECTING CHILDREN AT RISK

The child abuse inquiries of the late 1980s highlighted problems with the statutory framework for protecting children at risk. Part V of the Children Act provides local authorities and the police with statutory powers designed to protect children from abuse whilst also recognising the rights of parents by giving them the ability to challenge the use of law in this area.

The Department of Health's Introduction to the Act describes the objectives of these powers in the following terms:

> ... the Children Act tries to find a better balance between the need to protect children and the other interests of the individuals involved. The conditions which must be satisfied before an emergency protection or child assessment order may be made are closely linked to the purpose of these orders; where practicable parents and others are given a right of challenge; the duration of the orders is shorter than the place of safety order; and the legal effect of both of these orders is more clearly spelt out.

2.8.1 A duty to investigate

The Act imposes on local authorities a duty to investigate where they have reasonable cause to suspect that a child in their area is suffering or is likely to suffer significant harm.

Section 47(1) provides:

> Where a local authority –

   b) have reasonable cause to suspect that a child who lives, or is found,
      in their area is suffering, or is likely to suffer, significant harm,

the authority shall make, or cause to be made, such enquiries as they
consider necessary to enable them to decide whether they should take
any action to safeguard or promote the child's welfare.

2.8.2   Court orders

Three orders are provided by the Act; a child assessment order, an
emergency protection order and a recovery order. The latter order
is principally concerned with child abduction. Appropriate entry and
search warrants are also available.

Child assessment order

The order must be sought in a full court hearing by a local authority
or the NSPCC. The criteria for the grant of such an order are set
out in section 43(1):

43(1) On the application of a local authority or authorised person
for an order to be made under this section with respect to a child,
the court may make the order, if, but only if, it is satisfied that –

a) the applicant has reasonable cause to suspect that the child is
   suffering, or is likely to suffer significant harm;

b) an assessment of the state of the child's health or development,
   or of the way in which he has been treated, is required to enable
   the applicant to determine whether or not the child is suffering,
   or is likely to suffer, significant harm; and

c) it is unlikely that such an assessment will be made, or be satisfactory, in the absence of an order under this section.

Because the application is made at a full court hearing parents and
other interested parties are able to be present and resist the application if they so wish. If the order is granted the child must be
produced to the person named in the order and the order is likely to
include directions regarding the necessary assessments including a
medical examination. A child, with sufficient understanding to make
an informed decision, may refuse to consent to such an examination
or any other form of assessment.

Emergency protection order

Section 44(1) sets out the grounds on which such an order may be granted by the court:

> 44(1) Where any person (the applicant) applies to the court for an order to be made under this section with respect to a child, the court may make the order if, but only if, it is satisfied that –
>
> a) there is reasonable cause to believe that the child is likely to suffer significant harm if –
>
>   i) he is not removed to accommodation provided by or on behalf of the applicant; or
>
>   ii) he does not remain in the place in which he is then being accommodated.

In addition to this power local authorities may apply for an emergency protection order in the circumstances set out in part (b) of section 44(1):

> b) in the case of an application made by a local authority –
>
>   i) enquiries are being made with respect to the child under section 47(1)(b); and
>
>   ii) those enquiries are being frustrated by access to the child being unreasonably refused to a person authorised to seek access and that the applicant has reasonable cause to believe that access to the child is required as a matter of urgency; or
>
> c) in the case of an application by an authorised person:
>
>   i) the applicant has reasonable cause to suspect that a child is suffering, or is likely to suffer, significant harm;
>
>   ii) the applicant is making enquiries with respect to the child's welfare and;
>
>   iii) those enquiries are being frustrated by access to the child being unreasonably refused to a person authorised to seek access and the applicant has reasonable cause to believe that access to the child is required as a matter of urgency.

Applications for an emergency protection order are normally made by a local authority social worker but the section is wide enough to allow any person with an interest in the child to do so. Applications are normally made to the court but may be made to a single JP who is a member of the family proceedings panel. Where appropriate an order may authorise the applicant to enter specified premises and search for the child.

Under section 48(9) warrants may be issued by the court where attempts to exercise powers under an emergency protection order have been or are likely to be prevented. Such warrants authorise a police constable to assist the applicant for the order to exercise their powers under the order. The warrant may direct that the constable is accompanied by a doctor, nurse and/or health visitor.

Effect of the order

The order requires production of the child and it also authorises the removal of the child from, or retention in, particular accommodation. The order gives the applicant parental responsibility for the child.

There is a presumption that during the currency of the order reasonable contact will continue between parents and child though this may be limited by the court. The court may also direct (or prohibit) medical examinations and assessment of the child during the period of the order.

During the order the applicant is under a duty to return the child or allow him or her to be removed to the parents or the person who had care prior to the order being granted where it appears safe to do so. The child can be taken back again by the applicant, if that is necessary, so long as the order remains in force.

Duration and discharge of the order

The order is limited to a maximum of eight days though there are limited circumstances in which this may be extended for a further seven days. The parents, the child and other strictly specified people, may apply to the court to have the order discharged though only after the order has been in existence for 72 hours. No application to discharge may be made by anyone who had notice of the original application or by anyone who was present at the hearing.

Excluding the alleged abuser

The Family Law Act 1996, section 52 and Schedule 6, amends sections 38 and 44 of the Children Act 1989, to allow the court to make an 'exclusion requirement' when it makes an interim care order or an emergency protection order. The grounds for making such a require-ment are:

> ... where there is reasonable cause to believe that, if a person is excluded from the family home, the child will cease to suffer or be likely to suffer significant harm, and

> ... where another person living in the home (whether a parent or otherwise) is able and willing to give the child the care which it would be reasonable to expect a parent to give and s/he consents to the inclusion of this requirement.[21]

A power of arrest can be attached to such a requirement.

2.8.3 Police powers

The powers of the police in relation to children at risk are contained in section 46 of the Act and may be exercised without a court order on the basis that the officer has reasonable cause to believe that a child would be likely to suffer significant harm unless his or her powers were exercised.

In such circumstances police officers may take a child into police protection, for a maximum of 72 hours, by removing the child to suitable accommodation or by preventing the child's removal from a particular place. Responsibility for the child should be passed onto the local authority as soon as possible during the 72 hours though the police protection will last until an application is made for a court order. In such circumstances an application for an emergency protection order may be made by the police or the local authority.

Police protection under section 46 does not include a right of entry. If this is required it must be obtained by attaching a warrant to an emergency protection order. The police retain their power under section 17(1)(e) of the Police and Criminal Evidence Act 1984 which

---

21 See *Recent developments in children's law*, Nicola Wyld and Lindsey Mendoza, Legal Action, October 1996.

restates a common law power to enter and search premises for the purpose of saving life or limb.

3 THE CHILDREN ACT AND SOCIAL WORK: some issues for discussion

3.1 CONSULTING AND WORKING IN PARTNERSHIP WITH CHILDREN AND FAMILIES

Local authorities have, under the Children Act 1989, a general duty to safeguard and promote the welfare of children within their area who are in need and so far as is consistent with that duty to promote the upbringing of such children by their families. As parental responsibility for children is retained notwithstanding any court order short of adoption, local authorities must work in partnership with parents, seeking court orders when compulsory action is indicated in the interests of the child but only when this is better for the child than working with the parents under voluntary arrangements.[22]

The principle of partnership is central to social work practice under the Act and should be manifested in a number of ways including the provision of information, consultation with children and families, parental participation in reviews concerning children who are being looked after by a local authority and the drawing up of written agreements relating to children who are being accommodated.

Care proceedings under the Act may be seen as evidence that partnership between local authorities and families with children in need has not been successful. The Act has established significant harm as the criterion for making a care order with the proviso that the harm is attributable to the care provided for the child by his or her carers or parents. However, a number of the provisions of the Act make it clear that despite the criteria being established and a care order being granted to a local authority the options for work in partnership with parents remain.

22 *Working Together Under the Children Act. A guide to arrangements for inter-agency co-operation for the protection of children from abuse*, Home Office, Department of Health, Department of Education and Science, Welsh Office, (1991) HMSO. See also *Messages from Research, and Challenges of Partnership in Child Protection*, Department of Health (1995).

Under a care order parental responsibility for the child is taken by the local authority but it also remains with the parent(s) so that it is shared between them. The purpose of this arrangement is that the parents of children in care continue to be involved in making decisions concerning their upbringing. Section 34 requires local authorities to facilitate reasonable contact between a child in care and his or her parents and section 23(6) requires that a local authority looking after a child (this includes a child in care) shall make arrangements for the child to live with their family so far as this is consistent with their welfare. Section 22(4) sets out a duty under which a local authority should consult with the parents of children being looked after.[23] The expectation of the Act is that wherever possible partnership should continue even after a care order is made so that the order can be discharged where appropriate.

Despite considerable statutory 'encouragement' toward partnership and consultation with parents and children, underpinned by guidance, there remains concern that partnership is too often rhetoric rather than reality.

> The duty to give 'due consideration' to the wishes of children and parents may be interpreted broadly or restrictively. Authorities need not implement their wishes. Nor are they guided on the relative importance to attach to their respective views, other than that a child's age and understanding will affect the weight given to what the child says and wishes. Indeed, law and practice reflect an ambivalent attitude towards partnership with children.[24]

3.2 CHILD PROTECTION

Child abuse formed the focus for much public concern and comment prior to the passing and implementation of the Children Act. Concern about the need to protect children from abuse was tempered by concern not to intrude into family life unnecessarily. This concern has been taken up in guidance issued under section 7 of the Local Authority Social Services Act 1970. The preface to 'Working Together' declares:

---

23 Volume 3 of the Guidance on Family Placements and Volume 4 on Residential Care provide further details about the care of children being looked after by a local authority.
24 Braye, S and Preston-Shoot, M, *Practising Social Work Law*, (2nd edn), (1997) Macmillan.

It is important for all professionals to combine an open-minded attitude to alleged concerns about a child with decisive action when this is clearly indicated. Intervention in a family, particularly if court action is necessary, will have major implications for them even if the assessment eventually leads to a decision that no further action is required. Public confidence in the child protection system can only be maintained if a proper balance is struck avoiding unnecessary intrusion in families while protecting children at risk of significant harm.

Though the guidance is not law, local authorities are required to work to it unless exceptional local circumstances justify variations. 'Working Together' identifies a number of principles which should inform child protection work stressing that such work should be undertaken against a background of partnership between local authorities and families. The necessity for inter-agency co-operation is clearly stated as is the need to develop close working relationships between social services departments, the police service, doctors, community health workers, schools, voluntary agencies and others. Area Child Protection Committees are identified as the forum for developing, monitoring and reviewing child protection policies. This will include the monitoring of information contained on child protection registers. These registers are used to identify those children who are at risk because they have been abused or are at risk of abuse. Though the register has no formal legal status, its operation, particularly the decision to enter the name of an 'alleged or suspected' abuser, can be made accountable through an application for judicial review.[25] These committees are also responsible for promoting inter-agency working. Section 27 gives local authorities a power to request the help of other authorities, such as education, housing and health, in the exercise of their functions under Part III. When such a request is made these other authorities are under a duty to comply with the request so long as this is compatible with their other statutory functions and does not prejudice the discharge of these functions.

Child Protection Conferences are identified by Working Together as a central element in the child protection system:

> The child protection conference is central to child protection procedures. It is *not* a forum for a formal decision that a person has abused a child. That is a matter for the courts. It brings together the family and the professionals concerned with child protection and

25 *R v Norfolk County Council, ex p M* [1989] 2 All ER 359.

with the opportunity to exchange information and plan conference symbolises the inter-agency nature of treatment and the management of child protection. the child protection process, the work is conducted on agency basis and the conference is the prime forum for sharing information and concerns, analysing risk and recommending responsibility for action. It draws together the staff from all the agencies with specific responsibilities in the child protection process (health, social services, police, schools and probation), and other staff who can offer relevant specialist advice, for example psychiatrists, psychologists, lawyers, and provides them with the forum for conducting and agreeing their joint approach to work with the child and family.[26]

The guidance distinguishes between initial child protection conferences and the child protection review. It establishes that the former should be convened only after an investigation under section 47 has been carried out, and should decide on the level of risk of the children, on the need for registration, and on plans for the future. In contrast the purpose of child protection reviews is defined as: to review the arrangements for the protection of the child, identify the current level of risk, ensure that the child is adequately protected, review the effectiveness of inter-agency co-operation and the protection plan

It is clear that social work practitioners involved in child protection are required to work within a complex framework of statutory law, regulations, guidance and circulars from central government, and agency policy and practice. They continue to be accountable for their actions to families, parents and children; to the courts and ultimately to a society which imposes significant responsibility for preventing abuse to children on the social work profession.

3.3 APPLICATIONS UNDER THE CHILDREN ACT

The first Annual Report of the Children Act Advisory Committee, which was published late in 1992, reported on initial trends in the operation of the Act but warned against drawing firm conclusions from early experience. The Committee commented on the surprisingly few public law applications during the first six months of

---

26 Working Together under The Children Act, Home Office et al, (1991) HMSO, at page 41.

operation. The Children Act Report 1992, pub͟_____ in February 1993, tended to confirm this trend. S͟   irst year of operation show that there were 2,300 em͟   ion orders granted as against approximately 5,000 pla͟__   ders a year under the previous legislation. The figures for care orders show that 1,600 were made in the first year of the Children Act compared to 6,200 orders in the previous year, though the number of new care orders being sought during the year had risen.

The Committee published its final report in June 1997 with statistics for applications and orders made during 1996. During the year there were 5,600 care and supervision orders, 1% fewer than in 1995. There was a fall (16%) in the number of emergency protection orders and extensions to a figure of 2,565. Just over 1,000 residence orders were made. Applications for contact orders rose by just over 7%, while orders made rose by over 14% to 40,330. The number of residence orders made rose by over 8% to an estimated 27,660. 8,730 applications were made for prohibited steps orders, with 5,780 orders being made. The number of parental responsibility orders rose by over 27% to 5,680. The number of parental responsibility agreements registered rose by 4% to 3,590.

3.4   REPRESENTING THE CHILD – THE ROLE OF THE GUARDIAN AD LITEM

The Children Act provides for the appointment of a guardian ad litem in public law proceedings under the Act, most notably in applications for an emergency protection order and in care proceedings. The role of the guardian is to safeguard the interests of the child, so that section 41 provides that a guardian shall be appointed by the court unless it is satisfied that such an appointment is not necessary to safeguard the child's interests. Whilst the guardian is said to be the social work advocate for the child, the child will also be represented by a lawyer acting as the child's legal advocate. The former is concerned with the child's welfare, the latter with issues concerning the rights of the child and the justice of his or her case.[27]

> ... the guardian's role stands at the interface between conflicting rights
> and powers of courts, local authorities, and the child's natural or

---

27   See Judith Timms, *The Tension Between Welfare and Justice*, January [1997] Family Law, pp 38-47.

substitute parents. The guardian's main task is to secure the most positive possible outcome for the child. But the guardian also has to make a judgement between the potentially conflicting demands of children's rights, the protection of children, the autonomy of the family and the duty of the state.[28]

In order to discharge their welfare obligations the guardian will investigate the circumstances surrounding the court proceedings and present the court with a report identifying the guardian's view of the welfare of the child. In preparing this report the guardian will interview the child, the parents, local authority employees involved with the family and the child, and anyone else who may be relevant in establishing a view on the welfare of the child. The guardian has statutory authority (by section 42(1)) for access to local authority records concerning the child, and to examine and take copies of such records. This material is then admissible in court proceedings notwithstanding any rule of law or other provision which would otherwise have prevented it being admitted in court as evidence such as the hearsay rule.

It is clear that the guardian, who will be an experienced and independent social work practitioner, plays a central role, directed toward ensuring the welfare of the child, in those proceedings which are taken under Part IV and Part V of the Act. Their role is specified by the legislation and by Rules of Court and they have significant rights in relation to obtaining information and presenting evidence. Consequently their influence on the final decision by the court is considerable. Because they take an independent position in proceedings there may well be some tension between the interests of the local authority, and its social workers, and the guardian, though at the second stage of care proceedings all agencies and parties should be focused on the single issue of the child's welfare.

Guardians are appointed by the court from regional panels, with their funding being provided by local authorities. This financial structure continues to attract criticism largely on the grounds that it impinges on the independent role of the guardian.

---

28   Geoff Hoon MP, Parliamentary Secretary at the Lord Chancellor's Department, Speech to the National Conference of the National Association of Guardians Ad Litem and Reporting Officers, 3 November 1997.

3.5 THE COURT WELFARE OFFICER

In private law proceedings under the Act, a similar role to that of the guardian ad litem is provided by the court welfare officer. Section 7 gives the court a power to require a written or oral welfare report where it is 'considering any question with respect to a child'. Such reports are prepared by court welfare officers working for local authorities or a probation service. Most often welfare reports are prepared for the court when it is considering applications for orders under section 8 of the Act (contact, residence, specific issues and prohibited steps), and section 4 (parental responsibility). The court when it is deciding such cases is required to consider the welfare principles in section 1, and the welfare checklist in section 1(3) when the application is contested. Welfare reports will help the court decide on these issues and it is expected that the court will follow the recommendations of such reports; if it wishes to depart from these it is expected that reasons will be given.

3.6 THE TENSION BETWEEN THE COURTS AND LOCAL AUTHORITIES CONCERNING CHILDREN IN CARE

Historically the High Court has had responsibility for protecting the interests of those who were unable to do so for themselves. In relation to children wardship became a popular way for parents to challenge decisions concerning their children in the care of the local authority, and for local authorities wishing to circumvent or supplement their statutory powers. In *A v Liverpool City Council* [1982] AC 363 the House of Lords decided that the discretion of the local authority over children in its care should not generally be subject to interference by parents or by the courts through the use of wardship. The Children Act sought to consolidate and unify the law relating to children and therefore included provisions in section 100 which limit the use of wardship under the High Court's inherent jurisdiction so that there should not be alternative and parallel child law systems. The Act was founded on the single route into care provided by section 31 and on the parental responsibility of the local authority for children in its care.

Section 100 limits the High Court's inherent jurisdiction to make a child who is the subject of a care order, a ward of court. Local authorities are severely restricted in their ability to ask the High Court to exercise its inherent jurisdiction. This restriction reflects the fact that local authorities may only gain parental responsibility, and the authority that goes with it, over a child through the grant of a care order. Consequently the inherent jurisdiction should not provide an alternative method of gaining authority over a child except in very limited and necessary circumstances set out in the Act. Thus section 100(3) requires the court to grant leave to the local authority and subsection (4) sets out the only grounds on which leave may be granted: that no other appropriate order is available, and there is reasonable cause to believe that if the inherent jurisdiction were not used the child is likely to suffer significant harm.[29]

Tension between the courts and local authorities may also arise from the fact that the courts are responsible for considering the welfare of the child when determining any question, except those that arise in proceedings concerning Part III of the Act, with respect to the upbringing of the child (section1(1)(a)). Local authorities take over this function when granted a care order in relation to a particular child (section 22(3)). In practice the division of responsibility has not been so easy to allocate.

It is clear from case law (*Re KDT (a minor) (care order: conditions)* [1994] 2 FCR 721) that the court has no power under section 31 to impose conditions on a care order. Despite these limitations on the court's jurisdiction it is also clear from the cases that the court should carefully consider the issue of a child's welfare before granting a care order. The consequence of this principle is that courts will carefully scrutinise local authority care plans. In *Re C (a minor)(care proceedings)* [1992] 2 FCR 341 the court held that local authorities should:

> ... put all material facts before the court before inviting the court to pass to them the huge responsibility of the management of a full care order. The court should be slow to abdicate its responsibility until all the facts are known.

In *Re R (minors)(care proceedings; care plan)* [1994] 2 FCR 136, Wall J held that:

> ... the court should only pass responsibility over to the local authority by way of a final care order when all the facts are as clearly known as can be hoped. Thus, if the court, having heard the evidence, is not satisfied about material aspects of the care plan, the court should

---

29 The inherent jurisdiction is sometimes used to resolve issues arising from the medical treatment of children.

decline to make a care order. Local authorities should be left in no doubt at all that the care plan will in each case be subject to rigorous scrutiny.[30]

The issue of contact is one area where the Act, by section 34, gives the court a jurisdiction that runs to children in care. Consequently the court can investigate a care plan or the care of a child to the extent that it is concerned with the issue of contact.

> The proposals of the local authority, based on their appreciation of the best interests of the child, must command the greatest respect and consideration from the court, but Parliament has given to the court, and not to the local authority, the duty to decide on contact between the child and those named in section 34(1). Consequently the court may have the task of requiring the authority to justify their long-term plans to the extent only that those plans exclude contact between parent and child.[31]

A continuing series of reported cases provides evidence that this tension between the powers of the court and the discretion of local authorities will continue.[32] Social workers involved in the formulation of care plans and the issue of contact for children in care should be aware that their planning and decisions might be subject to scrutiny by the courts in the furtherance of their responsibility for the welfare of the child while a case is before them.

> So, we have now reached the position where, on the face of it, the court cannot direct the local authority in the exercise of its parental responsibility or maintain oversight of a case, unless a substantive application falls to be decided. From the vantage point of social workers and their managers this situation should feel like bliss! Once a care order is made they can get on with planning the child's future, arranging placements, deciding on rehabilitation or permanent substitute care, and so on, without subsequent judicial interference.

> However, in this context ignorance may well be bliss and social workers should be aware that what may look like a clear division of responsibility is, in practice, a contested frontier where a sense of territorial security may well be misplaced.[33]

---

30 [1994] 2 FCR 136.
31 *Re B (minors)(care: contact: local authority's plans)* [1993] 1 FLR 543.
32 See *Recent developments in children's law*, Nicola Wyld and Lindsey Mendoza, Legal Action, April 1997.
33 *Local Authorities and the Courts in Child Care Decisions*, Carole R Smith (Liverpool Law Review, 1997 Vol 19, No 2).

3.7 SOCIAL WORK IN AND FOR THE FAMILY PROCEEDINGS COURT

Care proceedings present a number of significant challenges for social work practitioners. These have been identified as including:[34]

- the preparation of an initial assessment report;

- the preparation of a full ('Orange Book') or risk assessment;

- negotiation with parents (or their representatives) of a written agreement for *(the administration of)* an interim care order;

- membership of a 'core' group of other key professionals;

- liaison with expert witnesses;

- liaison with guardians ad litem;

- statements covering other applications to the court (for example contact order, residence order);

- participation at case conferences;

- preparation (and in due course implementation of) a care plan.

Waller argues that these challenges are exacerbated by a deterioration in the relationship between social workers and the courts. He cites as examples, the increased use of expert witnesses, the considerable respect paid to guardians ad litem (as opposed to the lack of respect sometimes given to local authority social workers), hostile and aggressive cross-examination from lawyers, and the increasing tendency for lawyers to seek access to social services case files.[35]

In seeking to redress the balance Waller proposes a three year qualifying course which would enable social workers to be adequately prepared for child care work including necessary court work;

34 *Working in the Family Courts – A Social Work Perspective,* Brian Waller, March [1997] Family Law, pp 191-193.
35 It should also be acknowledged that courts have taken steps to limit the use of expert witnesses and have criticised guardians ad litem.

post-qualifying training to cater for the demands of complex child care cases; the provision of a more specialist social work service to the family proceedings courts; a recognition that operation of the courts can be dysfunctional for non-lawyers, including social workers; a review of the costs of care cases to identify whether the current level of legal costs is an appropriate charge on public expenditure; improving liaison between social services departments and the courts; and an extension of the work of the Children Act Advisory Committee to consider how the variety of agencies with responsibilities under the Children Act are working together.[36]

4 CASE STUDIES

1.   Marcus who is three years' old has been looked after by the local authority for the last two months because his mother, Sue, has been mentally ill. She is due to leave hospital today and has told the authority that she will come and collect Marcus early next week when she has had a chance to sort her flat out. You are seriously concerned about her ability to properly care for Marcus. Sue is not married. Her mother, who lives nearby and has been caring for Marcus at weekends since Sue went into hospital, has expressed the wish to care for him on a full time basis. She is convinced that Sue is not fit to care for him.

What statutory provisions under the Children Act are relevant to such circumstances?

2.   Derek and Jenny are married and have one child, Angela, who is four. Their relationship is often violent and as a result of information you have received from the health visitor you suspect that Angela may sometimes be assaulted by Derek. The health visitor has also expressed concern about Angela's emotional and psychological development.

Is the local authority under a duty to investigate the situation?

If Derek and Jenny refuse to allow a representative of the local authority (social worker) to see Angela or co-operate in any other

36   Waller's proposal for a three year qualifying diploma has been made before by many other commentators.

way, what powers does the authority have to facilitate an appropriate investigation?

3. The hospital has provided the local authority with the following information. Nicky is 18, single and a heroin addict. She has just given birth to a baby girl who is displaying all the signs of addiction. She lives in a squat with her boyfriend; he is not the father of the baby. Nicky has not sought or received any ante-natal care and is completely indifferent to her baby. She is due to leave hospital tomorrow. The father has contacted the authority because he is concerned about the welfare of the baby. Nicky has not been known to the authority prior to contact from the hospital.

Are the grounds for an emergency protection order satisfied?

Should the local authority seek such an order?

What is the position of the father if he expresses a wish to be concerned with the baby's future?

4. Jeanette is three years' old and has been accommodated by the local authority for the past four months since her mother left her with a neighbour and disappeared. It has now emerged that the mother is serving a prison sentence for drug and vice offences. She is due to be released in six months' time but has not enquired about Jeanette since her release date was fixed.

What are the powers and duties of the local authority in relation to Jeanette and what rights does the mother have?

On what grounds might the local authority seek a care order? Are these grounds satisfied in the circumstances identified?

5. Kylie is 18 months' old and is living with her mother Christine and the latest of a succession of boyfriends. You have been involved with the mother and daughter since Kylie's birth and you are concerned about the violent character of Christine's current boy-friend and in particular about the health and welfare of Kylie. At her last medical check-up the health visitor reported that she was failing to thrive and that she had old and faint bruises on her back and legs. Christine was very defensive and could not provide an adequate explanation about these. When you called at the flat last week (the day after the visit to the health visitor) to follow up these

concerns, the boyfriend told you that Christine and Kylie were asleep and refused you entry. They failed to keep an appointment to see you at the office the next day, and when you called at the flat in the afternoon the boyfriend refused you entry; he was abusive and threatened you with violence.

What are your powers under the Act in this situation?

6. Beverley is 17 years old and is currently living with her three-month old baby son in a mother and baby unit run by the local authority. She is obviously having great difficulty in coping with the baby and there is particular concern about her rough handling of the baby and her inability to control her own temper. She has had fights with other residents and has been heard to threaten to kill her baby if he doesn't stop crying. On three occasions before she came into the unit she asked that the baby be 'taken into care' as she was frightened that she would harm her son but on each occasion she took him back after a couple of days.

The local authority have now decided to seek a care order over her child and have told her that they have started court proceedings and the first hearing will be next month.

Beverley is angry and confused; she knows that she doesn't want her baby taken into care and that her father will do all he can to support her in this. She wants to know all about the proceedings: who will be involved, what could happen and what she can do to stop her baby being taken into care.

How will you answer her questions?

7. Sonia is a persistent school non-attender. Despite extensive work by an education welfare officer and the social services department Sonia is still not attending school. The local authority is also concerned about the sleeping arrangements in the two bedroom flat which Sonia shares with her younger sister and with her older sister and mother, both of whom have 'live-in' boyfriends. Whenever a social worker visits the home Sonia is in her bedclothes and her mother seems unable to get her to school even when transport is provided by the authority.

Explain the legal options available to the authority.

8.   Clive and Marrisa have a baby daughter, Cassie aged two. They have lived together as a family since she was born though Clive and Marrisa are not married. Last weekend Marrisa told Clive that she wished to end their relationship and Clive has moved out of the flat. He is very upset, and is particularly missing Cassie. Marrisa has told him that she wants to make a life for herself and Cassie without Clive.

Clive wants to see Cassie on a regular basis and to be involved in her upbringing. What can he do to secure these objectives? Will he be successful?

9.   The local authority is seeking a care order in relation to two children, aged three and five. The authority allege that they are at risk of significant harm because they live in a household with their mother and her boyfriend, where the boyfriend has been convicted of violent offences against children. The authority is concerned that both children are suffering from periodic physical abuse at the hands of the boyfriend. Evidence of minor injury is available from the family's doctor and the local hospital. The mother is denying that the injuries have been caused by assaults and is keen to protect her relationship with the boyfriend.

Identify the role of the guardian ad litem during the proceedings.

Are the grounds for a care order satisfied?

What matters will the court take into account when it is considering the welfare principles in section 1 of the Act?

Would your answers differ if it became clear that the relationship between the mother and the boyfriend had finished and he had left the family home?

5   ACTIVITIES

1.   In attempting to understand family proceedings there is no substitute for seeing such proceedings in the family proceedings court. The public are not admitted to such proceedings so permission will be needed. This may be arranged through placement

agencies or by means of a letter of introduction and request for permission to the Clerk to the Justices of the local magistrates' court.

Because of the complexity of the issues involved in care proceedings and the large number of people often involved such proceedings frequently last for two or three days. Applications for interim care orders are usually much shorter.

Provide an observation report of the proceedings you see. Identify the role and functions of those present in court and on the suitability of such proceedings for deciding the issues involved.

2.   Construct a flow chart or other diagram detailing the various legal steps in applying for an emergency protection order.

3.   Identify the different people who might be involved in care proceedings and their respective roles and functions.

4.   How is a child protection register compiled?

5.   Who may be present at a child protection conference and what is discussed?

6.   Write to the Children's Legal Centre and other organisations working in this area for their publication lists.

7.   Subscribe to, or look at Childright (published by the Children's Legal Centre) each month – this will keep you up to date with legal issues concerning child care practice.

8.   Write to the Family Rights Group for a publications list. The Group works to improve services for families and their children in public care or in contact with other statutory agencies. Membership includes receiving copies of all its publications.

9.   Get hold of a copy of the annual report of your Area Child Protection Committee and a copy of their local procedural handbook.

6   ADDRESSES

British Agencies for Adoption and Fostering
Skyline House, 200 Union Street
London SE1 0LX.
Phone: 0171 593 2000
Fax: 0171 593 2001
Web: www.vois.org.uk/baaf

Children's Legal Centre
University of Essex
Wivenhoe Park
Colchester
Essex CO4 3SQ.
Phone Advice line: 01206 873820
Fax: 01206 874026
E-mail: CLC@essex.ac.uk
Admin phone number: 01206 872466

Family Rights Group
The Print House
18 Ashwin Street
London E8 3DL.
Phone: 0171 923 2628
Helpline: 0171 249 0008
Fax: 0171 923 2683

Gingerbread
16-17 Clerkenwell Close
London EC1R 0AA.
Phone: 0171 336 8183
Advice: 0171 336 8184
Fax: 0171 336 8185
E-mail: ginger@lonepar.demon.co.uk
Web: www.lonepar.demon.co.uk

National Children's Bureau
8 Wakley Street
London EC1V 7QE.
Phone: 0171 843 6000
Fax: 0171 278 9512
E-mail: library@ncb.org.uk
Web: www.ncb.org.uk

National Council for One-Parent Families
255 Kentish Town Road
London NW5 2LX.
Phone: 0171 267 1361
Fax: 0171 482 4851

National Society for the Protection of Cruelty to Children (NSPCC)
42 Curtain Road
London EC2A 3NH.
Phone: 0171 825 2500
Freephone Helpline: 0800 800500
Fax: 0171 825 2525
E-mail: nspcc@dircon.co.uk
Web: www.nspcc.org.uk

7 MATERIALS

Official Publications, including guidance:

Annual reports of the Children Act Advisory Committee.

The Children Act 1989, Guidance and Regulations. In particular see:

Volume 2 – Family Support, Day Care and Educational Provision for Young Children, (1991).

Volume 3 – Family Placements, (1991).

Volume 4 – Residential Care, HMSO, (1991).

Department of Health, An Introduction to the Children Act 1989, HMSO.

Manual of Practice Guidance for Guardians ad Litem and Reporting Officers, HMSO, 1995.

Working Together Under the Children Act. A guide to arrangements for inter-agency co-operation for the protection of children from abuse, (1991) HMSO.

Books

Allen, N, *Making Sense of the Children Act 1989*, (1993) Longman.

Bainham, A, *Children – The Modern Law*, (1993) Family Law.

Hoggett, B, *Parents and Children*, (1993) Sweet and Maxwell.

John, M (ed), *A Charge Against Society: The Child's Right to Protection*, (1997) Jessica Kingsley Publishers.

Kaganas, F, King, M, and Piper, C (eds), *Legislating for Harmony, Partnership under the Children Act 1989*.

Preston-Shoot, M and Braye, S, *Practising Social Work Law*, (1997) Macmillan.

White, R, Carr, P and Lowe, N, *A Guide to the Children Act 1989*, (1990) Butterworths.

Wylde, N, and Carlton, N, *Family Emergency Procedures*, (1998) Legal Action

Journals

Childright, Published by the Childrens' Legal Centre.

The Legal Action Group monthly bulletin, Legal Action, publishes six monthly updates on developments in child care law.

Two journals, Family Law and Child and Family Law Quarterly, provide extensive coverage and discussion of child care law. The Journal of Social Welfare and Family Law provides regular coverage.

CHILDREN ACT PROCEEDINGS -COURT STRUCTURE

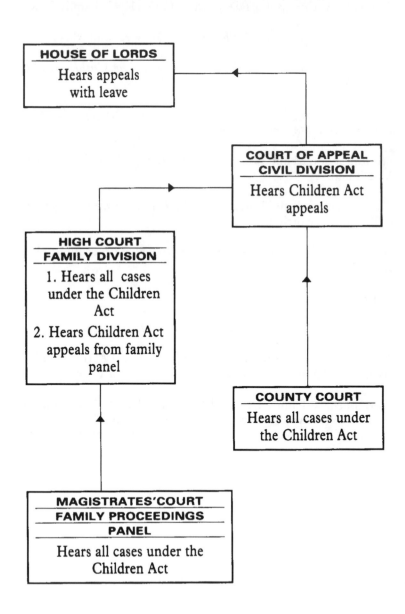

CHAPTER 4

Children with disability

1 INTRODUCTION

This chapter on children with disability follows on from the last chapter concerning child care law and practice under the Children Act 1989. The Act identifies particular groups of children as children in need and establishes local authority duties to provide services for them and their families. The Act makes it clear that a disabled child is a child in need, consequently local authorities are under a duty to provide services for disabled children and their families where appropriate.

Though the Children Act sought to consolidate child care law into one piece of legislation, the law concerning services for disabled children is to be found not only in the 1989 Act but in numerous other pieces of legislation ranging across such disparate areas as community care law, social security law, education law and health care law. Social work practitioners working with disabled children are therefore faced with a maze of legislation and a number of different messages about the status of the child and the rights of the child to assessment and services.

Volume 6 of the Children Act 1989 Guidance and Regulations, Children with Disabilities claims that the Act draws together:

> ... the SSD's functions towards children which existed under the Child Care Act 1980, the National Assistance Act 1948 and Schedule 8 of the National Health Service Act 1977 so that apart from the Chronically Sick and Disabled Persons Act 1970 and the Disabled Persons (Services, Consultation and Representation) Act 1986, the SSD's functions in respect of children with disabilities are covered by the Children Act.[1]

---

1 *The Children Act 1989 Guidance and Regulations*, Volume 6, *Children with Disabilities*, page 1, Department of Health, (1991) HMSO.

Practitioners are therefore already alerted to the fact that they have to work within the 1989 Act, the 1970 Act which deals with aids and adaptations to a child's home, the 1986 Act which is primarily concerned with the assessment of disability for services under the 1970 Act together with the inclusion of carers in that assessment. To this list there should now be added the Carers (Recognition and Services) Act 1995. Practitioners should also be aware that services for disabled children extend well beyond those provided by social services authorities and that any survey of such services should include education provision for children with special educational needs; health care services for children who are disabled or with long term illness, including children with learning disabilities or a mental disorder; the availability of disabled facilities grants to adapt housing, rights to accommodation where the family is homeless or threatened with homelessness and a child is vulnerable through their disability; and the rights of a disabled child who is themselves a carer.

Such a survey should also include reference to social security benefits which are often crucial to the financial circumstances of a family caring for a disabled child. Relevant benefits include disability living allowance, invalid care allowance, income support and the social fund.

This chapter will refer to this full range of statutory provision for disabled children within an argument that the different legislative schemes establish an inevitable series of paradoxical statements concerning the rights and status of disabled children, and that these paradoxes undermine any attempt by the Children Act to establish a unified and coherent structure for the provision of services for this often vulnerable group of people. An agenda for reform should consider whether all services for disabled children should be administered under the provisions of the Children Act thereby recognising the principle that disabled children are children first. Such a reform could take place at the same time as a consolidation of legislation providing services for disabled adults.

1.1   PRINCIPLES FOR PRACTICE

The Guidance sets out a number of principles for work with disabled children. The assertion is made that such work is to be governed by the general principles of the Children Act and that social services departments (SSDs) should seek to provide integrated services.

1.6 Work with children with disabilities in the context of the Children Act should be based on the following principles:

- The welfare of the child should be safeguarded and promoted by those providing services;

- A primary aim should be to promote access for all children to the same range of services;

- Children with disabilities are children first;

- Recognition of the importance of parents and families in children's lives;

- Partnership between parents and local authorities and other agencies; and

- The views of children and parents should be sought and taken into account.[2]

The Guidance supplements these principles by identifying the essential elements of work with disabled children: the assessment of need for services, the planning and co-ordination of services, service planning and provision in partnership with parents, working with the voluntary sector within the community, providing services for children living at home with their families, working with education and health care services, accommodation as a service for disabled children and their families, foster care and residential care for disabled children, child protection issues for disabled children, and the transition to adulthood.

2   THE LAW

The investigation of the law presented here starts with legislation which establishes rights, powers and duties that relate directly to disabled children and their families and are discharged by local authorities. These include the provision of services under the Children Act 1989, the Chronically Sick and Disabled Persons Act 1970, the Disabled Persons (Services, Consultation and Representation) Act 1986, the Education Act 1996, and the Carers (Recognition and

2   Ibid, page 2.

Services) Act 1995. Mental health services may be provided by local authorities and health authorities, whilst health services are provided under health authority legislation which is also thought of as community care legislation, that is the National Health Service Act 1977 and the National Health Service and Community Care Act 1990. Finally, mention will be made of financial benefits available to or for disabled children through the social security system.

2.1 THE CHILDREN ACT 1989

Part III of the Act deals with local authority support for children and families; section 17 establishes a general duty on local authorities to safeguard and promote the welfare of children within their area who are in need by providing services which are appropriate to those children's needs. Section 17(10) provides that a disabled child is a child in need and subsection 11 incorporates the definition of disability that is used in the National Assistance Act 1948:

> (11) For the purposes of this Part, a child is disabled if he is blind, deaf, or dumb or suffers from mental disorder of any kind or is substantially and permanently handicapped by illness, injury or congenital deformity or such other disability as may be prescribed.

Whilst section 17 establishes general duties, Schedule 2 of the Act provides more detailed powers and duties. These include:

- a pro-active duty on local authorities to identify children in need in their area (paragraph 1);

- a duty to open and maintain a register of disabled children within their area (paragraph 2);

- a duty to take reasonable steps to prevent children suffering ill-treatment or neglect (paragraph 4);

- a duty to provide services for a disabled child which are designed to minimise the effect of their disability and to give a disabled child the opportunity to lead a life that is as normal as possible (paragraph 5);

- a duty to provide particular services for children in need who are living with their families. These services include advice, guidance and counselling; occupational, social, cultural or recreational activities; and home help (which may include laundry facilities) (paragraph 8).

It is worth noting that local authority responsibilities toward disabled children are set out in Part III of the Act and in Schedule 2 which are headed Local Authority Support for Children and Families. This structure confirms the principle of the Act that disabled children are children in need and that services provided for them are part of mainstream children and family services, and re-affirms the point that disabled children are children first.

2.1.1 Assessment

Paragraph 3 of schedule 2 establishes an assessment power which allows local authorities to carry out joint assessments of children in need for services under the Children Act 1989, the Chronically Sick and Disabled Persons Act 1970, the Education Act 1996, the Disabled Persons (Services, Consultation and Representation) Act 1986, or any other Act (paragraph 3).

The paragraph should now be taken to include reference to an assessment under the Carers (Recognition and Services) Act 1995. This Act provides for the assessment of carers including disabled children who act as carers and of parents, and others, who care for a disabled child.

Section 1(2) of the 1995 Act provides for the assessment of the carer of a disabled child:

(2) ... in any case where –

(a) a local authority assess the needs of a disabled child for the purpose of Part 111 of the Children Act 1989 or section 2 of the Chronically Sick and Disabled Persons Act 1970, and

(b) an individual ('the carer') provides or intends to provide a substantial amount of care on a regular basis for the disabled child,

the carer may request the local authority, before they make their decision as to whether the needs of the disabled child call for the provision of any services, to carry out an assessment of his ability to provide and continue to provide care for the disabled child; and if he makes such a request, the local authority shall carry out such an assessment and shall take into account the results of that assessment in making that decision.

2.1.2   Services

Volume 6 of the Guidance identifies the range of duties, powers and services which are envisaged by the general duty to children in need under section 17(1):

> This general duty is supported by other specific duties and powers such as the facilitation of 'the provision by others, including in particular voluntary organisations of services' (section 17(5) and Schedule 2). These provisions encourage SSDs to provide day and domiciliary services, guidance and counselling, respite care and a range of other services as a means of supporting children in need (including children with disabilities) within their families. The Act recognises that some-times a child can only be helped by providing services for other members of his family (section 17(3)) 'if it [the service] is provided with a view to safeguarding or promoting the child's welfare' ... The SSD may make such arrangements as they see fit for any person to provide services and support 'may include giving assistance in kind, or in exceptional circumstances in cash' (section 17(6).

Whilst the 1995 'Carers' Act establishes a duty to assess carers, and thereby creates a right for carers to be assessed, it does not identify particular services that might follow from such an assessment. It has been suggested that the following services might be provided after such an assessment:

- services provided under the Children Act 1989; these can include services for the family of a disabled child;

- the provision of a home help under National Health Service Act 1977, Schedule 8 paragraph 3;

- Schedule 8 paragraph 2(1) of the National Health Service Act 1977 is also taken to empower local authorities to provide services to support carers;

- section 111 of the Local Government Act 1972 empowers local authorities to expend resources on carer support services. The section establishes a power to 'do anything (whether or not involving expenditure, borrowing or lending of money or the acquisition or disposal of any property or rights) which is calculated to facilitate, or is conducive or incidental to, the discharge of any of their functions'.[3]

2.1.3 Accommodation

Section 20 of the Children Act places a duty on local authorities to provide accommodation for children in need who appear to them to require such accommodation. This duty will be relevant to a disabled child where 'the person who has been caring for him being prevented (whether or not permanently, and for whatever reason) from providing him with suitable accommodation or care' (subsection (1)(c)).

If a local authority is providing residential care, or other accommodation, for a disabled child they are required by section 22(3)(a) to safeguard and promote the child's welfare; and by section 23(8) they shall, 'so far as is reasonably practicable, secure that the accommodation is not unsuitable to his particular needs'.

> Residential care should not be regarded as a failure but as a positive option where parents, families and friends have a continuing role. With the cessation of admissions to long-stay hospitals for residential care, SSDs should consider as a matter of urgency how they can work in partnership with their health and education counterparts to develop new patterns of residential services which provide good quality care in the local community. Such care may be provided through SSDs, DHAs, voluntary or independent agencies or by combinations and consortia according to local provision. Wherever the young person is placed, SSDs, DHAs and LEAs will have a continuing role and every effort should be made to ensure that any placement encourages development and offers opportunities for continuing education.[4]

2.2 THE CHRONICALLY SICK AND DISABLED PERSONS ACT 1970

This Act applies to disabled people of all ages including disabled children. Section 1 imposes a duty on local authorities to identify

---

3 For a fuller discussion of these assertions see Clements, L, *Community Care and the Law*, Chapter 7, Legal Action Group, 1996.
4 *The Children Act 1989 Guidance and Regulations*, Volume 6, *Children with Disabilities*, at page 51.

the number of disabled people in their area and to publish information about the services which are available under section 2 of the Act.

Section 2 of the Act sets out a number of services for disabled people, including disabled children, which the local authority are under a duty to provide where they are satisfied that the services are needed to meet the needs of the person or child concerned. The services are:

- practical assistance in the home;

- provision of, or assistance in obtaining radio, television, library or similar recreational facilities;

- lectures, games, outings or other recreational facilities outside the home, or assistance in taking advantage of educational facilities available;

- facilities for, or assistance in, travelling to and from home for various purposes;

- assistance in arranging adaptation to the home, or the provision of additional facilities designed to secure greater safety, comfort or convenience;

- facilitating the taking of holidays;

- meals, whether at home or elsewhere;

- provision, or assistance in obtaining, a telephone and any special equipment needed to enable the disabled person to use it.[5]

The House of Lords, in the case of *R v Gloucestershire County Council and the Secretary of State for Health, ex p Barry*, has recently considered whether local authorities are entitled to take their own financial resources into account when assessing or reassessing the needs of people with disabilities for services under section 2 of the Chronically Sick and Disabled Persons Act 1970.[6] Their Lordships

---

5 The bullet points are taken from *The Children Act 1989 Guidance and Regulations*, Volume 6, *Children With Disabilities*, page 55, Department of Health, (1991) HMSO.
6 [1997] 2 All ER 1.

have now decided that local authorities can take their financial resources into account when assessing a disabled person including a disabled child. Some commentators argue that the impact of this decision is to relegate the duty in section 2 to a mere power.

> In practice, cash-strapped local authorities, faced with growing demand, use eligibility criteria to tailor that demand to their resources. Eligibility criteria have been tightened as resources decrease further to restrict access to services. The House of Lords has now decided that this is lawful. Whether a disabled person has 'needs' as opposed to 'wants' will now depend, in part, on how much money a local authority has allocated to its community care budget.[7]

It can also be argued that the decision throws the emphasis onto the issue of needs in the sense that once a local authority has assessed a person and accepted that services should be provided to meet an assessed need, the authority is under a duty to provide for that need in some way.

2.3   THE DISABLED PERSONS (SERVICES, CONSULTATION AND REPRESENTATION) ACT 1986

Again this piece of legislation applies to disabled people of all ages. A disabled child is defined in Part III of the Children Act 1989.[8]

Section 4 establishes a duty on local authorities to assess a disabled person and/or their carer under section 8, for services provided under section 2(1) Chronically Sick and Disabled Persons Act 1970. The duty to assess is triggered by a request from the disabled person or their carer. Section 8 requires a local authority to take the continuing ability of a carer to care into account when assessing the needs of a disabled person for any services under 'any of the welfare enactments'.

Sections 5 and 6 impose a duty on education authorities to consult with social services authorities to establish whether a child who has been statemented under the Education Act 1996, may require social services support when they leave school. This section should be understood as an important element of the duty local authorities have in respect of the 'transition to adulthood'.

---

7   Ashton, K and Gould, J, *Community care: a duty to care?* Legal Action, May 1997.
8   See above at page 82.

2.4 EDUCATION ACT 1996

The Education Act 1996 contains provisions for the special educational needs of children whether these arise from physical disability
or illness, or from learning disability or mental disorder. The law
reflects the policy of the Warnock Report (1978) which concluded
that children with special educational needs should not be identified
as a distinct group but be recognised within a continuum of educational ability and needs. Consequently the Report argued for a
principle of integration within which the majority of children with
special educational needs should be educated in mainstream schools,
whilst also recognising the need for special schools for a minority of
children with particular needs. The Report envisaged that assessment
of children with special educational needs would identify those who
required a statement of special educational needs and of the special
provision needed to meet those needs, whether this was to be provided
in a mainstream school or in a special school, and a different category
of children who, though they had special educational needs, they were
not such as to require a statement. The needs of this category of child
were to be met within the ordinary structure of mainstream education.

These proposals were adopted by the Education Act 1981 and have
formed the basis of special educational needs provision ever since.
They are now incorporated in the 1996 Education Act.

Section 312 provides some basic definitions.

> (1) A child has 'special educational needs' for the purposes of this
> Act if he has a learning difficulty which calls for special educational
> provision to be made for him.
>
> (2) ... a child has a 'learning difficulty' for the purposes of this
> Act if –
>
> (a) he has a significantly greater difficulty in learning than the majority
>   of children of his age,
>
> (b) he has a disability which either prevents or hinders him from
>   making use of educational facilities of a kind generally provided
>   for children of his age in schools within the area of the local
>   education authority, or
>
> (c) he is under the age of five and is, or would be if special educational
>   provision were not made for him, likely to fall within paragraph
>   (a) or (b) when of or over that age.

(4) In this Act 'special educational provision' means –

(a) in relation to a child who has attained the age of two, educational provision which is additional to, or otherwise different from, the educational provision made generally for children of his age in schools maintained by the local education authority (other than special schools) or grant maintained schools in their area, and

(b) in relation to a child under that age, educational provision of any kind.

Local education authorities have a duty under section 321 to identify children who have special educational needs and to determine what special educational provision they need.

Section 323 is concerned with the assessment of educational needs, and section 324 sets out the procedure for making a statement, maintaining and ceasing to maintain a statement. The statement must provide details of the authority's assessment of special educational needs and the provision to be made to meet the assessed needs, and the school or other institution in which the authority propose that those needs be met.

A Code of Practice has been issued by the Department, and all those involved with special education have a duty to have regard to it.[9] This includes local education authorities, schools, health services and social services authorities. A number of fundamental principles are provided by the Code:

- the needs of all pupils who may have special educational needs either throughout, or at any time during, their school careers must be addressed; the Code recognises that there is a continuum of needs and a continuum of provision, which may be made in a wide variety of different forms

- children with special educational needs require the greatest possible access to a broad and balanced education, including the National Curriculum

---

9 *Code of Practice on the Identification and Assessment of Special Educational Needs*, Department for Education (1994). The Code is not issued under section 7 of the Local Authority Social Services Act 1970, consequently those to whom the Code applies have a duty to have regard to it, but it does not impose duties.

- the needs of most pupils will be met in the mainstream, and without a statutory assessment or statement of special educational needs. Children with special educational needs, including children with statements of special educational needs, should, where appropriate and taking into account the wishes of their parents, be educated alongside their peers in mainstream schools

- even before he or she reaches compulsory school age a child may have special educational needs requiring the intervention of the LEA as well as the health services

- the knowledge, views and experience of parents are vital. Effective assessment and provision will be secured where there is the greatest possible degree of partnership between parents and their children and schools, LEAs and other agencies.

The Education (Special Educational Needs) Regulations set a number of statutory time scales for the making of assessments and statements.

The 1993 Education Act established a new appeal structure and the Special Educational Needs Tribunal to hear appeals from parents. The grounds of appeal are now incorporated in the 1996 Act (sections 325 and 326); the constitution and outline procedure of the tribunal are contained in sections 333-336. There are six types of appeal for the Tribunal:

1. Against the local education authority's (LEA's) refusal to make a statement.

2. Against the assessment of the LEA, the provision specified in the statement, or the fact that no school is named in the statement.

3. Against the refusal of the LEA to make an assessment following a request to do so from a child's parents.

4. Against the refusal of an LEA to reassess a child who has a statement.

5. Against the decision of an LEA to cease to maintain a statement.

6. Against the LEA's decision not to change the name of the school specified in the statement.

The 1996 Act reflects the previous government's commitment to the principles of the 1981 Act despite considerable criticism of the structure and operation of the system of special needs education. The Audit Commission concluded their 1992 report, Getting in on the Act: Provision for Pupils with Special Educational Needs: the National Picture in the following terms:

> However there are some serious deficiencies in the way in which children with special needs are identified and provided for. These deficiencies are caused by three key problems:
>
> • lack of clarity both about what constitutes special educational needs and about the respective responsibilities of the school and the LEA
>
> • lack of clear accountability by schools and LEAs for the progress made by pupils, and accountability by schools to the LEA for the resources they receive
>
> • lack of incentives for LEAs to implement the 1981 Act.

Baroness Warnock, who chaired the original committee upon whose proposals the 1981 Act was based, is herself now critical of the principles behind that Act and their continued use in the 1993 Act (and by implication in the 1996 Act):

> The Government has proposals to amend the 1981 act to give parents better access to the processes of statementing and increased rights of appeal, to new style tribunals. But the drawback with such amendments is that they will be introduced against the background of the old ill-drawn line between those who do and those who do not merit statements. What happens to those whose needs still exist, but for whom the education authority has no statutory duty remains untouched. The suspicion must be that these children will be increasingly pushed to one side.[10]

2.5   HOUSING AND HOMELESSNESS

Where a disabled child is a member of a family which is homeless or threatened with homelessness the assessment of housing need can take place under the Children Act, and accommodation may be

10   *Special case in need of reform. Schools Report*, The Observer, 18 October 1992.

available under the broad duties of section 17 of the Children Act to children in need or under the specific accommodation duties of section 20(1)(c) identified above.[11]

The Housing Act 1996 places duties on housing authorities to provide accommodation where an applicant is homeless or threatened with homelessness, in priority need, and not intentionally homeless. The authority is under a duty to 'secure that accommodation is made available for occupation', section 193(2). The fact that a family in such circumstances includes a disabled child will be sufficient to establish their priority need.[12]

2.5.1 Disabled facilities grants

Disabled facilities grants are means-tested grants available under the Housing Grants, Construction and Regeneration Act 1996 for the purpose of adapting dwelling accommodation to facilitate the use of such accommodation by a disabled person. An application can be made for the benefit of a disabled child. The grants focus on works to improve heating, safety, cooking and access but an application cannot be approved by a local housing authority unless the authority is satisfied that the works are necessary and appropriate and it is reasonable to carry out the works, having regard to the age and condition of the building (section 24(3)).

2.6 MENTAL HEALTH SERVICES

It is only necessary here to identify the fact that the Mental Health Act 1983 applies to all age groups and its provisions therefore encompass a child who is disabled by reason of a mental disorder. Consequently the Act's provisions concerning compulsory admission to hospital, treatment for a mental disorder whilst in hospital and discharge from hospital may all apply to a child. In practice the use of the Mental Health Act 1983 in cases involving children is rare; services for children with a mental disorder should be provided under the provisions of the Children Act 1989.

---

11 See *R v London Borough of Tower Hamlets, ex p Bradford* (1997) 29 HLR 756, and *R v Northavon District Council, ex p Smith* [1994] 3 All ER 313.
12 For a fuller discussion of these issues see Chapter 13, Housing Rights.

It should also be noted that the provisions of the Mental Health (Patients in the Community) Act 1995 apply to children of 16 and over. This Act provides for compulsory supervision in the community for particular categories of patient upon discharge from hospital having been detained under the Mental Health Act 1983 for treatment. The purpose of the supervision is to ensure that he or she receives the after-care services which should be provided under section 117 of the Mental Health Act 1983.[13]

2.7 HEALTH CARE

This is an area where the law is currently being defined and re-defined through a series of court decisions concerning the extent to which children have independent rights to consent to or refuse medical treatment.

Disabled children of 16 or 17 have the same rights as other children under the Family Law Reform Act 1969 to consent to medical treatment on their own behalf so long as they have capacity (intellectual) to give a valid consent. Younger (disabled) children may have, in theory, equivalent rights as a result of the decision in *Gillick v West Norfolk and Wisbech Health Authority* [1985] 3 All ER 402 where the House of Lords held that a child of any age who has achieved sufficient maturity, in the sense that they fully understand what is proposed, has sufficient capacity to consent to (and refuse) medical treatment without reference to their parents or to any other person.

However these rights are subject to limitations which the courts have sought to define in a number of recent cases. In *Re W* [1993] 1 FLR 1 the High Court decided that it has inherent jurisdiction to authorise the medical treatment of children, irrespective of their age or their capacity to give their own consent. It is also clear from this decision that a refusal of treatment by a child, including a disabled child, may be overruled by the courts even where there is no doubt that the child had sufficient capacity to make their own decisions concerning treatment.

This development in the law has been both confirmed and extended by the High Court Family Division decision in *Re C (a minor)*

---

13   For a fuller discussion of these provisions see Chapter 7, Mental Health.

(medical treatment: court's jurisdiction) [1997] 13 LS Gaz R 29. The judge granted an application by the local authority for an order made pursuant to the High Court's inherent jurisdiction to detain a child aged 16 in a clinic so that the child could be treated for an eating disorder. It is thought that this is the first time the courts have used their inherent jurisdiction to allow a child to be detained for treatment.

The exercise of what is an essentially paternalistic jurisdiction in these particular circumstances has been criticised from a children's rights perspective:

> Does C's status as a minor justify her detention in circumstances where an adult would not have been detained? The Court has carefully protected the inherent jurisdiction, claiming that the special vulnerability of minors justifies greater powers of intervention in their lives. This justification becomes questionable when applied to a 16 year-old. Focusing on the special vulnerability of minors may simply be an excuse to deny minors the rights they deserve.[14]

Where a child is learning disabled so that they do not have capacity to make decisions concerning their health care it is accepted that such decisions are to be taken by their parents or by others with parental responsibility. Those making such decisions would be required to do so in the best interests of the learning disabled child and their decisions would be subject to review by the High Court in the exercise of its inherent (wardship) jurisdiction.

2.8 SOCIAL SECURITY BENEFITS[15]

Many families with a disabled child will derive part or all of their income from the social security system. Research has established a clear link between adult disablement and poverty[16] and the same link is also established where the disabled person is a child. In these circumstances it is important that both the disabled child and their

---

14 Carolyn Frantz, *Re C (a minor) – Is Forcible Detention of a Young Person Through the Court's Common Law Inherent Jurisdiction Acceptable Action?* Childright, May 1997, No 136.
15 Further details of these and other social security benefits are provided in Chapter 10.
16 *The Financial Circumstances of Disabled Adults Living in Private Households,* Office of Population and Censuses and Surveys, (1988) HMSO.

carers are receiving their full benefit entitlement. Those of particular relevance for disabled children are:

Disability living allowance

Disability living allowance is paid to a disabled person in respect of their care needs (the care component) and their mobility needs (the mobility component). Both components are available to disabled children though there are age rules for each.

There are series of disability tests for the care component which can be paid at three rates. The claimant must be so severely disabled physically or mentally that he or she requires from another person:

a)   during the day:

i)   frequent attention throughout the day in connection with bodily functions; or

ii) continual supervision throughout the day in order to avoid substantial danger to themselves or others;

b)   at night:

iii) prolonged or repeated attention in connection with bodily functions; or

iv) in order to avoid substantial danger to themselves or to others the claimant requires another person to be awake for a prolonged period or at frequent intervals for the purpose of watching over themselves;

c)   part time day care:

v)   the claimant requires in connection with bodily functions attention from another person for a significant portion of the day (whether during a single period or a number of periods); or

vi) the claimant cannot prepare a cooked meal for themselves if they have the ingredients.

The higher rate is paid where, in the circumstances of this chapter, a disabled child satisfies either or both i) and ii) *and* either or both iii) and iv).

The middle rate is paid where either or both i) and ii) *or* either or both iii) or iv) are satisfied.

The lower rate is paid where either or both v) and vi) are satisfied.

There is no lower age limit for the care component of disability living allowance though where the disabled child is under 16 there are additional tests:

- s/he has attention or supervision requirements that are substantially in excess of the normal requirements of a person of his age; or

- s/he has substantial attention or supervision requirements which younger persons in normal physical and mental health may also have but which persons of his age and in normal physical and mental health would not have.

Children under the age of 16 cannot found a claim for the care component on the basis that they satisfy the 'cooking test' set out in vi) above.

For the higher rate of mobility component the claimant must establish that they are suffering from a physical disability such that:

i)   they are unable to walk; or

ii)   are virtually unable to walk; or

iii) are both deaf and blind; or

iv)   are without feet or are a double amputee;

The higher rate is also available to claimants who are severely mentally impaired and have severe behavioural problems.

The lower rate of mobility component is payable where the claimant can show that although they are able to walk they are so severely disabled, physically or mentally, that, ignoring any familiar routes, they are unable to take advantage of their walking abilities out of doors without guidance or supervision from another person most of the time.

A disabled child of five years of age and over can claim the mobility component, subject to the additional criteria for the lower rate that, in addition to the ordinary conditions of entitlement, they show either that they require substantially more guidance or supervision than persons of their age in normal physical and mental health would; or that persons of their age in normal physical and mental health would not require such guidance or supervision.

Severe disablement allowance

Severe disablement allowance is a non-contributory benefit paid to those who became incapable of work before their twentieth birthday or are incapable of work and at least 80% disabled. The benefit is available to disabled children aged 16 and over who are not in full time education.

Invalid care allowance

Invalid care allowance is a benefit paid to carers of disabled people, including disabled children, where the disabled person is receiving either the higher or middle rate of the care component of disability living allowance and their care is regular and substantial. This condition is satisfied where the care is for 35 or more hours in each week. Invalid care allowance can be paid with both adult and child dependency additions.

Income jupport and job seekers (income based) benefit

Both means-tested benefits incorporate weekly premium additions to take account of the existence of a disabled child within the family. This premium is payable where the child is receiving disability living allowance.

3 DISABLED CHILDREN AND SOCIAL WORK: some issues for discussion

This survey has identified the law that is relevant to disabled children. It is possible to categorise different elements of this complex 'legal regime' for practitioners working with disabled children and their families and carers into personal social services (including assessment), education services, health care services, housing and accommodation services and financial support. It is clear that part of the complexity of the law arises from the different statutory duties and powers but it is also true that another element of the complexity facing practitioners is the existence of different messages about the status of the disabled child and their rights to services under different parts of the legal regime.

3.1   RIGHTS TO SERVICES?

The philosophy of the *Gillick* decision is reflected in the Children Act; it acknowledges the independent rights of a child and of the notion that the extent of these rights increases with a child's emerging maturity until a full rights status in law is achieved at the age of majority. This principle should apply equally to disabled children, a fact that is confirmed by Guidance to the Children Act which asserts that disabled children are 'children first' and are therefore entitled to be treated in the same way as other children under the Act. Though children with a learning disability may be unable to achieve full intellectual capacity they have an equivalent right to have their interests fully promoted and to the fullest opportunities to participate in decisions concerning their own lives.

The legal regime can also be examined to identify the extent to which the status, rights and interests of disabled children are promoted. It will become clear from an examination of the law that aspects of the legal regime are failing to achieve and deliver these rights.

Resources

One area of concern is the relevance of resources to the provision of services to disabled children. The recent House of Lords decision in *R v Gloucestershire County Council, ex p Barry* [1997] AC 584 makes it clear that a local authority may take the level of its resources into account when it is assessing a disabled person for services under section 2 of the Chronically Sick and Disabled Persons Act 1970 (aids and adaptations). Consequently services supposedly available to disabled children under this statutory duty are now subject to resource constraints on the local authority's assessment of need. In such circumstances it is entirely legitimate to suggest that such a decision undermines the notion of a right to such services. Lord Lloyd, in a dissenting judgment, suggested the consequences of such a decision:

> Suppose there are two people with identical disabilities, living in identical circumstances, but in different parts of the country. Local authority A provides for his needs by arranging for meals-on-wheels four days a week. Local authority B might also be expected to provide meals-on-wheels four days a week or its equivalent. It cannot, however, have been Parliament's intention that local authority B should be able to say 'because we do not have enough resources, we are going to reduce your needs'. His needs remain exactly the same. They cannot be affected by the local authority's inability to meet those needs. Every child needs a new pair of shoes from time to time. The need is not the less because his parents cannot afford them.[17]

A series of judicial review decisions in cases concerning local authority community care duties have recognised the fact that the provision of such services is subject to resource constraints though it can be argued that where a local authority has accepted that a need for services should be provided for, they are under a duty to provide, in some way that is not unreasonable, for the assessed need.[18]

Remedies

Legal enforceability is a key to the status of rights to services and to financial support for disabled children. The ability to enforce such rights must be both real and accessible. A brief examination of this notion of enforceability will however show that many of these rights are subject to processes of enforcement which are often problematic and sometimes inadequate.

Complaints procedures

Local authority complaint's procedures have been established under the Local Authority Social Services Act 1970, section 7B and the Children Act.[19] It is a matter of some debate whether complaints concerning the provision of services for disabled children should be

---

17   Judgment of Lord Lloyd in R v Gloucestershire County Council, ex p Barry.
18   See the chapter on Community Care Law for a fuller discussion.
19   For a discussion of the respective complaint's procedures see Chapter 6 on Community Care Law and Chapter 3 on Child Care Law.

heard by the Children Act procedure, or, if the services which have generated the complaint, are provided under the Chronically Sick and Disabled Persons Act 1970 and the Disabled Persons (Services, Consultation and Representation) Act 1986, whether a complaint should be heard by the procedure established under the 1970 Act. Though the procedures are similar the independent element for the children's procedure begins at the second stage. The objective of such pro-cedures is to resolve disputes and complaints informally. It is also established by case law that the recommendations of complaint's panels are not binding on local authorities though there would have to be very good reasons for departing from such a recommendation – *R v North Yorkshire County Council, ex p Hargreaves* (1994) 26 BMLR 121.

At least three observations can be made concerning the utility of complaint's procedures for the enforcement of the rights of disabled children to local authority services. First, their recommendations are not legally binding on the authority. Second, because each complaint is dealt with individually, it is impossible to build up a body of recommendations/decisions which articulate a right to services for disabled children. Third, guidance for the Local Authority Social Services Act 1970 procedure states that lawyers should not attend panel hearings in their professional capacity. In such circumstances there has to be some doubt concerning the ability of disabled children, their parents and/or their carers to properly represent their own position and interests in a panel hearing at which local authority officers will be present. Luke Clements comments on the current position of such procedures:

> Both the courts and the local government ombudsman are still assessing the effectiveness of the local authority complaints procedures and to an extent these procedures are therefore 'on probation'. They are not independent, and only time will tell whether they can develop into a system which commands the respect of service users and is objectively fair and effective.[20]

Tribunals

Other disputes involving the provision of services for disabled children are channelled through the tribunal system. Appeals concerning social

---

20   Luke Clements, *Community Care and the Law*, Chapter 12, at page 278, (1996) Legal Action Group.

security benefits are heard in Social Security Appeal Tribunals, with Disability Appeal Tribunals hearing appeals concerning disability living allowance; applications for discharge from compulsory detention in hospital can be heard by Mental Health Review Tribunals, and there are a series of grounds of appeal to Special Education Needs Tribunals (SENTs). Though appeal rights to SENTs are undoubtedly important, and a substantial improvement on the previous structure of limited appeals to local education authorities appeal committees, these rights are invested in parents and not in the child. In most circumstances this will not raise any concern as the parents are the best people to represent the interests of their child. There may be, however, circumstances in which this is not the case; where this is so the absence of an independent right of appeal vested in the child may mean that the child's interests are not properly represented. Comment should also be made concerning the fact that legal aid is not available to fund representation before SENTs. Such a position, which is shared by most tribunals, may seriously diminish the ability of parents to mount an effective challenge to the decisions of a local education authority before the tribunal.

Commissioner for Local Administration

Alternative paths for remedies are available through complaints to the Commissioners for Local Administration (local ombudsman). Complaints to the local ombudsman must be based on an allegation that the complainant has suffered injustice as a consequence of the local authority's maladministration. Such complaints can be very effective in ensuring the provision of services and for securing compensation. The annual reports of the Commissioners provide evidence of the increasing number of complaints against local authority social services departments concerning the provision of services for disabled people, including disabled children, and of the sometimes substantial compensation that is recommended. The Annual Report for 1995/96 provides clear evidence of the significant number of complaints concerning special educational needs. Delay in the completion of assessments and making the provision specified in the statement were the major causes of justified complaint.[21] One ombudsman reported on a complaint against South Bedfordshire District Council and Bedfordshire County Council where it was established that there had been a delay of at least six months in

21 *Local Government Ombudsman Annual Report 1995/96*, The Commission for Local Administration in England.

assessing a severely disabled teenager's needs for adaptations to the family home, and then that the application had been unreasonably refused. The recommendation of the Ombudsman was for an independent assessment of future care plans, that both Councils should consider whether to fund any provision recommended and to ensure that future decisions are made with full regard to the family's needs and wishes. Both Councils were recommended to pay compensation of £250 for time and trouble and the District Council to pay £150 compensation for distress caused by the failure to provide the adaptations needed.[22]

The same report also makes it clear that the local ombudsman will not normally investigate a complaint concerning social services unless the complainant has used, or sought to use, the local authority's complaints procedure.[23]

Judicial review

Judicial review is available as a procedure whereby the decisions of local authorities can be challenged in the High Court on the grounds that the process and procedure of a particular decision was in some way deficient and therefore unlawful. A disabled child can make an application for judicial review through a parent and/or a next friend, though it is clear that there is a general rule that applicants must have used established routes to secure a remedy before making an application for judicial review except where a point of law is involved. In *R v Birmingham City Council, ex p A (a minor)* [1997] 2 FCR 357, the court held that:

> Where neither facts not law were in dispute and the chief ground for complaint was the way in which a local authority had failed, through delay, to carry out its duties towards a child in need in its area, the appropriate course was to seek relief under the complaints procedure provided by section 26 of the Children Act 1989.

Though judicial review has a number of disadvantages as a procedure for securing services for disabled children, including the discretionary nature of leave to apply and of the available remedies, it has nonetheless become more frequently used as a route for securing such

---

22 Ibid, at pages 16-17.
23 See Legal Action, February 1996, at page 21 for summaries of findings of local ombudsman on community care and disability complaints.

services. This is partly because the other procedures are often ineffective and also because an application for leave to apply for judicial review has proved an effective strategy in persuading local authorities to provide services to disabled people who evidence their persistence and determination to secure such services through the use of legal remedies.

The range of available remedies for securing the provision of services to disabled children is itself complex and in turn compounds the complexity of the statutory regime of rights, powers and duties. The effectiveness of the available remedies and procedures in securing services, be they complaints procedures, tribunal hearings, complaints to the local ombudsman or judicial review, is often questionable.

To these two reservations, one more should be added: that is the extent to which such procedures properly provide for the 'voice of the disabled child' to be heard. The United Nations Convention on the Rights of the Child provides, in Article 12, for the right of a child, capable of forming his or her own views, to express those views and have them given due weight in accordance with his age and maturity. Whilst the Children Act establishes just such a principle for its complaints procedure (and for a competent child to refuse assessment) it may be less easy to guarantee in other procedures through which the right to services for disabled children is sought to be enforced. This is particularly the case in SENTs, where the right of appeal is vested in a child's parents, and where it seems that the child has no independent right to address the tribunal. Equal concern can be expressed about the way in which the courts seem to be using their inherent jurisdiction to overrule the articulated health care decisions of children who are 16 and over and who evidence Gillick competence.

In 'public law' court proceedings under the Children Act a guardian ad litem is appointed to represent the interests of the child to the court. There may well be an argument for the establishment of an equivalent to properly represent the interests of disabled children in securing the provision of services for their disability. In most circumstances this role is properly taken by the child's parents and in other circumstances it is taken by the Official Solicitor, for instance where the child's parents are unable, for whatever reason, to fulfil this function in court proceedings. A wider recognition of the right of the child to be heard may require the extension of this principle to all situations where the interests of a disabled child are to be decided by a court, tribunal or complaint's procedure.

3.2   THE QUALITY OF SERVICE DELIVERY

The statements of good practice which appear in Volume 6 of the Guidance on Children with Disabilities are also a set of objectives which local authorities, and others, should be working toward. In 1993 the Social Services Inspectorate carried out an inspection of four local authorities to assess their services to disabled children. The report of this inspection gives cause for concern.[24] There was poor development of policy and planning for services and an identification that such services suffered from the demands of child protection work. Partnership with parents was patchy and there was little if any evidence of co-ordinated assessments under the various statutes.

In relation to assessment, care planning, reviews and registers of disabled children there were serious deficiencies:

> In three SSDs there were no assessment procedures geared to establishing the needs of disabled children. Not all case files had evidence of assessments, but those that were seen were of an uneven quality. It was rare to see evidence of inter-agency assessments. In one SSD only three out of twelve case files contained written assessments.

> It was sometimes unclear who had responsibility for implementing and reviewing plans, and there was a need for a clear model of care management to be adopted.

> None of the authorities inspected were operating an effective register of disabled children ... However, at the time of the Inspection the lack of a register, or alternative up to date lists, had resulted in there being no reliable current information on the numbers, nature and distribution of disabled children in those authorities.[25]

These rather negative messages can be set against more positive findings concerning the placing of services for disabled children in the mainstream of children and family services, thus facilitating the Guidance principle that disabled children are children first. There was also clear evidence of a commitment to partnership with parents, to inter-agency liaison and the use of a register of disabled children as an important and effective planning tool.

---

24   *Report of the National Inspection of Local Authority Services to Disabled Children and Their Families*, Social Services Inspectorate, 1994.
25   Ibid, at page 6.

This inspection took place in 1993 and it is to be expected that significant improvements have been made in and to services for disabled children.[26] The Children Act has put in place a statutory framework for the provision of such services, but because it is only part of a fragmented and complex legal regime it is possible that this important area of practice will continue to be characterised by a lack of prominence among the priorities of social services and other responsible departments.

4   CASE STUDIES

1.   Remi is four years old and has a learning disability. He cannot walk and it seems unlikely that he will be able to go to the local school next year when he is five. He lives with his mother in an old house which is damp and has the bathroom and toilet on the first floor. His mother now finds it very difficult to carry Remi up and down the stairs.

Identify the various statutory assessment duties that are relevant to the circumstances outlined.

2.   On the basis of the same facts provide an explanation of the financial benefits which are available to this family under the social security system.

3.   Rachel is 10 years old and is being educated in her local primary school. She has a learning disability and her special educational needs are the subject of a statement which was made two years ago. She has recently been re-assessed and in the new statement the local education authority have identified a special school as the school in which her needs can be met. Her parents are adamant that they want her to continue her education in mainstream schools with her current friends.

What appeal rights do her parents have? Will Rachel have any opportunity to voice her own wishes in the appeal process?

---

26   See *Responding to Families in Need. Inspection of Assessment, Planning and Decision Making in Family Support Services*, (1997) Social Services Inspectorate.

4. Robby is 14 years old and has very recently been diagnosed as suffering from a degenerative muscle disease. He finds walking quite difficult sometimes. In the future he will be unable to get upstairs to the bathroom and his bedroom without help. His parents have been referred to the social services department and you have been allocated the case. They have asked you what services are available for Robby and the family. They want to care for him themselves and ensure that he continues with his education and that he has as much independence as possible. They also want to know what social security benefits they can claim, particularly if one of them has to give up their job to look after Robby.

Provide the necessary advice and outline the process of assessment and likely service provision.

5. On the basis of the same facts advise Robby and his mother and father in the situation where Robby can no longer get upstairs without being carried and the local authority decide that they will not provide a stair lift on the grounds that 'his needs are not sufficient to justify the allocation of limited resources'.

6. Natalie is 17 years old and has anorexia. She has been treated on a number of previous occasions but her condition is now much more serious and there are fears that she could cause herself substantial and permanent damage if she continues to eat as little as she is currently doing. She is refusing treatment. Natalie has clearly stated her decision to refuse treatment.

Should she be treated against her wishes?

In the event that she consents to treatment, should she be detained so that such treatment can take place? (On previous occasions she has absconded from the clinic where she would be treated and the managers are unwilling to admit her unless she can be detained.)

How might the necessary court orders be obtained?

5. ACTIVITIES

1. Obtain a copy of your local authority's Children's Plan. Identify the provision for disabled children.

2.   Obtain any information you can on your local education authority's policy and provision for special education needs.

3.   Does the local authority have any published material on the running of complaint's procedures under the Children Act and the Local Authority Social Services Act?

4.   Obtain Benefits Agency leaflets on benefits for disabled children.

5.   It may be possible to observe Special Educational Needs Tribunal and Disability Appeal Tribunal hearings when accompanying a local authority employee attending a tribunal and with the permission of the Tribunal.

6.   Become familiar with charitable and voluntary groups providing services for disabled children in your area.

7.   Put together a library of relevant materials. Update when necessary.

6   ADDRESSES

Advisory Centre for Education
1b Aberdeen Studios
22 Highbury Grove
London N5 2EA.
Phone: 0171 354 8321
Exclusion Helpline: 0171 704 9822

Children's Legal Centre
University of Essex
Wivenhoe Park
Colchester
Essex CO4 3SQ.
Phone Advice line: 01206 873820
Fax: 01206 874026
E-mail: CLC@essex.ac.uk
Admin. phone number: 01206 872466

Council for Disabled Children
c/o National Children's Bureau

8 Wakley Street
London EC1V 7QE.
Phone: 0171 843 6000
Fax: 0171 278 9512
Web: www.ncb.org.uk

Department of Health
PO Box 410
Wetherby
West Yorkshire
LS23 7LN.
Phone: 01937 840 250
Fax: 090 210 266
(For Local Authority Circulars (LACs), Local Authority Social
Services Letters (LASSLs) and Social Services Inspectorate Chief
Inspector (CIs) letters.)

Disability Alliance Educational and Research Association
Universal House
88-94 Wentworth Street
London E1 7SA.
Phone: 0171 247 8776
Fax: 0171 247 8765
Rights Advice Line: 0171 247 8763

Royal Association for Disability and Rehabilitation (RADAR)
12 City Forum
250 City Road
London EC1V 8AF.
Phone 0171 250 3222

Royal Society for Mentally Handicapped Children and Adults
(MENCAP)
123 Golden Lane
London EC1Y 0RT.
Phone: 0171 454 0454

7   MATERIALS

Clements, L, *Community Care and the Law* (1996) Legal Action
Group.

Cooper, J and Vernon, S, *Disability and the Law*, (1996) Jessica Kingsley Publishers.

Department for Education and the Welsh Office, *Code of Practice on the Identification and Assessment of Special Educational Needs*, (1994).

Department of Health, *Children With Disabilities. The Children Act 1989 Guidance and Regulations* Volume 6. (1991) HMSO.

Disability Rights Handbook. Annual editions published by the Disability Alliance Educational and Research Association.

Frantz, C, *Re C (A Minor) – Is Forcible Detention of a Young Person Through the Court's Common Law Inherent Jurisdiction Acceptable Action?* Childright, May 1997, No 136.

Friel, J, *Children with Special Needs. Assessment, Law and Practice – Caught in the Acts*, (1997) Jessica Kingsley Publishers.

Gilbert, G, *Children under the Housing Act*, Childright, June 1997, No 137.

Robinson, J, *Special educational needs, the code and the new tribunal. Education and the Law* Vol 8, No 1, 1996. (Contains references to the 1993 Act. The discussion is relevant to the 1996 Act as well.)

Social Services Inspectorate, *Report of the National Inspection of Local Authority Services To Disabled Children and Their Families*, (1994).

CHAPTER 5

Family breakdown

1 INTRODUCTION

The breakdown and ending of domestic relationships provides the site for a considerable amount of social work though there are relatively few specific statutory powers and duties. It is clear though that the personal, financial and child care complexities and difficulties experienced by those involved in the breakdown of a relationship are such that social work intervention is often needed. Problems involving accommodation, the care of children and the organisation of satisfactory financial arrangements, are all areas in which social workers can provide information and expertise in any short term crisis and in the longer term. The only real 'professional law' for social work in this area is that which arises from the fact that many court proceedings dealing with the breakdown of marriage and other domestic relationships are 'family proceedings' for the purpose of the Children Act 1989, and from the statutory responsibilities of local authorities in respect of child protection. There is also the important civil work of the probation service in which probation officers act as court welfare officers providing welfare reports for the courts in family proceedings. Through this statutory duty the probation service has become involved in the important development of mediation and conciliation services which seek to reduce the conflict often involved in matrimonial litigation and family proceedings. It is clear that mediation will be a central element of the new legal structure of divorce to be introduced in early 1999 by the Family Law Act 1996.

It is possible to suggest some examples of social work involvement in the legal aspects of relationship breakdown.

a)   A substantial number of existing service users, both adults and children, are also involved or have been involved in matrimonial and relationship breakdown. The breakdown of domestic relationships may involve emergency social work intervention to protect a child or children under the Children Act 1989 or arranging the accommodation of children under the same Act. It may also encompass work with women and children who are living in a refuge having left the matrimonial home because of domestic violence.

b) Where a court hearing family proceedings considers that a care or supervision order may be needed it can require a local authority to investigate the circumstances of the child to establish whether either order is appropriate (section 37 of the Children Act.)

c) Social workers may be involved in the supervision of contact orders made under the Children Act 1989 (section 16).

d) Probation officers or social workers may be involved in the administration of a family assistance order made under the Children Act 1989. The order requires the practitioner to advise, assist and befriend any person named in the order (section 7).

e) Work by probation officers as court welfare officers and the provision of welfare reports for the courts.

f) The development of conciliation and mediation schemes by the probation service as part of their civil work.

1.1 CONTENT

It is clear then that social work in the field of relationship breakdown is varied and can be complex. This chapter will give some explanation of the law which seeks to organise and provide for the consequences of such breakdown and will identify and explain the incidences of social work involvement required by both the law and by definitions of good practice.

It is necessary to look at divorce in the county court and its consequences for both spouses and for children and at the matrimonial jurisdiction of the magistrates' courts. The Children Act 1989 has had a substantial impact on this area of law and practice by defining court proceedings dealing with such issues as 'family proceedings'. The result is significant; where children are involved, for instance in a divorce, section 8 orders, such as residence and contact orders, are available; and section 1 principles apply so that the welfare of the child is paramount and there is a presumption of no order unless making an order is considered to be better for the child(ren).

The Child Support Act 1991 was implemented in April 1993 and a brief outline of the system of child support established by that Act and the Child Support Act 1995 will be provided.

Domestic violence will be considered as a separate matter as will the statutory duties of probation officers and social workers as report writers and the involvement of the probation service in the development of conciliation and mediation services.

2 THE LAW

2.1 DIVORCE

The facility of a divorce is only available to couples who are married. In this sense the law favours marriage as a form of domestic relationship by providing the services of the law to arrange and regulate the consequences of its breakdown. Such arrangements include the protection and enforcement of important rights for the divorcing spouses as well as for their children, such as accommodation, financial provision and appropriate care for children. In contrast to the favouring of marriage the law tends to disadvantage cohabitation. Couples who are not married cannot get divorced and are not able to avail themselves of all the facilities of the law outlined above though parents may apply for a section 8 under the Children Act to resolve disputes including those concerning contact and residence.

The Family Law Act 1996, Part II, provides a new legal structure for divorce; implementation of this part of the Act is planned for early 1999. Consequently the current law is described below and an outline of the new provisions will be provided in section 3.

2.1.1 Grounds

The Matrimonial Causes Act 1973 specifies that the sole ground for divorce is the irretrievable breakdown of marriage. This is to be established by one of five 'facts':

- that the respondent has committed adultery and the petitioner finds it intolerable to live with them;

- that the respondent has behaved in such a way that the petitioner cannot reasonably be expected to live with them;

- that the respondent has deserted the petitioner for a continuous period of two years;

- that the parties have lived apart for a continuous period of two years and that the respondent consents to the decree being granted;

- that the parties have lived apart for at least five years.

2.1.2   Petition stage

One of these facts, or a combination of two or more of them, will form the basis of the divorce petition which will be presented to a local divorce county court. A divorce petition may not be presented during the first year of marriage. Procedural rules specify the steps to be taken, and time limits for the conduct of what is known as the petition stage of a divorce. This stage does not involve a court appearance by the parties and legal aid is not available for this part of a divorce unless proceedings are contested, though advice and assistance under the green form scheme may be. As a result service users may need advice, assistance and support during this phase of divorce.

In the simplest divorce the petition is unopposed, there are no children and the parties have made mutually satisfactory arrangements for property and financial matters. In such circumstances the divorce court will be able to pronounce a decree nisi which can be made absolute after a short period of time. The spouses may remarry only after the divorce decree has been made absolute.

2.1.3   Ancillary proceedings

The unfortunate fact is that most divorces do not follow this simple path; the petition itself may be opposed, though this is rare these days; much more common is agreement between the parties about divorcing, but disagreement about the arrangements proposed for the matrimonial home, financial matters and the children. Such disputes are the basis of what are known as ancillary proceedings and legal aid is available for such proceedings.

If there are children of the marriage, the court, under section 41 of the Matrimonial Causes Act 1973, must consider whether, in the light of any arrangements that have been made for the children, to exercise any of its powers under the Children Act. These might include making a section 8 order, a family assistance order, or requiring the local authority to investigate the circumstances of the child.

The parties to divorce proceedings are encouraged to reach their own agreements on the issues of property, finance and children. In relation to any order it makes for a child the divorce court is subject to the principles set out in section 1 of the Children Act: primarily that the child's welfare is the paramount consideration and no order is to be made unless the court considers that doing so would be better for the child than making no order.

Where there is agreement concerning the arrangements for the children between the parties they must file a statement with the court setting out the terms of the agreement. Where the parties to a divorce are unable to reach agreement on issues concerning their children then either or both parents may apply for a section 8 order. The court may make a section 8 order on its own motion. A court hearing family proceedings may also direct the local authority to investigate the circumstances of the children where it considers that a care or supervision order may be needed (section 37).

In relation to property and finance, the parties are free to make their own arrangements. The terms of such agreements are subject to the provisions of the Child Support Act which means that maintenance arrangements must not be agreed which have the impact of reducing the liability of one party to maintain the children to the extent that the other party is required to claim social security benefits. Failing agreement the court has wide powers to make appropriate orders under the 1973 Act.

The litigation of such disputes is complex and often bitterly contested and it is only possible here to give the broadest outline of the relevant legal principles. It should also be noted that such disputes often arise before or at the time that a divorce petition is served so that disputes concerning the right to occupy the matrimonial home, the right to maintenance, or issues concerning the children need to be regulated by the divorce court during the divorce proceedings and pending any final resolution of the issues.

2.1.4   Property and financial orders

Property

Upon divorce, or a judicial separation, the court can make orders concerning the matrimonial home and the necessary financial arrangements. In relation to the matrimonial home the court has extensive powers to order the transfer of ownership of a home or the tenancy of a rented property between the parties, or it may order the sale of the property and allocate the proceeds of the sale between the parties, or order that the home be settled on trust so that its sale can be postponed until, for instance, the children reach adulthood or finish full time education. The court's powers in relation to the matrimonial home are wide and varied but under section 25 of the Matrimonial Causes Act 1973 it is under a duty, when making orders in relation to property and finance, to have regard to all the circumstances and to give its first consideration to the welfare of any child of the family.

Finance

The court is subject to the principle of section 25 described above and additionally to a series of specific statutory criteria in section 25 which the court is required to consider when deciding on an order for periodic (maintenance) and/or lump sum payments. These criteria include the financial resources and circumstances of the parties; their financial needs in the future which may depend on their age and health; any non-financial contribution made to the marriage e.g. child care and other domestic duties; the conduct of each of the parties if it would be unfair to ignore it and the value of any future financial benefits, such as a pension, which will be lost upon divorce. The court is also subject to a more general 'clean break' objective introduced by the Matrimonial and Family Proceedings Act 1984, and inserted in section 25A Matrimonial Causes Act 1973, which aims to terminate financial responsibility of one party for the other as soon as possible after the divorce.

The law is designed to provide principles which will allow the court to make arrangements and orders which are appropriate to the individual circumstances of any divorce. However, for many service users the reality of divorce is determined by the availability of local authority housing and the level of social security benefits for the parent who will care for the children after the divorce.

2.1.5   Children Act orders: residence and contact

The notion of parental responsibility emphasised by the Act is based on a responsibility for children that is continuing notwithstanding the divorce of a child's parents, so that both parents are expected to be involved in the major decisions about their child(ren). The expectation underlying the provisions of the Act is that divorcing parents will make their own arrangements for the care of their children after divorce, and that the courts will only intervene where the welfare of the child requires such intervention. Where disputes between divorcing parents arise and agreement cannot be reached, the court may have to consider making a section 8 residence or contact order. A residence order will regulate the arrangements for where a child is to live and may specify a situation where a child resides with both parents at different times. A contact order requires a person with whom a child is living to allow contact between the child and another person, the other parent for example.

Before the court makes such orders it may require a welfare report to be prepared by the court welfare service. There are a number of factors which are acknowledged to influence both the recommendations made in such reports and the orders ultimately made by the court. These factors are dominated by the welfare principle, and the welfare check list set out in section 1(3), but may also include the views of the child, a reluctance to disturb existing child care arrangements if they are working well, some evidence of a 'maternal preference', a concern with the behaviour of the parents only if it is relevant to the child's welfare, the standard of care available and a desire to keep siblings together.[1]

2.1.6   Care and supervision orders

Divorce proceedings are family proceedings for the purposes of the Children Act though it is not possible for the court to make a care

---

1   For a more detailed discussion of these issues and of the law concerning children and divorce see Dewar, J, *Law and the Family* (2nd edn, 1992).

or supervision order on its own motion. Such orders can only be made upon application by a local authority and then only on proof of the criteria set out in section 31(2) of the Children Act:

> A court may only make a care order or a supervision order if it is satisfied:
>
> a) that the child concerned is suffering, or is likely to suffer, significant harm; and
>
> b) that the harm, or likelihood of harm, is attributable to:
>
>> i) the care given to the child, or likely to be given to him if the order were not made, not being what it would be reasonable to expect a parent to give to him; or
>>
>> ii) the child's being beyond parental control.

Where the divorce court considers that either of these orders might be appropriate it will require the local authority to investigate the circumstances of the child(ren). If the local authority, as a result of its investigations, decides not to apply for a care or supervision order then it must inform the court of its reasons for not making such an application, and of the services it is providing for, and the work it is undertaking or intending to undertake with, the child(ren) and the family.

2.2   THE MATRIMONIAL JURISDICTION OF THE MAGISTRATES' COURTS

Divorce is a matter only for the county courts, but magistrates' courts have an important jurisdiction to deal with a number of matrimonial disputes short of divorce. This work is undertaken by the family proceedings panel of magistrates under the Domestic Proceedings and Magistrates' Courts Act 1978. The Act provides the court with a number of orders where a married applicant can establish that:

- the respondent has failed to provide reasonable maintenance for the applicant or the children of the family; or

- the respondent has behaved in such a way that the applicant cannot reasonably be expected to live with the respondent; or

- the respondent has deserted the applicant.

Subject to the provisions of the Child Support Act, which takes the majority of child maintenance matters out of the jurisdiction of the family proceedings court, orders can be made to provide maintenance for the applicant (and children). Orders can also be made for lump sum payments. When it is deciding on these orders the court is required to consider a number of criteria which are similar to those considered by the divorce courts when making property and financial orders. The magistrates also have a power to formalise agreements made by the parties themselves for maintenance and lump sum payments by means of a consent order.

Within this, now limited, jurisdiction the family proceedings court is required by section 8 of the Domestic Proceedings and Magistrates' Courts Act 1978 to consider whether to exercise any of its powers under the Children Act 1989. These powers include section 8 orders and the power to require a local authority to investigate the circumstances of the child(ren).

2.2.1 Child support

The Child Support Act 1991 was implemented in April 1993, and has been supplemented by the Child Support Act 1995; their provisions have had a significant impact on the issue of child maintenance. The objectives of the legislation are twofold; enforcing the obligation of parents to maintain their children, and thereby reducing the expenditure the state currently makes to fulfil that role where parents are defaulting on their responsibility. The normal situation will be where a child's parents have separated, the child is living with its mother and the father is not paying maintenance for the child. In such circumstances the mother of the child can apply to the Child Support Agency for a maintenance assessment against the father which the agency will collect and enforce if necessary. The assessment of maintenance is made on the basis of a means test and a formula detailed in regulations.

A parent, or person with parental responsibility, who is claiming Income Support, Income Based Job Seeker's Allowance, Family Credit or Disability Working Allowance is required to apply to the Agency for child maintenance and is therefore obliged to use its assessment, collection and enforcement services unless there are reasonable grounds for believing that compliance would involve a risk of harm or undue distress to the applicant or child. A person against whom an order is made has a right to have the decision reviewed and may appeal to a Child Support Appeal Tribunal.

The introduction of child support means that the courts have only a residual jurisdiction concerning child maintenance in a number of special circumstances where child support does not operate, for example in the case of step-parents. Divorcing couples are still able to agree on the issue of maintenance for their children post divorce though such agreements may not have the effect of increasing reliance on welfare benefits above the level which would be established if a child support assessment were in force.

2.3   THE WORK OF PROBATION OFFICERS IN THE COURT WELFARE SERVICE

2.3.1   Reports

The probation service has an important role providing, as the court welfare service, reports for the courts in a number of proceedings including divorce in the county courts, in domestic/family proceedings in the magistrates' courts under the Domestic Proceedings and Magistrates' Courts Act 1978, family proceedings under the Children Act 1989 and in wardship proceedings in the High Court. The function of the court welfare officer in this respect is to help the court resolve disputes so that the welfare of the child(ren) is promoted or safeguarded. This is achieved firstly by investigation and then by the submission of a welfare report to the court. Their work is determined by the principles set out in section 1 of the Children Act 1989, that the welfare of the child is the paramount consideration, that no order should be made unless the making of such an order is for the benefit of the child, and the principle that delay is likely to prejudice the interests of the child.

2.3.2   Mediation

In divorce and other family proceedings the investigation and inquiry process and the preparation of a welfare report is a difficult matter which requires sensitivity and skill. Where there are disputes between the parents over the children, the adversarial nature of divorce proceedings can mean that such disputes become entrenched and bitter. This feature of divorce litigation has been recognised for some time and a number of initiatives have been made with the broad objective of reducing conflict in disputes about children and of increasing areas of agreement between divorcing couples. It is thought that ultimately divorced parents are more likely to adhere to an agreement about the care of their children which has been mutually agreed than to an arrangement which has been imposed by court order. Underpinning the development of mediation schemes, designed to achieve these objectives where possible, is the belief that a child's welfare is better served by the continuation of a relationship with both parents after their divorce. Agreement between them about the care of their child is more likely to encourage such continuing relationships. The principle of continuing parental responsibility enshrined in the Children Act reflects these beliefs.

A number of mediation schemes have been developed 'out of court' in the sense that they are not formally connected to the divorce courts. The development of 'in court' conciliation schemes has largely resulted from an interpretation by some divorce court welfare officers of their professional role to encompass the promotion of agreement between divorcing couples on the future care of their children. It is argued that such agreement will in turn promote the welfare of the child. This development, and involvement in mediation services, is seen as the best method of achieving agreement and promoting the interests and welfare of children.

The availability of mediation services, both 'out of court' and 'in court' has grown significantly in recent years though the character of such schemes is varied. There are a number of well established criticisms of mediation and the courts have made it clear that court welfare officers should not combine the roles of mediator and report writer. Nonetheless the benefit of mediation is now widely accepted and it is clear that such processes will be at the centre of divorce proceedings when Part II of the Family Law Act 1996 is implemented early in 1999.[2]

2.4   THE IMPLICATIONS OF THE CHILDREN ACT 1989

The Children Act 1989 has a considerable impact on the way in which the law seeks to regulate the breakdown of domestic relationships.

---

2   For a fuller discussion of the role of mediation in the new law of divorce see: Dr Stephen Cretney, *Lawyers under the Family Law Act*, June [1997] Fam Law 405.

The breakdown of such relationships has a number of consequences and the Act provides a statutory code for all issues concerning children however they arise, eg as a result of divorce or as a result of domestic violence. So in divorce proceedings the Matrimonial Causes Act 1973 will provide for the issues concerning the parties, their property and their money and the Children Act provides principles and provisions for the divorce court to settle issues concerning the care of the children where this cannot be agreed by the divorcing parents.

A central concept of the Children Act is the notion of parental responsibility which is described as 'the collection of duties, rights and authority which a parent has in respect of his child'. In relation to marital breakdown the Act makes it clear, both in principle and in detail, that the parental responsibility of both parents for their children will continue despite their separation or divorce; it can only be restricted by specific orders of the court. The Act provides four orders under section 8, known as 'section 8 orders', which can be made to control and restrict parental responsibility where this is necessary for the welfare of the children. The important principles are that both parents will continue to exercise full parental responsibility for their children, except where that has been limited by a section 8 order, and that no order will be made unless it is necessary for the welfare of the child.

Section 8 orders are available in a wide range of family proceedings dealing with issues arising from the breakdown of domestic relationships. These family proceedings include divorce and separation proceedings under the Matrimonial Causes Act 1973, proceedings arising from domestic violence under Part IV Family Law Act 1996, matrimonial proceedings under the Domestic Proceedings and Magistrates' Courts Act 1978 and issues concerning the occupation of the matrimonial home under the Matrimonial Homes Act 1983. Section 8 orders can be made in family proceedings heard in the High Court, the county court and the magistrates' court.

The court may make a section 8 order itself without anyone having made an application though normally an application will be made by a parent, a guardian or a person with parental responsibility in whose favour a residence order has been made. These applicants do not need the leave of the court to make an application. The Act recognises that other people may have an interest in the upbringing of a child and provision is therefore made for a person with a genuine interest in the child's welfare to make an application with the leave of the court.

2.4.1 Family assistance orders

A family assistance order may be made under the terms of section 16. Such an order is designed to 'provide short-term help to parents following separation or divorce, to smooth the transition period for them and to encourage co-operation between them'.[3] The order is made in family proceedings and normally requires a probation officer or local authority social worker, or some other person, to advise, assist and befriend a person named in the order, ie parent, child, person with whom the child is living, or a person in whose favour a contact order has been made. The consent of anyone named in the order, except the child, is required and the order lasts for a maximum of six months. The order is directed to increasing co-operation between parents to the advantage of the children.[4]

2.5 DOMESTIC VIOLENCE

Domestic violence has been an important social issue during much of recorded history; as a legal issue it seems to have been rediscovered in the early 1970s. Domestic violence may well constitute a criminal assault and in theory such an assault can be prosecuted as a criminal offence. There is some evidence that the Crown Prosecution Service is reluctant to prosecute the perpetrators of such assaults where they believe that the victim may be unwilling to give evidence against their partners. Indeed it may be that the criminal law does not offer women sufficient protection from domestic violence for it is geared to the punishment of the assailant rather than the protection of the victim, with the result that a conviction and sentence may exacerbate the violence and increase the threat to women.

The disadvantages of the criminal law response to domestic violence led pressure groups working in this area in the early 1970s to look to the civil law for appropriate remedies and protections. A number of civil actions such as divorce provided the possibility of an injunction against a violent husband but because it was necessary to seek such orders as part of other proceedings they did not provide the speed, convenience and particular remedies sought by women who had been assaulted. The other important defect of using established matrimonial law actions was that they were unavailable to women who were not

---

3 Bainham, A with Cretney, S, *Children – The Modern Law*, (1993) Family Law.
4 Very few such orders have been made since the Act was implemented.

married to their partners. The inappropriateness of the criminal law and the disadvantages of the existing civil law procedure became the basis for a well orchestrated pressure group campaign to provide a specially designed civil law action for the victims of domestic violence. The campaign resulted in a private members' Bill becoming law as the Domestic Violence and Matrimonial Proceedings Act 1976.

Social workers have no specific powers or duties in relation to domestic violence though there are important duties under section 37 of the Children Act which require social work investigation where information is received that a child is suffering or likely to suffer significant harm. Social workers also have the right to apply for a child assessment order under section 43 of the Act and for an emergency protection order under the terms of section 44 of the Act.

2.5.1   Family Law Act 1996, Part IV

Part IV of the Act was implemented in October 1997; it seeks to provide:

> ... a comprehensive statutory scheme of protection by non-molestation injunctions and regulation of the occupancy of the home on relation- ship breakdown, widens the class of persons who are eligible to apply for protection and creates a unified statutory scheme covering the magistrates' (family proceedings) courts, county courts and High Court.[5]

Child abuse is one facet of domestic violence and the 1996 Act provides that non-molestation orders, occupation orders and ex- clusion requirements are all available to provide short-term relief and longer term remedies designed to protect a child from abuse.

Non-molestation orders

There is no statutory definition of molestation though in deciding to use its powers the court is required to consider all the circum- stances of the case, including the need to secure the health, safety and well-being of the applicant or the person for whose benefit the order would be made, and any relevant child.[6]

---

5   Victoria Teggin and Tracey Payne, *Family Law Act 1996: domestic violence provisions*, Legal Action, August 1997.
6   Section 42(5).

The orders can be general in nature or tied to specific acts of molestation, and may be granted for a specified period or 'until further order'. Where there is an immediate need for an order the court has a discretion to make an ex parte order. In deciding to make such an ex parte order the court is required by section 45(2) to consider all the circumstances of the case including:

(a) any risk of significant harm to the applicant or relevant child, attributable to the conduct of the respondent, if the order is not made immediately;

(b) whether it is likely that the applicant will be deterred or prevented from pursuing the application if an order is not made immediately;

(c) whether there is reason to believe that the respondent is aware of the proceedings but is deliberately evading service and that the applicant or a relevant child will be seriously prejudiced by the delay involved ...

An application for a non-molestation order may be made by a person 'who is associated with the respondent', and an application may be made on behalf of a relevant child. An associated person is defined by section 62 as a person who is associated because:

- s/he is a present or past spouse or cohabitant and living together as husband and wife;

- they live or have lived together in the same household, other than merely because one is the other's employee, tenant, lodger or boarder; [7]

- they are relatives;

- they have agreed to marry one another;

- they are parties to the same family proceedings;

- in relation to any child, they are both either the parents of or have parental responsibility for the child;

---

7   This category includes lesbians and gay men.

- any child who is living or who might reasonably be expected to live with either party to the proceedings;

- any child in relation to whom an order under the Adoption Act 1976 or the Children Act 1989 is in question in the proceedings; or

- any other child whose interests the court considers relevant [8]

Children aged 16-18 may make an application in their own right. Children under 16 will need the leave of the High Court to make an application for a non-molestation order. There are powers under section 60 for rules of court to allow third parties to make an application. These provisions have not been implemented.

The application for an order may be made on its own or as part of other family proceedings. The court may make an order without an application having been made if it considers that an order should be made for the benefit of any other party to the proceedings.

The court may attach a power of arrest to a non-molestation order where it appears to the court that the respondent has used or threatened violence against the applicant or a relevant child (section 47). There is a statutory presumption in favour of the attachment of a power of arrest in proceedings other than ex parte proceedings. Where a power of arrest has been attached a police officer may arrest, without a warrant any person they have reasonable cause to suspect has breached the order. Punishment for breach of an order may extend to custody.

Occupation orders [9]

Part IV of the Act also provides for the making of occupation orders to regulate the occupation of a home after relationship breakdown. The court can make an order to

- allow the applicant to enter and occupy the home;

---

8   Victoria Teggin and Tracey Payne, op cit.
9   Occupation orders are available in all cases of relationship breakdown and are not limited to cases involving domestic breakdown.

- to prevent eviction;

- to regulate either or both parties' occupation of the home;

- to exclude the respondent from the home or a surrounding area.

However the Act provides that the type of order made will reflect the applicant's existing rights of occupation, the respondent's right of occupation and the past and present relationship between the applicant and the respondent. For all applications the court must take into account:

- the housing needs and housing resources of each of the parties and of any relevant child;

- the financial resources of the applicant and the respondent;

- the likely effect of any order, or of the decision not to make an occupation order, on the health, safety or well-being of the parties and of any relevant child; and

- the conduct of the parties to each other and otherwise.

The range of available orders will reflect the occupation rights of the applicant and the respondent, and will determine the section of the Act under which an application can be made.

The complexities of the law concerning occupation orders are considerable; however three principles have been suggested:

> Applicants entitled to occupy are able to apply for orders for indefinite periods and against the full range of associated persons. Orders made in favour of applicants who are not entitled to occupy will be for a limited time and so will not be a permanent solution to their housing needs, unless a transfer of tenancy is successfully applied for before the orders expire ...

> The likelihood of significant harm attributable to the respondent's conduct will be a highly relevant factor ...

> Where there is no likelihood of harm, consideration of the criteria and the parties' respective entitlements to occupy will provide the

courts with the capacity to respond with great flexibility to a wide range of circumstances ... [10]

Powers of arrest may be attached to occupation orders where it appears to the court that the respondent has used or threatened violence against the applicant or a relevant child.

Exclusion requirements

The Family Law Act 1996 amends the Children Act 1989 by inserting new sections 38A and 44A giving the court the power to include an exclusion requirement in an interim care order or emergency protection order. This important power allows a suspected abuser to be excluded from the home. Powers of arrest may be attached to the order.

2.5.2   Harassment

The Protection from Harassment Act 1997, which came into force in June 1997, is designed primarily to deal with stalking. The Act prohibits harassment, except in strictly defined circumstances, and creates two criminal offences: a summary offence of criminal harassment; and an indictable offence involving harassment which causes fear of violence. The Act also creates a civil action for harassment (section 3) in which a victim may claim damages and/or an injunction in respect of actual or apprehended harassment. Arrest warrants may be issued under section 3(3) where the victim considers that the terms of the injunction have been breached. A breach of an injunction granted under section 3 by the civil courts is a criminal offence and may be punished in the criminal courts. Section 5 also gives the criminal courts powers to impose restraining orders on those who have been convicted of an offence under the Act prohibiting them from conduct which might be injurious to the victim.

In an attempt not to be caught by too narrow a definition, the Act does not define harassment other than to say that it will be constituted by behaviour which a reasonable person would consider to amount to harassment.

10   Victoria Teggin and Tracey Payne, *Family Law Act 1996: occupation orders*, Legal Action, September 1997.

These provisions are in addition to the availability of non-molestation orders under the Family Law Act 1996 so they are of particular significance to those who do not have access to such orders. Those covered by the 1996 Act are spouses, cohabitants, former spouses and cohabitants, and other associated persons.[11]

3   FAMILY BREAKDOWN AND SOCIAL WORK: some issues for discussion

3.1   REFORMING THE LAW OF DIVORCE AND SEPARATION

The Family Law Act 1996 makes significant changes to the law of divorce (and judicial separation). The Act has emerged from a highly contentious political process in which original proposals by the previous government for reform of divorce and domestic violence law were targeted by right wing campaigners, both inside and outside Parliament, as both 'anti-marriage' and 'anti-family'. The Act incorporates a number of principles in Part I which reflect the contentious political context and the desire of government to reduce legal aid expenditure on divorce matters. The Act removes matrimonial fault as a ground for divorce and promotes agreement between the divorcing parties on matters concerning children, property and finance, rather than reliance on court orders. Mediation becomes the central avenue through which attempts are to be made to preserve and save marriages, and, where this is impossible, to construct consensus about their dissolution and the consequences concerning children, property and financial matters.

Part II regulates divorce (and separation) by providing for a divorce order to dissolve the marriage (or a separation order). This order can only be made by the court where the marriage has irretrievably broken down. Such an order cannot be made unless:

• a statement of marital breakdown has been lodged with the court;

• a period of reflection and consideration has ended;

---

11   See above, p 124.

• an application for the divorce order has been made. The application must provide evidence of the parties' future arrangements and a declaration that the applicant believes that the marriage cannot be saved.

A party to the marriage cannot make a statement of marital breakdown during the first year of the marriage, and then not until three months after the parties have attended an information meeting which is designed to encourage them to attend marriage counselling. Two weeks after the statement of breakdown is lodged with the court a period of reflection begins which will run for nine months, or if there is a child of the family under 16, for fifteen months. At the end of the period of reflection either one of the parties, or both of them, can apply for the divorce order. As already identified this order will only be granted if the court is satisfied with the parties' arrangements concerning property, finances, and any children.

The court can also make an order which prevents the parties divorcing even where all the requirements have been satisfied. Such an order can only be made where the court is satisfied that dissolution would result in substantial financial or other hardship to the other party to the marriage or to a child of the family and it would be wrong in all the circumstances for the marriage to be dissolved.

3.2 MEDIATION

It appears that mediation will be central to the divorce process. Mediation is distinguished from counselling.

> Mediation is intended to enable couples to meet face to face to resolve their differences over issues relating to finance, property and children with the assistance of a trained mediator. If it appears that there is a chance of the marriage being saved, the mediator will be expected to refer the couple to trained counsellors who can help them achieve this. [12]

The importance of mediation to the new divorce process is emphasised by two elements of the legislation. Section 13(1) provides that the court may, after it has received a statement of marital breakdown, direct the parties to attend a meeting for the purpose of:

12   *A Guide to the Family Law Act 1996*, August [1996] Fam Law.

(i) enabling an explanation to be made as to the facilities available to the parties for mediation in relation to any disputes between them;

(ii) providing an opportunity for each party to agree to take advantage of these facilities.

Section 26 of the Act gives the Legal Aid Board powers to secure mediation services by contracting for the provision of such services. An amendment to the Legal Aid Act 1988 allows legal aid to be available to pay for mediation in family matters.[13]

It appears that mediation will take over some of the role of legal representation at least for those parties who would be entitled to legal aid and who agree to seek to settle their differences and disputes with the help of the services of a mediator. However legal aid will still be available to pay for legal advice and assistance and for representation where it is necessary. Such legal help may be as an alternative to mediation or in support of it.

The decision to place mediation centre stage in family matters is significant and raises a number of questions. Will mediation be compulsory? Will legally assisted persons have a choice between mediation and law? Which proceedings are more suitable for legal representation? What will be the impact on the civil work of the probation service acting as court welfare officers?

The Lord Chancellor argued for the voluntariness of mediation in the House of Lords debate on the Bill:

> ... where either party to the proceedings is not prepared to take part in mediation, mediation is not suitable to the dispute, the parties and all the circumstances, I cannot see that a mediator could possibly regard mediation as suitable for a dispute where either party was not prepared to take part in it.[14]

Despite these assurances the Legal Aid Board, when it is deciding whether it is reasonable for a person to be granted legal aid in family matters, must have regard to whether mediation is a suitable alternative and for this purpose must have regard to the outcome of a

13   'Family matters' includes the availability of mediation in respect of issues arising under Parts I to V of the Children Act 1989.
14   Hansard, 25 January 1996, vol 568, no 32, col 1214.

meeting with a mediator. This meeting is required by the Legal Aid Act 1988, section 15(3)F, inserted by the Family Law Act 1996, which specifies that a person will not be granted legal aid for legal representation in family matters unless they have attended a meeting with a medi-ator to determine whether mediation is suitable to the parties, the dispute and all the circumstances of the case, particularly whether mediation can take place without either party being influenced by fear of violence or other harm.

Section 15(3)G of the Legal Aid Act 1988, again inserted by the Family Law Act 1996, specifies certain cases as not appropriate for mediation, and consequently provides that in these cases a person does not have to attend a meeting with a mediator before being granted legal aid for legal representation. These specified proceedings include those under Part IV of the Family Law Act 1996 (occupation of the family home, prevention of molestation and other related matters) and Part IV or V of the Children Act 1989 (care and supervision, and the protection of children).

The emphasis on mediation in the new law concerning relationship breakdown will necessitate the availability of appropriately trained mediators. Over the years considerable expertise has been developed in the mediation of disputes concerning children, despite a chronic lack of funding and consistent organisation. The new law requires much more: mediators will be required to mediate in disputes concerning property, financial matters and children; they will be partly publicly funded through the legal aid scheme; and to some extent mediation will be asked to fulfil a role alternative to that of lawyers. It is to be expected that appropriate training and qualification standards will be put in place. Some lawyers will also be expert mediators, but any attempt by the legal profession to seek to annex mediation for the profession in order to protect legal aid income should be firmly resisted.

For a number of years the probation service has provided a court welfare service in the family proceedings courts. Such work involves the preparation of welfare reports in family law proceedings concerning private law applications under Part I and Part II of the Children Act. The majority of these reports are made in respect of applications under section 4 for a parental responsibility order and under section 8 of the Act for contact and residence orders. Such work clearly requires work with parents who are in dispute with each other and has inevitably led to the involvement of the probation service in mediation work.

What will happen to this expertise within the new legal structure for relationship breakdown is difficult to predict. Parts I and II of the Children Act are family law matters for the purposes of the Family Law Act 1996, consequently mediation funded through legal aid will be available in those disputes which have hitherto given rise to the need for welfare reports commissioned from the probation service by the family proceedings court. There may remain a residual need for such reports where mediation is unsuccessful or not used and a disputed matter comes before the courts. More intriguingly the probation service could establish itself as an expert mediation service funded through legal aid. A further prospect is that those court welfare probation officers supportive of mediation and themselves expert mediators will resign from the probation service and seek employment as independent mediators. It is to be hoped that the new law on relationship breakdown does not mean that valuable expertise in the probation service is lost to a family law system which will need just such skills in abundance.

3.3   DOMESTIC VIOLENCE, THE LAW AND SOCIAL WORK PRACTICE

Domestic violence provides an example of how the quality of social work practice in a particular area can be enhanced by an appropriate understanding of the law. In work with the victims of domestic violence the boundaries of such knowledge are not restricted to legal provisions designed to deal with domestic violence itself but also include an understanding of legal services, the law on child protection, the law relating to relationship breakdown, social security and housing law.

A very brief pathway can be indicated as an example to illustrate the need for a social worker to develop legal knowledge and practice skills which together provide the basis for good social work in the field of relationship breakdown. A woman service user who has been assaulted by her partner may benefit from the support of a social worker designed to (in no particular order of priority):

- contact the police;

- find a place in a refuge for the woman and her children;

- contact a sympathetic lawyer with appropriate knowledge and skills;

- arrange for medical attention;

- trigger the emergency child protection measures in the Children Act; if there is an application for an emergency protection order or an interim care order an exclusion requirement may be attached to the order which would exclude the assailant from the home;

- provide help, information and support at any court hearing where a non-molestation order or occupation order is sought;

- provide evidence to the court of injuries sustained;

- support and possibly assist the service user in claiming social security benefits where necessary.

Longer term involvement may involve dealing with the housing authority in securing accommodation under the homelessness provisions of the Housing Act 1996 and supporting the service user during divorce proceedings. The complexity and variety of legal knowledge is clear and most if not all of the work described above involves the law in one way or another. An understanding of the legal implications of a service user's situation will enable the social worker to make appropriate practice decisions and with the help of a sympathetic lawyer, to provide the necessary support and protection.

4   CASE STUDIES

Here are a series of case studies which may be used to consolidate work done in the areas covered in this chapter and in the previous chapter on the Children Act 1989. Reference will need to be made to the provisions of the Children Act.

1.   Desmond and Barbara have been married for ten years and have two children, Rufus, eight, and Rebecca, six. They have been separated for three years and Barbara wishes to get divorced. The children have been sharing their time between both parents and want to continue doing this. The matrimonial home is owned by Desmond who has been living with his new girlfriend in her flat for the last two years. You became involved with Barbara and her children when they encountered harassment on the estate where they live.

Barbara is anxious about how to proceed with the divorce and about what might happen to the house and the children. Barbara does not work and has been living on money given to her by Desmond.

What advice would you give to Barbara?

Would your advice be any different if Barbara tells you that Desmond has threatened to beat her up if she continues to ask for money from him?

2.   Rosanna has three children and lives with Mick. She rings the office from a local refuge where she is staying with her children after leaving her local authority flat because Mick has assaulted her and the children and has threatened her and the children should they return.

Rosanna 'wants him out' of her flat and 'her life', and asks you what can be done.

3.   Neil and Ruby have been married for 16 years and have one child, Charlie, eleven. Ruby has petitioned for divorce but she and Neil are in dispute over what should happen to Charlie who is currently living with Ruby.

If Neil and Ruby cannot agree, what orders are available under the Children Act to provide for the children and what principles will the court take into account when it makes any decision about Charlie? Provide some information on the role of the court welfare officer in this process.

Answer these questions by reference to current divorce and family proceedings law, and then by reference to the new legal structure in the Family Law Act 1996.

4.   Ricky and Lauren have been married for five years and have one child, Steven, aged three. As the duty social worker you receive a phone call from a call box; Lauren is very upset but manages to tell you that Ricky has assaulted both her and Steven. You tell her to come to the office where in conversation it transpires that there has been a long history of violence. Lauren is scared to go back to the home (a local authority flat with a joint tenancy) and she fears for her and Steven's safety in the light of threats made to them by Ricky.

What advice and assistance would you be able to provide in the short term crisis situation and in the longer term?

What are the statutory duties of the local authority in this situation?

5.   Terry and June have one child, Hannah, aged six. Terry left the matrimonial home (which they jointly own and which is subject to a substantial mortgage) two years ago and June has begun divorce proceedings. Terry is delighted as he has moved in with a new girlfriend. Terry has been seeing Hannah on a weekly basis but June does not want Hannah to meet his new girlfriend and so she has refused to let Hannah see Terry.

How might this dispute be resolved?

6.   Marcus and Lorretta, who are married, have lived in a council flat for five years and they have three children aged five, three and two. One month ago they had yet another row and Marcus left. Lorretta has heard nothing from him since, though she knows that he is staying with a friend of his. She has no money and has been living on her child benefit and money borrowed from her mother. She is getting desperate for money but has decided that she does not want Marcus to return or see the children because his aggressive behaviour upsets them and since he has been away they have been much better. Lorretta is a devout Roman Catholic and would not contemplate beginning divorce proceedings.

What can she do?

5   ACTIVITIES

1.   Ring your local divorce county court and ask whether they produce a booklet to help people undertake their own divorce petitions.

2.   Look in your local telephone book and see if there is a local divorce mediation scheme. Look under 'mediation', 'conciliation' or 'divorce'. If so contact them for any information they might be able to provide. The addresses and phone numbers for national organisations working in this area are set out below.

3. Contact your local probation service and ask for any information they can provide on their civil work. It may be possible to spend
a day with a court welfare officer.

4. With the help of the local social services department, women's
refuge (if there is one), CABx and any other sources try and compile
a list of local lawyers who undertake child and family work, and
you would feel able to refer a service user to.

5. Is there a law centre in your area? Does it deal with domestic
violence work?

6. If you have access to the internet you can contact the web page for
the Lord Chancellor's Department. This site has a considerable amount
of information on the Family Law Act 1996 and on the law regarding
domestic violence. The web site address is: www.open.gov.uk/lcd

7. Try to keep up to date with the phased implementation of the
new divorce law of the Family Law Act 1996. Journals to look at
include Legal Action, published monthly by the Legal Action Group,
and the specialist law journal, Family Law. Implementation is
currently set for early 1999.

8. Get hold of the 1995 Home Office Circular on inter-agency co-
ordination to tackle domestic violence from the Home Office
Communications Directorate.

6 ADDRESSES

Association of Chief Officers of Probation
212 Whitechapel Road
London E1 1BJ.
Phone: 0171 377 9141
Fax: 0171 375 2100

Children's Legal Centre
Essex University
Wivenhoe Park
Colchester
Essex CO4 3SQ.
Phone Advice Line: 01206 873820

Fax: 01206 874026
E-mail: CLC@essex.ac.uk
Admin phone number: 01206 872466

Communications Directorate
Home Office
Room 156
Queen Anne's Gate
London SW1H 9AT.
Phone: 0171 273 3000
Fax: 0171 273 4660

Family Mediation Service
Institute of Family Therapy
24-32 Stephenson Way
London NW1 2HX.
Phone: 0171 391 9150
Fax: 0171 391 9169

Legal Aid Board
5th and 6th Floors
29-37 Red Lion Street
London WC1R 4PP.
Phone: 0171 813 5300

Lord Chancellor's Department
Family Policy Division
Selbourne House
54-60 Victoria Street
London SW1E 6QW.
Web: www.open.gov.uk/lcd

National Council for Family Proceedings
Centre for Socio-Legal Studies, Centre for Policy Studies
Bristol University.
Phone: 0117 974 1117
Fax: 0117 973 7308

National Council for One Parent Families
255 Kentish Town Road
London NW5 2LX.
Phone: 0171 267 1361
Fax: 0171 482 4851

Women's Aid Federation
PO Box 391
Bristol BS99 7WS.
Phone: 0117 944 4411 (admin.), 0117 963 3542 (helpline).

7   MATERIALS

Allen, N, *Making sense of the Children Act*, (1992) Longman.

Association of Chief Officers of Probation, *Probation Services and Domestic Violence*. Available from the Association or on the internet at www.penlex.org.uk/pbposdo.html

Bainham, A with Cretney, S, *Children: The Modern Law*, (1993) Family Law.

Cretney, S, *Lawyers under the Family Law Act*, June [1997] Fam Law.

Department of Health, *An Introduction to The Children Act 1989*, (1989) HMSO.

Dewar, J, *Law and the Family* (1992) Butterworths.

Douglas, G, Murch, M and Perry, A, *Supporting children when parents separate – a neglected family justice issue or mental health issue*, Child and Family Law Quarterly, Vol 8, No 2, 1996.

Family Law, *A Guide to the Family Law Act 1996*, August [1996] Fam Law.

Freeman, M D A, *Divorce Gospel Style*, June [1997] Fam Law.

Lawson-Cruttenden, T and Addison, N, *Harassment and Domestic Violence*, June [1997] Fam Law.

Legal Aid Board, *Legal Aid Guide*.

Lord Chancellor's Department, *Undefended divorce. A guide for the petitioner acting without a solicitor*. Available free from county courts.

Lord Chancellor's Department, *A Guide to Part IV of the Family Law Act 1996 For Agencies and Professionals Helping Victims of Domestic Violence*, (1997). Available as a booklet from the Lord Chancellor's Department or on the Internet at www. open.gov.uk/lcd/dvbook_.htm

Moroney, L and Harris K, *Relationship breakdown and housing: a practical guide*, (1997) Shelter.

Mullender, A, *Rethinking Domestic Violence. The social work and probation response*, (1996) Routledge.

Murphy, J, *Domestic Violence: The New Law*, The Modern Law Review [Vol 59, November 1996].

Teggin, V and Payne, T, *Family Law Act 1996: domestic violence provisions*, August 1997; *occupation orders*, Legal Action, September 1997.

CHAPTER 6

Community care law

This chapter is divided into two sections. Section 1 is concerned with the broad context of community care law as it relates to all potential service users. Section 2 discusses the law as it relates to vulnerable service users. It should be recognised that many services for this group of users will be provided under the breadth of community care law, however there are areas of law that relate specifically to vulnerable service users and these are identified and discussed in Section 2. This section will also consider the proposals of the Law Commission on reform of the law to provide for the personal welfare of vulnerable service users. Reference will be made to the Green Paper issued by the Lord Chancellor's Department in December 1997, *Who Decides? Making decisions on behalf of mentally incapacitated adults*. The paper seeks views on the direction of law reform proposed by the Law Commission.

Service users may be vulnerable because of their mental incapacity. In these circumstances they may be provided with services under community care law. Section 1 identifies legislation that may be of relevance to such service users, but reference should also be made to the chapter on mental health and in particular to Section 2 of the chapter which discusses mental incapacity.

SECTION 1
COMMUNITY CARE LAW

1 INTRODUCTION

Historically this area of social work, and the law which regulates much of it, has received relatively little attention. This situation began to change in the early 1980s due in many respects to the work of pressure groups such as Age Concern, the Disability Alliance,

MENCAP and the Royal Association for Disability and Rehabilitation (RADAR), who succeeded in increasing public recognition of
the interests of people who are chronically ill or disabled.

Public concern about community care services, and the media
attention that has developed around this concern, has given this
area of local authority services an importance that properly reflects
its cost and the number of service users involved. Social work in
this area and with this group of service users constitutes an important element of professional practice. It is regulated by a complex,
and ever increasing variety of statutory provisions, some imposing
duties, some according rights and others giving discretionary
powers to local authorities. The National Health Service and
Community Care Act 1990 (hereafter identified as the Community
Care Act), which was implemented between April 1991 and April
1993, established local authorities as the lead agency in the provision of community care services but did nothing to reduce the
complexity of the law which regulates this area of practice. In fact
the Act increased the level of complexity by grafting new powers
and duties on to those that were already in place under existing
legislation such as the Chronically Sick and Disabled Persons Act
1970. This process has unfortunately continued with the implementation of the Mental Health (Patients in the Community) Act
1995, the Carers (Recognition and Services) Act 1995 and the
Community Care (Direct Payments) Act 1996. Community care
law is in urgent need of reform; at the very least the complex legal
regime needs consolidation into a single Community Care Act.

1.1   COMMUNITY CARE: ORGANISATION AND REFORM

Community care is not new. So, for example, it is possible to understand the provisions of the Chronically Sick and Disabled Persons Act
1970 as being directed to allowing people with a disability to live
relatively independent lives in their own homes with the help of services
provided by local authority social services departments. The trend in
social policy toward care in the community rather than in residential
institutions was confirmed by the Disabled Persons (Services, Consultation and Representation) Act 1986 (hereafter identified as the
Disabled Persons Act 1986) and by the programme to close many long
stay psychiatric hospitals which was implemented during the 1980s
and early 1990s. The introduction of the Social Fund can also be
understood as part of a rolling community care programme that is

itself seen by some commentators as an element of the privatisation and domestication of the welfare state. This 'rolling programme' of community care has been implemented in an incremental fashion, often without proper resourcing. The failure to implement the key sections of the Disabled Persons Act 1986 can be seen as an example of this.

In 1986 an Audit Commission report on community care provided an alarming picture of escalating demand for services, increasing costs, particularly for residential provision, and gross underprovision of community care services and facilities. In many ways the Audit Commission's work provided the initiative for the 1988 report on community care by Sir Roy Griffiths which identified confusion in responsibility for community care which was shared between local and national government, the national health service, the voluntary and private sector and informal carers. The Griffiths report re-commended that local authorities, through their social services departments, should become the lead agency for community care. Griffiths argued that local authorities should not be the monopoly providers of community care services but act as the arrangers and purchasers of them:

> Elected local authorities are best placed, in my judgement, to assess local needs, set local priorities and monitor local performance ... What is needed is strengthening and buttressing of their capacity to do this by clarifying and where necessary, adjusting responsibilities and to hold them accountable. [1]

The Griffiths report was published in March 1988 but it is thought that the recommendation of a lead role for local authorities was not well received by government and it was not until November 1989 that a White Paper was published setting out government legislative proposals for the organisation of community care services. 'Caring for People – Community Care in the Next Decade and Beyond' proposed that a substantial element of care services be supplied by the voluntary and private sectors with local authority social services departments organising and purchasing individual provision in response to their assessment of individual need.

Provision by the voluntary and private sector was to be extended beyond residential care to include those domiciliary care services

---

1 *Community Care: An Agenda for Action*, (1988) HMSO.

provided by social services departments. The White Paper fell short of requiring competitive tendering for care provision and recognised that local authorities should retain the power to provide care services themselves particularly for people with high level specific needs. To encourage the use of the voluntary and private sectors the government required local authorities to produce a three year community care plan with annual updates. The Secretary of State has the power to intervene by issuing directions and giving guidance.

Part III of the Community Care Act 1990, which was fully implemented in April 1993, provides a central element of the legislative framework for community care in England and Wales. The full legal regime extends beyond the 1990 Act to encompass legislation in place before its implementation and legislation that has been implemented since. We can describe a 'narrow' concept of community care law to cover the provision of personal social services; this chapter will concentrate on this narrow definition of community care law though discussion will range beyond this boundary. From the perspective of the service user the experience of community care may well extend beyond the provision of personal social services to include social security benefits and housing provision. This wider concept of community care law will be identified though the details are discussed elsewhere in the book.

1.2 LEGAL STRUCTURE

The complex legal structure of community care is built upon a range of powers and duties imposed principally on local authorities and health authorities. The law contains a number of duties on local authorities to provide services. However the extent to which these duties are absolute, or contain elements of discretion, is increasingly becoming the subject matter of litigation. There are also some discretionary legal powers where local authorities can decide whether they wish to do something, eg section 31 of the National Assistance Act 1948 gives a local authority the power to decide whether it wishes to give funds to voluntary organisations for the provision of recreational facilities or meals for old people. It appears that the issue of resources is emerging as the main problematic issue for local authorities who are seeking to satisfy increasing demand for services from reducing and cash limited resources. Increasingly this dilemma is ending up in the courts as service users seek to enforce their 'rights' to community care services against local authorities who argue that their resources must be a relevant factor in deciding how competing claims for services are to be met.

In identifying the substance of community care law (sometimes known as the legal mandate), it is necessary to extend the description beyond statute to include case law, directions and guidance. The importance of directions and guidance in community care law needs to be identified.

The Local Authority Social Services Act 1970, section 7A(1) requires local authorities to exercise their social services functions in accordance with Directions issued by the Secretary of State. An example is the Complaints Procedure Directions 1990 which determine important elements of the procedure for community care complaints.

The legal status of guidance is problematic. The Local Authority Social Services Act 1970 provides that:

> 7 - (1) Local authorities shall, in the exercise of their social services functions, including the exercise of any discretion conferred by any relevant enactment, act under the general guidance of the Secretary of State ...

In *R v Islington London Borough Council, ex p Rixon* [1997] ELR 66, Sedley J held that:

> Parliament in enacting section 7(1) did not intend local authorities to whom ministerial guidance was given to be free, having considered it, to take it or leave it. A local authority was required to follow the path charted by the Secretary of State's guidance, with liberty to deviate from it where the local authority judged on admissible grounds that there was a good reason to do so, but without freedom to take a substantially different course.

It now seems that a distinction is being drawn between policy guidance, which is issued under section 7(1), and practice guidance. Policy guidance has a higher status than practice guidance. The former is said to tell a local authority what it must do, whilst practice guidance suggests how it might be done. In the field of community care law *Community Care in the Next Decade and Beyond: Policy Guidance* was issued under section 7(1), whereas *Care Management and Assessment, Guidance for Practitioners and Managers* does not have such status though it must be considered by a local authority.

2   THE LAW

2.1   THE LEGISLATIVE STRUCTURE OF COMMUNITY CARE LAW (IN CHRONOLOGICAL ORDER)

There are a number of core statutory provisions which together constitute the boundaries and framework for social work practice with community care service users. [2]

2.1.1   National Assistance Act 1948

Section 29(1) enables local authorities to make arrangements to promote the welfare of:

> ... persons aged eighteen and over, who are blind, deaf or dumb (or who suffer from mental disorder of any description) and other persons who are substantially and permanently handicapped by illness, injury or congenital deformity or such other disabilities as may be prescribed by the minister.

This power is subject to directions from the Secretary of State which currently appear in LAC(93)10 so that local authorities are directed to make arrangements for the provision of welfare services for the service users identified by section 29.

Section 21: a general power to provide residential accommodation:

> ... a local authority may with the approval of the Secretary of State, and to such extent as he may direct, shall make arrangements for providing:

> (a) residential accommodation for persons aged eighteen and over who by reason of age, illness, disability or any other circumstances are in need of care and attention which is not otherwise available to them and ...

The Secretary of State has directed, by LAC (93)10, that services under this section shall be provided by local authorities. The provision therefore establishes a general duty to provide residential services for the groups of people identified, and who are ordinarily resident in the

---

2   See Chapter 7 for a more detailed discussion of community care for service users who have a mental disorder or who have a learning disability or mental incapacity.

authority's area or are in urgent need of residential accommodation.

The local authority can provide its own residential accommodation under the powers in section 21, it can place service users in accommodation provided by another local authority, or make arrangements, under the provisions of section 26, with other persons (the private or voluntary sector) for them to provide accommodation.

Section 21 duties can also be met by a placement in a nursing home (with the consent of the relevant health authority).

2.1.2   Health Services and Public Health Act 1968: section 45: the promotion of the welfare of old people

Section 45 gives local authorities the power to promote the welfare of old people. DHSS Circular 19/71 identifies the range of services that local authorities are enabled to provide. They are: meals and recreation in the home or elsewhere; information on elderly services; travel assistance to participate in section 45 services; assistance in finding boarding accommodation; social work support and advice; home help and home adaptations; subsidy of warden costs; and warden services.

2.1.3   Chronically Sick and Disabled Persons Act 1970

Section 1 requires a local authority to identify the needs of those persons identified in section 29 of the National Assistance Act 1948. Section 1 also requires the local authority to publish information about the services it provides for these service users.

Section 2 places a duty on local authorities to provide a range of services for those who fall within the ambit of section 29 National Assistance Act 1948 and who have a need for any or all of the services specified in section 2. These services are:

• practical help in the home, eg a home help; providing or help in obtaining a radio, television, library or other similar recreational facilities;

• lectures, games, outings, or other recreational facilities outside your home and any help needed to take advantage of educational facilities;

- help with travelling to any of these or similar activities;

- any adaptations, such as a ramp or lift, or special equipment needed in the home 'for greater safety, comfort or convenience';

- holidays;

- meals, either in the home or elsewhere;

- a telephone, and any special equipment necessary to use a telephone.

The underlying purpose of s 2 was undoubtedly to convert the vaguely worded, generally discretionary services under s 29 of the 1948 Act into a set of specific services to which individual disabled people had an enforceable right. [3]

2.1.4   National Health Service Act 1977, Schedule 8

Schedule 8 provides for three distinct services: services for expectant and nursing mothers (paragraph 1); domiciliary care services for the prevention of illness, and the care and after-care of those who are or have been ill (paragraph 2); and for home help and laundry services (paragraph 3). These services are to be provided by social services authorities.

Services under paragraph 1 are discretionary. Under paragraph 2, services that relate to mental disorder have been directed by the Secretary of State, whilst those that relate to non-mental illness are discretionary. Paragraph 3 services cover a duty to provide adequate home help services for households where such help is required for a person who is suffering from illness, lying in, an expectant mother, or handicapped as a result of having suffered from illness or congenital deformity. Laundry services for the same group of service users is the subject of a discretionary power.

The provisions of the schedule apply to service users of all ages.

---

3   Luke Clements, *Community Care and the Law*, (1996) Legal Action Group, at page 118.

2.1.5 Mental Health Act 1983, section 117

Section 117 imposes a duty on health authorities and local social services authorities to provide after-care services for patients who have been discharged from hospital having been detained for treatment under section 3 of the Act, or mentally disordered offenders detained for treatment under section 37, or those transferred to hospital from prison under sections 47 or 48.

The Code of Practice issued under the Act, identifies the possible elements of after-care:

> ... day care arrangements, appropriate accommodation, out-patient treatment, counselling, personal support, assistance in welfare rights, assistance in managing finances, and if necessary, in claiming benefits, ...

It appears that the duty to provide after-care services under section 117 is a duty that is owed to individual patients. This is confirmed by the judgment of Otton J in *R v Ealing Health Authority, ex p Fox* [1993] 3 All ER 170:

> I consider s 117(2) as mandatory: ... The duty is not only a general duty but a specific duty owed to the applicant to provide him with after-care services until such time as the district health authority and local social services authority are satisfied that he is no longer in need of such services.

After-care services for patients who are discharged from hospital without having been detained are provided under the care programme approach introduced by the joint health and social services Circular HC (90)23/LASSL (90)11 (updated by *Guidance on the Discharge of Mentally Disordered People and their Continuing Care in the Community*, HSG (94)27/LASSL (94)4). Health authorities are to take lead responsibility in the provision, together with social services authorities, of equivalent services to those provided under section 117 for detained patients.

2.1.6 Disabled Persons (Services, Consultation and Representation) Act 1986

Section 4 of the 1986 Act provides a duty on local authorities to assess the needs of disabled people for services provided under section 2 of the Chronically Sick and Disabled Persons Act 1970.

The duty to assess is triggered by a request for assessment from the disabled person and/or their carer.

Section 8 provides that the assessment for services must take the abilities of the carer into account.

2.1.7 National Health Service and Community Care Act 1990

Section 46 requires local authorities to publish community care plans which are subject to review and modification. Local authorities are required to consult a wide constituency before initial publication and in keeping the plan under review, including health authorities and the voluntary and private sectors.

Section 47(1) establishes the central duty to assess.

(1) Subject to subsections (5) and (6) below, where it appears to a local authority that any person for whom they may provide or arrange for the provision of community care services may be in need of any such services, the authority –

(a) shall carry out an assessment of his needs for those services; and

(b) having regard to the results of that assessment, shall decide whether his needs call for the provision by them of any such services.

Section 46(3)) defines the term 'community care services' to cover services provided under:

• Part III of the National Assistance Act;

• section 45 of the Health Services and Public Health Act 1968;

• section 21 of and Schedule 8 to the National Health Service Act 1977;

• section 117 of the Mental Health Act 1983.

Section 47(2) provides that if at any time during an assessment under subsection 1, it appears to the local authority that the person being assessed is a disabled person, then the authority shall also assess, under the Disabled Persons (Services, Consultation and Representation) Act, the person's needs for services under section 2 of the Chronically Sick and Disabled Persons Act 1970.

2.1.8 Mental Health (Patients in the Community) Act 1995 [4]

The Act provides, by amendments to the Mental Health Act 1983, for supervised discharge orders for certain patients discharged from hospital following detention for treatment under the Act. The duty is imposed jointly on health authorities and social services authorities.

The Act establishes a new category of patients that are subject to compulsory after-care in the community. The order empowers health and social services authorities to require a patient to live at a specified place, to attend for medical treatment, and for occupation, education and training. The after-care must be kept under review and where the patient neglects or refuses to comply with the arrangements made the authorities are required to consider whether the patient should be admitted to hospital.

2.1.9 The Carers (Recognition and Services) Act 1995

The Act is a recognition of the important role played by carers in the provision of community care services and of the rights that flow from this role. It provides for an assessment of the needs of a carer when an assessment is being undertaken under the National Health Service and Community Care Act 1990.

Section 1(1):

> ... in any case where –
>
> (a) a local authority carry out an assessment under section 47(1)(a) of the National Health Service and Community Care Act 1990 of the needs of a person for community care services, and
>
> (b) an individual (carer) provides or intends to provide a substantial amount of care on a regular basis for the person,
>
> the carer may request the local authority, before they make their decision as to whether the needs of the ... person call for the provision

---

4   Further details are provided in Chapter 7 on Mental Health.

of any services, to carry out an assessment of his ability to provide and continue to provide care for the ... person; and if he makes such a request, the local authority shall carry out such an assessment and shall take into account the results of that assessment in making that decision.

2.1.10   The Community Care (Direct Payments) Act 1996

The Act empowers local authorities to make payments to community care service users (adults, not children) so that they can buy their own services directly. Direct payments can only be made to people who have been assessed as needing community care services; they must also be disabled. Certain groups are excluded from receiving direct payments:

- older service users over the age of 65;

- patients detained under mental health legislation who are on leave of absence from hospital;

- conditionally discharged detained patients subject to Home Office restrictions;

- patients subject to guardianship under the Mental Health Act 1983 and those subject to a supervised discharge order made under the provisions of the 1995 Act;

- people who are receiving any form of after-care or community care which constitutes part of a care programme initiated under a court order; and

- offenders serving a probation or combination order subject to an additional requirement to undergo treatment for a mental health condition or for drug or alcohol dependency.

2.2   A WIDER COMMUNITY CARE LAW CONTEXT

2.2.1   Guardianship under the Mental Health Act 1983

The guardianship provisions of the Mental Health Act are contained in sections 7–10 and provide a mechanism by which the interests of someone who is over 16 and has a mental disorder can be protected. (The definition of mental disorder utilised for these provisions is the same as that used in section 3 for an admission for treatment.) This protection is afforded by placing the person in the guardianship of the local authority social services department or some other person approved by them. The guardian will have considerable control over that person's life.

Reception into guardianship can only take place where it is for the welfare of the patient or the protection of other people and requires a diagnosis of mental disorder as defined by the Mental Health Act 1983. This requires a diagnosis of mental illness, or severe mental impair-ment, or mental impairment or psychopathic disorder. The utility of guardianship orders in the provision of care for people with a learning disability is restricted by the definition of mental impairment in the Act. This is defined as a state of arrested or incomplete development of mind (not amounting to severe mental impairment) which includes significant impairment of intelligence and social functioning and is associated with abnormally aggressive or seriously irresponsible conduct of the person concerned. As a result a service user with a learning disability who does not display abnormally aggressive or seriously irresponsible conduct is not mentally impaired for the purposes of the Act and therefore cannot be received into guardianship under it.

These limitations have had the effect of severely restricting the use of guardianship by local authorities though it also seems that many authorities are reluctant to use guardianship because of its cost, the compulsion attached to it, and the limited powers of the guardian. A Department of Health Press Release (97/139) indicates that during the year ending on 31 March 1996, 291 guardianship cases were closed and 357 new cases opened. This meant that at the end of that year the number of guardianship cases in force increased from 170 to 624.

2.2.2 The management of property and affairs for those unable to do so themselves

A sometimes difficult aspect of illness or learning disablement concerns the ability of people to manage their own property and financial affairs either temporarily or permanently. The law provides a number of procedures and facilities to overcome this problem.

The weekly collection of social security benefits or pensions for service users, including those who are physically disabled, may be undertaken by someone nominated as an agent. This may be the local authority where a long term agent is needed for someone living in Part III accommodation. Where a person is unable to undertake more complex dealings with the Department of Social Security or the Benefits Agency, eg claiming benefit, because of their incapacity then the Department may appoint someone else (an appointee) to exercise that person's rights in respect of social security benefits. Dealings with banks or building societies may require what is known as a third party mandate; essentially a permission to act on behalf of the person.

Power of Attorney

Broader powers to act on behalf of someone else may be given under a Power of Attorney; the power may be limited to specific matters or unlimited. The power may only be given and exercised while the donor of the power has mental capacity in the sense that they are able to understand what they are doing and what the effects will be. A Power of Attorney will come to an end when the donor no longer has the necessary mental capacity as described.

Enduring Power of Attorney

This disadvantage, which is considerable, has been addressed by the Enduring Powers of Attorney Act 1985. Under the Act a person with mental capacity (the donor) may appoint someone else (the attorney) to manage their affairs when they lose the mental capacity to do so themselves. The form of this appointment is governed by regulations. When the donor becomes mentally incapable the Enduring Power of Attorney must be registered with the Court of Protection. Notice of the intention to register must be given by the attorney to the donor and to at least three of the donor's nearest relatives. Both the donor and his or her relatives are entitled to object to the registration or to the attorney. The attorney must act on behalf of the donor and in their interests and the Court of Protection will consider complaints against an attorney.

The Court of Protection and the Public Trust Office [5]

The task of the Court of Protection is to protect and manage the financial affairs and property of people who are unable to do so themselves because of their mental incapacity. The Court is regulated by the Mental Health Act 1983 and the Court of Protection Rules.

5   The Court of Protection is discussed in Chapter 7. The work of the Court is obviously an important element of any broad concept of community care law and so it is also considered in this chapter.

The Protection Division of the Public Trust Office is responsible for the day-to-day administration of those cases under the jurisdiction of the Court.

An application to have someone placed under the jurisdiction of the Court may be made by anyone, including a local authority, though normally it will be by the nearest relative. There must be a medical diagnosis that the person is 'incapable, by reason of mental disorder, of managing and administering his property and affairs'. A person under the jurisdiction of the Court is known as a patient. The Court is likely to appoint a Receiver to manage the patient's property; this may be a relative, solicitor, bank or the Director of a local authority social services department. Before appointing a Receiver the Court will notify the patient of what is proposed so that objections can be made. The task of the Receiver is to administer the patient's money and affairs in their best interests and according to the Court's instructions. The patient may make a valid will if the Court considers that they have 'testamentary capacity'; if this is not the case then the Court will make a statutory will on their behalf. Receivers must normally submit annual accounts to the Court and administration fees are payable to the Court. A receivership will end on the death of the patient or on recovery of mental capacity.

Where the estate is small or the administration is simple the Public Trustee may make directions authorising the patient's assets to be used in particular ways for the benefit of the patient.

There has been some concern over the jurisdiction and work of the Court:

> It is also a matter of concern that the jurisdiction is premised on an assumption that capacity is an all-or-nothing status. No provision is made for a partial intervention in a person's affairs limited in scope because the person has partial or fluctuating capacity. It can be difficult for a patient to obtain a discharge, ... Nor does the Court permit a patient to execute an enduring power of attorney over any of his or her property, since this would conflict with the global approach it takes to each case ... Those to whom receivership powers are delegated must usually give security and submit detailed yearly accounts.

The costs of this highly protective system are charged to the patients. [6]

6   *Mental Incapacity*, No 231 Law Commission, (1995) HMSO. See National Audit Office, *Looking after the Financial Affairs of People with Mental Incapacity*, National Audit Office, (1994) HMSO.

2.2.3 Social security benefits

Entitlement to benefit is an issue of considerable importance to community care service users. Despite concerted pressure by a number of pressure groups representing such claimants (and service users) and notwithstanding the introduction of disability living allowance, there is still no unified disability benefit available, instead claimants have to establish entitlement to individual benefits designed to meet specific need. Some of these benefits are contributory in the sense that entitlement depends in part on adequate national insurance contributions, others are non-contributory; whilst the basic benefit of income support is means tested.

The chapter on Social Security Benefits provides a discussion of those benefits of most concern to social work practitioners and service users, though some comment is made here on the Social Fund.

The social fund

The discretionary social fund is comprised of community care grants, budgeting loans and crisis loans. Community care grants can be made to 'promote community care' which is defined by the department to include helping someone establish themselves in the community after discharge from residential or institutional care, or helping someone remain in the community rather than be admitted to residential or institutional care. Such grants are said to be designed to complement, not replace, provision by health authorities and social services departments. Budgeting loans are designed to assist claimants meet occasional expenses for which it might be difficult to budget. They are repayable. Crisis loans can be made from the fund to help with expenses following an emergency or disaster.

The statutory social fund provides entitlement to grants paid in respect of maternity expenses, funeral costs and cold weather.

2.2.4 Adaptations to accommodation

The Housing Grants, Construction and Regeneration Act 1996 contains provisions for the making of disabled facilities grants. These grants are designed to help pay for adaptations to accommodation for disabled people. These adaptations are designed to facilitate a disabled person's use of a dwelling. The focus is on works to improve heating, safety, cooking and access facilities.

The Act provides that:

A local housing authority shall not approve an application for a disabled facilities grant unless they are satisfied –

(a) that the relevant works are necessary and appropriate to meet the needs of the disabled occupant, and

(b) that it is reasonable and practicable to carry out the relevant works having regard to the age and condition of the dwelling or building.

In considering the matters mentioned in paragraph (a) a local housing authority which is not itself a social services authority shall consult the social services authority.

3   COMPLAINTS AND OTHER REMEDIES FOR SERVICE USERS

3.1   COMPLAINTS

Section 50 National Health Service and Community Care Act 1990 inserted a new section 7B in the Local Authority Social Services Act 1970 the effect of which is to give the Secretary of State the power to require social services authorities to establish a complaints procedure to investigate complaints concerning the exercise of their social services functions. The Secretary of State has exercised this power and has also issued the Complaints Procedure Directions 1990 which determine the form and procedure of these complaints procedures. Further (policy) guidance is provided in *The Right to Complain* (1991).

The Directions specify a three stage process with a first stage designed to facilitate an informal resolution of the complaint. The second formal stage involves the registration of the complaint which should be in writing. The Directions make it clear that local authorities should provide appropriate information and assistance to help complainants. Authorities are required to respond to the complaint within 28 days if possible, and within a maximum of three months.

The authority should investigate the complaint and report the result to the complainant in writing.

The review stage may be triggered by a written request from the complainant within 28 days of receiving the report of the investigation from the formal stage. The authority must convene a panel to hear the complaint. The panel is chaired by an independent person though the other two members of the panel are not required to be independent and are often comprised of a councillor and an officer. The hearing must follow the rules of natural justice and the Policy Guidance provides that the complainant may be accompanied by another person who should not be a lawyer. The panel is required to come to a decision within 24 hours of the hearing which should be recorded in writing. The panel's recommendations, and the reasons, must be communicated to the local authority, the complainant and any other person with a sufficient interest.

The authority has twenty eight days to decide what response to make, but is not bound to accept the recommendation. Case law has however made it clear that local authorities must have very good reasons if they are to fail to comply with a recommendation.

> ... where a panel has given a careful reasoned decision adverse to the local authority on the subject of a complaint and the local authority rejects the panel's recommendation without itself giving a rational reason for doing so, then there is a strong prima facie case for quashing the local authority's decision as unlawful. (Dyson J in *R v North Yorkshire County Council, ex p Hargreaves* (1994) 26 BMLR 121.)

3.2 DEFAULT POWERS

Section 7D of the Local Authority Social Services Act 1970 provides the Secretary of State with powers to declare an authority to be in default by failing to comply with their social services duties. The declaratory order may contain directions for fulfilling the duty concerned and these directions can be enforced by the courts.

Though these default powers may appear attractive to the dissatisfied service user this is an illusion. The Secretary of State has never used the powers available under section 7D and they are probably reserved for the situation where there has been a complete breakdown of the statutory social service function.

3.3 COMPLAINT TO THE LOCAL AUTHORITY MONITORING OFFICER

The function and responsibilities of the monitoring officer are established by section 5 of the Local Government and Housing Act 1989. The officer is required to report to the authority on any matter in which the authority may have contravened the law or any code of practice made or approved under statute, or on any maladministration or injustice which falls within the remit of the local government ombudsman.

Such action may be sufficient to resolve a complaint, including a complaint concerning community care services, and will give a local authority a chance to respond to a complaint before it becomes the subject of other action such as a formal complaint to the local government ombudsman or even an application for judicial review.

3.4 COMPLAINT TO THE LOCAL GOVERNMENT OMBUDSMAN

Commissioners for Local Administration may investigate a complaint against a local authority by a person who claims to have suffered injustice as a result of the authority's maladministration. Maladministration is commonly accepted to encompass 'bias, neglect, inattention, delay, incompetence, ineptitude, perversity, turpitude, arbitrariness and so on'. [7]

Complaints to the local ombudsman cannot be investigated unless they have already been made to the local authority concerned and the authority has been given the chance to investigate the complaint and respond to it. Equally the local ombudsman cannot investigate a complaint where there is already an existing remedy, such as court proceedings or tribunal hearing. It appears that where complaints concern community care services the local ombudsman will decline to investigate unless the complainant tried to utilise the statutory complaints procedure and has found this to be defective.

Following a finding of injustice arising from local authority maladministration, the local ombudsman can recommend the payment

---

7 This list is known as the Crossman list.

of compensation to the person who has suffered the injustice. The reports of such investigations are published. However there is evidence that the local ombudsman is often reluctant to accept complaints for investigation, that less than 5% of complaints result in a final report, and that investigations are lengthy, averaging 18 months. Despite these difficulties the local ombudsman is dealing with increasing number of complaints concerning social services, including community care services, and the operation of local authority complaints procedures. In 1995/96 complaints concerning social services constituted 6.1% of all complaints received by the local commissioners.

3.5 APPLICATIONS FOR JUDICIAL REVIEW

Judicial review is a public law procedure which may be used to challenge the legality of discretionary decision making by public bodies, including local authorities. Judicial review can be used to challenge the legality of decisions about entitlement to assessment, assessment itself, service provision and the use of the complaints procedure.

An application for leave is made to the Divisional Court of the Queens Bench Division of the High Court and is considered by a single judge. This 'filter process' is used to decide whether the applicant has a meritorious application, whether the matter is one of public law and whether the applicant has sufficient standing (locus standi) to make the application. If leave is granted a full hearing takes place to decide whether a decision should be judicially reviewed. If the application is successful the court may grant a number of orders though the normal result is to quash the original decision.

The grounds for an application for judicial review are said to encompass a public body, including a local authority, having acted ultra vires (beyond its powers), illegally and unreasonably in the sense of irrationality. These examples from the field of community care law are taken from Community Care and the Law. [8]

Irrelevant considerations: decision makers must take account of relevant considerations and ignore irrelevant factors. In *R v Avon*

8   Clements, L, op cit, (1996) Legal Action Group, Chapter 12.

County Council, ex p M [1994] 2 FCR 259, judicial review was granted against the county council on the grounds that when deciding on the appropriate residential placement for M they had not taken his psychological needs into account.

Inappropriate weight given to one factor: in *R v Gloucestershire County Council, ex p Mahfood* (1995) 30 BMLR 20, DC, the council had withdrawn services to various disabled people because the council's resources had been cut. The judge held that this amounted to making one factor determinative; 'this amounted to treating the cut in resources as the sole factor to be taken into account, and that was, in my judgement, unlawful'.

Unlawful delegation: authorities must not delegate their own decision making powers to others unless they have the power to do so. For example decisions to provide assistance to clients/service users under section 2 of the CSDPA 1970 must not be determined solely by the grant of a disabled facilities grant. The two matters are independent of each other.

Procedural impropriety: decision makers must act fairly, must not be biased, must allow a party time to prepare his or her case, must ensure that a party has a proper opportunity to be heard, and in appropriate situations, must give reasons for their decisions.

Examples include:

Duty to consult – *R v Devon County Council, ex p Baker and Durham County Council, ex p Curtis* [1995] 1 All ER 73:

> First that the consultation must be at a time when proposals are still at a formative stage. Second that the proposer must give sufficient reasons for any proposal to permit of intelligent consideration and response. Third ... that adequate time must be given for consideration and response and, finally, fourth, that the product of consultation must be conscientiously taken into account in finalising any proposals.

Duty to act in accordance with mandatory requirements – includes a duty to follow procedures laid down by statute and by mandatory guidance, that is section 7(1) guidance. In *R v North Yorkshire County Council, ex p Hargreaves* (1994) 26 BMLR 121 the council failed to take account of the applicant's sister's preferences when assessing his sister's needs. This is required by the Policy Guidance, issued under section 7(1), which the court held were mandatory.

Duty to give reasons – present in the Complaints Procedure Directions and therefore mandatory to give reasons. In the absence of an express provision requiring the giving of reasons, they may nevertheless be required, if, for instance, the decision would otherwise be unintelligible, or would contravene the minimum standards of fairness.

3.6 BREACH OF STATUTORY DUTY

It would seem logical that breaches of statutory duty, including duties on local authorities imposed by social services legislation, should be enforceable by an action for damages. However it has long been accepted that this is not the case largely because these statutory provisions are to be seen as general duties, or target duties, to provide certain services for people rather than duties owed to particular individuals.

Despite these reservations it seems that the duty to provide after-care services under section 117 of the Mental Health Act 1983 is a duty owed to an individual who can therefore sue for damages for breach of statutory duty.[9] Lord Clyde, in his judgment in *R v Gloucestershire County Council and the Secretary of State for Health, ex p Barry* [1997] AC 584, uses similar language to talk about the duty to make welfare provision for a disabled person under section 2(1) of the Chronically Sick and Disabled Persons Act 1970:

> ... section 2(1) imposed a duty on the local authority to make welfare arrangements for an individual where they are satisfied that in the case of that individual it was necessary in order to meet his needs to make the arrangements. This was not a general but a particular duty and it gave a correlative right to the individual which he could enforce in the event of a failure in its performance. Such a provision is this area of the legislation is not common. We were referred only to one other example of it, in section 117 of the Mental Health Act 1983.

---

9   *R v Ealing District Health Authority, ex p Fox* [1993] 3 All ER 170.

4 COMMUNITY CARE, THE LAW AND SOCIAL WORK: some issues for discussion

4.1 ASSESSMENT, NEEDS AND RESOURCES

The concepts of assessment and need are central to community care law. Essentially social services authorities are required by legislation to assess the needs of potential and existing service users for services and, on the basis of the assessment, to determine the nature and level of services to be provided. This seemingly simple process has been rendered as exceedingly complex by confusion over the extent of assessment duties and service provision duties, and by questions concerning the relevance of local authority resources to the performance of these statutory duties.

Section 2 of the Chronically Sick and Disabled Persons Act 1970 is central to the provision of services for those who come within the group of service users identified by section 29 of the National Assistance Act 1948. For a number of years there existed some doubts over the nature of the duty to assess under section 2 of the 1970 Act. This doubt was resolved by the implementation of section 4 of the Disabled Persons (Services, Consultation and Representation) Act 1986 which provided for an assessment upon the request of a disabled person or their carer.

To this assessment duty another has been added by the 1990 Act which establishes a more pro-active duty to assess, this time for community care services, in circumstances where the person's need has come to the knowledge of the local authority, and the person concerned falls within the category of people for whom community care services can be provided, and the person could benefit from the provision of community care services.

The assessment of need under section 47(1) is subject to guidance issued by the Secretary of State. There is policy guidance – *Community Care in the Next Decade and Beyond* – and practice guidance – *Care Management and Assessment, A Practitioners' Guide* and *Care Management and Assessment, A Managers' Guide*. Both forms of guidance talk about a 'needs led assessment' and make the point that such assessments are to be distinguished from the past practice of service led assessment.

Despite this identification of a distinct duty to assess needs under the 1990 Act there is still doubt about the nature of the context within which an assessment for need should take place. Policy guidance suggests:

> Assessment does not take place in a vacuum: account needs to be taken of the local authority's criteria for determining when services should be provided, the type of service they have decided to make available and the overall range of services provided by other agencies, including health authorities. [10]

Nonetheless there is a separation between assessment and need within section 47 of the 1990 Act to the extent that the assessment is directed to establishing needs only for community care services. Once these needs have been established through the assessment process, the local authority has a distinct duty to decide which needs call for the provision of services, and further to decide what services will 'satisfy' the needs they have decided to provide for. In making these decisions the local authority may take local eligibility criteria into account.

> 13. An authority may take into account the resources available when deciding how to respond to an individual's assessment. However, once the authority has indicated that a service should be provided to meet an individual's need and the authority is under a legal obligation to provide it or arrange for its provision, then the service must be provided. It will not be possible for an authority to use budgeting difficulties as a basis for refusing to provide the service.

> 14. Authorities can be helped in this process by defining eligibility criteria, i.e. a system of banding which assigns individuals to particular categories, depending on the extent of the difficulties they encounter in carrying out everyday tasks and relating the level of response to the degree of such difficulties. Any 'banding' should not, however, be rigidly applied, as account needs to be taken of individual circumstances. Such eligibility criteria should be phrased in terms of the factors identified in the assessment process. [11]

Within the community care regime of the 1990 Act resources are clearly a relevant criteria for a local authority in setting eligibility criteria and when deciding how to respond to the outcome of an individual assessment. This situation is now confirmed by the House of Lords judgment in *R v Gloucestershire County Council and the Secretary of State for Health, ex p Barry* [1997] AC 584.

---

10 *Community Care in the Next Decade and Beyond*, Department of Health 1990.
11 CI(92)34, *The Laming Letter* (From the Chief Inspector of the Social Services Inspectorate to directors of social services).

The question now arises as to whether the assessment and provision of services for disabled people under section 2(1) of the Chronically Sick and Disabled Persons Act 1970 is in any way different. It should be remembered that section 47(1) of the 1990 Act deals with the assessment and provision of community care services, whilst section 47(2) provides that if such an assessment for community care services identifies the fact that the person being assessed is a disabled person, then the local authority must decide whether their needs call for the provision of services under section 2 of the 1970 Act.

The relationship between assessment, need and resources, as it relates to section 2, has been considered by the House of Lords in *Ex p Barry*. Michael Barry was born in 1915. He had suffered from several heart attacks, had had a stroke and had poor eyesight. He lived at home on his own and got around with the help of a zimmer frame as a result of a previous hip fracture. In 1992 his needs were assessed by the local authority as 'home care to call twice a week for shopping, pension, laundry, cleaning. Meals-on-wheels four days a week'. A year later his needs were assessed as being the same. In September 1994 the local authority wrote to Mr Barry informing him that they could no longer meet his full needs as they had been assessed, and they would be withdrawing his cleaning and laundry services. The letter explained that the authority had had their resources from central government cut by £2.5 million. Mr Barry and others challenged the decision of the authority by judicial review, arguing that their needs remained the same and that the authority was under a duty to provide services to meet those needs. The authority argued that in assessing Mr Barry's needs they were entitled to have regard to their resource position.

After hearings in the Divisional Court and in the Court of Appeal, the House of Lords, in a majority decision, held that a local authority may take its resources into account when assessing needs under section 2(1) of the 1970 Act. Lord Nicholls argued that:

> ... needs for services cannot sensibly be assessed without having some regard to the cost of providing them. A person's need for a particular type or level of service cannot be decided in a vacuum from which all considerations of cost have been expelled.

> Thus depending upon the authority's financial position, so the eligibility criteria, setting out the degree of disability which must exist before help will be provided with laundry or cleaning or whatever, may properly be more or less stringent.

This interpretation does not emasculate section 2(1). The section was intended to confer rights upon disabled persons. It does so by giving them a valuable personal right to see that the authority acts reasonably in assessing their needs for certain types of assistance, and a right to have their assessed needs met so far as it is necessary for the authority (as distinct from others) to do so. I can see no basis for reading into the section an implication that in assessing the needs of disabled persons for the prescribed services, cost is to be ignored. I do not believe Parliament intended that to be the position.

The impact of the majority decision has been criticised by a number of commentators arguing from the perspective of disabled people and service users.

> Eligibility criteria have been tightened as resources decrease further to restrict access to services. The House of Lords has now decided that this is lawful. Whether a disabled person has 'needs' as opposed to 'wants' will now depend, in part, on how much money a local authority has allocated to its community care budget. [12]

However, it should be recognised that when a local authority, following an assessment of need, accept that they should provide services in response to the assessed need, then a duty arises to provide some form of services

Many of the recent community care cases decided on applications for judicial review such as *Ex p Barry* and *R v Sefton Metropolitan Borough Council, ex p Help the Aged* (1997), are essentially conflicts generated by the lack of resources for community care services and the attempt by local authorities to reconcile the equation of limited resources and increasing and almost unlimited demand for community care services.

4.2   ENFORCING RIGHTS TO COMMUNITY CARE SERVICES

The difficulty of enforcing rights to community care services has been a cause for concern for many years. The situation now seems to be that the 'mixed economy' of community care is matched by a 'mixed economy' of enforcement procedures. Service users may choose

---

12   Karen Ashton and Jean Gould, *Community care: a duty to care?* Legal Action, May 1997, at page 23.

between complaints procedures, local ombudsman complaints and judicial review applications, The possibilities are varied, though some questions should be raised concerning the utility of such processes for establishing and enforcing rights to community care services.

The preferred avenue for service users is the complaints procedure. This procedure is designed to resolve 'complaints' within a process that encourages informality at the beginning and only provides an independent element at the final stage. It should be remembered that the 'recommendations' (not 'decisions') are not binding on local authorities, though they must have cogent and material reasons for any refusal to accept the recommendation.

Where the use of complaints procedures are inappropriate or defective a service user may have recourse to the local ombudsman, if they have suffered injustice due to local authority maladministration. The jurisdiction of the local ombudsman is limited and few complaints are accepted for full investigation. Even fewer investigations reach a final report. The process is slow though compensation can be paid and future practice may be improved.

Attempts to enforce rights to community care through applications for judicial review often receive wide publicity though they must remain a minority choice because of the cost and legality associated with High Court applications. Applications without real merit and those that can be better settled by alternative methods such as the complaints procedure, will be rejected at leave stage. Even cases which are 'won' are the subject of discretionary remedies; most often limited to an order to quash the original decision, which can then be taken again.

An action for damages for breach of statutory duty remains limited to those 'community care' duties which are understood as being owed to individual service users. To date this appears to include only duties under section 117 of the Mental Health Act 1983 and possibly to duties under section 2(1) of the Chronically Sick and Disabled Persons Act 1970.

Many of those who need community care services to live an independent and fulfilling life are disabled and often elderly. As a group they have historically been disadvantaged and even discriminated against; they are frequently disempowered. Community care legislation has established at least a limited right to an assessment and to services. These rights should be legally enforceable. The current state of the law does not establish such a level of enforcement and as such it is difficult to properly describe a 'right to community care'.

The establishment of a Community Care Appeal Tribunal would go some way to achieving such an objective. A model already exists in the Special Education Needs Tribunals which determine appeals within a system which is based upon the assessment of needs followed by a proposal for services. A Community Care Appeal Tribunal could have jurisdiction over all disputes concerning community care assessment and service provision which could not be resolved by informal means. Such a jurisdiction would properly establish legally enforceable rights to community care for a group of service users whose disadvantage would be reduced by the establishment of such a forum. It is likely that two things would need to be resolved prior to such a development. Firstly, community care law would need to be consolidated in the same way that child care law has been by the Children Act. Secondly, the issue of resources needs to be legally clarified. Are rights to community care to be made conditional upon the resources of local authorities, themselves subject to grant from central government? Whatever the outcome to the second issue the establishment of such a tribunal would go some way toward establishing firm and enforceable rights for an important and historically disadvantaged group of service users.

4.3 RESIDENTIAL CARE

The Wagner Report (1988) emphasised the positive role of residential care, and its place within the structure of community care. [13]

Caring: this should be personal, and residents should feel valued, safe and secure.

Choice: each resident's right to exercise choice over their daily life should be respected.

Continuity: this includes both consistency of care from staff, and the maintenance of links with a resident's previous life.

13   Wagner, G, *Residential Care: A Positive Service*, (1988) HMSO.

Change: for residents, the opportunity for continued development; for staff, a commitment to respond to changing needs.

Common values: ensuring that practice is based on a shared philosophy and values.

The Registered Homes Act 1984 provides for the registration of independent sector residential care homes, nursing homes and mental nursing homes. Local authorities are the registration authority for residential care homes, while nursing homes and mental nursing homes must be registered with the appropriate district health authority. Residential care homes are those that provide board and personal care for residents. They must be registered under the 1984 Act and the Registered Homes (Amendment) Act 1991 provides a less rigorous registration system for homes with less than three residents.

The requirements for registration are set out in the 1984 Act and the Residential Care Homes Regulations 1984: the applicant must be a fit person and the premises must be suitable for the purposes of the home. Applications may be refused where these criteria are not fulfilled. Conditions may be attached to the registration under section 5(3), relating to number, age, sex and category of residents. A breach of a registration condition or of the Regulations is a ground for the cancellation of registration and a criminal offence. Such breaches may also establish the unfitness of the proprietor. Where an application for registration is refused or the registration authority gives notice of its intention to cancel registration, an appeal lies to the Registered Homes Tribunal. Registration may be cancelled in an emergency under section 11 where there is a serious risk to the life, health, or well-being of residents.

Inspection of all private and public sector residential care homes must be carried out by the Inspection Unit of the social services authority at least twice a year. Though the unit is accountable to the Director of Social Services, it is not part of the department and undertakes its work as a free standing agency. The Department of Health Social Services Inspectorate has published an Inspection Workbook, *Homes are for living in*, which stresses the rights of residents which contribute to their quality of life. Closure is the ultimate sanction for failure to meet required standards, though both the registration and inspection of residential care homes should be directed toward the care and quality of life enjoyed by residents.

Home Life: A Code of Practice for Residential Care is said to enjoy the same status as guidance issued under section 7 of the Local Authorities Social Services Act 1970 and establishes the working principles and practices for residential care. It is used extensively by local authorities as guidance for decisions on registration and inspection. Nursing homes are registered and inspected by District Health Authorities working under the *Code of Guidance, Registration and Inspection of Nursing Homes: A Handbook for Health Authorities.*

The regulation of private residential and nursing homes takes place under the provisions of the Registered Homes Act 1984. The 1984 Act provides for the registration of private residential and nursing home accommodation where 'board and personal care are provided in residential accommodation for those in need of such personal care by reason of old age, disablement, past or present dependence on alcohol or drugs, or past or present mental disorder'. For residential accommodation the registration authority is the local authority whose duties are exercised by the social services department. The registration and inspection of residential care homes is concerned with the quality and safety of facilities and services and is influenced by the Code of Practice, *Home Life,* issued by the Department. [14] The Code establishes principles of care that can be seen as a set of entitlements for residents, ie fulfilment, dignity, autonomy, individuality and esteem.

Small residential care homes (where board and personal care for fewer than four persons is provided) have been brought within a modified system of registration by the Registered Homes (Amendment) Act 1991. [15]

In relation to private nursing homes the supervision and registration are carried out by health authorities under the terms of the Act and

14   *Home Life: A Code of Practice for Residential Care,* (1986) Centre for Policy on Ageing. See also Alison Brammer, *The Registered Homes Act 1984: Safeguarding the Elderly?* Journal of Social Welfare and Family Law No 4, 1994.
15   For critical comment on the Registered Homes Act 1984 see Carson, D, *Registering Homes: Another Fine mess?* (March 1985) Journal of Social Welfare Law.

the influence of the *Code of Guidance: Registration and Inspection of Nursing Homes; A Handbook for Health Authorities.*

The National Health Service and Community Care Act 1990 provided for a new system for charging for residential accommodation. Local authorities are required to charge residents who are placed in accommodation under section 21 the standard rate fixed for the accommodation, unless the resident can establish that they are unable to pay at such a rate. In this circumstance the authority must assess the financial circumstances of the resident and fix the charge accordingly. In practice all residents are financially assessed and charged accordingly. Their income and capital resources, subject to various disregards, are taken to contribute to the cost of accommodation, but only to the extent that all residents are left with a personal weekly allowance, currently set at £14.10. Where accommodation is in the independent sector, the local authority will fund the gap between the residents' contribution from their financial resources, and the cost of the accommodation up to the standard fixed rate.

SECTION 2
VULNERABLE SERVICE USERS

1   INTRODUCTION

The legal mandate for work with vulnerable service users is largely derived from the community care law discussed in Section 1 of this chapter. However, because the concept of vulnerability is part of the language of practice and is used in the debate about the reform of the law concerning this group of service users, it is necessary to provide a discreet discussion of the legal mandate for work with vulnerable service users, which will nonetheless compliment the discussion in Section 1.

Vulnerability is not currently defined in English law though the concept will encompass all those who fall within Part III (sections 21 and 29) of the National Assistance Act 1948, section 45 of the Health Services and Public Health Act 1968, section 3 and Schedule 8 of the National Health Services Act 1977, and section 117 of the Mental Health Act 1983. [16]

16   See Part 1, section 2.1 on the legislative structure of community care law.

The Law Commission has proposed the following definition:

> ... any person of 16 or over who (1) is or may be in need of community care services by reason of mental or other disability, age or illness and who (2) is or may be unable to take care of himself or herself, or unable to protect himself or herself against significant harm or serious exploitation. [17]

Such a definition recognises the breadth of this group of potential service users by acknowledging that the causes of vulnerability are varied, but include mental disability, disability arising from other causes, age and illness.

Recognition of the rights and interests of vulnerable people is now well established though this has not always been the case. Equally acknowledgement of the importance of work with this wide group of service users is a fairly recent feature of social work organisation and practice. Both developments reflect a number of factors, including:

- the disability surveys reported on by the Office of Population and Census Studies in 1988 identified a level of disability which, although it was possibly understated, surprised many people;

- the Griffith Report, Community Care: Agenda for Action (1988) raised public and professional concern about the care of vulnerable people, whether caused by their physical or mental disability, or their age;

- the work of the Law Commission on reforming the law on mentally incapacitated adults which began with the publication of Fourth Programme of Law Reform: Mentally Incapacitated Adults, in 1989;

- the greater acknowledgement and recognition of 'elder abuse' which has gradually taken place in the last fifteen years. [18]

Increasingly, work with vulnerable service users has heightened awareness of the lack of a coherent legal structure to protect the

---

17   *Mental Incapacity*, Law Commission No 231, (1995) HMSO.
18   The Social Services Inspectorate has published guidance on the issues raised for social services managers and for practitioners: *No Longer Afraid: The safeguard of older people in domestic settings*, (1993) Social Services Inspectorate, Department of Health, HMSO.

rights and interests of vulnerable people. Indeed, the Law Commission has recognised that there are particular gaps in the law concerning the personal protection of vulnerable people:

> In the report we also discuss the extent of the powers which should be available to public authorities to intervene and protect adults who are at risk of abuse or neglect. The existing law in this area is patchy and out of date. Such powers as are available are little used, and as a result vulnerable people may not be getting all the help and protection they need and deserve. [19]

2 THE LAW FOR WORK WITH VULNERABLE SERVICE USERS

2.1 COMMUNITY CARE LAW

The broad spectrum of community care law will provide a range of assessment duties for vulnerable service users. This will include the duties owed to disabled people by virtue of their inclusion in the category of service users defined by section 29 of the National Assistance Act 1948:

> ... persons aged eighteen and over, who are blind, deaf or dumb (or who suffer from mental disorder of any description) and other persons who are substantially and permanently handicapped by illness, injury or congenital deformity or other such disabilities as may be prescribed by the minister.

Statutory powers and duties for the provision of services are established across the range of community care legislation, including the Chronically Sick and Disabled Persons Act 1970. [20] Particular mention should be made of the assessment and services provisions of the National Health Service and Community Care Act 1990, section 47(1):

> (1) Subject to subsections (5) and (6) below, where it appears to a local authority that any person for whom they may provide or arrange for the provision of community care services may be in need of any such services, the authority –

19 *Mental Incapacity*, Law Commission No 231, (1995) HMSO, at page 1.
20 See section 1 of this chapter for a detailed discussion of the range of duties and powers for assessment and services which may be relevant for vulnerable service users.

(a) shall carry out an assessment of his needs for those services; and

(b) having regard to the results of that assessment, shall decide whether his needs call for the provision by them of any such services.

Arrangements for the provision of residential care by a local authority under section 21 of the National Assistance Act 1948 is a community care service which may be of particular use for a vulnerable person.

> ... a local authority may with the approval of the Secretary of State, and to such an extent as he may direct, shall make arrangements for providing ... residential accommodation for persons aged eighteen or over who by reason of age, illness, disability or any other circumstances are in need of care and attention which is not otherwise available to them.

The necessary approvals and directions have been given by the Secretary of State so that the provision of residential accommodation for people who are ordinarily resident in their area is a local authority duty.

Assessment for residential care takes place under section 17 of the National Health Service and Community Care Act 1990.

2.2   PERSONAL WELFARE

The personal welfare of service users who are vulnerable is protected by the assessment and service duties of community care law, and in some emergency situations by section 47 of the National Assistance Act 1948. This provides for the compulsory removal of a person from where they are living if the person is:

(a) suffering from grave chronic disease or, being aged, infirm or physically incapacitated, are living in insanitary conditions, and

(b) they are unable to devote to themselves, and are not receiving from other persons, proper care and attention.

An application must be made by the local authority to the magistrates' court for the order to remove the person to hospital or residential care. The application must be supported by written evidence from a medical officer of the health authority to the effect that the removal of the person is necessary in the interests of that person or to prevent injury to the health or serious nuisance to others. Seven days' notice of the application must be given to the person concerned or some other person in charge of him or her. The order may last for a maximum of three months and may be extended for further periods of up to three months each.

The National Assistance (Amendment) Act 1951 provides a mechanism whereby an order may be made 'ex parte', that is without the seven days' notice being given or the appearance of the person concerned. Such a procedure can be used where the medical officer and another doctor certify that the removal of the person without delay is necessary in their interests. The application for such an order can be made to a single magistrate, but the order may only be made for a maximum of three weeks.

The Law Commission has considered the utility of these provisions for the protection of vulnerable people.

> We invited comment on how the balance between protection from harm and respect for individual rights, which is particularly delicate in this area of our project, should be struck and maintained. To the basic question of whether any reform of these emergency powers was needed our consultees responded with a resounding affirmative. The existing law was said to be ineffective in protecting elderly, disabled and other vulnerable people from abuse and neglect, and inadequate in its approach to issues of autonomy and individual rights. It appeared to be counter-productive, being so draconian that it was rarely used.[21]

Where a person's vulnerability is caused by their mental disorder, the Mental Health Act 1983 emergency place of safety orders may be of use.

Section 135(1) provides:

> If it appears to a justice of the peace, on information on oath laid by an approved social worker, that there is reasonable cause to suspect that a person believed to be suffering from mental disorder –
>
> (a) has been, or is being, ill-treated, neglected or kept otherwise than under proper control, in any place within the jurisdiction of the justice, or

21   *Mental Incapacity*, Law Commission No 231, (1995) HMSO.

(b) being unable to care for himself, is living alone in such a place, the justice may issue a warrant authorising any constable to enter, if need be by force, any premises specified in the warrant in which that person is believed to be, and, if thought fit, to remove him to a place of safety with a view to the making of an application in respect of him under Part II of this Act, or of arrangements for his treatment or care.

Section 136(1) provides:

If a constable finds in a place to which the public have access a person who appears to him to be suffering from mental disorder and to be in immediate need of care or control, the constable may, if he thinks it necessary to do so in the interests of that person or for the protection of other persons, remove that person to a place of safety within the meaning of section 135 above.

A place of safety is defined to encompass residential accommodation provided or arranged under Part III of the National Assistance Act, a mental health hospital, a police station, a mental nursing or care home, or any other suitable place.

Both sections contain a 'diagnosis threshold' of mental disorder. This is defined in section 1(2) of the Act to encompass:

... mental illness, arrested or incomplete development of mind, psychopathic disorder and any other disorder or disability of mind.

The two provisions only provide for short term place of safety powers. Neither is therefore appropriate for the long term care of vulnerable people.

2.3 ELDER ABUSE

There is little doubt that some vulnerable people are subject to abuse at the hands of those who care for them. [22] One facet of this depressing phenomena is the abuse of elderly people defined in the following terms:

---

22 See Department of Health, *No Longer Afraid: The safeguard of older people in domestic settings*, Social Services Inspectorate, (1993); and Turk, V and Brown, H, *The Sexual Abuse of Adults with Learning Difficulties: Results of a Two Year Incidence Survey*, (1993) 6 Mental Handicap Research 193.

> Abuse may be described as physical, sexual, psychological or fin-
> ancial. It may be intentional or unintentional or the result of neglect.
> It causes harm to the older person, either temporarily or over a period
> of time. [23]

Widespread public concern about child abuse was one of the
factors which led to the major reforms of child law brought about
by the Children Act 1989. Whilst there is public concern about
the abuse of vulnerable, often elderly, people it has not led to
reform of the law. Currently, English law provides no specific
remedies or protections against such abuse, but rather a ragbag
of legal remedies designed for other purposes, including section
47 of the National Assistance Act 1948. The criminal law can be
used to prosecute abusers guilty of physical, sexual or financial
abuse, or of theft. Civil actions for damages may also be available.
The domestic violence provisions of the Family Law Act 1996,
which offer protection to an abused person in the domestic
setting, may be used to obtain non-molestation injunctions and
occupation orders.

It has to be recognised that the victims of these crimes and civil
wrongs are often not able or capable of activating the law in their
own interests. In this sense, their vulnerability is all encompassing.
Even in situations where an abused person could utilise legal protections or remedies the very process of doing so may exacerbate
their vulnerability and open them up to further danger of abuse. The
tensions between paternalism and autonomy should also be acknowledged. Protective measures should not impinge upon the legitimate
exercise of self-determination even where such decisions mean that
a vulnerable person remains in an actual or potentially abusive
environment.

2.4   MENTAL HEALTH LAW

The provisions of the Mental Health Act 1983 may be relevant where
a person's vulnerability is related to their mental disorder or mental
incapacity. For the moment it is necessary only to identify the fact
that a mentally incapacitated person can be compulsorily admitted
to hospital for treatment only if they evidence abnormally aggressive

---

23   Department of Health, *No Longer Afraid. The safeguard of older people in
     domestic settings*, (1993), at page 3.

or seriously irresponsible conduct. (Other provisions of the Act concerning the property and financial affairs of vulnerable people who are mentally incapable are considered in Section 2 of the chapter on Mental Health.)

3 REFORMING THE LAW

The Law Commission's original overview paper established guiding principles for reforming the law:

> ... that proper safeguards should be provided against exploitation and neglect, and against physical, sexual or psychological abuse. [24]

The Law Commission has taken the child protection provisions of the Children Act as a model for its recommendations.

Where a local authority have reason to believe that a vulnerable person in the area is suffering or likely to suffer significant harm or serious exploitation they shall make such enquiries as they consider necessary to enable them to decide:

(1) whether the person is in fact suffering or is likely to suffer such harm or exploitation and

(2) if so, whether community care services should be provided or arranged or other action taken to protect the person from such harm or exploitation.

A 'vulnerable person' is defined as:

> ... any person of 16 or over who (1) is or may be in need of community care services by reason of mental or other disability, age or illness and who (2) is or may be unable to take care of himself or herself, or unable to protect himself or herself against significant harm or serious exploitation.

Harm is defined as:

---

24   Consultation Paper No 119, para 4.27 quoted in *Mental Incapacity*, Law Commission No 231, (1995) HMSO.

... ill-treatment (including sexual abuse and forms of ill-treatment that are not physical); the impairment of, or an avoidable deterioration in, physical or mental health; and the impairment of physical, intellectual, emotional, social or behavioural development.

The duty to investigate would be supported by powers of entry under warrant, and assessment orders. The Law Commission also recommends the creation of a temporary protection order if the vulnerable person is likely to be at risk unless removed and kept in protective accommodation.

The balance between paternalism and autonomy is struck by the recommendation that a vulnerable person with appropriate mental capacity may refuse community care services and other protective services and interventions. Vulnerable people without such capacity would not be able to exercise a refusal of services or protection.

The government's Green Paper raises a number of questions concerning the need for reform in this area of law:

> The Government considers that there may be merit in some of the recommendations made in this area, but is not convinced that there is a pressing need for reform. Whilst it is important to protect vulnerable adults, the Government also believes that regard should be had to the rights of individuals to live in isolation if they choose, even if at some degree of risk to themselves. The question of fitness to object is also very difficult to judge. A number of initiatives have been undertaken to address the particular problem of elder abuse, and these cannot yet be fully evaluated. In the light of these concerns, the Government would particularly welcome views from local authorities, carers and mental health and learning disability organisations, on whether there is a need for legislation along the lines recommended by the Law Commission. If it is felt that such legislation is necessary, views would be welcomed on the practicalities of the proposals. [25]

The Law Commission has made a number of other proposals for reforming the law on mental incapacity. These proposals will be of interest where a service user's vulnerability is consequent upon their mental incapacity. These proposals are described in Section 2 of Chapter 7 on Mental Health.

---

25   *Who Decides? Making decisions on behalf of mentally incapacitated adults*, (1997) Lord Chancellor's Department.

The publication of the Lord Chancellor's Green Paper is a welcome indication that the valuable work of the Law Commission will not be wasted. It is clear that the government is broadly supportive of the proposals in the Law Commission's report and it is to be hoped that legislation on the basis of the draft Bill included in that report will be laid before Parliament in the not too distant future.

4 CASE STUDIES

These case studies can be used in a number of ways. A strict legal analysis of the facts will allow the identification of the detail of relevant community care law. An alternative, and probably more appropriate task, is to invite an analysis which covers issues of practice and the law which permits, facilitates, controls or determines professional practice. This analysis can be attempted as one exercise or divided into a 'practice issues' analysis and a legal analysis, with a discussion on the impact of the one on the other. This allows some general reflection on the nature of the relationship between professional practice and the law.

1.   Florence is 75; she is frail and sometimes forgetful and confused. She finds it very difficult to climb stairs and she has not been able to walk to the local shops for the last month. It is difficult for her to cook for herself. She lives in her own home where the bathroom and toilet are situated on the first floor. Florence is a very independent woman who is determined to cope if she can.

2.   Bill is 64 and is suffering from Parkinson's Disease. He is very slow in his movements and sometimes stumbles and falls. He can use the toilet, but now uses the shower rather than the bath. He finds it difficult to dress himself or to use kitchen utensils to prepare food. He is particularly concerned about how he will be able to look after himself in the future as his illness gets worse. His bathroom and main toilet are upstairs though there is an outside toilet which he uses during the day.

3.   Ranjit is 46. He has had a bad car accident which has left him paralysed from the waist down. He is still in hospital but his condition is such that he can be discharged. He lives with his wife in a terraced house which is in poor condition; it is damp and does not have central heating. The bathroom and toilet are on the ground

floor but down a small flight of steps at the rear of the house. His wife, who speaks very little English, suffers from angina and high blood pressure.

4. Roberta is 23, she was born with very little hearing. She has diabetes and has been blind for the last three years. She has always lived with her mother, Bella, who provided and cared for her. Roberta has never worked and has few domestic skills. Her mother has recently suffered a stroke and is likely to be in hospital and convalescing for a substantial period of time. It is unlikely that she will regain full use of her left arm and leg. Bella is increasingly concerned for Roberta's welfare and worries about her safety in the house.

5. Abdul is 4 and has cerebral palsy with associated slight learning difficulty and moderate visual impairment. His walking ability is severely limited. His family have provided support for his care and mobility needs with very little reference to outside agencies. They are though finding it increasingly difficult to look after Abdul.

6. Joan is an elderly woman living in a small house with her daughter Mary. The house is owned by Joan. In the past year Joan has developed a condition that has made it very difficult for her to get up the stairs to the bedroom and bathroom. Joan has written to the council for help, but they have told her that the waiting list for a visit is nine months due to lack of staff. Joan can no longer get out to the shops because she cannot walk that far and can no longer do any housework. Mary, who is out at work all day, is becoming very worried about Joan's mobility and her general condition. Joan lives on her pension.

You work for a charity that provides advice to elderly people and Mary has approached you with a number of specific enquiries:

a) will the council install a stairlift?

b) will the council provide a home help for her mother?

c) will the council provide and install a personal alarm for her mother?

d) as a last resort will the council provide a place in a residential home for Joan?

e) what social security benefits are available for their situation?

7.   Alice is 84 years old and lives on her own in a local authority flat. She has been referred to the social services department for the first time by her GP and the case has been allocated to you. She has very bad arthritis and her flat is damp and draughty and has not been modified in any way to help her. She has trouble using the bath and the toilet and she cannot get out to collect her pension.

Identify the statutory provisions which you would consider in determining the ways in which you could help Alice continue to live in her own flat. In what circumstances would she be entitled to residential accommodation?

8.   Marcus is 24 years old, blind, deaf and has learning difficulty. Since he left his special school at the age of 19 he has lived at home and been cared for by his mother. Over the last two years it has become increasingly difficult to visit Marcus; his mother is very aggressive and refuses to allow anyone to enter the house. Last year you were so concerned that you managed to get Marcus admitted to psychiatric hospital for assessment but he was discharged three days later, after his mother pleaded with the psychiatrist to let him return home. You understand from Marcus's elder sister that he spends all his time lying on a sofa in the front room in squalid conditions and she is concerned about the standard of care being provided for him by their mother who she thinks is mentally ill. The house is in a bad state of disrepair and is owned by the local authority.

As a local authority field social worker what can you do?

9.   Robert is 73, he is slightly confused. His mobility is poor and he can no longer get upstairs to the bathroom, out to the shops, or to collect his pension. He lives with his son who provides a very basic level of care for his father. Robert is frequently ill with bronchitis and other conditions which his doctor puts down to 'neglect'. The doctor has referred Robert to the social services department and the case has been allocated to you for assessment for community care services. You arranged an appointment to see Robert last week. You were met by Robert's son, who was drunk and verbally abused you. When you finally got to see Robert you were shocked by his condition and the state of his room. He was clearly unwell and was living in a squalid and unhealthy environment. There was an overfull commode, dirty clothes, damp bed and old food on the floor. Your first impressions were that he could not look after himself and didn't really know what was happening to him. He accused his son of 'hitting me' and 'taking my money'. Robert has a black eye and his son collects his pension.

Robert's son told you not to come back again; if you did he would refuse you access to his father.

a) How are you going to secure entry to the house so that you can see Robert again?

b) Would you seek to remove Robert from his home? If so, which legal provisions are available to you?

c) How might you seek to protect Robert from neglect and abuse?

d) Identify current legal provisions which might be relevant to the issues of community care assessment and service provision.

e) Indicate how your powers and duties would be altered if the Draft Mental Incapacity Bill were to become law?

5 ACTIVITIES

1. Get a copy of your local authority's community care plan and identify the various arrangements it has made for the provision of community care services.

This will give you a picture of provision by the statutory, voluntary and private sector.

2. How are the private sector and the voluntary and charitable sector involved in the provision of community care services?

What arrangements are in place for consultation with service users and carers?

Write to the pressure groups and voluntary organisations working with the service users discussed in this chapter and get hold of their publication lists.

RADAR has a comprehensive publications list.

The Disability Alliance ERA produces an annual edition of its *ESSENTIAL Disability Rights Handbook*.

3. How does the complaints procedure work in your local authority?

4. How does the inspection system work in your local authority?

5. Subscribe to RADAR's monthly Bulletin.

6. Get hold of a copy of LASSL(97)15 – List of Current Local Authority Circulars (LACs) and Local Authority Social Services Letters (LASSLs) – from the Department of Health publication unit. (See below for details.)

7. How does the local authority satisfy its duty to provide residential accommodation? Do they run their own homes? Are there independent sector homes?

8. Contact Age Concern to get hold of copies of relevant fact sheets, eg Local Authority Charging Procedures for Residential and Nursing Home Care; and Finding Residential and Nursing Home Accommodation.

9. Get hold of a copy of *No Longer Afraid: The safeguard of older people in domestic settings*, Social Services Inspectorate, Department of Health, (1993).

10. Does the local authority Inspection Unit provide any information about their work? Do they publish an annual report?

6 ADDRESSES

Age Concern
Astral House
1268 London Road
London SW16 4EJ.
Phone: 0181 640 5431

Centre for Policy on Ageing,
25–31 Ironmonger Row
London EC1V 3QP.

Court of Protection
The Public Trust Office, Protection Division

Stewart House
24 Kingsway
London WC2B 6JX.
Phone: 0171 269 7000
Fax: 0171 404 1725

Department of Health
PO Box 410
Wetherby
West Yorkshire LS23 7LN.
Phone: 01937 840 250
Fax: 01937 845 381

Help the Aged
St James's Walk
London EC1R 0BE.
Phone: 0171 253 0253
Freephone Advice: 0800 650065
Fax: 0171 250 4474
E-mail: HTA@dial.pitex.com
Web: www.helptheaged.org.uk

MENCAP
123 Golden Lane,
London EC1Y 0RT.
Phone: 0171 253 9433.

National Association for Mental Health (MIND)
Granta House
15-19 Broadway
London E15 4BQ.
Phone: 0181 519 2122.

The Disability Alliance Educational and Research Association
Universal House
88–94 Wentworth Street
London E1 7SA.
Phone: 0171 247 8776
Fax: 0171 247 8765
Rights Advice Line: 0171 247 8763

The Royal Association for Disability and Rehabilitation (RADAR)
12 City Forum

250 City Road
London EC1V 8AF.
Phone: 0171 250 3222
Fax: 0171 250 0212

7 MATERIALS

Clements, L, *Community Care and the Law*, (1996) Legal Action.

Cooper, J and Vernon, S, *Disability and the Law*, (1996) Jessica Kingsley Publishers.

Decalmer, P and Glendenning, F (eds), *The Mistreatment of Elderly People*, (1997) Sage.

Fish, D, *Community care: duties towards mentally ill people and their families*, Legal Action, November 1995 and May 1996.

Griffiths, A and Roberts, G (eds), *The Law and Elderly People*, (1995) Routledge.

Mandelstam, M with Schwehr, B, *Community Care Practice and the Law*, (1995) Jessica Kingsley Publishers.

Guidance and Circulars

Care Management and Assessment: Managers' Guide, (1991) Social Services Inspectorate.

Care Management and Assessment: Practitioners' Guide, (1991) Social Services Inspectorate.

Carers (Recognition and Services) Act 1995, LAC (96)07.

Community Care in the Next Decade and Beyond, (1990) Department of Health.

Community Care (Direct Payments) Act 1996, LASSL(97)09.

Community Care (Direct Payments) Act 1996. Policy and Practice Guidance, (1996) Social Services Inspectorate.

Home Life: A Code of Practice for Residential Care, Department of Health Circular, LAC (89) 8. Published by Centre for Policy on Ageing. (CPA). The CPA have also published *A Better Home Life* (1996).

Homes are for living in, (1989) Social Services Inspectorate HMSO.

No Longer Afraid: The safeguard of older people in domestic settings, (1993) Social Services Inspectorate, Department of Health.

Other materials

Age Concern Factsheets, eg No 22 – Legal arrangements for managing financial affairs; No 29 – Finding residential and nursing home accommodation; No 32 – Disability and ageing: your rights to social services.

Dealing With The Estates of People Suffering From Mental Disorder, Public Trust Office.

Disability Rights Handbook 'Disability Alliance' (New edition published annually in April/May.)

Enduring Powers of Attorney, Public Trust Office.

Handbook for Receivers, Public Trust Office.

Mental Incapacity, Law Commission No 231, (1995) HMSO.

Your local authority Community Care Plan.

Legal Action, a monthly journal published by the Legal Action Group, has regular articles on community care law.

Important material is now available on the Internet. The Department of Health has a web site at http://www.open.gov.uk/doh and this site provides press releases, guidance and other material on community care.

CHAPTER 7

Mental health

This chapter is divided into two sections. Section 1 considers the professional social work law arising from the duties and powers specified in the Mental Health Act in relation to patients/service users who have a mental disorder. Section 2 considers the law concerning those patients/service users who have a mental incapacity. Such patients/service users may also be vulnerable because of their mental incapacity. The law concerning vulnerable service users is discussed in Section 2 of the chapter on community care law.

SECTION 1
MENTAL DISORDER

1 INTRODUCTION

Mental health is one of the major 'professional law' areas of social work practice. The Mental Health Act 1983 allocates to social workers a number of legal rights, powers and duties which partly determine the boundaries and nature of practice with people who have a mental disorder. Additionally the Act defines the legal position of patients in relation to their compulsory admission to hospital, their treatment whilst detained, their rights whilst in hospital and their discharge from hospital.

This area of practice is marked out by the law in the sense that a number of these important rights, powers and duties are invested in a social work practitioner called an 'approved social worker' who is required by the Act to have been specially trained and qualified. The post qualification training required for this role is mandatory for all those wishing to practise as approved social workers so that they have 'appropriate competence in dealing with persons suffering from mental disorder' – section 114(2).

Social work practice with service users who have a mental disorder extends well beyond the statutory boundaries of the Mental Health Act 1983 and may involve other legislation concerning people who are elderly, those who have a chronic illness, a disability, people who are homeless, welfare rights issues, aspects of community care provision and criminal justice matters. The emphasis of this chapter will be on work within the provisions of the Mental Health Act 1983 though some indication will be given of this wider frame of practice.

The 1983 Act replaced the 1959 Mental Health Act and the 1982 Mental Health (Amendment) Act and was seen partly as a product of pressure group politics in which MIND (the National Association for Mental Health) played a leading role. Their concern was to increase the rights of patients who were compulsorily detained in psychiatric hospital. Other concerns raised in the debate about the reform of the law included those of the health service trade unions who wanted a clearer definition of the legal position for their members working in this area and the desire of other groups to remove people with a learning disability from the long term detention provisions of the existing legislation. The search for a clearer definition of the legal rights and duties affecting workers and patients was the dominant objective of reform. In many respects this clearer definition has been achieved though views on the nature of the legal rights and duties set out by the Mental Health Act 1983 reflect different professional interests and individual positions on issues such as civil liberties. There are, of course, a number of issues arising from the operation of the current mental health system which are of concern to social work practitioners and others working in the area. Examples include the over-representation of women and members of the ethnic communities diagnosed as having a mental disorder, concern about the regimes within special hospitals, and a recognition that the legislation is institution-centred in an era when most patients with a mental disorder are now cared for and treated in the community.

This chapter provides only a brief outline of the law because those wishing to practise as approved social workers will undergo further post-qualification training where the details of the legislation constitute a substantial part of the course. Nonetheless it is necessary to have some knowledge of the main legislative provisions and of the issues they raise for social work practice, and for the rights of patients and service users.

2 THE LAW

2.1 THE MENTAL HEALTH ACT 1983

The Mental Health Act 1983 specifies procedures for the compulsory admission of patients to hospital; it further defines the
position and rights of patients whilst in hospital, the circumstances of their treatment, the procedures for their continued
detention and finally for their discharge. The Act has recently
been amended by the Mental Health (Patients in the Community)
Act 1995 to provide for the compulsory supervision of particular
categories of patient discharged from hospital following detention
for treatment. Within these specifications the Act details the legal
position of patients and of those working within and with the
mental health service. An attempt has been made in this section
to identify and discuss areas of the law where social workers have
or may have a part to play.

The Act makes provision in relation to people who have a 'mental
disorder'; this is a generic concept which is further defined by the
Act in terms of four categories.

The four categories of mental disorder are mental illness, severe
mental impairment (both of which are considered to be major
disorders), mental impairment and psychopathic disorder (both of
which are considered to be minor disorders so that the treatability
condition for admission and detention applies to them). *Mental
illness* is not defined by the Act. The other three categories are defined
in section 1(2) in the following terms:

• *severe mental impairment* – 'a state of arrested or incomplete
development of mind which includes severe impairment of intelligence and social functioning and is associated with abnormally
aggressive or seriously irresponsible conduct';

• *mental impairment* is defined in the same terms except that the
word 'significant' is used instead of the word 'severe';

• *psychopathic disorder* – 'a persistent disorder or disability of
mind (whether or not including significant impairment of
intelligence) which results in abnormally aggressive or seriously
irresponsible conduct'.

It is important to note that section 1(3) of the Act clearly specifies that a person cannot be classified as mentally disordered 'by reason only of promiscuity, or other immoral conduct, sexual deviancy or dependence on alcohol or drugs'.

People with a learning disability are not subject to compulsory admission to, and detention in hospital for treatment unless they exhibit seriously irresponsible or abnormally aggressive behaviour.

There is no minimum age limit for admission to hospital under the provisions of the Mental Health Act 1983 though the Code of Practice for the Act sets out the difficult issues raised by the admission of children and young persons to hospital and their treatment whilst in hospital:

> ... any intervention in the life of a young person, considered necessary by reason of their mental disorder, should be the least restrictive possible and result in the least possible segregation from family, friends, community and school.[1]

The Code of Practice provides guidance to statutory authorities on how they, and their employees, should discharge their responsibilities under the Act. The introduction to the Code provides some broad principles for work under the Act:

> ... that people being assessed for possible admission under the Act or to whom the Act applies should:
>
> − receive respect for and consideration of their individual qualities and diverse backgrounds − social, cultural, ethnic, and religious;
>
> − have their needs taken fully into account though it is recognised that, within available resources, it may not always be practicable to meet them;
>
> − be delivered any necessary treatment or care in the least controlled and segregated facilities practicable;
>
> − be treated or cared for in such a way that promotes to the greatest practicable degree, their self-determination and personal responsibility consistent with their needs and wishes;

---

1 *Code of Practice, Mental Health Act*, Department of Health and the Welsh Office, (1993) HMSO.

– be discharged from any order under the Act to which they are subject immediately it is no longer necessary.

2.2   VOLUNTARY PATIENTS

It should be appreciated that the vast majority of patients in psychiatric hospital are voluntary patients and as such they are in substantially the same position as patients in hospital for a physical illness; so for instance they may refuse treatment and may discharge themselves at any time. For psychiatric patients this latter right is subject to short term holding powers exercised by designated doctors and nurses under section 5 of the Act. The doctor in charge of a voluntary patient's psychiatric treatment has a 72 hour power to detain a patient if s/he reports to the hospital managers that an application for compulsory admission under the Mental Health Act 1983 ought be made in respect of the patient. A qualified mental health nurse has a similar holding power for six hours if they consider that a patient is suffering from a mental disorder to the extent that it is necessary for their health or safety, or for the protection of others, for the patient to be immediately restrained from leaving the hospital. This power can be exercised only when the doctor treating the patient is not available.

Voluntary patients (whether in- or out-patients) cannot be treated without their valid consent. It should be noted though that the common law would allow treatment to be administered in cases of necessity. This concept is said to include life saving treatment where the patient is unable to consent and their wishes are not known, and it may extend to an emergency intervention to restrain a violent patient where there is a serious and immediate danger to the patient or to others.

2.3   THE WORK OF THE APPROVED SOCIAL WORKER

Under the Act an approved social worker has legal independence and acts in a personal capacity. The rights, duties and powers of an approved social worker are central to the Act and constitute the statutory boundaries of substantial areas of social work practice in relation to those people with a mental disorder. Pre-eminent is the duty to make an assessment, possibly but not necessarily leading to an application for compulsory admission under section 13.

2.3.1 The application for admission: assessment

Section 13 of the Act places a duty on the approved social worker to make an application for admission to hospital or reception into guardianship in respect of any patient if s/he is satisfied that such an application should be made. Behind this statutory duty is the important principle that the approved social worker will have an independent professional view as to whether an application for admission is necessary. The section requires the patient to be interviewed before the application is made so that the approved social worker can 'satisfy himself that detention in a hospital is in all the circumstances of the case the most appropriate way of providing the care and medical treatment of which the patient stands in need' – section 13(2). The objective of this requirement is to identify the personal circumstances of the patient and thereby to be able to assess whether there are alternative community based treatment facilities available. The Act is based on the assumption that compulsory admission to hospital should be very much a last resort and one of the tasks of the approved social worker is to investigate all other treatment and care opportunities.

The section requires the interview to be carried out in a 'suitable manner' and the Act thereby acknowledges that there will be circumstances in which it is impossible to gain the necessary information from a patient. It may even be necessary to use the emergency powers available under section 135 to obtain a warrant to search for and remove a patient so that an attempt can be made to interview the patient.

If a patient's nearest relative[2] so requests, a local social services authority must, under section 13(4), direct an approved social worker to consider whether an application for compulsory admission should be made. Again the law requires the formulation of an independent professional opinion by the approved social worker who may decide for or against making an application.

2.3.2 The application

An approved social worker, subject to section 13, has a duty to apply for the compulsory admission of a patient to hospital in three closely

---

2 Nearest relatives are defined by section 26 of the Act in descending order of seniority as being: a) husband or wife, b) son or daughter, c) father or mother, d) brother or sister, e) grandparent, f) grandchild, g) uncle or aunt, h) niece or nephew. A cohabitee of more than six months is regarded as a spouse.

defined circumstances specified in Part II of the Act. In all of these circumstances the nearest relative also has the right to apply for admission independently of the approved social worker though provisions in the legislation make it clear that wherever possible the approved social worker and the nearest relative should be in agreement over the necessity to make an application.[3] This agreement is important for an approved social worker is likely to have a continuing relationship with the patient and their family who may be looking after them upon their discharge from hospital. The Code of Practice identifies the approved social worker as the preferred applicant because of their professional training, knowledge of the legislation and of local resources. The Code also raises concern about the relationship between the nearest relative and the patient where the application for admission is made by the patient's nearest relative.

The medical recommendation for admission is normally made by an 'approved' doctor; this is a doctor approved by the Secretary of State under section 12(2) of the Act as having special experience in the diagnosis or treatment of mental disorder. An application for admission is made so that the patient may be compulsorily detained in hospital.

The Act specifies powers of detention in three sets of circumstances:

i)   in an emergency to protect the patient or to protect others;

ii) to allow an assessment of the condition of the patient; and

iii) to allow the longer term treatment of a patient.

The maximum length of the detention and the rights of the patient vary in each circumstance and these provide a sliding scale of 'seriousness'. Thus the procedures and criteria of admission for treatment are far stricter than for an emergency admission.

2.3.3   Admissions in an emergency

Section 4 provides for an admission in an emergency.

The application may be made by an approved social worker or the nearest relative.

---

3   Section 3 requires that the nearest relative does not object.

The application should be supported by the medical recommendation of a doctor who has previous knowledge of the patient though the recommendation of an authorised doctor is acceptable. The doctor must certify that:

a)   the patient is suffering from a mental disorder of a nature or degree which warrants the detention of the patient in a hospital for assessment (or for assessment followed by medical treatment) for at least a limited period; and

b)   he ought to be so detained in the interests of his own health or safety or with a view to the protection of other persons (section 2(2)).

The additional major criteria for an application for admission in an emergency are the urgent necessity for detention and that going through the requirements for an admission for assessment would cause undesirable delay.

The diagnostic criteria are the same as those for an admission for assessment but the Code of Practice distinguishes the two forms of admission by specifying that an emergency situation is evidenced by a significant risk of mental or physical harm to the patient or others, or the danger of serious harm to property or the need for the patient to be physically restrained.

The person making the application must have seen the patient during the 24 hours prior to the application and the admission must take place within 24 hours of the medical examination or the application whichever is the earlier. The patient may be detained for up to 72 hours under this section though it is possible to convert an emergency detention to detention for assessment with the requirement of a second medical opinion. If it is thought appropriate that a patient detained in an emergency should be detained for treatment under section 3, then an application under that section should be made. In such circumstances the full requirements of a section 3 application would need to be fulfilled.

The Code of Practice stresses that emergency applications should not be made on the basis of convenience merely because the procedures for such applications are less rigorous than for an admission for assessment.

2.3.4   Admission for assessment

Section 2 provides for an admission and detention for assessment upon the application of an approved social worker or the nearest relative.

The application must be supported by the medical recommendations of two doctors, one of whom is approved. The doctors must certify that the patient is suffering from mental disorder of a nature or degree which warrants his detention in a hospital for assessment, or for assessment followed by treatment, for at least a limited period, and he ought to be detained in the interests of his own health or safety or with a view to the protection of others.

The applicant must have seen the patient within the 14 days before the application. The patient may be detained for up to 28 days under this section. During this period an application for detention for treatment may be made if the requirements of section 3 are satisfied. In such circumstances the full requirements for such an admission must be complied with. It should be noted that some compulsory treatment of the patient may be permitted where a patient is detained under section 2, though section 2 should never be used for the purpose of an admission for detention in hospital for treatment.

2.3.5   An admission for treatment

Section 3 provides for an admission and detention for treatment. The application may be made by the approved social worker or the nearest relative. Before making an application the approved social worker must, where practicable, seek the agreement of the nearest relative. If this is refused then the approved social worker cannot make the application unless the county court 'displaces' the nearest relative under the grounds identified in section 29; essentially that the agreement is being unreasonably withheld.

The application must be supported by two medical recommendations, with one of the doctors being approved under section 12(2).

The criteria for admission and detention are:

a)   that the patient is suffering from one of the four categories of mental disorder and that this is of a nature or degree which makes it appropriate for him to receive medical treatment in hospital; and

b) in the case of psychotic disorder or mental impairment, such treatment is likely to alleviate or prevent a deterioration of his condition; and

c) it is necessary for the health or safety of the patient or for the protection of others that he should receive such treatment and it cannot be provided unless he is detained under this section.

The applicant must have seen the patient within the 14 days before admission. The patient may be detained for up to six months under this section. There are powers to renew detention for treatment for a further six months and then for periods of one year at a time. Renewal of the order requires a report from the responsible medical officer to the hospital managers that the original criteria for admission still exist. In addition the 'treatability' condition set out in b) above is satisfied, except that where a patient is suffering from mental illness or severe mental impairment and cannot be treated they may nonetheless be detained where they are unlikely to be able to care for themselves or to obtain the care that they need, or to guard themselves against serious exploitation.

2.4 GUARDIANSHIP

A patient over 16 may be received into guardianship under section 7 as an alternative to admission to and detention in hospital. The criteria to be established are that the patient is suffering from one of the four forms of mental disorder, and it is of a nature or degree which warrants reception into guardianship, and it is necessary in the interests of the welfare of the patient or for the protection of others that s/he should be so received. The application is by the nearest relative or the approved social worker and must be supported by two medical recommendations. The guardian will be the local social services authority or a person accepted by the authority. The guardian has power to require the patient to live in a specified place and to attend for treatment, occupation, education or training. Patients under a guardianship order have the same common law rights as voluntary patients to refuse treatment.

Guardianship orders are rarely made. A Department of Health Press Release (97/139) indicates that during the year ending on 31 March 1996, 291 guardianship cases were closed and 357 new cases opened.

At the end of that year the number of guardianship cases in force was 624.

2.5 EMERGENCY POWERS

There are two very important emergency powers under the Act designed to deal with particular situations in which it is necessary to intervene to protect or control someone who has a mental disorder. In both circumstances approved social workers will be working closely with the police.

Section 136 allows a person in a public place to be taken to a place of safety by a police officer where it appears to the officer that the person is 'suffering from mental disorder' and is 'in immediate need of care and control'. This power of detention, which runs for a maximum of 72 hours, is used to allow a medical examination and interview by an approved social worker so that appropriate arrangements for the patient can be made, such as an application for admission to hospital. (A place of safety includes a police station or a hospital.)

Section 135 gives power to an approved social worker to apply to a magistrate for a warrant which allows the police, together with a doctor and the approved social worker, to enter private premises and remove a person to a place of safety. When applying for the warrant the approved social worker must have reasonable cause to believe that the person is suffering from a mental disorder and 'has been, or is being, ill treated, neglected or kept otherwise than under proper control, or is living alone and is unable to care for himself'. This provision allows the person to be removed to a place of safety for up to 72 hours so that the necessary examinations and interviews can take place and appropriate arrangements made if necessary.

2.6 PEOPLE WITH A MENTAL DISORDER AND THE CRIMINAL JUSTICE SYSTEM

The Mental Health Act 1983 makes particular provision for people with a mental disorder who have been charged or found guilty of a criminal offence. Again this is a lengthy, complex and therefore specialist area of law and only an outline can be provided here.

There are a small number of special hospitals which are established for patients who have been detained under the Mental Health Act 1983 and who require treatment under specially secure conditions because of their 'dangerous, violent or criminal propensities'.

The Home Office Circular 66/90, *Provision for Mentally Disordered Offenders*, establishes the principle of diversion from the criminal justice system. The aim of the circular is to ensure that a mentally disordered person who has offended against the criminal law, but only in a minor way, and where the public interest does not demand prosecution, is not charged or brought to trial, but diverted to the psychiatric health care service for care and treatment.

2.6.1 Suspects, detention and questioning

The provisions of the Police and Criminal Evidence Act 1984 establish the appropriate adult system for suspects who have a mental disorder or learning disability.

> If an officer has any suspicions or is told in good faith that a person of any age, whether in custody or not in custody, may be suffering from a mental disorder, or is mentally handicapped, or cannot understand the significance of questions put to him or his replies, then he shall be treated as a mentally handicapped person. (Police and Criminal Evidence Act, Code C.)

The Code provides that a police surgeon (forensic medical examiner) should be called when the police need an opinion on the mental health of a suspect or whether the person concerned needs an appropriate adult. An appropriate adult, who may be an approved social worker, should be informed of the detention of the person concerned and asked to attend at the police station to ensure that the person's rights are fully protected during questioning and detention.

2.6.2 Remands for assessment and treatment

Sections 35 and 36 allow people who have been accused of a criminal offence to be remanded to hospital for reports or very occasionally for treatment. The objective of the remand for reports power is to allow a psychiatric medical report to be prepared so that the court can properly decide how to proceed. More often such defendants will be diverted from a remand in custody by the making of a 28-

day order for assessment or an order for treatment under sections 2 and 3 respectively.

2.6.3 Sentencing mentally disordered offenders

A probation order with a treatment condition may be imposed by the courts as a community sentence. The offender's mental condition must be such as to require and be susceptible to treatment, but not such as to warrant a hospital order.

The main provision is contained in section 37 and provides the criminal courts with the power to make a hospital order on an offender who is suffering from one of the four categories of mental disorder. The effect of a hospital order is that the offender is admitted to and remains in hospital in circumstances which are similar to those for an admission and detention for treatment under section 3 of the Act. One of the implications of this is that the offender can be discharged, without reference to the courts, by the hospital managers or a Mental Health Review Tribunal, but not by the nearest relative, in the same way as any other patient.

The detention and release of an offender on a hospital order can be controlled by the imposition of a restriction order under section 41. This order is made by the Crown Court on the basis that it is necessary to protect the public from serious harm by restricting the release of the offender either for a specified time or without limit. Such offenders can only be released by the decision of the Home Secretary or a Mental Health Review Tribunal.

Sections 47 and 48 allow remand and serving prisoners to be transferred from prison to hospital where the Secretary of State (Home Office) is satisfied that the person concerned is suffering from a mental disorder which requires detention in hospital for treatment.

2.6.4 Insanity and unfitness to plead

The criminal law has established two general defences to a criminal prosecution for those who have a mental disorder; in addition a finding of diminished responsibility will reduce a conviction for murder to one for manslaughter. These defences are: that the defendant is unfit to plead, and that the defendant is not guilty by reason of insanity.

The consequences for raising these defences used to be that the defendant would be sentenced to a hospital order with restrictions. The Criminal Procedure (Insanity and Unfitness to Plead) Act 1991 has ameliorated this result by providing a range and choice of responses for the court. The court may still impose a hospital order with restrictions, or it may make an ordinary hospital order, a guardianship order, a supervision and treatment order, or even an absolute discharge.

2.7 PATIENTS' CIVIL RIGHTS

Although the principle underpinning the Mental Health Act 1983 is that compulsorily detained patients should not have their civil rights curtailed there are some important restrictions on the rights of such patients. Implicit within the discussion of the admission procedures and those relating to emergencies is the principle that such procedures must be administered within the law. Approved social workers have substantial rights, powers and duties, the exercise of which may result in the loss of liberty for significant periods of time. The Mental Health Act 1983, section 139 provides a limited protection to anyone acting within the provisions of the Mental Health Act 1983 by restricting the access of compulsory patients to the courts. In order to take a civil action a patient must obtain the leave of the High Court by establishing that there are reasonable grounds for their accusation that the person acted in bad faith or without reasonable care. Consent for the bringing of criminal proceedings must be given by the Director of Public Prosecutions. There are also restrictions on the sending and receiving of correspondence and on voting rights.

Under section 132 detained patients have a specific right to be informed of their rights by the hospital managers. Patients must be informed in writing of their rights in respect of treatment, application to the Mental Health Review Tribunal, correspondence, and of the basis for their detention.

It should also be acknowledged that patients who have spent some time in hospital having been detained because of their mental disorder may well suffer from a long term disadvantage relating to the stigmatisation that surrounds mental illness. Such disadvantage may extend to employment prospects, housing and other aspects of independent living.

2.8 TREATMENT

The treatment of patients with a mental disorder is one of the issues which most concerned those arguing for reform of the Mental Health Act 1959. MIND argued that the 1959 Act was never clear as to whether psychiatric treatment could be lawfully administered to compulsorily detained patients without their consent. Nonetheless it was clear that such treatments were administered under the old legislation on the basis that patients could not give the necessary consent because of the nature of their mental disorder.

Voluntary patients are required to give their consent to treatment for their mental disorder in the same way that treatments for physical illness or injury require the consent of the patient. The difficulty centres on whether a patient's mental disorder is such that they are unable to give a consent which is valid in law. The validity of such a consent is based on three elements:

i)   the provision of sufficient information about the nature and purpose of the treatment including any side effects;

ii) the patient must be able to understand what s/he has been told about the treatment; and

iii) consent must be given voluntarily.

The psychiatric treatment of patients who have been compulsorily detained is closely regulated by a series of statutory safeguards in Part IV of the Act and in particular in sections 57 and 58. The principle is that procedural safeguards must be satisfied before specific treatments can be administered. The more significant the nature of the intervention through treatment the tighter the safeguards.

Section 57, which applies to psychosurgery and sex hormone implant treatment, requires a patient's valid consent and an independent certification that the consent is valid and that the treatment is appropriate. This 'second opinion' certification procedure is provided and controlled by the Mental Health Act Commission.

Section 58 applies to electro-convulsive therapy (or other specified treatments) and to a course of medication three months after it is first administered. The patient's valid consent is required and the validity of the consent must be confirmed by the responsible medical officer or an independent doctor appointed by the Mental Health Act Commission. If the patient refuses to consent or is not able to give a valid consent then these treatments can be administered only if a doctor appointed by the Mental Health Act Commission certifies (after consultation with two others from the care team) that 'the patient is not capable of understanding the nature, purpose and likely effects of that treatment or has not consented to it but that, having regard to the likelihood of its alleviating or preventing a deterioration of his condition, the treatment should be given'. Social workers may be involved in the consultations required.

Section 63 provides that medical treatment for a mental disorder, not being treatment falling within sections 57 or 58, may be given without consent. In *B v Croydon Health Authority* [1995] Fam 133, the Court of Appeal decided that feeding by naso-gastric tube for an eating disorder comes within the definition of medical treat-ment for a mental disorder, and could therefore be administered under section 63 without the consent of the patient.

> The general law is that an adult person of full mental capacity has the right to choose whether to eat or not. Even if the refusal to eat is tantamount to suicide, as in the case of a hunger strike, he cannot be compelled to eat or be forcibly fed. On the other hand, if a person lacks the mental capacity to choose, by the common law the medical practitioner who has him in his care may treat him (and by this I include the artificial administration of food) according to his clinical judgement of the patient's best interest. In addition, under section 63 of the Mental Health Act 1983, the consent of a patient liable to be detained under the Act is not required for 'any treatment given to him for the mental disorder from which he is suffering...'. Lord Justice Hoffman.[4]

Patients admitted in an emergency are not subject to the provisions of Part IV and cannot be treated without their consent except where minimal emergency intervention is necessary to protect the patient or other people.

---

4   See also the case of *Re C (adult ...refusal of treatment)* [1994] 1 WLR 290. The Divisional Court decided that an in-patient at Broadmoor who was a schizophrenic had the necessary capacity to refuse consent to an operation to amputate his leg below the knee. The surgery had been recommended to prevent the further development of gangrene.

2.9 DISCHARGE FROM HOSPITAL

There are a number of ways in which patients who have been compulsorily detained in hospital may be discharged from their detention. Subsequently they may remain in hospital as voluntary patients and as such may discharge themselves at any time.

Section 23 provides that a patient who has been detained for assessment or treatment may be discharged by order of the responsible medical officer, or the hospital managers, or by the patient's nearest relative. The section does not provide any statutory criteria for such a decision. The power of the nearest relative to discharge the patient is limited by the provisions of section 25 which requires that they provide the hospital managers with at least seventy-two hours' written notice of their intention. During this period the responsible medical officer can prevent the discharge by certifying to the hospital managers that the patient would be a danger to himself/herself or to others if discharged. Where the nearest relative's attempt to discharge the patient is so prevented, the nearest relative may not seek such a discharge again for at least six months, though by section 66 they then have access to a Mental Health Review Tribunal to apply for the patient's discharge.

2.9.1 Mental Health Review Tribunals

Mental Health Review Tribunals have an important jurisdiction to consider applications for discharge from hospital or guardianship from patients, and in some circumstances from the nearest relative. Applications are normally heard by a three person tribunal comprising a legally qualified chairperson, a doctor and a lay person with relevant knowledge or experience. Cases for hearing may also be referred to the tribunal by the Secretary of State for Health, or the Home Secretary in the case of restricted patients. Section 66 specifies the circumstances in which patients and nearest relatives may apply for discharge, including the right to a tribunal hearing for patients admitted and detained for assessment under section 2.

Section 72 sets out the powers of the tribunal. They include a discretionary power to discharge any patient detained under the Act, and mandatory duties to discharge if particular criteria are established.

For patients detained under section 2, the tribunal must order their discharge if they are satisfied:

(i) that he is not then suffering from mental disorder or from mental disorder of a nature or degree which warrants his detention in a hospital for assessment (or for assessment followed by medical treatment) for at least a limited period; or

(ii) that his detention as aforesaid is not justified in the interests of his own health or safety or with a view to the protection of other persons.

For patients detained under other sections of the Act the tribunal is under a duty to discharge if they are satisfied:

(i) that he is not then suffering from mental illness, psychopathic disorder, severe mental impairment or mental impairment or from any of those forms of disorder of a nature or degree which makes it appropriate for him to be liable to be detained in a hospital for medical treatment; or

(ii) that it is not necessary for the health or safety of the patient or for the protection of other persons that he should receive such treatment; or

(iii) in the case of an application by virtue of paragraph (g) of section 66(1) above, that the patient, if released, would be likely to act in a manner dangerous to other persons or to himself.[5]

The tribunal has a variety of powers; it may discharge a patient, although this may be subject to a delay to facilitate the arrangement of appropriate after-care facilities; grant a leave of absence; or order a transfer to another hospital or into guardianship. Legal aid is available for the representation of patients before tribunal hearings.

It appears from the decision in *R v Managers of South Western Hospital, ex p M* [1994] 1 All ER 161 that a patient discharged by a tribunal may be compulsorily admitted on the same day so long as the criteria of the chosen admission section are fulfilled.

Patients who are the subject of a hospital order with restrictions imposed under section 41, may be conditionally released by the tribunal, but are subject to recall by the Home Secretary.

---

5   Section 66(1)(g) – involves the blocking of a nearest relative discharge by a report from the responsible medical officer.

2.10   THE MENTAL HEALTH ACT COMMISSION

The Commission, which was established by the 1983 Act, is charged with a number of statutory functions:

* to appoint independent doctors and others whose certificates are needed before certain treatments are administered;

* to receive reports from responsible medical officers concerning all treatments given to detained patients under section 57 and all treatments given without the patient's consent under section 58. The Commission can cancel the certificates which have been granted for treatment;

* to 'keep under review the exercise of the powers and the discharge of the duties conferred or imposed by this Act so far as relating to the detention of patients or to patients liable to be detained ...' This function covers the admission and detention process and the conditions in which patients are detained and treated;

* to visit and interview all detained patients;

* to investigate complaints;

* to prepare and update the Code of Practice under the Act;

* to review the censorship of mail;

* to publish a biennial report to be laid before Parliament.

2.11   THE COURT OF PROTECTION

The Court of Protection has jurisdiction to look after the property and affairs of anyone who is unable to do so for themselves because of their mental disorder. Details in relation to the court are contained in Part VII of the Mental Health Act 1983. An application for the court to invoke its jurisdiction can be made by anyone who is interested in the patient so that a social worker may be involved. The court is likely to appoint a Receiver to manage the patient's property and affairs over which the court has exclusive powers. Much of the work of the Court is administered on a day-to-day basis by the Public Trust Office. Fees and other expenses are recovered from the property which together with any other interests are managed for the benefit of the patient.

2.12   CARE IN THE COMMUNITY

There are a substantial and increasing number of people with a mental disorder who are not in hospital but who are living, and being treated and cared for in the community. This situation has come about as a result of a number of factors including the switch to a policy of community care and the programme of closure of long stay psychiatric hospitals. As a result a significant and increasing element of social work practice with service users who have a mental disorder or a learning disability, takes place outside the psychiatric hospital. Such work, which is not restricted to approved social workers, takes place within the general power of local authorities under section 29 of the National Assistance Act 1948 to promote the welfare of people with a disability and under a number of other specific statutory provisions.

a)   The Chronically Sick and Disabled Persons Act 1970, section 2, requires social services departments to arrange for the provision of services to anyone who has a need because of their permanent and substantial handicap. The relevant services are help in the home, recreational facilities in and outside the home, assistance with transport to such facilities, appropriate aids and adaptations to the home, holidays, meals and the installation of telephones.

b)   Under the National Health Service Act 1977 the Secretary of State has a general duty to provide health services and under the same Act a duty has been imposed on local authority social services departments to provide prevention, care and after-care services in relation to physical and mental illness.

c)   More specifically the Mental Health Act, section 117, requires a district health authority and the social services department to provide after-care services and facilities for patients who have been discharged from hospital after detention for treatment under sections 3, 37, 41, 47 and 48. The Code of Practice describes the objectives and process in the following terms:

Objectives

27.1 The purpose of aftercare is to enable a patient to return to his home or accommodation other than hospital or nursing home, and to minimise the chances of him needing any future in-patient hospital care.

Process

27.6 When a decision has been taken to discharge or grant leave to a patient, it is the responsibility of the RMO to ensure that a discussion takes place to establish a care plan to organise the management of the patient's continuing health and social care needs. This discussion will usually take place in multi-professional clinical meetings held in psychiatric hospitals and units. If this is not possible, administrative support should be available to the RMO to assist in making arrangements.

The multi-professional discussion should establish an agreed outline of the patient's needs and assets taking into account his social and cultural background, and agree a time-scale for the implementation of the various aspects of the plan. All key people with specific responsibilities with regard to the patient should be properly identified. Once plans are agreed it is essential that any changes are discussed with others involved with the patient before being implemented. The plan should be recorded in writing.

27.11 The care plan should be regularly reviewed. It will be the responsibility of the key worker to arrange reviews of the plan until it is agreed that it is no longer necessary. The senior officer in the key worker's agency responsible for section 117 arrangements should ensure that all aspects of the procedure are followed.

The Code also identifies a number of factors to be considered as part of any decision concerning after-care:

- the patients wishes and needs;

- the views of relevant relatives, friends and supporters;

- the necessity for an agreement from the receiving authority if different from the discharging authority;

- the possible involvement of other agencies;

- the establishment of a care plan (to include, resources permitting and if appropriate, day care arrangements, appropriate accommodation, out-patient treatment, counselling, personal support, assistance in welfare rights and personal finance);

- the appointment of a key worker from either of the statutory agencies to monitor the care plan's implementation, liaise and co-ordinate where necessary;

- the need to identify any unmet need.

In the case of *R v Ealing District Health Authority, ex p Fox* [1993] 3 All ER 170 the Divisional Court held that services under section 117 are owed individually to patients and are not merely a target duty owed to a group of people defined by statute. In theory this decision opens up the possibility of a patient/service user taking an action in the courts in respect of a failure to provide such after-care services, or in respect of any other deficit in the performance of this duty.

d) The Disabled Persons (Services, Consultation and Representation) Act 1986 provides important rights through which the interests of people with a disability can be protected and promoted. The definition of a disabled person includes a person with a learning disability and those with a mental disorder within the terms of the Mental Health Act 1983. The 1986 Act was designed to provide an assessment of the needs of disabled people by a local authority who must give a written statement of the results of the assessment. The Act is largely designed to secure the provision of local authority services under section 2 of the Chronically Sick and Disabled Persons Act 1970.

Section 7 of the Disabled Persons (Services, Consultation and Representation) Act 1986 is specifically directed to patients who have been detained in a psychiatric hospital for at least six months for treatment and are to be discharged. The section requires the hospital managers to inform the relevant district health authority, local authority and education authority of the patient's date of discharge so that an appropriate assessment of needs may be made. Section 7 has never been implemented.

e) The community care provisions of the National Health Service and Community Care Act 1990 were implemented in April 1993. The provisions of the Act are imposed on top of legislation already in force and are directed to the provision of community care services for those who are assessed as having a need for such services. The provision of services is the responsibility of social services authorities, who are the lead authority, though community care plans are to be drawn up in consultation with health authorities, education authorities, housing authorities, voluntary organisations and organisations representing users and carers. People with a mental disorder, including those with a learning disability, are likely to be among those who will need community care services and will therefore be assessed under the 1990 legislation.

f)   The provisions of the Housing Act 1996 in relation to homelessness are important for social work practice. The Act specifies that anyone who is vulnerable because of their disability has a priority need for accommodation; it should be accepted that patients who have a mental disorder and are homeless or threatened with homelessness are clearly within such a category of priority need.

g)   Section 17(10) of the Children Act 1989 defines a child in need.

For the purposes of this Part a child shall be taken to be in need if –

a) he is unlikely to achieve or maintain, or to have the opportunity of achieving or maintaining, a reasonable standard of health or development without the provision for him of services by a local authority under this Part;

b) his health or development is likely to be significantly impaired, or further impaired, without the provision for him of such services; or

c) he is disabled,

...

(11) For the purposes of this Part, a child is disabled if he is blind, deaf or dumb or suffers from mental disorder of any kind or is substantially and permanently handicapped by illness, injury, or congenital deformity or such other disability as may be prescribed; and in this Part –

'development' means physical, intellectual, emotional, social or behavioural development; and 'health' means physical or mental health.

As a result of this definition children who have a mental disorder or a learning disability are brought within the provisions of the Act which specifies their entitlement to local authority support and services under Part III and Schedule 2 of the Children Act, and other legislation which includes the Chronically Sick and Disabled Persons Act 1970 and the Mental Health Act 1983.

h)   The Mental Health (Patients in the Community) Act 1995 has introduced supervised discharge orders for certain patients discharged from hospital having been detained for treatment under the 1983 Act. The 1995 Act amends the 1983 Act to impose duties jointly on social services and health authorities which amount to compulsory after-care in the community.

A patient's responsible medical officer may apply to the health authority for an order in respect of a patient who is suffering from a mental disorder and there is substantial risk of serious harm to the health or safety of the patient or others, or of the patient being seriously exploited if he or she were not to receive after-care under supervision. The application must be supported by a social worker and a second medical recommendation. The order empowers the health and social services authorities to require the patient to live at a specified place and to attend for medical treatment, occupation, education or training. The after-care must be kept under review and where the patient neglects or refuses to comply with the arrangements made for him or her, the authorities are required to consider whether the patient should be admitted to hospital. If it is so decided, a full application for admission is required.

i)   The Care Programme Approach, which was introduced in 1991, requires health authorities, in collaboration with local authority social services departments, to put in place specified arrangements for the care and treatment of mentally ill people in the community.[6] The Department of Health has identified four main elements to the care programme approach:

*   systematic arrangements for assessing the health and social needs of people accepted by the specialist psychiatric services;

*   the formulation of a care plan which addresses the patient's identified health and social care needs;

6   Further detail appears in Guidance HSG(94)27/LASSL(94)4, *Guidance on the Discharge of Mentally Disordered People and their Continuing Care in the Community*.

- the appointment of a key worker to keep in close touch with the patient and monitor care;

- regular review, and if need be, agreed changes to the care plan.

j)   Supervision Registers. Health Service guidance published in 1994 (HSG(94)5), required health authorities to introduce supervision registers by October 1994 to identify those patients known to be at serious risk to themselves or to others.

3   MENTAL HEALTH LAW AND SOCIAL WORK: some issues for discussion

3.1   BLACK AND MINORITY ETHNIC PATIENTS

> ... it is clear that the black population generally perceives the psychiatric services on offer as unwelcome, unsupportive and alien to their culture and needs. The higher admission rates for schizophrenia in this group may possibly reflect the fact that black people usually come for help from the services at a time when they are in crisis, having received little or no help from primary care services, outpatient services or community mental health teams.[7]

Racism is a continuing and concerning issue in the mental health care system. Research over the years, commented on by MIND, identifies the fact that black people are more likely than white people to be removed by the police to a place of safety under the provisions of sections 135 and 136; are more likely to be admitted and detained in hospital under the provisions of sections 2, 3 and 4 of the Act; are more likely to be detained in locked wards, to be given higher doses of medication, diagnosed as suffering from schizophrenia or other forms of psychotic illness.[8] The 1994 Reed Report[9] confirms a similar experience for black mentally disordered offenders who are more likely than their white counterparts to be remanded in custody for psychiatric reports; subject to restrictions on hospital orders; detained in higher degrees of security for

---

7   Mental Health Act Commission, Sixth Biennial Report, Ch 8, at p 85.
8   MIND's Policy on Black and Minority Ethnic People and Mental Health, (1993) MIND.
9   Review of Health and Social Services for Mentally Disordered Offenders and Others Requiring Similar Services, Vol 6 (HMSO).

longer; and be referred from prison to medium secure units or special hospitals.

Such researched and well documented evidence of racism in the psychiatric health care system poses a considerable challenge for the system and for those who work within it. Such a challenge may well weigh particularly heavily on social work professionals working within or for the psychiatric health care system because of the commitment of the profession to anti-discriminatory practice.

The Mental Health Act Commission has commented, in response to the Orville Blackwood Report[10] that the Report:

> ... highlights very dramatically the serious consequences arising from the failure by mental health services to adequately recognise the fact that psychiatry tends to reflect white, middle class and eurocentric values which can act as real barriers to the provision of relevant and effective care and treatment.[11]

3.2   CARE IN THE COMMUNITY

The last two biennial reports of the Mental Health Act Commission have raised concerns about the ability of the community care system to provide appropriate levels of care and support for patients and mental health service users who are living in the community. The Fifth Report highlighted problems with the performance of after-care duties imposed by section 117 of the Mental Health Act 1983, and with the implementation of the Care Programme Approach.[12] The Audit Commission has also expressed a continuing concern about the provision of community mental health care services.[13] The report into the treatment and care of Christopher Clunis, the Ritchie Report 1994, comments on the inadequate services available to patients who are suffering from schizophrenia and who may pose a threat to themselves and to others. The Sixth Biennial Report of the Commission confirms

---

10   Inquiry into the Death of Orville Blackwood, Special Hospital Service Authority, (1993).
11   Fifth Biennial Report 1991–1993, Mental Health Act Commission, (1993) HMSO.
12   See Fifth Biennial Report 1991–1993, Mental Health Act Commission, (1993) HMSO, Ch 14, Care in the Community.
13   Finding a Place, Review of Mental Health Services, (1994) Audit Commission.

a continuing concern about section 117 services and the care programme approach.[14]

Problems still reported include:

* poor recording of care plans, particularly unmet needs;

* meetings being arranged at the last minute;

* difficulties in arranging section 117 meetings prior to discharge;

* no flagging of reviews of section 117 meetings;

* a scarcity and lack of variety in the range of services in the
  community. The principles of Community Care have in many
  places not been easy to achieve because of restrictions imposed
  by lack of resources.

The problems of resourcing assessment and service provision are
common throughout community care but are exacerbated in the field
of mental health where there has been some public hostility to the
concept and experience of caring for people with a mental disorder
in the community.

The financing of services has been helped by the mental illness
specific grant, first provided in 1991/92. The objective of the annual
grant is explained in LAC (96)6:

> ... to enable local authority social services departments to improve
> the social care of people with a mental illness who need specialist
> psychiatric care. It supports the Care Programme Approach in-
> cluding the introduction of Supervision Registers for the provision
> of community care for all in-patients considered for discharge, and
> all new patients accepted by the specialist psychiatric services.

Concern about the care of particular groups of patients in the
community who might be a threat to themselves or others continues
to engender much public debate. For some years the issue of compulsory treatment in the community had attracted considerable

---

14   Sixth Biennial Report 1993-1995, Mental Health Act Commission, (1995)
     HMSO, Ch 10, Community Care.

interest. Ultimately the government shied away from such legislation preferring to deal with public concern through the introduction of Supervision Registers, and by the introduction of supervised discharge under the provisions of the Mental Health (Patients in the Community) Act 1995. The Act does not provide for compulsory treat-ment in the community though patients who are subject to supervision under the Act may be admitted to hospital if they fail to adhere to the conditions of their supervision including those concerning treatment. However such an admission is not an automatic 'sanction', the full requirements of the admission sections of the Act must be satisfied. This is entirely appropriate from the perspective of the civil rights of the patient, but it might suggest that the legislation has a greater symbolic force than practical impact. There is no doubt that incidents, such as the murder of Jonathan Zito by Christopher Clunis, generate significant public concern. In the face of such concern government often feels the need to respond. The introduction of supervision registers and supervised discharge can be understood as part of such a response.

The Mental Health Act Commission has expressed some concern about the operation of supervision registers.[15]

> Initial implementation of the registers has thrown up problems of interpretation of the guidance relating to inclusion on the register, to informing the patient of inclusion and concerning access to the registers. These are all areas in which Commission members have noted a wide variation in practice.

> For example, members on one visit found that a criterion for inclusion appeared to be that an individual was thought to have committed a crime, and on another it was discovered that the local policy provided for the police to be notified of everybody placed on the register. On a number of occasions, a lack of understanding amongst professional groups not employed by the Health Service, including Approved Social Workers, as to how they relate to the registers has been apparent.

The shift away from hospital based care and treatment to care in the community is now significant and well established. The challenge for the mental health service and for social services departments lies in the provision of services that are appropriate for increasing

---

15   Ibid, at p 134.

numbers of patients and service users, in a climate of restricted resourcing and public concern that periodically develops into hostility.

3.3 REFORM OF THE LAW AND THE ORGANISATION OF PSYCHIATRIC AND SOCIAL SERVICES FOR PEOPLE WITH A MENTAL DISORDER

It has been apparent for some time that the basic legislation concerning the care and treatment of people with a mental disorder needs reform. This discussion will consider two major themes which constitute part of the agenda for reform. They are the development of the community as the environment within which most patients are cared for and treated, and the dual responsibility of health authorities and social services departments for service planning and provision leading to an emphasis on inter-agency working for the care and protection of mentally ill people.

In its Fifth Biennial Report the Mental Health Act Commission identified a shift from service provision in hospital to a community based mental health service, and argued that the legislative framework for the provision of such services should reflect this shift.

> It is at the very least arguable that the radical transformation of mental health services, from being primarily hospital based to community focused, should be reflected in the legislative framework.[16]

Among the specific reasons for a review of the law, the Commission identified:

- the disappearance of many of the institutions on which the services of the 1983 (and 1959) Act are based;

- the need for legislation to address the concept of entitlement to a reasonable standard of care and treatment;

- the interrelation between the 1983 Act and the Children Act, and the needs of people with learning disability;

---

16 Ibid, at p 102.

- the interrelation between the 1983 Act and the 1990 National Health Service and Community Care Act.

To these issues, which were identified in the Fifth Report, should also be added the impact of a series of enquiries listed in the Sixth Report: Clunis, Buchanan, Robinson and Laudat. All these enquiries exposed what the Commission called 'fault-lines in the co-ordination of care', and have led to a public distrust in the ability of community care to ensure the safety of patients and the public.

The passing and implementation of the Mental Health (Patients in the Community) Act 1995 is a response to some of these issues, particularly to the problem of ensuring after-care. The Act is certainly not the significant reform of mental health law that has been called for, indeed its provisions have drawn criticism from a number of commentators, including MIND and the Commission. MIND, arguing from a largely human rights perspective, points to the fact that provisions in the Act conflict with the European Convention on Human Rights, that it fails to adequately provide for patient consultation and involvement, lacks provisions for patient advocacy, has very limited grounds for access to the Mental Health Review Tribunal, and that the Act endangers the relationship of trust that is necessary for proper care in the community.[17] The Commission, in its Sixth Biennial Report, expresses disappointment that the encroachment on individual liberty, introduced by the Act, has not been accompanied by an equivalent protection of the individual's rights and interests.

The switch to the delivery of services to the majority of patients in the community has, in turn, placed a greater emphasis on the dual responsibilities of health authorities and social services departments, on their organisation of services, and on the variety of agencies involved in service delivery. The provision of after-care services under section 117 of the Act is a prime example of such joint responsibility. The Department of Health responded to the Report of the Inquiry into the Care and Treatment of Christopher Clunis (the Ritchie Report), in part by the publication of Building Bridges in its Health of the Nation series. This guide to inter-agency working is concerned to improve the care of people who are severely mentally ill and living in the community.

17 Kate Harrison, *Patients in the community*, New Law Journal, 24 February 1995.

The message of guidance contained in Building Bridges was taken up by the previous government in its Green Paper 'Developing Partnerships in Mental Health', published in February 1997.

> It is clear, says the Green Paper, that people with severe mental illness do not always receive a safe, effective and seamless service. This results in a reduced quality of care, occasionally with tragic results. Poor service co-ordination also causes anxiety and concern for relatives, staff and the public. It says that the challenge in delivering seamless services is perhaps greater for people with mental health problems than for any other group.[18]

The Green Paper considers proposals to encourage joint work between health authorities and local authorities. It identifies the merits attached to the publication of joint mental health plans, and complimentary funding arrangements. Four structural changes are set out:

Option one: mental health and social care authorities; accountable directly to the Secretary of State for Health and responsible for planning, commissioning and purchasing health and social services for working age adults with severe mental illness.

Option two: single authority responsibility; accountable to either health authorities or local authorities and responsible for planning, commissioning and purchasing mental health and social care.

Option three: a joint health and social care body; accountable to health and local authorities who would establish a joint body to plan, commission and organise the contractual framework for delivering mental health and social care services.

Option four: agreed delegation; a new statutory authority, accountable to health and local authorities would be able to delegate particular functions and responsibilities to each other. For example, a local authority may ask the health authority to undertake commissioning for specific social services.

The impact of the change of government on these and other reform proposals remains to be seen. What is clear is that care in the community is now the focus for the care and treatment of the majority of patients with a mental disorder. Inter-agency work will therefore remain the key to effective work with this vulnerable and

18   Press Release – 97/030, Department of Health, 4 February 1997.

important group of patients and service users. If this objective is not realised public opinion may well call for a more restrictive and institutional response.

SECTION 2
MENTAL INCAPACITY

1 INTRODUCTION

Work with service users with a mental incapacity is recognised as an important element of social work practice. The legal mandate for such work is largely derived from community care law, but may also be drawn from mental health law.

Recognition of the rights and interests of service users with a mental incapacity is now well established though this has not always been the case. The work of the Law Commission on reforming the law on mentally incapacitated adults, which began with the publication of Fourth Programme of Law Reform: Mentally Incapacitated Adults in 1989, has been instrumental in raising both professional and public consciousness. During its research the Law Commission identified an alarming underdevelopment in the law concerning people with a mental incapacity:

> It is widely recognised that, in this area, the law as it now stands is unsystematic and full of glaring gaps. It does not rest on clear or modern foundations of principle. It has failed to keep up with social and demographic changes. It has also failed to keep up with developments in our understanding of the rights and needs of those with mental disability.[19]

2 THE LAW

2.1 DEFINITIONS

There are two significant and related difficulties in this area of law; the problem associated with definitions, and the fact that English

19   *Mental Incapacity*, Law Commission No 231, (1995) IIMSO, at p 1.

law recognises a variable test of capacity. The Mental Health Act 1983 utilises the concept of mental disorder as a generic concept to encompass mental illness, arrested or incomplete development of mind, psychopathic disorder and any other disorder or disability of mind (section 1(2)). Consequently people with a mental incapacity are drawn under the provisions of the Act wherever a threshold criteria of 'mental disorder' on its own is specified. Such situations include the exercise of place of safety emergency powers under sections 135 and 136, and the short term compulsory admission powers under sections 2 and 4.

In contrast, section 3 of the Act provides that a compulsory admission for treatment requires a diagnosis of one of the four forms of mental disorder, ie mental illness, severe mental impairment, mental impairment and psychopathic disorder, and further that mental impairment, severe mental impairment and psychopathic disorder must be associated with abnormally aggressive or seriously irresponsible conduct. The consequence of this is that a person with a mental incapacity cannot be compulsorily admitted to hospital for long periods, or into guardianship, unless they exhibit seriously irresponsible or abnormally aggressive behaviour.

English law utilises a number of different definitions of mental incapacity; generally the greater the legal significance of a decision the greater the capacity required of its parties.

> Generally, there is a presumption that the person is capable until proved otherwise, and capacity is judged in relation to the particular decision, transaction or activity involved. There is also a basic common law test of capacity, to the effect that the person concerned must at the relevant time understand in broad terms what he is doing and the likely effects of his action. Thus, in principle, legal capacity depends upon understanding rather than wisdom: the quality of the decision is irrelevant as long as the person understands what he is deciding.[20]

It is also important to recognise that a person who is suffering from a mental disorder may still retain the mental capacity to make a number of legally enforceable decisions. In the case of *Re C (adult ... refusal of treatment)* [1994] 1 WLR 290 the Divisional Court decided that an in-patient at Broadmoor who was a schizophrenic

---

20 *Mentally Incapacitated Adults and Decision-Making: An Overview*, (1991) Consultation Paper No 119, HMSO.

had the necessary capacity to refuse consent to an operation to amputate his leg below the knee. The surgery had been recommended to prevent the further development of gangrene.

2.2   THE CURRENT LEGAL STRUCTURE

The Law Commission provides a tripartite analysis of the law as it applies to mental incapacity; health care, property and financial matters, and personal welfare.

2.2.1   Health care matters – medical treatment and personal care

In law any interference with a person's body without their consent constitutes a battery. This amounts to a civil wrong which can be compensated by an award of damages for trespass to the person; it may also amount to a criminal assault.

English law requires a valid consent to medical treatment and to any other bodily interference such as that which is part of personal care. Such a valid consent is established where:

• the consent is given voluntarily;

• the patient/service user must be able to understand what he or she has been told about the treatment or care;

• the patient/service user must have been given sufficient and appropriate information about the nature, purpose and impact of the treatment or care.

These strict legal principles are predicated upon the patient or service user having sufficient capacity to give a valid consent. This may not be possible where the patient or service user has a learning disability or is suffering from dementia or another condition which has an impact on their mental capacity. Until the case of *Re F (mental patient: sterilisation)* [1990] 2 AC 1 English law provided no procedure whereby any other person or court could take a medical or personal care decision involving bodily interference on behalf of a patient or service user without sufficient capacity. The only exception to this rule was provided by a doctrine of urgent necessity which certainly applied to medical treatment and may have also applied to personal care:

15.18 A patient can be given treatment without consent when he is incapable of giving consent because he is unconscious and is in urgent need of treatment to preserve life, health or well-being (unless there is unequivocal and reliable evidence that the patient did not want that treatment), provided that it is necessary that the treatment be administered while the patient is still unconscious.[21]

The law of wardship does not extend to adults, the treatment provisions of the Mental Health Act 1983 cover only treatment for a mental disorder, and the jurisdiction of the Court of Protection applies only to financial and property matters and did not extend to medical treatment or personal care.

The case of *Re F* involved a proposed sterilisation operation on a 36 year-old woman with learning disability to the extent that she was unable to give her consent to the operation. The High Court was asked to give a declaration that the operation would be lawful despite the absence of the patient's consent. The declaration was granted by the High Court and their decision was upheld by the Court of Appeal and the House of Lords.

In its judgments the House of Lords established the general principle that medical treatment and personal care can be administered without the consent of a patient/service user, who is unable to consent, only where such treatment or care would be in the best interests of the patient.

> ... a doctor can lawfully operate on, or give treatment to, adult persons who are incapable ... of consenting to his doing so, provided that the operation or other treatment concerned is in the best interests of such patients. The operation or other treatment will be in the best interests if, but only if, it is carried out in order either to save lives, or to ensure improvement or prevent deterioration in their physical or mental health.[22]

Lord Goff's judgment provides further guidance to the breadth of the principle:

> When the state of affairs is permanent or semi-permanent, action properly taken to preserve life, health or well-being of the assisted

---

21   *Code of Practice, Mental Health Act 1983*, (1993) Department of Health and Welsh Office.

22   From the judgment of Lord Brandon.

person may well transcend such measures as surgical operation or substantial medical treatment and may extend to include such humdrum matters as routine medical or dental treatment, even simple care such as dressing and undressing and putting to bed.

It now seems to be the law that in circumstances such as those faced daily by staff and carers in residential care homes, in nursing homes and in psychiatric hospitals, and by friends and relatives providing care at home, where the patient or service user does not have the capacity to consent, intervention in terms of medical treatment or personal care will be permitted without their consent so long as it is in the best interests of the person concerned.

Despite the articulation of the 'best interests' principle the determination of patient's or service user's capacity might still be problematic. The task of determining capacity is ultimately one for a doctor though information from carers, relatives, social workers, nurses and others should be an important element of the decision making process. It is clear that because capacity is a variable standard, an assessment of a person's capacity must be made in relation to the particular treatment or other matter proposed. Capacity may also vary over time so that an assessment of capacity should be proximate to the matter proposed. Equally every opportunity for the patient or service user to consent should be constructed so that, for example, information is given in a form that is most likely to be understood.

2.2.2 Property and financial affairs

Learning disability may mean that a service user has never had the capacity to manage his or her own financial and property affairs. Other service users, including many who are elderly, may lose this ability, physically or intellectually, through illness or disability.

The collection of social security benefits may be undertaken by a person other than the claimant, appointed as an agent. This agent may be an employee of the local authority. Social security legislation empowers the Secretary of State to appoint another person to act on behalf of a service users/claimants who are unable to act for themselves because of their mental incapacity.[23] This appointee procedure encompasses all matters relating to entitlement to benefit.

23   Social Security (Claims and Payments) Regulations 1987.

Any person with sufficient mental capacity (the donor) may establish a power of attorney under which another person (the donee) may act on their behalf. A power of attorney may be limited to certain specified matters or may be general. A power of attorney will come to an end upon the donor's loss of mental capacity.

The limited use of such powers has been addressed by the Enduring Powers of Attorney Act 1985. Any person with capacity may establish an enduring power of attorney which will come into effect upon the loss of capacity, by reason of mental disorder, of the donor, and the registration of the enduring power of attorney with the Court of Protection. Upon registration the attorney has exclusive power to administer the property and financial affairs of the donor within the terms of the power. Registration is subject to notice being given to the donor and to their nearest relatives, and to their objections.

Where a person is suffering from a mental disorder so that they are incapable of managing their own property and financial affairs, their property and other financial affairs may be managed on their behalf by the Court of Protection. The work of the court is administered on a day-to-day basis by the Public Trust Office. An application to the court will normally be made by a relative of the patient, but may be made by others such as a friend, a social worker or a solicitor. The Court will appoint a Receiver, often a relative or close friend of the patient, to manage the property and financial affairs of the patient and the Public Trustee may be appointed as the Receiver if there is no other suitable person.

The Receiver exercises the powers of a judge of the Court. These powers are established by section 95 of the Mental Health Act 1983:

(1) The judge may, with respect to the property and affairs of a patient, do or secure the doing of all such things as appear necessary or expedient–

(a) for the maintenance or other benefit of the patient,

(b) for the maintenance or other benefit of members of the patient's family,

(c) for making provision for other persons or purposes for whom or which the patient might be expected to provide if he were not mentally disordered, or

(d) otherwise for administering the patient's affairs.

Where the assets of the patient are small, and there is no need for a receiver, the Public Trustee may issue directions concerning the administration of a patient's estate.

The Law Commission has been critical of the jurisdiction and work of the Court:

> ... the jurisdiction is premised on an assumption that capacity is an all-or-nothing status. No provision is made for a partial intervention in a person's affairs, limited in scope because the person has partial or fluctuating capacity. It can be difficult for a patient to obtain a discharge, ... Nor does the Court permit a patient to execute an enduring power of attorney over any of his or her property, since this would conflict with the global approach it takes to each case ... Those to whom receivership powers are delegated must usually give security and submit detailed yearly accounts. The costs of this highly protective system are charged to patients.[24]

2.2.3 Personal welfare

Where a person with mental incapacity is at risk the Mental Health Act 1983 emergency place of safety orders may be of use.

Section 135(1) provides:

> If it appears to a justice of the peace, on information on oath laid by an approved social worker, that there is reasonable cause to suspect that a person believed to be suffering from mental disorder –
>
> (a) has been, or is being, ill-treated, neglected or kept otherwise than under proper control, in any place within the jurisdiction of the justice, or
>
> (b) being unable to care for himself, is living alone in such a place, the justice may issue a warrant authorising any constable to enter, if need be by force, any premises specified in the warrant in which that person is believed to be, and, if thought fit, to remove him to a place of safety with a view to the making of an application in respect of him under Part II of this Act, or of arrangements for his treatment or care.

---

24   *Mental Incapacity*, Law Commission No 231, (1995) at p 10.

Section 136(1) provides:

> If a constable finds in a place to which the public have access a person who appears to him to be suffering from mental disorder and to be in immediate need of care or control, the constable may, if he thinks it necessary to do so in the interests of that person or for the protection of other persons, remove that person to a place of safety within the meaning of section 135 above.

A place of safety is defined to encompass residential accommodation provided or arranged under Part III of the National Assistance Act, a mental health hospital, a police station, a mental nursing or care home, or any other suitable place.

Both sections contain a mental disorder threshold and only provide for short term place of safety powers. Neither is therefore appropriate for the long term care of vulnerable people.

Many community based services for mentally incapacitated people are provided under the range of statutory powers and duties described in 2.12, section 1 'Care in the Community'.

2.3   REFORM OF THE LAW

It is clear that the law in relation to mental incapacity needs reform. Section 1 has identified the need to reform mental health law to take account of the dominance of the switch to care and treatment in the community, and the unacceptable complexity of community care law. The Law Commission's proposals for reform of the law concerning mental incapacity were based on thorough research and consultation. However the Lord Chancellor's Department issued a Green Paper, *Who Decides? Making decisions on behalf of mentally incapacitated adults,* in December 1997 to consult on the direction and details of the Law Commission's proposals. The government has indicated its acceptance of the need for reform and it is to be hoped that a new legal framework will be legislated for in the not too distant future. If, as seems likely, the new law were to follow the Law Commission's model, then there will be increased statutory duties for social services authorities, particularly in the area of the personal welfare.

The Law Commission's original overview paper established three guiding principles which reflect the challenges of legislating in this difficult area:

(i) that people are enabled and encouraged to take for themselves those decisions which they are able to take;

(ii) that where it is necessary in their own interests or for the protection of others that someone else should take decisions on their behalf, the intervention should be as limited as possible and should be concerned to achieve what the person himself would have wanted; and

(iii) that proper safeguards should be provided against exploitation and neglect, and against physical, sexual or psychological abuse.[25]

2.3.1 Incapacity and best interests

The Law Commission has recommended a single definition of incapacity. A person is without capacity if at the material time he or she is:

(1) unable by reason of mental disability to make a decision on the matter in question, or

(2) unable to communicate a decision on that matter because he or she is unconscious or for any other reason.

The Commission's proposals establish the 'best interests' criteria as the fundamental principle for any form of substitute decision making. Consequently any decision taken on behalf of a person without capacity must be taken in their best interests.

… in deciding what is in a person's best interests regard should be had to:

(1) the ascertainable past and present wishes and feelings of the person concerned, and the factors that the person would consider if able to do so;

(2) the need to permit and encourage the person to participate, or to improve his or her ability to participate, as fully as possible in anything done for or any decision affecting him or her;

25 Consultation Paper No 119, para 4.27, quoted in *Mental Incapacity*, Law Commission No 231 (1995) HMSO.

(3) the views of other people whom it is appropriate and practicable to consult about the person's wishes and feelings and what would be in his or her best interests;

(4) whether the purpose for which any action or decision is required can be effectively achieved in a manner less restrictive of the person's freedom of action.

The Lord Chancellor's Green Paper indicates that the government supports the Commission's recommendations in principle.

2.3.2 A general authority to act reasonably

The Law Commission utilises the principle of necessity described in the judgment of Lord Goff in Re F as the basis for recommending the creation of a general authority to act reasonably in respect of people without capacity.

> ... not only (1) must there be a necessity to act when it is not practicable to communicate with the assisted person, but also (2) the action taken must be such as a reasonable person would in all the circumstances take, acting in the best interests of the assisted person.[26]

The Commission makes the following recommendation:

> ... that it should be lawful to do anything for the personal welfare or health care of a person who is, or is reasonably believed to be, without capacity in relation to the matter in question if it is in all the circumstances reasonable for it to be done by the person who does it.

The provision, which would clarify an uncertain area of law, would be subject to the best interests principle. Such a provision would be particularly important for many families and carers who are involved with the everyday care and treatment of people without mental capacity.

The Green Paper accepts the argument for establishing such a general authority, but asks for comment on the definition of such an authority.

26   *Re F (mental patient: sterilisation)* [1990] 2 AC 1, 75.

2.3.3   Continuing Powers of Attorney and a new Court of Protection

These powers, which would build on and replace Enduring Powers of Attorney, would cover matters of personal welfare, health care, property and financial affairs. An attorney acting under such a power would be under a duty to act in the best interests of the donor, and would not be allowed to undertake any acts of confinement or coercion. The operation of Continuing Powers of Attorney (CPA) would be monitored by the Court of Protection.

The Green Paper indicates the government's acceptance of the objective behind these proposals – to encourage people to take for themselves those decisions which they are capable of. However the government seeks further advice on whether the CPA should extend to health care and personal welfare matters.

2.3.4   Public law protection for vulnerable people at risk

The Law Commission has taken the child protection provisions of the Children Act as a model for its recommendations. These powers could be triggered to protect a person who is vulnerable because of their mental incapacity.

> Where a local authority have reason to believe that a vulnerable person in the area is suffering or likely to suffer significant harm or serious exploitation they shall make such enquiries as they consider necessary to enable them to decide:
>
> (1) whether the person is in fact suffering or is in such harm or exploitation and
>
> (2) if so, whether community care services should be provided or arranged or other action taken to protect the person from such harm or exploitation.

A 'vulnerable person' is defined as:

> ... any person of 16 or over who (1) is or may be in need of community care services by reason of mental or other disability, age or illness and who (2) is or may be unable to take care of himself or herself, or unable to protect himself or herself against significant harm or serious exploitation.

Harm is defined as:

> ... ill-treatment (including sexual abuse and forms of ill-treatment that
> are not physical); the impairment of, or an avoidable deterioration in,
> physical or mental health; and the impairment of physical, intellectual,
> emotional, social or behavioural development.

The duty to investigate would be supported by powers of entry
under warrant, and assessment orders. The Law Commission also
recommends the creation of a temporary protection order if the
vulnerable person is likely to be at risk unless removed and kept
in protective accommodation.

The balance between paternalism and autonomy is struck by the
recommendation that a vulnerable person with appropriate mental
capacity may refuse community care services and other protective
services and interventions. Vulnerable people without such capacity
would not be able to exercise a refusal of services or protection.

The government's Green Paper raises a number of questions concerning the need for reform in this area of law:

> The Government considers that there may be merit in some of the
> recommendations made in this area, but is not convinced that there is
> a pressing need for reform. Whilst it is important to protect vulnerable
> adults, the Government also believes that regard should be had to the
> rights of individuals to live in isolation if they choose, even if at some
> degree of risk to themselves. The question of fitness to object could
> also be very difficult to judge. A number of initiatives have been under-
> taken to address the particular problem of elder abuse, and these cannot
> yet be fully evaluated. In the light of these concerns, the government
> would particularly welcome views from local authorities, carers and
> mental health and learning disability organisations, on whether there
> is a need for legislation along the lines recommended by the Law
> Commission. If it is felt that such legislation is necessary, views would
> be welcomed on the practicalities of the proposals.[27]

2.4 CONCLUSION

The Law Commission proposes to extend the jurisdiction of the
Court of Protection so that it was able to deal with the full range of

---

27 *Who Decides? Making decisions on behalf of mentally incapacitated adults*,
(1997) Lord Chancellor's Department.

issues caused by a person's lack or loss of capacity. Such jurisdiction would encompass personal welfare, health care, financial and property matters, and would exercised through the making of single orders or the appointment of a manager.

The Law Commission's proposals were published in February 1995 together with a draft Mental Incapacity Bill. In 1996 the last government, acting through the Lord Chancellor's Department, declared that it had decided not to legislate on the basis of the Commission's proposals. This depressing decision might have reflected the fact that the government did not wish to bring such radical and potentially controversial proposals to a Parliament in which it held the slenderest of majorities. It is also possible that a significant reform of the law concerned with the interests of mentally incapable people was not perceived as being a priority.

Reform of the law as envisaged by the Law Commission's proposals would have a significant impact on the lives of mentally incapable people, and on the practice of social workers involved with this group of service users. There is no doubt that the Children Act has had a huge impact on social work with children and families; it is entirely possible that the legislating of the Mental Incapacity Bill would have a similar impact on social work with mentally incapable adults. The proposals of the Law Commission were well researched and developed with the assistance of significant professional and expert consultation. The law needs reform and the publication of the current Lord Chancellor's Green Paper is to be welcomed as an indication that the argument for reform of the law has now been accepted by government. It is also to be hoped that legislation will reflect the principles of the Law Commission's work so that the interests of this important group of service users will be properly protected and promoted.

3 CASE STUDIES

Here are a number of case studies which can be used to consolidate work done on mental health law. They concentrate on areas of practice in which approved social workers will be involved.

1. Mike is a frequent cannabis user with a history of psychiatric illness. He often sleeps rough. You are an approved social worker and you have dealt with Mike on a number of occasions. You

have formed the opinion that he needs in-patient treatment for his illness and treatment for his drug use. He is very reluctant to enter any psychiatric hospital having been assaulted whilst a voluntary patient last year. He has recently disappeared and you suspect that he is living with a number of addicts in a local squat which is known to you. You have serious fears about his well-being. His family live in the town but have declined to get involved on previous occasions.

What powers are available to you under the Mental Health Act 1983 to deal with this situation?

2.   Sonia is 20 and is learning disabled. She has lived at home all her life and has been cared for by her mother. She attends a day centre but her behaviour has recently become increasingly erratic and aggressive and the workers at the centre have expressed doubts about her being able to continue there. You are an approved social worker and on duty in the area office when you receive a phone call from the centre telling you that Sonia has attacked two of the workers with a pair of scissors and has now locked herself in the toilet and refuses to come out.

In what way, if at all, are your powers under the Mental Health Act relevant to Sonia's condition?

3.   Ricky, is 24 and has been receiving community care services for a number of years. He has a long criminal record for petty theft and burglary. He has been severely depressed since he was 18 and has been in the local psychiatric hospital on a number of occasions as a voluntary patient but has always discharged himself after a few days. Yesterday Ricky was arrested by the police and has been charged with yet another burglary. He came to see you this morning having been released on bail by the police and says that he wants to go into hospital and get himself 'properly sorted out for once and for all'. He has said this before and you know that the hospital will not accept him as a voluntary patient again. You have just received a phone call from Ricky's solicitor who says that her client is going to plead guilty and that he may well receive a custodial sentence unless something can be done to persuade the court to keep him out of prison.

Discuss how you, as a local authority social worker might work with Ricky both in the short and longer term.

4. Roy has been convicted by the Crown Court on the charge of grievious bodily harm. The court has received reports from Roy's social worker and his psychiatrist which identify the fact that Roy is suffering from schizophrenia. What sentencing and disposal powers does the court have?

5. Robby is 36 and has a learning disability. He takes things from shops and is well known to the police though he does not appreciate that this amounts to stealing or that stealing is a crime. He has just been arrested by the police for stealing toys from Woolworths and they have rung you as Robby's social worker to tell you that this time he will be charged and the papers passed to the Crown Prosecution Service. How might you intervene to protect Robby's interests?

6. Richard has a long history of petty offending though he has never been given a custodial penalty. Three years ago he was diagnosed, during a remand for psychiatric reports, as suffering from schizophrenia. Since his diagnosis he has been a voluntary patient on two occasions and has been successfully treated and subsequently discharged. He is currently living in bed and breakfast accommodation and has begun drinking to excess. When he gets drunk he has a tendency to get agitated though up to now he has only one conviction for violence.

The police have been called to a disturbance outside Richard's flat. He is shouting and swearing.

a) What rights do the police have under the Mental Health Act 1983 to deal with such a situation?

b) In the event that Richard is taken to the police station for questioning, what protections are available to him.

c) In the event that you, as an approved social worker, are asked to assess Richard for a possible admission to hospital, identify the issues that will need to be considered before such a decision can be made.

d) Does Richard satisfy the statutory criteria for a compulsory admission?

e) In the event that the incident outside his flat involves a serious assault by Richard on a neighbour and he is brought before the courts on a charge of grievous bodily harm, how might he be diverted from the criminal justice system at this stage?

f)   Is diversion an appropriate response to the situation in which a person with a mental disorder commits a criminal offence?

g)   If Richard were convicted of the offence and sentenced to a hospital order how might he secure his release from hospital?

h)   Three months after his detention in hospital, the RMO concludes that Richard could be released if made subject to compulsory after-care. How might this be established? Does Richard fulfill the statutory criteria?

i)   What sanctions can be applied to Richard if he is made subject to such an order and he fails to comply with its conditions?

7.   Christopher has schizophrenia. He is due to be discharged from hospital next week having been detained under section 3 of the Mental Health Act 1983 four months ago. Under medication his condition has improved significantly since his admission.

a)   What after care duties apply to Christopher? What sort of services should be provided for him? Indicate the statutory basis for the provision of these services.

b)   Two weeks after his discharge Christopher is arrested by the police for assaulting a person in a pub fight. What provisions apply to his detention and questioning in the police station?

c)   Three weeks later Christopher has stopped taking his medication, he is sleeping rough and is displaying anti-social and aggressive behaviour; he is in possession of crack cocaine. What powers do the police have to take him to a place of safety?

d)   In the event that he is charged with possession of a controlled drug and makes his first appearance in court, can he be diverted at this stage; if so, how might this be achieved?

e)   Christopher has been diverted into the psychiatric system by a civil admission under section 3. He was admitted 2 weeks ago and is refusing his medication. Can he be treated against his wishes? Would your answer be different in three months' time?

f) Explain the system of supervised discharge orders. Would Christopher's interests be better protected if he were subject to such an order?

8. Paula has schizophrenia and has been detained for treatment under the Mental Health Act 1983. Her RMO has concluded that she could be discharged from her section in the near future.

Identify the statutory assessment and after-care duties that apply in such a case and outline the contents of an appropriate care plan and/or care programme for Paula.

She is 38, has no living relatives and no accommodation of her own.

9. Geoff is a detained patient under section 3 of the MHA. His RMO has suggested to Geoff that ECT might help his long term depressive illness.

What consent provisions apply? Would your answers be any different if Geoff were an informal patient?

10. Peter is 73 years old and is living in an independent sector residential care home. He is becoming increasingly confused and is regularly drawing money from his small building society account and offering it to the staff in the home. He hides food in his room, telling his son that he will need it when 'the war starts'. He can no longer get down to the post office to draw his pension and income support and he has no idea about paying for his care from his benefit.

a) His son asks you for an explanation of the possible legal arrangements that can be made for his father.

b) Consider the situation if Peter were in good physical and mental health but is concerned that in the near future he may begin to lose his mental faculties and not be able to manage his personal and financial affairs.

c) Provide answers to both a) and b) that reflect the current law AND indicate what the answer might be if the Law Commission's draft Mental Incapacity Bill were to be implemented.

4 ACTIVITIES

Here are a number of activities which are suggested to increase knowledge and experience of social work practice within the context of mental health law. The information collected can be used to expand any existing collection of materials.

1. Get hold of a copy of the Mental Health Act Code of Practice published by the Department of Health and the Welsh Office in 1993.

2. Write to MIND (National Association for Mental Health) for a copy of their publications list and any other materials they distribute.

3. Obtain a series of free leaflets available from the Court of Protection giving information about its work.

4. Within the context of community care mental health, what services are provided by a partnership of health authorities, local authority social services and housing departments, and by the voluntary sector? Get hold of a copy of the Community Care Plan published by your local authority.

5. Obtain copies of the forms used for applications for admission to hospital under the provisions of the Mental Health Act 1983. These will help in understanding the process and the procedures that must be gone through before someone can be admitted to hospital compulsorily.

6. Design a 'flow chart' or other diagram to explain the admissions process and the role of the approved social worker and the nearest relative.

7. Identify the services that are available for people with a mental incapacity. Do these services strike a proper balance between the principles of paternalism and autonomy?

8. Contact Age Concern to get hold of copies of relevant fact sheets, eg Local Authority Charging Procedures for Residential and Nursing Home Care; and Finding Residential and Nursing Home Accommodation.

9. Contact MENCAP for a publication list.

5 ADDRESSES

Alzheimer's Disease Society
Gordon House
10 Greencoat Place
London SW1P 1PH.
Phone: 0171 306 0606
Fax: 0171 306 0808
E-mail: 101762.422@compuserve.com
Web: www.vois.org.uk/alzheimers

MENCAP
123 Golden Lane
London EC1Y 0RT.
Phone: 0171 454 0454
Fax: 0171 608 3254

MIND. National Association for Mental Health
Granta House
15-19 Broadway
London E15 4BQ.
Phone: 0181 519 2122

National Schizophrenia Fellowship
28 Castle Street
Kingston upon Thames
Surrey KT1 1SS.
Phone: 0181 547 3937
Fax: 0181 547 3862
Advice line: 0181 974 6814
E-mail: Info@nsf.org.uk
Web: www.nsf.org.uk

SANE
199 Old Marylebone Road
London NW1 5QP.
Phone: 0171 724 6520
Saneline London: 0171 724 8000
Saneline outside London: 0345 67 8000
Web: MKN.co/help/charity.sane/index

Schizophrenia Association of Great Britain
Bryn Hyfryd

The Crescent
Bangor
Gwynedd LL57 2AG.
Phone/Fax: 01248 354048
E-mail: Sagb@btinternet.com
Web: www.btinternet.com/~sagb

The Mental Health Act Commission
Maid Marion House
56 Hounds Gate
Nottingham, NG1 6BG.
Phone: 01602 504040
Fax: 01602 505998

The Court of Protection
The Public Trust Office
Protection Division
Stewart House
24 Kingsway
London WC2B 6JX.
Phone: 0171 269 7000
Fax: 0171 404 1725

6 MATERIALS

Ashton, G and Ward, G, *Mental Handicap*, (1992) Sweet and Maxwell.

Clements, L, *Community Care and the Law*, (1996) Legal Action, 1997

Cohen, J and Ramon, J, *Social Work and the Mental Health Act 1983*, Macmillan and BASW.

Fish, D, *Community Care: duties towards mentally ill people and their families*, Legal Action November 1995 and May 1996.

Gostin, L, *A Practical Guide to Mental Health Law*, (1983) MIND.

Griffiths, A and Roberts, G (eds), *The Law and Elderly People*, (1995) Routledge.

Hoggett, B, *Mental Health Law*, (1996) Sweet and Maxwell.

Jones, R, *Mental Health Act Manual*, (1996) Sweet and Maxwell.

O'May, N and Biggs, N, *Mentally disordered offenders*, Legal Action, January 1993.

Prins, H, *Can the Law Serve as a Solution to Social Ills? The Case of the Mental Health (Patients in the Community) Act 1995*, Medicine, Science and the Law (1996) Vol 36, No 3.

Age Concern Factsheets, eg No 22 Legal arrangements for managing financial affairs; No 29 Finding residential and nursing home accommodation.

Building Bridges, (1995) Department of Health.

Dealing with the Estates of People Suffering from Mental Disorder, Public Trust Office.

Enduring Powers of Attorney, (1995) Public Trust Office.

Handbook for Receivers, Public Trust Office.

Mental Health Act Code of Practice, Department of Health and the Welsh Office (1993).

Mental Health Act Commission, Biennial Reports, HMSO.

Mental Incapacity, Law Commission No 231, (1995) HMSO.

MIND Rights Guides 1-4: Civil Admission and Discharge; Patients Involved in Criminal Proceedings; Your Rights in Hospital; Mental Health Review Tribunals.

CHAPTER 8

The criminal justice system

1 INTRODUCTION

1.1 SOCIAL WORK INVOLVEMENT IN THE CRIMINAL JUSTICE SYSTEM

Social work involvement in the adult criminal justice system centres on the work of the probation service. Other social workers may also have service users who are facing a criminal prosecution, are victims of a crime or are seeking to discharge a sentence of the court such as a fine. This chapter, which is concerned with the adult criminal justice system,[1] will provide information specifically concerned with probation work but will also give an outline of the jurisdiction of the criminal courts and of criminal procedure. The sentencing options of the courts will be discussed and the principles of sentencing outlined. The chapter does not provide a comprehensive discussion of probation work.

Whilst the probation service provides specialist social work skills in the criminal justice system the involvement of other social workers most often takes place vicariously through service users. For practitioners to give service users the information and support they may need as they face the criminal justice system it is necessary to have a reasonable knowledge of the system. For example: does the service user know at what stage they are in the system; do they know what might happen next; do they appreciate the significance of what has happened; should they be legally represented; can they appeal?

1.2 REFORM OF THE SYSTEM

The criminal justice system has always been the site of political controversy with public concern centering on crime rates and

---

1   Defendants between the ages of 10 and 17 inclusive are dealt with in the youth court.

sentencing practice, and government policy concerning itself with the costs of the system and the image of the 'law and order' industry. Other issues, such as the public accountability of the police and the nature and impact of policing policies, continue to interest commentators on the criminal justice system.

Change is a characteristic of the criminal justice system. Since the beginning of this decade there has been a series of important new legislation, eg the Criminal Justice Act 1991, importantly amended by the Criminal Justice Act 1993, the Criminal Justice and Public Order Act 1994, the Crime (Sentences) Act 1997, the Protection from Harassment Act 1997. This trend of frequent and significant change in the law looks set to continue with the government determined to radically reform the youth justice system and other parts of the criminal justice system through the provisions of the Crime and Disorder Bill 1997. It reflects the importance of criminal justice within the political agenda of both government and opposition, and within the concerns of the media. The increased politicisation of criminal justice, and the rate of change, is a matter of some concern, particularly for those working within the administration of criminal justice who are confronted with a system in an almost permanent state of change. Despite this the development of models of good practice has continued with the publication of National Standards for the Supervision of Offenders in the Community establishing a comprehensive standard for significant aspects of the work of the probation service and others working with offenders in the community.

1.3 PRINCIPLES OF CRIMINAL JUSTICE AND CRIMINAL LAW

Most criminal offences have two elements which have to be established for a defendant to be found guilty. The prosecution must establish both the actus reus, the commission of the criminal act, and the mens rea, the necessary criminal intent. There are, however, a number of offences, which are described as strict liability offences, where a criminal intent is not required as an element of the crime, eg going through a red traffic light.

There is a presumption of innocence in the criminal law. A defendant is innocent of a charge until s/he has been proved guilty. The burden of proof is therefore on the prosecution who must prove their allegations beyond a reasonable doubt. The Criminal Justice and

Public Order Act 1994 introduced important changes in the law relating to what is known as the 'right to silence'. Since the implementation of the Act an accused person may continue to choose to remain silent during questioning or at their trial; however if they choose to do so the court (jury or magistrates) may draw appropriate inferences from the accused's silence.

Criminal procedure in the English legal system is adversarial in character. This means that any trial is by way of a contest between the prosecution and the defence in which the prosecution is seeking to establish its allegations by evidence and the defence is seeking to undermine the worth of the allegations and the evidence. There is no objective finding of truth by the court which has to rely on the prosecution and the defence for the evidence on which it must make a decision. If the prosecution is unable to bring evidence of its allegations the case must be dismissed.

2 THE LAW

2.1 THE CATEGORIES OF CRIMINAL OFFENCES

Criminal prosecutions are decided in either the magistrates' courts or the Crown Courts. The venue will depend on the type of offence and in certain circumstances on the choice of the defendant.

2.1.1 Summary offences

These are the least serious criminal offences and they can only be dealt with in the magistrates' courts.

2.1.2 Either way offences

Such offences may be tried in the magistrates' court or in the Crown Court. The venue for trial will be decided in the magistrates' court and is subject to the 'plea before venue' procedure introduced by section 49 of the Criminal Procedure and Investigations Act 1996. This procedure allows a defendant to indicate whether they will plead guilty or not guilty before the decision is taken on whether the trial should be in the magistrates' court or the Crown Court. Where a guilty plea is indicated the magistrates will deal with the case themselves, or commit the defendant to the Crown Court for sentence where they do not consider their sentencing powers to be sufficient.

Where the defendant indicates a not guilty plea, or no plea, then the magistrates proceed to what is called a 'mode of trial' hearing in which brief facts of the allegation will be given to the magistrates and they will decide whether the case is suitable to be heard by them or whether the nature of the allegation or their limited powers of sentencing require that it be heard by the Crown Court. If the magistrates decide to 'accept jurisdiction' then the defendants must decide whether they wish the case to be heard at the magistrates' court or at the Crown Court. In such circumstances defendants are therefore able to choose to be tried by a judge and jury, or by the magistrates.

2.1.3 Indictable offences

These are the most serious criminal offences and they can only be tried in the Crown Court. In relation to such offences magistrates have a preliminary jurisdiction to commit the case to the Crown Court. In essence a committal hearing is designed to establish that the prosecution have a case of sufficient worth for the defence to have to answer the allegation. In practice most committals these days are completed by the prosecution serving the case papers on the court and the defence, and the magistrates announcing to the defendants that they are committed for trial at the Crown Court.

2.2 BAIL

The issue of bail is of fundamental importance for the refusal of bail means that a person is deprived of their liberty despite a presumption of innocence. Initially bail is granted or refused by a senior police officer but as soon as a defendant appears in court for the first time the issue is one for the court. The Criminal Justice and Public Order Act 1994 gives the police powers to impose conditions on the grant of bail where the officer believes that such conditions are necessary to prevent the accused failing to surrender to bail, committing further offences whilst on bail, or interfering with witnesses.

The Bail Act 1976 provides that a person charged with an imprisonable offence shall be granted bail unless one of the exceptions
specified in the Act is established. These are:

> ... there are substantial grounds for believing that the accused would,
> if released on bail:
>
> i) fail to surrender to custody; or
>
> ii) commit an offence while on bail; or
>
> iii) interfere with witnesses or otherwise obstruct the course of justice,
>   whether in relation to himself or any other person.

Bail may be granted unconditionally or subject to conditions such
as residence or a surety designed to ensure that grounds set out in
the Bail Act are not broken. Where bail is refused the defendant will
be remanded in custody. Because bail is such an important issue
defendants should be legally represented where there is a chance that
they could be remanded in custody following an unsuccessful bail
application. Such representation may be provided by the duty
solicitor where a defendant does not have his or her own solicitor.
Where a defendant is refused bail by the magistrates they may apply
to a Crown Court judge for bail.

The Bail (Amendment) Act 1993 gave the Crown Prosecution Service
limited rights to appeal against a bail decision made in the magistrates' courts. The Criminal Justice and Public Order Act 1994
provides for an automatic remand in custody for those charged with
murder, manslaughter or rape who have previously been convicted
of such offences. The presumption in favour of bail does not extend
to those charged with murder, manslaughter, rape, attempted murder
or attempted rape.

A number of probation committees provide bail hostels though the
availability of hostel places varies throughout the country and the
conditions of acceptance are often very specific. Nonetheless the availability of a place in a probation hostel is often influential in persuading
magistrates to grant bail with a condition of residence at the hostel.
Probation services will also be involved in the provision of bail information
to the Crown Prosecution Service. This information may be crucial in
the decision of the CPS to oppose or support bail. This work is governed
by a National Standard for Bail Information Schemes.

2.3 PRE-TRIAL PROCEDURE

The prosecution of minor summary offences may be dealt with in a single court hearing without the need for the defendant to be represented. However, in many cases an adjournment of the proceedings may be needed so that the defendant's solicitor can take instructions from his or her client. Such adjournments may be for a short period of time enabling the case to progress on the same day or for a week or more where such time is necessary for the defence solicitor to consider the strength of the prosecution's case as disclosed by 'advance disclosure' and to take appropriate instructions from the defendant. The defence is entitled to advanced disclosure from the prosecution in all either way and indictable offences. On the basis of such instructions, and the legal advice given, the defendant will plead guilty or not guilty to the allegation as put by the prosecution.

A plea of not guilty means that a date for trial must be fixed and the proceedings adjourned so that witnesses may attend court to give evidence. Upon any adjournment of a case where the offence is imprisonable, the issue of bail will need to be decided. If the defence in an either way matter decides to opt for a jury trial the case must be committed for trial at the Crown Court and the arrangements for such a hearing will normally require another adjournment.

In indictable offences the pre-trial procedure will be the same as for an either way offence where the defence opts for a jury trial except there will be no mode of trial hearing. It should be borne in mind that the more serious the offence the more likely it is that bail will be a contested issue.

This very brief outline of the pre-trial procedures will serve to show that it is only in the simplest matters that a defendant will appear in court, have the allegation put to them, plead guilty and be sentenced at one hearing. Criminal prosecutions can often be protracted matters particularly where there is a trial, a finding of guilt and a request for pre-sentence reports.

2.4 THE CRIMINAL TRIAL

2.4.1 The magistrates' court

The majority of prosecutions in the magistrates' courts are conducted by the Crown Prosecution Service. A trial will be opened by the crown prosecutor outlining the allegations to a bench of lay magistrates or to a single stipendiary magistrate. The evidence to sustain the allegations will be presented by prosecution witnesses who will be taken through their evidence by the crown prosecutor. Once they have given their evidence each prosecution witness will be available to be cross-examined by the advocate for the defence. After cross-examination the prosecution may re-examine their witnesses and the magistrate(s) may question witnesses to clarify issues of doubt in the evidence they have given. The case for the prosecution will close when all their witnesses have given their evidence and any cross-examination and re-examination has taken place.

At the end of the case for the prosecution the defence may address the magistrate(s) on the basis that the prosecution have failed to make out a case for the defence to answer. This will be the situation for example, where the defence is of the opinion that the evidence brought by the prosecution fails to establish either of the elements, the actus reus or mens rea, of the crime. If the magistrate(s) agrees then the case will be dismissed at this stage. If they reject this application by the defence the case continues with the evidence of the defence witnesses. Again each witness is available to be cross-examined by the crown prosecutor and may be re-examined by the defence advocate.

When all the evidence has been presented the defence will address the magistrate(s) on the evidence, the burden of proof and points of law if necessary. The prosecution may also address the magistrate(s) on points of law. The magistrate(s) will normally retire to make their decision on the facts as they find them and on the law which will be explained to them by their clerk. If they find the defendant not guilty that is the end of the matter, unless the issue of costs needs to be decided, and the defendant is free to leave the court. If the finding is one of guilt the offender (as s/he now is) must be sentenced for the offence. The options available to the magistrate(s) are considered below but prior to sentence the defence advocate may wish to address the magistrate(s) in mitigation of the offender and the crown prosecution will provide information about the offender's criminal record, if any.

The magistrate(s) may decide, and in some circumstances must decide, to adjourn for the preparation of reports before deciding upon the sentence. Pre-sentence reports, which are prepared by the probation service, may be supplemented by psychiatric or other reports.

2.4.2   The Crown Court

In essence the procedure of a trial in the Crown Court is the same as that in the magistrates' court though for those involved it is a very different experience. A defendant who pleads not guilty to a charge in the Crown Court will be tried by a jury. The first task is therefore to choose a jury; their task is to decide the question of guilt on the basis of the evidence presented and the law as explained to them by the judge. In the Crown Court the judge decides questions of law while the jury decides questions of fact.

The presentation of evidence by witnesses and their cross-examination and re-examination is essentially the same as in the magistrates' court though the questioning is done by barristers instructed by defence solicitors and by the Crown Prosecution Service, and it proceeds much more slowly. At the end of the presentation of evidence both the prosecution and defence will address the jury. The judge will then direct the jury by explaining the law and by reviewing the evidence. The jury will retire to reach a verdict. Juries are expected to reach a unanimous verdict though if that proves impossible the judge may be willing to accept a majority (10–2) verdict.

If the jury find the defendant not guilty that is the end of the matter except for the issue of costs. A finding of guilt means that the judge must consider the question of sentence. Again it may be necessary to adjourn the case for the preparation of reports as in the magistrates' court. Maximum sentences are set by Parliament but judges have considerable discretion in the choice and severity of sentence. The Crime (Sentences) Act 1997 has restricted that discretion in the sense that it specifies mandatory sentences for second serious violent or sexual offences (life), and a minimum of at least seven years for a third offence of class A drug trafficking.

2.5   SENTENCING IN THE ADULT CRIMINAL COURTS

The Criminal Justice Act 1991 is the major piece of legislation concerning sentencing in the criminal courts. Despite being declared as a 'coherent statutory framework for sentencing which is based on a coherent set of principles'[2] the legislative framework for

---

2   John Patten MP, Minister of State, Home Office 'The Criminal Justice Act 1991', 23 November 1991, Justice of the Peace.

sentencing has been supplemented by the Criminal Justice Act 1993, which amended the 1991 Act, the Criminal Justice and Public Order Act 1994 and by the Crime (Sentences) Act 1997.

The Guide to the Act identifies six principles that form the basis of the Act and therefore should determine the sentencing practice of the criminal courts and influence the practice of those working within the criminal justice system:[3]

(i) the severity of the sentence in an individual case should reflect primarily the seriousness of the offence which has been committed. Whilst factors such as preventing crime or the rehabilitation of the offender remain important functions of the criminal justice process as a whole, they should not lead to a heavier penalty in an individual case than that which is justified by the seriousness of the offence or the need to protect the public from the offender;

(ii) a sharper distinction than hitherto should be drawn between property offences and offences against the person – that is crimes of a sexual or violent nature. The Act recognises that additional restrictions may need to be placed on the liberty of a sexual or violent offender in order to protect the public from serious harm from the offender;

(iii) the procedures for administering sentences once they have been imposed should be both rigorous and fair so as to ensure that the sentencer's intentions are properly reflected in the way in which the sentence is served;

(iv) community penalties should play a full part in their own right in the structure of penalties. They should not be viewed as 'alternatives to custody';

(v) the way in which young people are dealt with in the criminal justice system should more closely reflect their age and development, as should the extent to which their parents should be expected to take responsibility for their actions;

(vi) criminal justice services should be administered as efficiently as possible, and without discrimination on improper grounds, particularly those of race and sex.

---

3   A full quotation from the Home Office Guide to the Act, paragraph 1.2 is
    provided here.

The link between the seriousness of the offence and the severity of the punishment, sometimes known as the principle of proportionality or 'just deserts' has the impact of shifting the emphasis of sentencing policy away from the overt objectives of crime prevention and rehabilitation and firmly toward the principle of sentencing to punish. The explicit distinction that is made between offences against property and violent or sexual offences is important, for in respect of offences against the person the Act recognises that the principle of sentencing to fit the seriousness of the crime may not be sufficient to provide proper protection to the public and provides for more severe sentencing when such protection is necessary. Community sentences are recognised by the Act as a category of sentences in their own right and not as alternatives to custody.

The Act establishes that sentences under the Act are to be understood in terms of their restriction on liberty. Custody clearly falls within this notion and fines may be seen as restricting the offender's liberty to choose how his or her resources are spent. Community sentences are required by section 6(2) to be 'such as in the opinion of the court are commensurate with the seriousness of the offence' and should also be understood as restricting liberty.

The Act can be understood to provide for three categories of sentence, discharges (absolute and conditional) and fines, community sentences and custody. The principle of sentencing commensurate with the seriousness of the offence operates across the range of sentences so that a community sentence can be imposed only if the offence concerned is serious enough to justify the level of restriction of liberty involved in complying with the sentence. Equally custody can be ordered only where the offence is so serious that only a custodial sentence can be justified for it or where the offence is a violent or sexual offence so that only a custodial sentence would provide adequate protection for the public from serious harm from the offender.

When a court imposes a community sentence it must be satisfied, in addition to the requirement that the sentence is commensurate with the seriousness of the offence, that the particular sentence chosen is also the most suitable for the offender.

In deciding the seriousness of an offence the court must take account of all aggravating and mitigating circumstances. Section 28(1) provides that in mitigating a sentence the court may take into account any matters which it considers to be relevant. The same section allows the sentencing court when it is sentencing an offender for more than one offence to consider the total impact of the orders.

Section 29 deals with the effect of previous convictions and of offending while on bail. When a court is considering the seriousness of any offence it may take previous convictions of the offender into account, and any failure of the offender to respond to previous sentences. The court is under a duty to treat the commission of an offence whilst on bail as an aggravating factor.

The sentencing principles of the Act will shape the sentencing practice of the criminal courts and therefore must be taken into account in the preparation of pre-sentence reports by the probation service.

2.6 SENTENCES AVAILABLE IN THE ADULT COURT

2.6.1 Discharges and financial penalties

Absolute and conditional discharges

An absolute discharge is a decision by the court, following a plea of guilty or a finding of guilt, that no punishment is necessary. A conditional discharge is a decision by the court that it will not impose a sentence for the offence committed on condition that the offender commits no further offence during the period of discharge (a maximum of three years). Should a further offence be committed during that period the offender is liable to be sentenced for the original as well as the subsequent offence.

Fines

Section 18 of the Criminal Justice Act 1991 provides general rules for the fixing of fines:

• the court is required to enquire into the financial circumstances of the offender before setting the level of fine;

• the amount of the fine shall reflect the seriousness of the offence;

• in fixing the amount of any fine the court is required to take into account the circumstances of the case including the financial circumstances of the offender so far as they are known or appear to the court; (this provision applies irrespective of whether it has the effect of increasing or reducing the amount of the fine).

The same factors will also be relevant in fixing the terms upon which the fine is to be paid. Fines can be paid at regularly periods over an extended period though this should not normally be more than twelve months.

Fines are generally unlimited in the Crown Court. In the magistrates' courts maximum fines are subject to a structure of offence levels currently set at:

Level 1 – £100

Level 2 – £200

Level 3 – £1,000

Level 4 – £2,500

Level 5 – £5,000.

The Act provides that fines may be recovered by the attachment of income support subject to a maximum deduction.[4] Other means of payment and enforcement are available; attachment of earnings, distress warrants, and money payment supervision orders. The ultimate means of enforcement is committal to prison where the court has determined that non-payment is due to wilful refusal or culpable neglect.

Compensation orders

Financial orders to compensate the victims of crime may be made together with other sentences or as an order in its own right. By the Powers of Criminal Courts Act 1973 courts are under a duty to give reasons for not making a compensation order when they have an opportunity to do so. Where an offender has limited means a

---

4   It is presumed that this power also now applies to income-based job seekers' allowance.

compensation order will take precedence over a fine as a sentence choice and in payment. The value of a compensation order should reflect the loss of the victim but must also take the offender's means to pay into account. There is no limit to the amount of a compensation order made in the Crown Court; in the magistrates' courts the limit is £5,000.

2.6.2 Community sentences

Probation

A probation order may be made on adult offenders for a minimum of six months and a maximum of three years. The offender need not consent to the order. Section 8(1) of the Criminal Justice Act 1991 substitutes a new section 2 into the Powers of Criminal Courts Act 1973 specifying the conditions for making a probation order:

> ... supervision of the offender by a probation officer is desirable in the interests of –

> a) securing the rehabilitation of the offender; or

> b) protecting the public from harm from him or preventing the commission by him of further offences.

There are now six types of additional requirements which may be included in an order: residence; to refrain from or take part in specified activities; attend a probation centre; a requirement that sexual offenders take part in specified activities or attend a probation centre; to submit to treatment for a mental condition; to submit to treatment for drug or alcohol dependency.

Community service

Such an order is available as a sentence for an imprisonable offence and requires the offender to undertake unpaid work for the community. Orders can vary between 40 hours and 240 hours work to be completed in one year and are carried out under the supervision of a community service organiser. National Standards identify the objective of such orders to be the re-integration of the offender into the community through positive and demanding unpaid work and reparation to the community.

Combination order

This order, introduced by section 11 of the Criminal Justice Act 1991, combines probation supervision and community service. The Home Office's General Guide to the Act sets out the thinking behind this order:

> The combination order is intended for offenders who the courts believe should make some reparation to the community, through a community service order, and who also need probation supervision to tackle problems that underlie their offending and thus to reduce the risk of further offending in the future. Given the considerable restriction on liberty inherent in a combination order, such an order will be appropriate for amongst the most serious offenders likely to be given a community sentence.

The order is available for offenders who have committed an imprisonable offence. The probation element is for a minimum of twelve months and a maximum of three years and the community service element for between 40 and 100 hours.

Attendance centre order

Attendance centre orders may be made on offenders under the age of 21. The minimum sentence is for 12 hours and the maximum for 36 hours. The order is served by attendance at the centre, normally on a Saturday afternoon, to undertake directed activities in a disciplined environment usually run by the police. Such orders cannot be made where there is no centre geographically available for the offender to attend.

Curfew orders

This order was introduced by section 12 of the Criminal Justice Act 1991 which also provides, by section 13, for such orders to be electronically monitored by 'tagging'. The order is for a minimum of two hours and a maximum of twelve hours a day; it may be made for any period up to six months. The order, which requires the offender to be in a specified place at and for a specified time, cannot be made unless the offender is willing to comply with it. (These orders are not yet in force.)

Pre-sentence reports

The sentencing court must obtain a pre-sentence report from a probation officer before it can make a probation order with additional requirements, a community service order or a combination order. The Criminal Justice and Public Order Act 1994 has modified this rule to the extent that the Crown Court need not order a report in the case of an indictable only offence if the court considers it unnecessary in all the circumstances, or in all other cases if there is a previous report available to be considered.

The preparation of such reports is covered by the National Standards for the Supervision of Offenders in the Community which specify that a report should address the current offence, relevant information about the offender, a conclusion and where relevant, a proposal for the most suitable community sentence.

Enforcing and revoking community sentences

Offenders who breach the requirements of a community sentence may be fined up to a maximum of £1,000, or receive up to 60 hours community service, or be given an attendance centre order if they are under 21. If the court is of the opinion that the breach is serious it may revoke the original order and sentence anew for the original offence. Where the court finds that the offender has wilfully and persistently failed to comply with the order then the court may assume that the offender has not consented to a community order thus leaving the offender liable to a custodial sentence.

The commission of a further offence whilst an offender is serving a community sentence does not, in itself, constitute a breach of the order but may be the basis for revoking the order and re-sentencing for the original offence.

Community orders may be revoked in the interests of justice and Schedule 2 of the 1991 Act specifies that a probation order may be revoked under this provision on the grounds of the good progress of the offender. Applications for the revocation of community orders may be made by the offender subject to the order or by the supervising officer.

2.6.3 Custodial sentences

Custodial sentences for summary and either way offences can only be imposed after the court has obtained a pre-sentence report. In the case of indictable only offences the court must obtain a pre-sentence report unless, in the circumstances of the case, the court considers it is unnecessary. The court must consider and take into account the contents of the report, other information about the offence and the offender that is available, including aggravating and mitigating factors, before deciding on sentence.

Section 1 of the Criminal Justice Act 1991 sets out the criteria which must be met for a custodial sentence to be imposed:

(2) Subject to subsection (3) below, the court shall not pass a custodial sentence on the offender unless it is of the opinion

a) that the offence, or the combination of the offence and one or more offences associated with it, was so serious that only such a sentence can be justified for the offence; or

b) where the offence is a violent or sexual offence, that only such a sentence would be adequate to protect the public from serious harm from him.

(3) Nothing in subsection (2) above shall prevent the court from passing a custodial sentence on the offender if he fails to express his willingness to comply with a requirement which is proposed by the court to be included in a probation order or a supervision order and which requires an expression of such willingness.

In reaching its conclusion that the offence is so serious that only a custodial sentence can be justified, the sentencing court may take into account one or more associated offence. Such offences are defined by section 31(2) to cover:

a) the offender is convicted of it in the proceedings in which he is convicted of the other offence, or (although convicted of it in earlier proceedings) is sentenced for it at the same time as he is sentenced for that offence; or

b) the offender admits the commission of it in proceedings in which he is sentenced for the other offence and requests the court to take it into consideration in sentencing him for that offence.

Section 3 sets out a number of procedures that must be gone through before it can impose a custodial sentence. In reaching the conclusion that an offence is so serious that only a custodial sentence is justified the court is required to take aggravating and mitigating factors into account. When deciding that a custodial sentence is necessary to protect the public from serious harm from a violent or sexual offender, the court may take into account any information it has about the offender. The court is required to obtain a pre-sentence report and consider its contents before making either of these two decisions, though there is no obligation to do so in indictable only cases where the court considers that it is unnecessary to have a report.

Section 4 sets out additional requirements to safeguard the interests of offenders who have a mental disorder.

In cases where custody is a possible sentence the pre-sentence report is particularly important. Such a report will contain information concerning aggravating and mitigating factors surrounding the commission of the offence. The Guide to the Criminal Justice Act 1991, published by the Home Office, in the section on Custodial Sentences and the Sentencing Framework, suggests factors which should be considered by the court and which must therefore be canvassed in a pre-sentence report: '... the presence or absence of pre-meditation, or whether the offender was the ringleader or a junior partner in the crime'. Such reports must cover the issue of the risk of harm to the public posed by a violent or sexual offender.

Courts may impose suspended custodial sentences under the amended provisions of section 22 of the Powers of Criminal Courts Act 1973. The power to suspend is limited to cases where custody is firstly an appropriate sentence and suspension can be justified by the exceptional circumstances of the case. The second criterion can only come into play if the first criterion is satisfied. Where a court suspends custody it must consider whether to additionally impose a fine or compensation order. Custodial sentences on offenders under 21 cannot be suspended.

2.7 THE CRIMINAL JUSTICE WORK OF THE PROBATION SERVICE

The probation service was first put on a statutory footing by the Probation of Offenders Act 1907. It now employs approximately 6,500 probation officers, most of whom have a social work qualification. It is funded largely by the Home Office and is administered locally by committees comprising magistrates, local authority representatives, a Crown Court judge and other co-opted members.

The duties of the probation service are now consolidated in the Probation Service Act 1993. Probation officers provide a number of services which derive from responsibilities identified in the Probation Service Three Year Plan 1994–97:

- To provide the courts with advice and information on offenders to assist in sentencing decisions.

- To implement community sentences passed by the courts.

- To design, provide and promote effective programmes for supervising offenders safely in the community.

- To assist prisoners, before and after release, to lead law-abiding lives.

- To help communities prevent crime and reduce its effects on victims.

- To provide information to the courts on the best interests of children in family disputes.

- To work in partnership with other bodies and services in using the most constructive methods of dealing with offenders and defendants.

The government has made it clear that it sees the probation service as a lead agency in the administration of the criminal justice system and much of this work is now subject to the 'National Standards for the Supervision of Offenders in the Community' published by the Home Office in 1995.

The foreword to the first National Standards, published in 1992, set out Ministerial intent:

> The publication of these national standards is an important step ... We now have a clear statement of expected practice setting out the objectives of supervision. This forms a broad and consistent framework, within which probation and social services staff can exercise the initiative and professional judgement essential for the effective supervision of offenders in the community.
>
> In addition, the standards are an important statement to which sentencers, offenders and the public can look as the basis on which such work should operate.

Aims for the Standards are set out in Chapter 1:

> The aims of these National Standards are to strengthen the supervision of offenders in the community, providing punishment and a disciplined programme for offenders, building on the skill and experience of practitioners and service managers:

- by setting a clear **requirement** for supervision, understood by all concerned

- by enabling service practitioner's **professional judgement** to be exercised within a framework of **accountability**

- by encouraging the adoption of **good practice** including the development of local practice guidelines (which should be in line with the requirements set by the standards)

- by ensuring that supervision is delivered **fairly, consistently and without improper discrimination**

- by setting a priority on the **protection of the public** from re-offending (and from the fear of crime)

- by establishing the importance of considering the **effect of crime on victims**

- by ensuring the public can have confidence that supervision in the community is an **effective punishment** and a means to help offenders become responsible members of the community.

2.7.1 Probation orders

Probation orders are made under sections 2 and 3 of the Powers of Criminal Courts Act 1973 as amended by the Criminal Justice Act 1991. The criteria for making such an order are:

> ... supervision of the offender by a probation officer is desirable in the interests of (a) securing the rehabilitation of the offender; or (b) protecting the public from harm from him or preventing the commission by him of further offences.

The purpose of supervision under a probation order is identified by section 2(1) of the Powers of the Criminal Courts Act 1973:

- securing the rehabilitation of the offender;

- protecting the public from harm from the offender;

- preventing committing further offences.

National Standards indicate the desired objectives of such an order:

- confronting offending behaviour, challenging the offender to accept responsibility for his or her crime and its consequences;

- making offenders aware of the impact of the crimes they have committed on their victims, the community and themselves;

- motivating and assisting the offender towards a greater sense of personal responsibility and discipline, and to aid his or her re-integration as a law-abiding member of the community;

- intervening to remedy practical obstacles preventing rehabilitation (eg education, training, skills needed for employment and action to counter drug or alcohol misuse, illiteracy or homelessness) and to help the offender acquire relevant new skills; and

- ensuring that the supervision programme for the offender is demanding and effective.

2.7.2 Community service orders

The probation service is responsible for establishing, managing and operating community service orders. These responsibilities are subject to the National Standards which specify that the aims and objectives of the order are to prevent further offending by re-integrating the offender into the community through punishment and reparation to the community.

2.7.3 Combination orders

Combination orders are supervised by the probation service with the objective of securing the rehabilitation of the offender; protecting the public from harm from the offender; and/or preventing the offender from committing further offences. National Standards specify that there should be a supervising officer for the order who is responsible for reviewing the order every three months in consultation with other officers involved.

2.7.4 Supervision orders

Under the provisions of the Criminal Justice Act 1991 the probation service is involved in the supervision of offenders sentenced to a supervision order in the Youth Court. This work is discussed in the chapter on youth justice.

2.7.5 Management of approved probation and bail hostels

The probation service is responsible for the day to day running of probation and bail hostels under the direction of area probation committees or voluntary management committees. Probation hostels provide residential facilities for offenders who require enhanced supervision to live in the community. Such hostels are provided for, among others, high risk offenders who have been released from custody, or offenders on a probation order with an additional residence requirement order. Bail hostels provide accommodation for defendants on bail with a condition of residence at the hostel as an alternative to a remand in custody.

The management of such hostels is subject to the National Standards which specify appropriate objectives:

Hostel staff should develop a regime in consultation with their committee and the local probation service. This should provide a structured and supportive environment which will seek to:

- ensure that the requirements of the court are met;

- promote a responsible and law-abiding lifestyle, and respect for others;

- create and maintain a constructive relationship between the hostel's staff and its residents;

- facilitate the work of the probation service and other agencies aimed at reducing the risk that residents will offend or re-offend in the future;

- assist hostel residents to keep or find employment and to develop their employment skills;

- encourage and enable residents to use the facilities available in the local community and to develop their ability to become self-reliant in doing so;

- enable hostel residents to move on successfully to other appropriate accommodation at the end of the period of residence;

- establish and maintain good relations with neighbours and the community in general.

National Standards also set clear specifications relating to supervision and enforcement which require staff to respond firmly and quickly to deal with non-compliance.

2.7.6 Supervision before and after release from custody

The probation service is involved with offenders while they are serving a custodial sentence and upon release from a prison establishment. The release provisions of the Criminal Justice Act 1991 establish a system under which custodial sentences are served partly in prison and partly in the community but subject to recall. Supervision by a probation officer is a central part of that part of a custodial sentence served in the community. National Standards set objectives for work with offenders in custody and after release as:

- the rehabilitation of the offender;

- the protection of the public from harm from the offender;

- the prevention of further offending.

Standards also specify liaison between the supervising probation officer, the prison probation officer and prison staff from the beginning of a sentence to facilitate preparation for and supervision after release. Further standards are set for the enforcement of licence conditions and for breach and recall to prison.

2.8 THE PREPARATION OF PRE-SENTENCE REPORTS BY THE PROBATION SERVICE

Pre-sentence reports are produced for the sentencing court to assist that court in determining the most suitable method of dealing with an offender. 'They provide a professional assessment of the nature and causes of a person's offending behaviour and the action which can be taken to reduce re-offending' (National Standards). Pre-sentence reports should be structured around a set of headings specified in the National Standards: introduction, offence analysis, relevant information about the offender, risk to the public of re-offending, conclusion.

The introduction should summarise the sources of information used to compile the report and should identify whether the offender is known to the report author, the probation service or the social services department.

Offence analysis is designed to provide the court with information to explain why the offender committed the offence at this time. It should include an analysis of the offence including comment on culpability and premeditation, the context in which the offence occurred, the impact on the victim, an assessment of the offender's attitude to the offence and the victim, and comment on the offender's awareness of the consequences of the crime. There might also be an assessment of the implications of any special circumstances, such as a family crisis, which were directly relevant to the offending.

The section of the report specifying relevant information about the offender is concerned

> ... to give a concise assessment of the offender's personal and social circumstances which could assist the court in deciding on the suita- bility of relevant sentencing options in the case concerned. (National Standards)

Any personal or social information on the offender should be concerned with offending behaviour, the prospect of further of- fending and with the offender's capacity for change. The section may contain information an any relevant community care assessment that has been made.

The section on the risk to the public of re-offending should provide an assessment of the risk of re-offending and of the risk of harm to the public. This assessment should specify the nature and seriousness of possible further offences, and the likelihood of their occurring.

The conclusion of the pre-sentence report should reflect the content of the report and might include a proposal for a community sentence where this is appropriate given the content of the report. If such a proposal cannot be made the report should indicate why this is the conclusion. The proposal for a community sentence should:

- have regard to the range of programmes and activities available locally (in partnership with the independent sector where appropriate) and the type of offender for whom they are most suited;

- have regard to the individual offender's personal and social circumstances, as already assessed;

- have regard to which community order is most suitable for the offender and most likely to be completed without the commission of a further offence;

- contain a degree of restriction on liberty matching the nature of the offence.

(National Standards)

If the report contains a proposal for a probation order, supervision order or combination order it should also include an outline of the supervision plan proposed for the offender. If custody is a likely sentencing option for the court, the pre-sentence report should identify any likely adverse effects of custody for the offender and his or her family, adverse effects on the offender's education or employment, and any other considerations that might be relevant to the length of custodial sentence.

3 CRIMINAL JUSTICE AND SOCIAL WORK: some issues for discussion

3.1 REFORM OF THE CRIMINAL JUSTICE SYSTEM

The criminal justice system continues to be an issue of media and public concern, and of political debate. Consequently it also continues to be a site for reform and legislative initiative. The politicisation of criminal justice shows little sign of abating. Recent law reform ranging from the Criminal Justice Act 1991 through to the Protection from Harassment Act 1997 was identified in the introduction to this chapter; such a range of legislation reflects the twin priorities of criminal justice policy: the punishment of the offender and the protection of victims and the community. If the former priority dominated legislation in the early years of this decade, protection of victims and the community has been established as the most recent priority. The government has published a number of consultation papers in which there is a local community emphasis, and is proposing to legislate for local initiatives in crime prevention and anti-social behaviour orders through the pro-visions of the Crime and Disorder Bill 1997.

Getting to Grips with Crime: A New Framework for Local Action (Home Office, September 1997), proposed new duties on local authorities and the police service to develop statutory partnerships to help prevent and reduce crime. They would have a joint duty to:

i) conduct an audit of local crime and disorder issues and consult collectively about these with other local agencies and with the voluntary sector, local businesses and the residential community ('other partners');

ii) consult collectively with local agencies and the other partners on targets for reducing crime and disorder, and agree with relevant agencies or partners responsibility for targets and timescales;

iii) publish a local community safety strategy with details of:

- consultation;

- analysis of crime and disorder in the area;

- long and short term targets for crime and disorder reduction;

- timescales for each element of the plan;

- responsibility for delivery of targets;

and then to consult with the other local agencies and the other partners annually on progress towards the targets, reviewing and revising then as necessary to reflect this progress;

iv) from time to time (possibly after three years) revisit the basic process of joint audit, and produce a new strategy.

Commenting on the nature and purpose of the proposals the con-sultation document argued that:

The proposals set out in this paper are not about requiring local government to deliver a major new service, or to take on substantial new burdens. Their aim is to give the vital work of preventing and reducing crime a new focus across a very wide range of local services, including – as paragraph 13 makes clear – those provided by local authorities. It is a matter of putting crime and disorder considerations at the heart of decision making, where they have always belonged.

The government believes that there will be real, tangible benefits for local authorities and the police service if these proposals are implemented. In other words, an effective strategy for preventing and reducing crime, coupled with a more central position for crime and disorder considerations across the whole range of local government business, promises to produce substantial savings for local authorities.

The shift of focus toward the local community is also evidenced by the consultation paper 'Community Safety Order', published by the Home Office in September 1997. The proposed order would be available to combat identified threats to community safety.

Anti-social behaviour causes distress and misery to innocent, law-abiding people – and undermines the communities in which they live. Neighbourhood harassment by individuals or groups, often under the influence of alcohol or drugs, has often reached unacceptable levels, and revealed a serious gap in the ability of the authorities to tackle this social menace. The Government is committed to tackle this problem to allow people to live their lives free from fear and intimidation.

The consultation paper proposes that local authorities and the police should have the power to apply to the courts for a community safety order on the grounds that the order was needed to deal with conduct which:

- causes harassment to a community;

- amounts to anti-social criminal conduct, or is otherwise anti-social;

- disrupts the peaceful and quiet enjoyment of a neighbourhood by others;

- intimidates a community or a section of it.

If the court were to grant an order it would be addressed to named individuals and would prohibit the person named in the order from carrying out any conduct specified in the order. Any breach of the terms of the order without reasonable excuse would be an indictable criminal offence punishable by imprisonment and/or an unlimited fine. The orders would be available against a young offender over the age of criminal responsibility (ten years and above).

The community safety order is directed to dealing with harassment which is directed toward a community rather than the Protection from Harassment Act 1997 which is designed to provide remedies for an individual who is the subject of individual harassment of a specific kind.

The Crime and Disorder Bill 1997 contains provisions in Clause 1 for these proposals, but renames the order as an 'anti-social behaviour order'.

3.2 RACE AND CRIMINAL JUSTICE

The National Association for the Care and Resettlement of Offenders has reported that:

> ... while black people are over represented as suspects, defendants and offenders, they are under-represented in the criminal justice agencies themselves, especially at the higher levels.[5]

More specifically, research reviewed in 1991 and 1992 revealed that young black people were more likely to be stopped, less likely to receive a caution and more likely to be prosecuted than comparable white offenders, and that black defendants were more likely to be remanded in custody than white defendants.[6]

Concern about this evidence may have been partly responsible for the inclusion of section 95 in the Criminal Justice Act 1991 which requires the Home Secretary to annually publish information which would help those involved in the administration of criminal justice fulfil 'their duty to avoid discriminating against any persons on the ground of race, sex or any other improper ground'.

5 *Black People's Experience of Criminal Justice,* (1991) NACRO.
6 Ibid, and *Race Policies into Action,* (1992) NACRO.

The first section 95 report was published in 1992 and commented that:

> At present there is only limited information available on any part of this subject. Research findings to date have been patchy in their coverage. Both statistics and research findings, however, provide evidence which supports the concerns which have been expressed about differential treatment of Afro-Caribbeans (that is, people of West Indian or African origin) ...[7]

Research since this report confirms the existence of discrimination on the grounds of race in the administration of elements of the criminal justice system. A study of sentencing by the Crown Court in the West Midlands found that black males were 17% more likely to receive a custodial sentence than white males. There were disparities in the use of sentences other than custody. Black adults received higher tariff sentences, were more likely to receive a suspended prison sentence and less likely to be given a community service or probation order.[8]

More recent research, reviewed by the Penal Affairs Consortium, confirms these trends.[9] This convincing and depressing research paints a picture of a racist criminal justice system which discriminates against black suspects, defendants and offenders. The problem is compounded by the under-representation of members of ethnic minority groups in the staffing of the system. This feature runs through the judiciary, the magistracy, courts clerks, the Crown Prosecution Service, lawyers, the police, the Prison Service and the Probation Service, though it is clear that the position is improving as a result of policies to recruit from ethnic minorities.

Awareness of the problem has led to initiatives in many criminal justice agencies including race issues training for the judiciary and the magistracy, Race Relations Committees for the Bar and the Law Society, equal opportunities policies in the probation service, the police and the CPS. The Prison Service has a significant race relations policy and the Justices' Clerks' Society has a policy to promote racial equality in the magistrates' courts.

---

7 *Race and Criminal Justice*, (1992) Home Office; reported in *Race and Criminal Justice*, Penal Affairs Consortium.

8 Hood, R, *Race and Sentencing: A Study of the Crown Court*, (1992) Clarendon Press.

9 *Race and Criminal Justice*, Penal Affairs Consortium.

Social workers working within and around the criminal justice system will be aware of the legacy and history of discrimination within the system, and will see day-to-day evidence of the impact on service users from the ethnic minorities. Despite 'official' recog-nition of the existence and effect of discrimination, the criminal justice system is still an overwhelmingly white in-stitution. Con-sequently social workers and probation officers working in the system must transcend the history of dis-crimination within the system to become agents of change. Though anti-discriminatory practice is good personal and pro-fessional practice the challenge of working in the criminal justice system is considerable.

> The comprehensive programme of action needed to combat discrimin-ation in the criminal justice process includes appropriate training for decision makers (both race training and training in rigorous structured decision making); the redoubling of efforts to recruit and retain black staff in criminal justice agencies; work to ensure a non-discriminatory approach in all areas of policy and practice; comprehensive racial monitoring of every aspect of decision making; and feeding back the results of monitoring to decision makers so that areas of discrimination can be identified and action plans drawn up to put right what is going wrong.

> In recent years, criminal justice agencies have taken substantial steps to monitor their activities and to identify and combat discrimination in the process. But much more needs to be done if we are to ensure that the duty to avoid discrimination, enshrined in section 95 of the 1991 Criminal Justice Act, is fully met throughout the criminal justice process.[10]

3.3   RACIAL VIOLENCE

The government is proposing to strengthen the law concerning racially motivated crimes. In a consultation document, Racial Violence and Harassment, the government cites the increase in racial incidents from 4,383 in 1988 to 12,222 in the period April 1995–May 1996 as evidence of a significant problem that requires a legislative response. The proposals take the form of establishing new statutory offences of racial crime to be punished more severely than their non-racial equivalents. As an example the government proposes

10   Ibid, at p 10.

that a racially motivated assault occasioning actual bodily harm would be punishable by a maximum term of imprisonment of seven years – two years more than the non-racial offence.

The consultation paper argues that the new Protection from Harassment Act 1997, introduced primarily to deal with stalking, can be seen as part of the package of racial offences which will so include current offences under the Public Order Act 1986, and therefore proposes increased sentences for racially motivated harassment under both Acts.

The proposals in the document, which are to be legislated for in the Crime and Disorder Bill are to be seen as an element in a package which also includes the proposal to establish a community safety order. As such they are part of the policy initiative toward the interests of the community and the victims of crime as well as an element in strengthening the powers of the courts to punish offenders who are guilty of offences that pose a threat to social, community and racial cohesion. Part II of the Bill deals with racially aggravated offences by defining racial aggravation and identifying a series of racially aggravated assaults, public order offences and harassment offences (Clauses 22–25).

4 CASE STUDIES

1. Doug Richards is twenty-three and has been found guilty of burglary for the second time in two years. The magistrates have decided to adjourn the case for two weeks for a pre-sentence report having indicated that they think the offence serious enough for a community sentence.

Identify the issues which your report will have to address.

If you were to recommend a probation order identify the role of the probation officer and the offender in the administration of such an order.

2. Mary Lewis has pleaded guilty to her first offence, theft by shoplifting. Mary is 34 and a single parent and has indicated to the magistrates that she took some food from an Iceland store because

she had nothing to give her daughter for tea and no money to buy anything. She lives in a local authority flat; income support and child benefit are her sole source of income and she has significant debts. She has told the magistrates that she wants some help and they have asked for a pre-sentence report.

Indicate the issues you would address in your report particularly in view of your conclusion that this offence does not warrant a community sentence.

In the event that a one year probation order is made what powers are open to you if Mary fails to keep any of the appointments you make with her?

What could the consequences be for Mary?

3.   Martin, who is 25, has been given 240 hours' community service having been found guilty of a 'domestic' burglary. On two occasions he has failed to turn up for work as directed and when he does turn up his work is unsatisfactory.

As a community service officer what powers do you have?

What might be the consequences for Martin in the circumstance that he admits his breach of the order? Martin has a lengthy record of offences including theft, burglary and assaults. He has served one prison sentence of six months, imposed last year for an assault on a bus driver.

4.   You are a probation officer on court duty in your local magistrates' court. An 18 year old is brought up to the court from the cells. He was arrested by the police last night and has been charged with the theft of £1,000. He is clearly confused but tells the magistrates that he is guilty and wants the matter dealt with today. When he is asked if he wants a lawyer he refuses. The bench is clearly concerned and decides to put the case back for an hour so that 'you can have a chance to speak to the probation officer'. They indicate that they do not think he realises the seriousness of his position and ask you whether you can help.

When you see him he has no idea of what is going on and asks you to explain what could happen to him.

What are you going to tell him?

What are you going to tell the magistrates when he appears in court again in an hour?

5 ACTIVITIES

1. Any Diploma student who has a probation placement will obviously have the very best experience of probation work. Other students might be able to arrange to visit a local probation office or sit in court with the duty probation officer and thereby gain some understanding of the nature of probation work and the criminal process.

The addresses and phone numbers of probation services in England, Wales and Northern Ireland appear in the back of 'Supervision in the Community: Probation Working' published by the National Association of Probation Officers.

2. Most probation services provide information and publications which explain their work. Get hold of as much information as possible from the probation service for your area. What particular schemes do they run for offenders?

3. Some understanding of the criminal justice system at work can be achieved by undertaking observation reports of the magistrates' courts and the Crown Court. Particular attention might be paid to the role of the duty solicitor, other defence lawyers, the probation officer and the impact of recommendations in pre-sentence reports.

Those who are able to visit both the magistrates' courts and the Crown Court will notice substantial differences in the character and nature of proceedings in both courts. What is the quality of the summary justice provided in the magistrates' courts?

4. Get publication lists from:

Association of Chief Officers of Probation;

Howard League for Penal Reform;

National Association for the Care and Resettlement of Offenders;

National Association of Probation Officers;

Liberty;

Penal Affairs Consortium;

Prison Reform Trust.

These organisations produce high quality pressure group material on issues concerned with the criminal justice system. With a selection of the available materials it is possible to put together a substantial package of information about the criminal justice system which will be useful in social work practice.

Many of these organisations are accessible through the internet. A good start is through the Penal Lexicon Web Site at www.penlex. org.uk

5.   If you are thinking of working in the criminal justice system as a probation officer or social work professional you should get hold of a copy of the National Standards from the Home Office.

6   ADDRESSES

Association of Chief Officers of Probation
212 Whitechapel Road
London E1 1BJ.
Phone: 0171 377 9141
Fax: 0171 375 2100

Home Office, Probation Service Division
50 Queen Anne's Gate
London SW1H 9AT.
Phone: 0171 273 3262

Howard League for Penal Reform
708 Holloway Road
London N19 3NL.
Phone: 0171 281 7722
Fax: 0171 281 5506
E-mail: Howard.League@ukonline.co.uk

National Association for the Care and Resettlement of Offenders
169 Clapham Road
London SW9 0PU.
Phone: 0171 582 6500
Fax: 0171 735 4666

National Association of Probation Officers
2-4 Chivalry Road
Battersea
London SW11 1HT.
Phone: 0171 223 4887
Fax: 0171 223 3505

Liberty
21 Tabard Street
London SE1 4LA.
Phone: 0171 403 3888
Fax: 0171 407 5354
E-mail: liberty@GN.atc.org

Prison Reform Trust
The Old Trading House
15 Northborough Street
London EC1V 0AH.
Phone: 0171 251 5070
Fax: 0171 251 5076
E-mail: Prisonreform@prisonreform.demon.co.uk

7 MATERIALS

Davies, M, Croall, H and Tyrer, J, *Criminal Justice*, (1995) Longman.

Gibson, B and Cavadino, P, *Introduction to the Criminal Justice Process*, (1995) Waterside Press.

Wasik, M and Taylor, R, *Blackstone's Guide to the Criminal Justice Act 1991*, (1994) Blackstone.

Wasik, M and Taylor, R, *Blackstone's Guide to the Criminal Justice and Public Order Act 1994*, (1995) Blackstone.

Gender and the Criminal Justice, (1992) Home Office.

Home Office press releases and consultation papers from the internet: www.homeoffice.gov.uk

NACRO Factsheets.

National Standards For The Supervision of Offenders In The Community, (1995) Home Office.

Race and Criminal Justice, Penal Affairs Consortium.

CHAPTER 9

Youth justice

1 INTRODUCTION

1.1 SOCIAL WORK INVOLVEMENT IN YOUTH JUSTICE

The involvement of social workers in the youth justice system is both varied and extensive and it may be useful to start this chapter by identifying some of the areas of practice which bring social workers into contact with the criminal justice system as it affects children (10–13) and young persons (14–17).

In many areas social services and probation work with young people involved with the criminal justice system is organised through a youth justice team[1] which is responsible for court duty services, assessment for and the preparation of pre-sentence reports, supervision of community sentences, the development of bail information and support facilities, the cautioning panel, and the supervision of young offenders before and after release from young offender institutions.

The variety of practice outlined above is 'reactive' in the sense of responding to a child or young person already involved with the youth justice system either as a suspect, defendant or as an offender. In another, equally important respect, social work practice is also 'proactive' in its concern and work designed to keep children and young people out of the criminal courts, and in a more general sense 'out of trouble'. The Children Act 1989, in Schedule 2, places a duty on local authorities to take reasonable steps to reduce the need to bring criminal proceedings against children and young persons and to encourage children in their area not to commit criminal offences. The Crime and Disorder Bill 1997 makes it clear that the government is concerned to enhance the objective of preventing offending;

---

1 Youth justice teams will be replaced by youth offender teams when the provisions of the Crime and Disorder Bill are implemented.

consequently the pro-active duties of local authorities will be increased by the Bill. Local authorities, together with the police, will be required to prepare strategies for reducing crime and disorder; and together with other interested agencies, publish an annual youth justice plan.

The establishment, in a number of areas, of inter-agency or cautioning panels which bring together the police, the social services, probation, the education welfare service and others with the common objective of keeping child and young offenders out of court, has been an important element in what are known as 'diversionary schemes'. The use of the official police caution as an alternative to prosecution can be seen as part of this diversionary objective though it can only be used where a child or young person admits an offence.

1.2 THE POLITICS OF YOUTH JUSTICE

Youth justice is a site for political controversy and as a result has experienced, or suffered, the effects of significant shifts in penal and social policy. The variety of constituencies with an interest in the youth justice debate is considerable and includes the 'caring professions', politicians, the media, the 'law and order lobby', the legal profession, the police, the prison service, the magistracy, the courts service and others. The periodic domination of particular constituents in the debate has been reflected in these shifts in policy so that the essential character or philosophy of the youth system is difficult to define. Youth justice is currently the most controversial element of criminal justice policy with its politicisation spanning the period before and after the 1997 general election. The Crime and Disorder Bill contains significant legislative initiatives to reform the youth justice system; it remains to be seen whether the implementation of its provisions will mark a period of calm in youth justice. The history of this aspect of the criminal justice system suggests that this is unlikely.

1.3 A MODEL FOR YOUTH JUSTICE?

The search for 'models' to explain the principles and operation of the youth justice system continues. By simplifying the debate it has hitherto been possible to identify two alternative models, the welfare model and the justice model. The welfare model sees intervention based on welfare or treatment as the appropriate response to a child or young person who commits a criminal offence. Offending is seen as symptomatic of some underlying problem which needs to be identified and responded to. 'Treatment' is provided by the caring professions so that power in this model lies with the social work profession and its allies. The alternative model argues that the welfare response to youth crime contains far too much discretionary power in the sense that the offender could become a 'victim' of the caring professions as one of the unintended consequences of welfarism. Critics of the welfare model see the adult criminal justice system, which operates on the basis of rights for the defendant and determinate sentences for the offender, as the appropriate model for the youth justice system.

This debate, which has been deliberately simplified, is overlaid by many other considerations. Government is required to be seen to be doing something about the criminal behaviour of young people. Children and young people who offend are currently being 'demonised' at the same time as their parents are labelled as lacking responsibility for their children. Social workers and probation officers are being used as scapegoats for a system that is failing to deliver a reduction in youth crime and juvenile delinquency. Youth courts are under pressure to be more punitive in sentencing, and the Home Office Circular 18/1994, *The Cautioning of Offenders*, has called for a reduction in the use of cautioning.

The historical difficulty in determining a coherence in policy under-pinning the youth justice system has been exacerbated in the 1990s. While the Children Act emphasises the welfare of children both in the community and in court proceedings, the youth justice system appears to be heading in the opposite direction, toward a much more punitive model for persistent offenders.

Practice for those working with children and young people in the criminal justice system continues to require careful negotiation of conflicting principles and practices. However the 'welfare principle' of section 44 of the Children and Young Persons Act 1933 remains in force:

> Every court in dealing with a child or young person who is brought before it, either as an offender or otherwise, shall have regard to the welfare of the child or young person ...

The provision has survived numerous legislative changes to the youth justice system; it should continue to inform all social work practice despite increasing threats to undermine its message.

1.4 THE PRINCIPLES OF THE CRIMINAL JUSTICE ACT 1991

The 1991 Act provides a sentencing framework for all criminal offenders and established a youth court to administer that framework for offenders aged 10 to 17. There are a number of features of the Act which, put together, may be said to constitute an important statutory element in a philosophy for youth justice:

- the principle of proportionality between the seriousness of the offence and the severity of the sentence applies to the sentencing of children (10–13) and young persons (14–17);

- this principle is to be balanced with the welfare principle of section 44 of the Children and Young Persons Act 1933 which continues to apply in all courts dealing with children and young people;

- an emphasis on the responsibility of parents for the behaviour of their children under the age of 16;

- the establishment of a new category of offender; the 16–17 year old 'near adult' offender subject to the full range of sentences;

- the introduction of National Standards to establish a base of good practice for the supervision of offenders in the community and for the preparation of pre-sentence reports;

- a statutory duty on all those working in the criminal justice system to avoid discriminating on improper grounds including race or gender;

- an encouragement to inter-agency co-operation in the development of diversionary initiatives and in the supervision of offenders in the community.

2 THE LAW

This section describes the current law and legal processes. Significant changes are envisaged by the provisions of the Crime and Disorder Bill 1997. The direction and substance of these reforms are discussed in section 3.3.

2.1 THE CHILD AND YOUNG PERSON AS SUSPECT

The age of criminal responsibility is set by the Children and Young Persons Act 1933 at ten years of age. Below that age children are deemed incapable of committing a criminal offence. In these circumstances it is not possible for a child under the age of ten to be arrested.

The Police and Criminal Evidence Act 1984 provides special safeguards which control how children and young people up to the age of 17 may be detained and questioned. In particular Code C, The Detention, Treatment and Questioning of Persons by Police Officers, determines the way in which a suspect under the age of 17 is treated while being detained and questioned at a police station. The Code gives all suspects (including those under 17) in police custody the right to have a person informed of their arrest; the right to obtain legal advice; and the right to consult a copy of the codes of practice (paragraph 3.1). Section 58(1) of the Act provides a right for anyone (including a juvenile) detained at a police station to consult a solicitor at any time. Advice from a police station duty solicitor is free.

Where the police detain a suspect under the age of 17 (a juvenile) they must inform the person responsible for their welfare (including the supervising officer if the juvenile is subject to a supervision order) that he or she has been arrested, why they have been arrested and where they are being detained. (Code C, pararaph 3.7.)

The custody officer must inform an appropriate adult (who may or may not be the person responsible for the juvenile's welfare) of the grounds for the juvenile's detention and his whereabouts, and ask the adult to attend at the police station (paragraph 3.9). The role of the appropriate adult is to advise and assist the juvenile (paragraph 3.12), and facilitate communication with the juvenile being interviewed.

Paragraph 1.7 establishes who may take on the role of the appropriate adult (in what seems to be an order of priority):

i) his parent or guardian (or, if he is in care, the local authority or voluntary organisation. The term 'in care' is used in this code to cover all cases in which a juvenile is 'looked after' by a local authority under the terms of the Children Act 1989);

ii) a social worker;

iii) failing either of the above, another responsible adult aged 18 or over who is not a police officer or employed by the police.

It is inappropriate for any person, including a social worker, to act as the appropriate adult if they have received an admission of guilt from the juvenile.

The Code provides important rights for the appropriate adult: to read the custody record; consult with the juvenile in private at any time, and instruct a solicitor at any time on behalf of the juvenile or instruct a solicitor to advise him or her while performing the role of appropriate adult.

Questioning of the child or young person cannot begin before the arrival of the appropriate adult who must be present during the questioning. The child or young person is also entitled to have a solicitor present at the police station, and during questioning. Children and young people should not be detained in a cell.

These are important rights and it may fall to a social worker to make sure that they are in place.

2.1.1   Bail, remand to local authority accommodation and remands to custody

Once charged a child or young person should be released on bail by the police. Section 47(1A) of the Police and Criminal Evidence Act 1984 gives the custody officer the power to impose conditions on bail where he or she is satisfied that conditions are necessary for the purposes of preventing the accused from:

- failing to surrender to bail;

- committing an offence while on bail;

- interfering with witnesses;

- otherwise obstructing the course of justice.

If the juvenile is refused bail then they should be transferred to local authority accommodation to await their first appearance in court unless:

- it is impracticable for the custody officer to do so; or

- in the case of a juvenile aged 12 to 16, no secure accommodation is available and keeping him/her in other local authority accommodation would not be adequate to protect the public from serious harm from him/her.[2]

When a juvenile has been transferred to local authority accommodation the local authority then has the decision where to place the juvenile. This could be with remand foster parents, at home with parents, in a residential children's home or in secure accommodation. The local authority can only place a juvenile received from the police in secure accommodation if it appears that any accommodation, other than that provided for the purpose of restricting liberty is inappropriate because the child is likely to abscond from such other accommodation; or the child is likely to injure him/herself or other people if s/he is ekpt in such other accommodation (Children (Secure Accommodation) Regulations 1991). If the local authority decide to keep a juvenile in secure accommodation they may do so for a maximum of 72 hours without court authority.

Once the child or young person has appeared in court, decisions concerning bail will be taken by the court under the provisions of the Bail Act 1976. The Act is said to establish a right to bail. However bail may be refused in a number of circumstances including those where the court finds that there are substantial grounds for believing that, if granted bail, the defendant would abscond, commit further offences, interfere with witnesses or otherwise interfere with the course of justice.

Where bail is refused the child or young person will be remanded to local authority accommodation and the court has powers to require the young person to comply with conditions that could be imposed under the Bail Act 1976, such as a condition of residence or a curfew. The court can also require the local authority not to place the child or young person with a named person.

Section 23 of the Children and Young Persons Act 1969 allows the youth court to remand young people aged 15 or 16 to local authority accommodation with a requirement that they are held in secure accommodation. Such remands can only be made in particular circumstances:

---

2   Police and Criminal Evidence Act 1984, s 38(6).

A court shall not impose a security requirement except in respect of a young person who has attained the age of fifteen, and then only if –

a) he is charged with or has been convicted of a violent or sexual offence, or an offence punishable in the case of an adult with imprisonment for a term of fourteen years or more; or

b) he has a recent history of absconding while remanded to local authority accommodation, and is charged with or has been convicted of an imprisonable offence alleged or found to have been committed while he was so remanded,

and (in either case) the court is of the opinion that only such a requirement would be adequate to protect the public from serious harm from him (Section 23(5)).

The power to remand with a security requirement will only be implemented when enough local authority secure accommodation is available. Until that time 15 and 16 year old boys can be remanded to a remand centre or prison accommodation in the circumstances set out in section 23(5).

The White Paper *No More Excuses – A New Approach to Tackling Youth Crime in England and Wales* (1997), discussed the non-implementation of these pro-visions. The Crime and Disorder Bill, in Clauses 80 and 81, provides for court ordered secure remands, and extends the lower age limit to twelve years old.

The decision to bail a juvenile defendant is crucial. Bail information and support schemes are operated by many local authority social services departments/youth justice teams. Bail information schemes are designed to provide the CPS, defence lawyers and the court with appropriate information to facilitate a fully informed decision on a bail application. Juveniles on bail may benefit from a bail support scheme designed to enable them to comply with the terms and conditions of their bail.

2.1.2   Legal aid

A child or young person charged with a criminal offence is entitled to legal advice and assistance under the green form scheme and to apply for criminal legal aid for representation in court. If a child or young person is not represented on a first appearance in court s/he may be helped and represented by the court duty solicitor.

2.2 THE JURISDICTION OF THE YOUTH COURT

The youth court is part of the magistrates' court system but is constituted separately from the adult court and there are strict rules which seek to prevent children and young people coming into contact with adult defendants at court. The general principle is that criminal proceedings against youth defendants should be heard in the youth court. The major exception to this principle relates to grave crimes as defined by section 53 of the Children and Young Persons Act 1933, that is an offence punishable in the case of an adult with imprisonment for fourteen years or more, indecent assault upon a woman contary to section 14 of the Sexual Offences Act 1956, and (for offenders who have attained the age of 14) offences of causing death by dangerous driving or whilst under the influence of drink or drugs. Homicide charges must be tried on indictment at the Crown Court. For prosecutions concerning section 53 grave crimes, the youth court must decide whether to commit the defendant for trial. In such mode of trial hearings the youth court should consider the following:

> Age 10–14: Is the offence so serious that a custodial sentence would be merited?

> Age 15–17: Is the offence so serious that in the case of a young offender aged 18–20 years a custodial sentence of substantially more than two years would be merited?[3]

If the answer to either is in the affirmative, the defendants should be committed to the Crown Court for trial.

A child or young person may be tried in the adult criminal courts when s/he is jointly charged with an adult.

The age of criminal responsibility is set by Parliament at ten. The principle of *doli incapax* applies to defendants under the age of 14; it establishes a presumption that the defendant is incapable of committing a crime. This presumption can be rebutted by the prosecution bringing evidence to establish beyond a reasonable doubt that the child defendant knew at the time of the offence that

---

3   Ashford, M and Chard, A, *Defending Young People in the criminal justice system*, (1997) Legal Action Group, at p 149.

the criminal act was seriously wrong.[4] Young people aged 14 to 17 are fully responsible for their criminal acts.

2.3 THE YOUTH COURT

The lay magistrates who make up the 'youth court panel' are selected from the magistrates in a petty sessional area as having appropriate experience and knowledge of the circumstances of children and young people. They should normally be under the age of 50 when appointed and they receive special training as youth court magistrates. Benches of no more than three magistrates hear the majority of cases in the youth court though a single magistrate may hear a bail application or sit as an examining magistrate for the purposes of a committal hearing. A stipendiary magistrate will normally sit with lay magistrates in the youth court but may sit alone if it is not in the interests of justice to adjourn the hearing. The public are not admitted to the youth court though the press may report criminal proceedings so long as such reports do not allow the identification of the defendant.

Youth courts are under a statutory duty to require a parent or parents to attend court hearings involving children and young people between the ages of 10 and 15, unless satisfied that it would be unreasonable to do so. Where the young person is 16 or 17 this duty is relegated to a power. These provisions are set out in section 34A of the Children and Young Persons Act 1933 which also places local authorities in the same position as natural parents where the authority has parental responsibility for the juvenile.

2.4 COURT PROCEEDINGS

Children and young people charged with a criminal offence may plead guilty or not guilty. If there is a plea of guilty the Crown Prosecution Service will outline the facts of the case and the offender

---

4 The presumption will be abolished by the implementation of the Crime and Disorder Bill 1997. The proposal to abolish was canvassed in: *Tackling Youth Crime*, Home Office, September 1997, and confirmed in *No More Excuses – A New Approach To Tackling Youth Crime in England and Wales*, Home Office, November 1997.

and/or their legal representative will be given an opportunity to address the court about the offence and about their personal circumstances before the magistrates decide on sentence. Representations on behalf of the offender may be made by their legal representative though often the magistrates will want to hear from the child or young person directly.

A plea of not guilty will mean that a date for trial has to be fixed. At the trial the prosecution will seek to prove the charge by bringing evidence. Prosecution witnesses may be cross-examined by the defence who will bring their own evidence to refute the charge. The defence is likely to include the evidence of the defendant who, with other defence witnesses, will be open to cross-examination by the prosecution. After all the evidence has been heard and the defence has addressed the magistrates they will retire to reach their decision with the benefit of legal advice from the court clerk.

The burden of proof is on the prosecution to prove the charge beyond a reasonable doubt. If the defendant is found not guilty then that is the end of the matter, but if there is a finding of guilty the decision on sentence may be delayed for the preparation of a pre-sentence report.

The Criminal Justice and Public Order Act 1994 allows the court to draw 'such inferences as appear proper' from the failure of the defendant, before charge, to mention a relevant fact relied on in his or her defence at trial (section 34). Similarly section 35 allows the court to draw proper inferences from the failure of the defendant to give evidence or refuse to answer questions while in the witness box. Section 35 will not apply when the accused is under 14, or where their mental or physical condition makes it inappropriate for them to give evidence, or the appropriate statutory warning has not been given to the accused. The accused must be warned of the consequences of his or her refusal to give evidence or answer questions in court.

2.5 PRE-SENTENCE REPORTS

Very often in the youth court the magistrates will want further information about the child or young person before they decide on sentence; in a number of circumstances reports are required before sentence is imposed. The necessary information will be obtained through pre-sentence reports prepared by the probation service, or by a youth justice team. Magistrates may also request a school report prepared by teachers and processed by the education welfare service.

Section 3(1) of the Criminal Justice Act 1991 requires both the youth court and the Crown Court to obtain and consider a pre-sentence report before imposing a custodial sentence. This requirement has been amended by the Criminal Justice and Public Order Act 1994 to the extent that:

i)   the offence is an indictable only offence and the court thinks such a report is unnecessary in the circumstances of the case; or

ii) in all other cases, a previous report is available to the court.

It is also clear from case law that a report is not necessary where the court is imposing a custodial penalty because the offender has refused to consent to a community penalty.[5] Section 7 of the Criminal Justice Act 1991 requires the youth court to obtain and consider a pre-sentence report before it forms an opinion on the suitability of the offender for the more serious community sentences, ie probation order with additional requirements, community service, a combination order, or a supervision order which includes requirements imposed under the 1969 Children and Young Persons Act.

The preparation of pre-sentence reports is subject to the National Standards for the Supervision of Offenders in the Community which require the report to address the current offence, to provide relevant information about the offender and a conclusion which may include a proposal for the most suitable community sentence.

2.6   SENTENCING YOUTH OFFENDERS

In some respects the sentences available to the sentencing court are the same as those which can be made in the adult criminal court, though supervision orders are exclusive to courts sentencing youth offenders. The welfare principle contained in

5   *R v Meridith* [1994] Crim LR 142.

section 44(1) of the Children and Young Persons Act 1933 applies to sentencing youth offenders.

The Criminal Justice Act 1991 established 16 and 17 year old offenders as a special category for sentencing purposes:

> The inclusion of 17 year old offenders within the jurisdiction of the youth court and the recognition of 16 and 17 year old offenders as a category of 'near adults' for sentencing purposes has resulted in a sentencing regime which identifies the 10 to 15 age group as distinct from the 16 and 17 year old offenders. Courts will have more flexible sentencing arrangements for them (16 and 17 year old offenders), reflecting the fact that offenders of this age are at a transitional stage between childhood and adulthood. Some will be more developed and independent than others. Bringing all offenders of this age group within the jurisdiction of the youth court, and providing the youth court with a flexible range of disposals for offenders of this age, will enable the penalty given in each case to reflect the individual's development and circumstances.[6]

The principle of 'just deserts' or proportionality requires that the choice of sentence reflects the seriousness of the offence. A continuum of seriousness applies so that sentencers are required to establish:

- that an offence is serious enough for a community sentence;

- that custody can only be imposed when the offence is so serious that only a custodial sentence can be justified; or

- that the offence is a violent or sexual offence and that only custody is adequate to protect the public from serious harm from the offender.[7]

There is one exception to this principle of sentencing thresholds. A supervision order with a requirement of intermediate treatment is available as an alternative to custody. In this circumstance alone

---

6   Criminal Justice Act 1991, Children and Young Persons, Guide published by the Home Office, December 1991.
7   The youth court cannot impose a custodial sentence on an offender under the age of 15.

a community sentence can be imposed in circumstances where the court considers the offence to be so serious that custody is justified.

Sections 28 and 29 of the Criminal Justice Act 1991 apply to sentencing youth offenders. Section 28 provides that the court can take into account any factors which it considers to be relevant in mitigation of a sentence. Section 29(1) provides that previous offences or a failure to respond to previous sentences may be taken to aggravate the seriousness of the current offence.

Social workers and probation officers preparing pre-sentence reports for the sentencing court are required to work within the terms of the National Standards but must also take account of the sentencing principles of the Criminal Justice Act 1991 identified above. In addition report writers should understand the factors and interests that youth court magistrates regard as important and which therefore influence their sentencing practice. Magistrates welcome concise, coherent reports where they see any proposals as realistic in relation to the offence and the offender. They are also concerned about what they see as their duty to the community; a duty which requires sentences to have some public credibility.

2.6.1 Binding over

The Criminal Justice Act 1991, section 58(2) and (3), gives the sentencing court duties and powers to bind over the parents or guardian of youth offenders in addition to sentencing the offender. The purpose of the bind over is to require parents or guardians to take proper care and exercise control over the offender; and where a community sentence has been passed, to ensure that the offender complies with the requirements of the sentence.

For offenders under the age of 16 the court is under a duty to bind over parents where to do so is in the interests of preventing the commission of further offences by the child or young person. For offenders who are 16 or 17 the court has a power rather than a duty to bind over parents or guardians. The maximum recognisance for such a bind over is £1,000. Parents or guardians are required to consent to be bound over and may be fined if they refuse and the court finds the refusal to be unreasonable. Bind overs may be varied or revoked upon application by the parent or guardian where the court concludes that to do so is in the interests of justice.

2.7 THE RANGE OF SENTENCES

2.7.1 Discharges and fines

Discharges

An absolute discharge is a decision by the court that no punishment is necessary. A conditional discharge means that the youth offender is not sentenced for the offence but discharged for a period of time (maximum of three years) on condition that s/he does not re-offend during that period. If the child or young person re-offends during the period of the discharge then the court may re-sentence for the original offence as well as for the new offence.

Fines

The sentencing court is required by section 18 of the Criminal Justice Act 1991, to take the seriousness of the offence and the means of the offender into account when fixing the level of a fine. The exception to this rule is the situation where the fine is to be levied against the offender's parents or guardian. In these circumstances the means of the parent or guardian are taken into account. The court has a duty to require the payment of fines to be made by the parents of 10 to 15 year old offenders unless they cannot be found or it would be unreasonable to order them to pay. In respect of 16 and 17 year old offenders the court has a power rather than a duty to order parents to pay. Local authorities may be required to pay the fines of those offenders for whom it has parental res-ponsibility though the level of the fine is subject to a different financial formula.

Where the parent or guardian is fined the maximum level of fines is the same as applies to adult offenders.[8] Where the fine is imposed on an offender under the age of 14 the maximum fine is £250; where the offender is aged 14 to 17 the maximum fine is £1,000. The Crown Court is not subject to these scale maxima.

Compensation order

The court can award a compensation order as a sentence in its own right or in addition to another sentence. Parents, guardians and local

---

8   See the scale set out in Chapter 8.

authorities are responsible for compensation orders in the same circumstances as they are for fines. The level of compensation will reflect the monetary value of the damage caused by the offence and the ability of the parent or guardian to pay when the order is levied against them, or the offender when the order is made against them.

2.7.2 Community sentences

Section 6(1) of the Criminal Justice Act 1991 specifies the availability of community sentences:

> A court shall not pass on an offender a community sentence ... unless it is of the opinion that the offence, or the combination of the offence and one or more offences associated with it, was serious enough to warrant such a sentence.

Having decided that the 'serious enough' threshold has been crossed, the court is then required by section 6(2) to choose the sentence that is both suitable for the offender and commensurate with the seriousness of the offence.

Supervision orders

This order is exclusive to youth offenders and is available for those from 10 to 17 years of age. A supervision order, which is made under the Children and Young Persons Act 1969, places the child or young person under the supervision of a social worker or probation officer, for a specified period up to a maximum of three years. There are a number of varieties of supervision order ranging from the minimum order, with no special requirements, through to the supervision order which includes specified activities as a direct alternative to custody:

- to attend a specified place at specified times (intermediate treatment): s 12(2)(b);

- to take part in specified activities (intermediate treatment): s 12A(3)(a);

- to remain at a specified place or places between 6pm and 6am (a night restriction): s 12A(3)(b);

- to refrain from taking part in specified activities: s 12A(3)(c);

- to live at a particular place: (residence as specified): s 12(2)(a) and s 12A(3)(a);

- to live in local authority accommodation: s 12AA;

- to receive psychiatric treatment: s 12B

- to attend school or comply with other arrangements for his/her education: s 12C

It is also possible for the court to declare that a supervision order with an additional requirement of specified activities is being made as a direct alternative to custody (s 12D).[9]

The Children Act 1989 allows the court to include a residence requirement in a supervision order under which an offender is required to live in accommodation provided by or on behalf of a local authority for a period of up to six months. The availability of this requirement is limited to offenders who have committed a serious offence, the commission of the offence was due to a significant extent to the circumstances in which the offender had been living and that when the offence was committed the offender was subject to a supervision order with additional requirements other than those relating to mental treatment or school attendance.

Under section 15(3)(a) of the Children and Young Persons Act 1969 breaches of the terms of the supervision order or of any requirements made under the order can be dealt with by the court by the imposition of a fine or an attendance centre order (see below). Where the supervision order included a specified activities requirement as an alternative to custody its breach can result in the youth offender being re-sentenced for the original offence with custody being a possible new sentence.

The supervision order has been the cornerstone of developments in relation to juvenile offenders. The aims and objectives of such an order are set out in the National Standards:

- to encourage and assist the child or young person in his or her development towards a responsible and law abiding life, thereby promoting the welfare of the offender and seeking

9 Ashford, M and Chard, A, *Defending Young People in the criminal justice system*, (1997) Legal Action Group, at p 338.

– to secure the rehabilitation of the offender

– to protect the public from harm from the offender

– to prevent the offender from committing further offences.

To achieve these aims and ensure effective supervision, supervising officers and those working under their direction should address the following objectives:

– enabling and encouraging the young offender to understand and accept responsibility for his or her behaviour and its consequences;

– ensuring the involvement, wherever possible, of the parents, guardian, family or other carers in the supervision of the young offender;

– helping the young offender to resolve personal difficulties linked with offending (eg problems within the family or at school) and to acquire positive new skills;

– making the young offender aware of the impact of the crime committed on its victim, the community and the offender himself or herself;

– motivating and assisting the young offender towards a greater sense of personal responsibility, discipline and self respect, and to aid re-integration as a law-abiding member of the community;

– ensuring that the young offender understands the difference between right and wrong; and

– ensuring that the supervision programme is demanding and effective.

Attendance centre orders

Youth offenders who have committed an offence for which an adult could be imprisoned may be ordered to attend at an attendance centre for a minimum period of 12 hours; the maximum period is 24 hours for offenders up to 15 years old and 36 hours for offenders aged 16 or 17. If the offender is under 14 the order may be for less than twelve hours where it is thought that a twelve hour order would be excessive. At the centre the offender will be required to take part in activities run by the police in a disciplined environment for two or three hours usually on a Saturday afternoon. If a child or young person fails to comply with the order they can be fined and the order allowed to continue, or the order can be revoked and the offender re-sentenced for the original offence.

Community service orders

Community service orders are available for youth offenders aged 16 and 17 who have committed an offence for which an adult could be sent to prison. The offender is interviewed by a community service officer to establish their suitability for unpaid work for the community. The minimum number of hours is 40, and the maximum for a youth offender is 240.

Where the offender has failed to comply with the order breach proceedings may be taken. If the breach is established then the court may fine the offender, make a community service order for not more than 60 hours, make an attendance centre order, or revoke the order and re-sentence for the original offence. If the court finds that the offender has wilfully and persistently failed to comply with the order then it may conclude that the young person has failed to give his or her consent to a community sentence; such a finding allows the court to impose a custodial sentence.

Probation

The sentencing court can make a probation order on an offender aged 16 or 17 for a minimum of six months and a maximum of three years. By section 2(1) of the Powers of Criminal Courts Act 1973 before making such an order the court must be:

> ... of the opinion that the supervision of the offender by a probation officer is desirable in the interests of –
>
> a) securing the rehabilitation of the offender; or
>
> b) protecting the public from harm from him or preventing the commission by him of further offences, ...

A number of additional requirements can be included in the order: to live at a particular place such as a bail hostel; to undergo psychiatric treatment for a mental condition; to attend a probation centre; to take part in specified activities or schemes organised by the probation service; to undergo treatment for drug or alcohol dependency or a requirement not to do particular things during a period of time (a 'refraining order').

Breach of a probation order may be dealt with in the same way as the breach of a community service order.

Combination order

This order is available for 16 and 17 year old offenders who have committed an imprisonable offence. Section 11(2) of the Criminal Justice Act 1991 requires the court to be of the opinion that the order is desirable in the interests of:

a) securing the rehabilitation of the offender; or

b) protecting the public from harm from him or preventing the commission by him of further offences.

The order requires the offender to be supervised by a probation officer for a period of one year minimum and three years maximum and to perform between 40 and 100 hours community service. Failure to comply with a combination order has the same implications for the offender as a failure to comply with a probation or community service order.

Curfew order (not yet in force)

The court may impose a curfew order on offenders aged 16 or 17. The offender is required to remain at a specified place for a minimum of two hours and a maximum of twelve hours per day. Before making the order the court must obtain and consider information about the place where the offender will be curfewed and the attitude of people at that place who will be affected by the presence of the curfewed offender. The offender need not consent to the order and the order should not, as far as is reasonably practicable, conflict with the offender's religious beliefs, any requirements of another community sentence or with the offender's work or attendance at an educational establishment. The Criminal Justice Act 1991 stipulates that a person must be made responsible for monitoring the order and provides for the electronic monitoring (by 'tagging') of offenders subject to curfew orders.

Failure to comply with curfew orders is dealt with in the same way as for probation, community service and combination orders.

Reports

The 1991 Criminal Justice Act requires the court to consider a pre-sentence report before passing the more serious of the community sentences, ie probation order with additional requirements, community service order, combination order or a supervision order with requirements. The Criminal Justice and Public Order Act 1994 has changed the circumstances in which a pre-sentence report is required to the extent that the court need not require a report:

- in the case of an indictable-only offence, if the court considers it unnecessary in all the circumstances; or

- in all other cases, if a previous pre-sentence report is available to be considered (if more than one report is available the most recent should be considered).

National Standards

The preparation and writing of pre-sentence reports and the super-vision of community sentences are subject to the National Standards for the Supervision of Offenders in the Community. Published by the Home Office, these required standards of practice for probation services and social services departments in England and Wales identify an expectation that the guidance and requirements contained in them are followed.

2.7.3 Custody

The Criminal Justice Act 1991 sets out the criteria for custodial sentences for all age groups so that the same conditions apply in the adult court and in the youth court. Section 1(2) provides that a court shall not pass a custodial sentence (in a young offender institution) unless it is of the opinion:

a) that the offence, or the combination of the offence and one or more offences associated with it, was so serious that only such a sentence can be justified for the offence; or

b) where the offence is a violent or sexual offence, that only such a sentence would be adequate to protect the public from serious harm from him.

Section 1(3) provides that:

> (3) Nothing in subsection (2) above shall prevent the court from passing a custodial sentence on the offender if he fails to express his willingness to comply with a requirement which is proposed by the court to be included in a probation order or a supervision order and which requires an expression of such willingness.

An associated offence is another offence which the offender is convicted of at the same hearing or another offence which the offender is sentenced for at the same hearing.

Custody by the youth court

The minimum age for a custodial sentence in the youth court is 15. The minimum custodial sentence in the youth court is two months and the maximum is six months for one offence and twelve months for any two or more indictable offences.

Where the youth court considers it does not have sufficient sentencing powers it may commit an offender to the Crown Court for sentencing. (In these circumstances the Crown Court may impose a custodial sentence of up to 24 months.)

Custody in the Crown Court

The Crown Court can impose a term of up to 24 months where the offender has been committed from the youth court to the Crown Court for sentence.

Where an offender was tried on indictment for a grave crime as specified by section 53 of the Children and Young Persons Act 1933, the Crown Court may impose a custodial sentence on an offender aged 10 to 17 for a period not exceeding the maximum which could be imposed on an adult offender for the same offence.

Under the provisions of section 53 of the Children and Young Persons Act 1933 anyone under 18 convicted of murder will be detained at Her Majesty's Pleasure (the equivalent of a life sentence).

2.7.4 Secure Training Orders (not yet in force)

These new orders are established by the Criminal Justice and Public

Order Act 1994. They are designed as a custodial and supervisory sentence for persistent young offenders. Section 1(5) provides:

The court shall not make a secure training order unless it is satisfied –

(a) that the offender was not less than 12 years of age when the offence for which he is to be dealt with by the court was committed;

(b) that the offender has been convicted of three or more imprisonable offences; and

(c) that the offender, either on this or a previous occasion –

(i) has been found by a court to be in breach of a supervision order under the Children and Young Persons Act 1969, or

(ii) has been convicted of an imprisonable offence committed whilst he was subject to such a supervision order.

The minimum length of the order is six months and the maximum is two years. Half of the order will be served in a secure training centre and half under supervision, normally by a social worker or probation officer. Failure to comply with the supervision requirements may trigger breach proceedings. If a breach is established the offender may be detained in a secure training centre for up to three months or for the remaining period of their order, whichever is the shorter.

2.8 APPEALS

An appeal by a youth offender against conviction and sentence by the youth court may be made to the Crown Court where the case will be re-heard. It is argued that social workers and probation officers have an important role to play in advising children and young people and their parents of rights to appeal against a custodial sentence and in encouraging solicitors to make appeals in such cases.

3 YOUTH JUSTICE AND SOCIAL WORK: some issues for discussion

3.1 THE CAUTIONING OF YOUTH OFFENDERS

The Home Office Circular to Chief Constables (14/1985) declared:

It is recognised both in theory and in practice that delay in the entry of a young person into the formal criminal justice system may help to prevent his entry into that system altogether.

It is now widely accepted that there is considerable value in reducing the number of children and young people prosecuted in the youth court. The various methods of keeping such offenders out of court are known as 'diversionary schemes or procedures'. Though the police control the exercise of major elements of the prosecution system, where 'cautioning panels' exist, social workers who are members of these panels can have an important role to play in the decision to prosecute or caution.

Juvenile bureaux, inter-agency or cautioning panels have been established for some time in a number of areas and these have allowed social services departments to influence, to a greater or lesser extent, the decision of the police in relation to the action to be taken against a child or young person who has come to their notice. As a result of such consultation a caution may be administered as an alternative to prosecution. Police cautioning has become the dominant method of diversion and is in essence a 'serious and strict telling off' and there is widespread agreement that cautioning has been successful in delaying and sometimes preventing the entry of a child or young person into the formal criminal justice system.[10]

Different models of police cautioning have developed over time and those which exclude consultation with other agencies therefore preclude social work influence. So for example an 'instant caution' is administered by the police within a very short time of offending or arrest and is most often given without consulting other agencies. Cautioning by letter is increasingly used as a means of saving time and money. More formal cautions may be given after consideration by an inter-agency or multi-agency panel which may include representatives from the police, the probation service, education welfare service, social services, education and the youth service. In such panels there is clearly considerable scope for social work practitioners to influence the decision whether to prosecute a youth offender. In some areas such panels have the benefit of the extra facility of what is termed 'cautioning plus' described by NACRO as:

10 It should be noted that cautions are recorded and in practice are included in an offender's record which is presented in court at any subsequent hearing.

... some form of support or additional activity as an adjunct to a caution. This may include a recommended activity, an apology to the victim or some sort of reparation. It might also include the offer of social work assistance for the young person or the family or some other kind of welfare provision.[11]

The central position of the police in the cautioning decision has been re-iterated by the most recent Home Office Circular on cautioning.

The decision to caution is in *all* cases one for the police, and although it is open to them to seek the advice of multi-agency panels, this should not be done as a matter of course. It is important that cautions should be administered quickly, and where such advice is sought it must not lead to unnecessary delay.[12]

The Circular, which was issued in 1994, evidenced government concern about the use of cautioning at a time when youth offending had become a major 'law and order' issue. There is little doubt that the intention of the Circular was to reduce the use of cautions, particularly multiple cautions, though their use as an effective disposal was recognised. In this sense the Circular reflected the political mood of the times in which young offenders, particular persistent young offenders, were being targeted for tougher and more punitive responses to their offending.[13]

Despite the findings of the Audit Commission's report, *Misspent Youth*, which confirmed and emphasised the benefit and success of diversion schemes and cautioning, the current government is proposing to replace the cautioning scheme for young offenders with a system of police reprimands and Final Warnings.

When a young person aged 10–17 offends and admits guilt, the police will have the choice of issuing a formal police reprimand (if the offence is minor), issuing a Final Warning or charging the individual. The police will always have the option of pressing charges. In serious cases, the presumption will be that the child or young person should be charged.[14]

---

11 *Diverting Juvenile Offenders from Prosecution*, NACRO Juvenile Crime Committee, Policy Paper 2, 1989.
12 Home Office Circular 18/1994, *The Cautioning of Offenders*.
13 In part this newer and tougher regime was legislated for in the Criminal Justice and Public Order Act 1994, particularly in the provision for secure training orders for persistent offenders in the 12–14 age range.
14 *Tackling Youth Crime*, (1997) Home Office, at para 50.

It is envisaged that the use of the Final Warning will also result in additional intervention to be designed and delivered by the new local Youth Offender Team.

> The Final Warning will usually result in the offender being placed on a programme of interventions prepared by the local Youth Offender Team. The purpose of the programme would be to help the offender (and his or her family) to change the attitudes and behaviour which led to the offending so as to prevent any further offending. The programme could include:

> • an assessment of the young person to establish the reasons for offending behaviour including any problems requiring attention;

> • work with parents to help them become more effective in supervising their child;

> • short term counselling or group work with the young offender to bring about behavioural change;

> • reparation to victims; supervised community or youth activities; or

> • work to improve attendance and achievement at school.[15]

It is to be hoped that the introduction of this new structure will ensure that the benefits of cautioning are not lost. There must however be some concern that young offenders (and their families) who receive a Final Warning and are subject to a Youth Offender Team intervention, may be treated disproportionately when compared to an adult offender who is convicted and sentenced for the same offence. The interventions envisaged by the government's consultation paper, and provided for in clause 53 of the Bill, are significant when compared to a fine or even to some community penalties.

3.2 THE YOUTH COURT

The existence of the youth court is a result of both the Children Act 1989 and the Criminal Justice Act 1991. The youth court has a

---

15   Ibid, at para 56.

specifically criminal law jurisdiction in contrast to the sometimes difficult mix of care and criminal jurisdiction administered by the old juvenile court. Though the youth court might have become a catalyst in the emergence of a distinct philosophy of youth justice it has become apparent that the work of the court reflects the tensions and conflicts that have historically characterised the philosophy and politics of juvenile and youth justice.

Any census of the various factors that influence the work of the court, and those working in the field of youth justice, will include:

• the principles of the Criminal Justice Act 1991: the just deserts principle and the practice of sentencing that reflects the growing maturity and responsibility of the offender;

• the increased punitivism of the Criminal Justice and Public Order Act 1994, evidenced by, among other things, the provisions for secure training orders;

• the increased emphasis on parental responsibility;

• the increased use of the Crown Court to try and sentence young offenders;

• the continuing existence of section 44 of the Children and Young Persons Act 1933, the welfare principle;

• specific provisions of the Children Act which require local authorities to reduce the need to bring criminal proceedings against children in their area; and

• the general welfare orientation of the Children Act.

It is clear that the youth court has become a politicised arena for the administration of youth justice. The trend of legislation is toward a more punitive response to second time and more persistent youth offending. The White Paper envisages a more interventionist youth court and other proposals, for later legislation, describe a distinct system for dealing with first time offenders who plead guilty, based upon such offenders undertaking 'contract style' obligations concerning reparation and future offending. Continuing and increasingly difficult tensions between 'welfare' and 'justice' will have to be negotiated in the planning of services and in the every day work of youth justice practice.

3.3 REFORMING THE YOUTH JUSTICE SYSTEM

There is now little doubt that the youth justice system is about to undergo significant reform. The government issued three consultation papers in September and October 1997 and a White Paper in November. All gave an indication of the type of youth justice system that the government envisages, and the publication of the Crime and Disorder Bill in December has confirmed their intentions.

The agenda for reform was set by the identification of the current problems:

- it lacks public credibility and clear aims;

- the current system of repeat cautions is not working;

- re-offending continues on bail;

- the youth justice system is too cumbersome and slow;

- there is a lack of supervised community based interventions programmes aimed at changing the behaviour of young offenders early in their careers;

- the current system of custodial orders and facilities is disjointed and variable and needs radical overhaul;

- there is an absence of national strategic direction.[16]

The three consultation papers, Tackling Youth Crime, New National and Local Focus on Youth Crime and Tackling Delays in the Youth Justice System were together concerned with reform to the law, to court procedure and to the services structure for young offenders. The substance of the proposals were replicated in the White Paper and largely reproduced in the Crime and Disorder Bill published in December 1997. (The relevant clauses of the Bill are identified in the discussion below.) If all these proposals become law the youth justice system will be significantly different.

Tackling Youth Crime specified three problem areas:

16   *Tackling Youth Crime*, (1997) Home Office, at p 2.

i) taking responsibility;

ii) being tough on youth crime and its causes; and

iii) preventing youth crime;

and suggests ways in which they can be tackled.

In 'taking responsibility' the government argued that young offenders must face up to the consequences of their offending for themselves and for others, by taking responsibility for their actions. It also argued that parents must recognise their responsibility for the actions of their children. The paper proposed the abolition or reform of the doctrine of *doli incapax*,[17] and the introduction of a new Reparation Order which would require young offenders to make some form of reparation to the victim of their crime or to the community at large (see Clause 54). In relation to parental responsibility, it proposed to introduce a Parenting Order to give the courts powers to deal effectively with parents who wilfully neglect their responsibilities, or who need help and support in fulfilling them (see Clauses 8 and 9).

In 'Tough on youth crime and on the causes of youth crime' the consultation paper presented two arguments.[18]

Firstly:

> When young people offend, the response of the youth justice system should be rapid, consistent and effective. No young person should be allowed to feel that he or she can offend with impunity. By intervening early and effectively before crime becomes a habit, we can prevent young offenders from graduating into adult criminals.

> While cautioning works well with most first time offenders (about 80% of whom do not re-offend within two years), it becomes progressively less effective once a pattern of offending sets in. If cautioning is used inconsistently or repeated without positive intervention to reverse offending habits it will not be effective.

17 The principle provides a rebuttable presumption that children aged 10 but under 14 cannot be guilty of a criminal offence. To overturn the presumption the prosecution must establish that the child knew that what they were doing was seriously wrong. The White Paper opted for abolition and this is confirmed by the terms of Clause 27 of the Bill.

18 *Tackling Youth Crime*, (1997) Home Office, at p 3.

Secondly:

> Punishment is important as a means of expressing society's condemnation of unlawful behaviour and as a deterrent. Punishment should be proportionate to the offence but progressively tougher if young people continue to offend. To ensure the protection of the public, punishment should be complemented by intervention to change their behaviour and prevent them offending again.

In response to these problems government proposed to replace the use of cautions with a system of police Final Warnings which will normally include guidance and support to reduce the risk of re-offending (see Clause 53). Action Plan Orders will combine reparation, punishment and rehabilitation to prevent re-offending, and will involve the parents of the young offender (see Clauses 56 and 57). Supervision orders are to be strengthened to allow the inclusion of reparation; by reinforcing breach arrangements and by simplifying enforcement (see Clauses 58 and 59).

In 'Preventing youth crime' reference is made (at page 3) to Home Office research[19] which argues that:

> ... the strongest influences on starting to offend are low parental supervision, persistent truancy and associating with offenders. Effective intervention to prevent children and young people turning to crime, and if they do, to prevent re-offending, needs to address the causes of offending as well as punishing the offender.

Government proposed a Child Safety Order and a Local Curfew Order (see Clauses 11–15). Under the former order the courts will be able require children under ten to be home by a certain time or avoid a certain area; such orders will used to protect children under ten who are at risk of becoming involved in crime. The latter order will allow local authorities to impose temporary curfews on children under ten to prevent criminal and anti-social behaviour.

The second consultation paper, New National and Local Focus on Youth Crime dealt with structural proposals for organising and administering the local response to youth offending. The implementation of the proposals in this paper will have a considerable impact on the responsibilities of local authorities and on the work of

---

19 *Aspects of Crime, Young Offenders 1995*, Home Office, January 1997.

probation officers and social workers working in the youth justice system. The main proposals were to establish inter-agency Youth Offender Teams to deliver community based intervention with and supervision of young offenders, and a new Youth Justice Board for England and Wales to co-ordinate the work of the youth justice system (see Clauses 28–33).

Local authorities with social services and education responsibilities are to be responsible for ensuring that appropriate services are provided through the Youth Offender Teams, and for the publication of an annual youth justice plan. This duty is to be discharged in partnership with the probation service, the police and health authorities.

Youth Offender Teams should include social workers, probation officers, police officers, and education and health authority staff, and may also include other appropriate representatives including those from the voluntary sector. The teams should be responsible for:

- assessment and intervention work in support of the Final Warning;

- supervision of community sentences;

- provision of the appropriate adult service;

- provision of bail information;

- providing bail supervision and support;

- the placement of young people in open/secure accommodation, remand fostering, approved lodgings etc;

- court work and the preparation of reports;

- involvement in throughcare during a custodial sentence, and in post-release supervision;

- the supervision of some parenting and child safety orders.

The third consultation paper was concerned with delays in the youth justice system. The rationale for speeding up the system, from offence to sentence, is provided in the Introduction to the paper:

It currently takes an average of 4.5 months for a young person who commits an offence to be sentenced. In the worst cases, offenders are not dealt with until a year or more after the offence was committed. The Audit Commission in its study of Misspent Youth (November 1996) found that 4 out of 5 cases observed in that study were adjourned.

Delays of this kind anger, frustrate and distress the victims. They do not help the young offender. The link between his or her offence and society's response to that offence, through the sentencing process, is broken. During the time that young people are awaiting trial on bail they all too often continue their offending so that by the time the case comes to trial they have not just one but a string of offences to answer for. It is in young people's own best interests that swift and effective action is taken in response to offending. They need to face up to the consequences of their behaviour and understand why it is wrong. Early action needs to be taken to help prevent further offending.[20]

The major proposal in this paper was for the introduction of statutory time limits in cases involving young offenders (see Clauses 34–37). The limits will apply to three stages of the criminal justice process, ie arrest (or where there is no arrest, laying of information) to first listing; first listing to start of trial, and conviction to sentence.

Taken together the proposals in the three consultation papers added up to a radical reform of the youth justice system. They were confirmed in the government's subsequent White Paper (CM 3809) *No More Excuses – A New Approach to Tackling Youth Crime in England and Wales*, published in November 1997.

The White Paper set out the Government's programme of reform for the youth justice system and identified the aims of reform:

- a clear strategy to prevent offending and re-offending;

- that offenders, and their parents, face up to their offending behaviour and take responsibility for it;

- earlier, more effective intervention when young people first offend;

20 *Tackling Delays in the Youth Justice System: A Consultation Paper*, (1997) Home Office, at p 1.

- faster, more efficient procedures from arrest to sentence;

- partnership between all youth justice agencies to deliver a better, faster system.

The White Paper confirmed the tenor and the details of the proposals raised in the consultation papers. Additionally the government included details of a new Detention and Training Order (DTO) as a generic sentence to replace detention in a Young Offender Institution and the secure training order (see Clauses 60–65):

> It will be subject to the restrictions on the use of custody laid down in the 1991 Criminal Justice Act, ie courts may impose the order only where the offence or offences in question are so serious that only custody is justified. For 10 and 11 year olds, the power to make an order would be available only in response to persistent offending and only where the court considers that a custodial sentence is necessary to protect the public from further offending by that child. For 12–14 year olds, the DTO could be imposed only in relation to persistent offending. For 15–17 year olds, it would be available for any imprisonable offence sufficiently serious to justify custody under the 1991 Act.[21]

Half such orders will be spent in custody and half under community supervision by a member of the appropriate Youth Offending Team. Orders will range from a minimum of four months to a maximum of two years. The use of such orders for 10 and 11 year olds will only be possible if the Home Secretary lays an order before Parliament. The Crown Court will retain its current sentencing powers in relation to grave crimes under the provisions of section 53 of the Children and Young Persons Act 1933.

The White Paper also makes some significant proposals concerning the organisation and function of the youth court.

> A frank assessment of the current approach of the youth court must conclude that, all too often, inadequate attention is given to changing offending behaviour. This is not the fault of individuals working within the system. It is encouraged by the court's very structures and procedures. The government is determined to tackle these failings head on. The purpose of the youth court must change from simply

---

21 *No More Excuses – A New Approach to Tackling Youth Crime in England and Wales*, Cm 3809, (1997) Home Office, at p 24.

deciding guilt or innocence and then issuing a sentence. In most cases, an offence should trigger a wider enquiry into the circumstances and nature of the offending behaviour, leading to action to change that behaviour. This requires in turn a fundamental change of approach within the youth court system.[22]

In addition to the substantive proposals identified in the consultation papers, the White Paper encourages magistrates in the youth court to engage directly with young offenders and their parents. It also proposes increasing the openness of proceedings through increasing access of the public and lifting some reporting restrictions. The government also proposes that defence services will be provided by a selected group of lawyers working under contracts with the Legal Aid Board.

However, in a radical model for future legislation, the White Paper outlines a distinct system for first time 'non-serious' offenders who plead guilty.

The Government considers that it will be necessary to reshape the criminal justice system in England and Wales to produce more constructive outcomes with young offenders. Its proposals for reform build on principles underlying the concept of restorative justice:

- **restoration**: young offenders apologising to their victims and making amends for the harm they have done;

- **reintegration**: young offenders paying their debt to society, putting their crime behind them and rejoining the law abiding community; and

- **responsibility**: young offenders – and their parents – facing the consequences of their offending behaviour and taking responsibility for preventing further offending.

The new approach is intended to:

- ensure the most serious offenders continue to be dealt with in a criminal court to provide punishment, protect the public and prevent re-offending;

- provide an opportunity for less serious offending to be dealt with in a new non-criminal panel, enforced by a criminal court;

22   Ibid, at p 32.

- involve young people more effectively in decisions about them – encouraging them to admit their guilt and face up to the consequences of their behaviour;

- involve the victim in proceedings, but only with their active consent; and

- focus on preventing re-offending.

In this model the first-time offender who pleads guilty would be convicted by the youth court and then referred to a youth panel. The members of the panel and the offender would draw up a contract concerning the ways in which the offender would make reparation to the victim or the community, and proposals for preventing future offending. The panel would oversee the contract performance and would refer the offender back to the youth court if the terms were breached. The panel would be made up of a mixture of youth justice practitioners, including a magistrate, a member of the Youth Offending Team and possibly a police officer. The parents of offenders under the age of 16 would be required to attend panel sessions, and the parents of offenders aged 16 and 17 would be encouraged to attend. Victims would also be able to attend.

Government claims that these reforms of the youth court will:

> ... help to shape a more effective youth justice system for the next century. The approach combines the principles of restorative justice with more traditional punitive measures, which must be available to the courts in order to protect the public. The overall result should be a more streamlined and effective system, with a clearer focus on preventing offending.[23]

Given the government's current parliamentary majority it is likely that the Crime and Disorder Bill, which is to be the vehicle for these and other criminal justice reforms, will become law without significant amendment. The likely impact of the reforms is difficult to judge, but it is probable that more young people and their parents will be brought within the youth justice system; the net-widening impact of the proposals is clear. Such an impact will inevitably construct a wider group of service users for the new youth offender teams. Despite the increased punitivism of the reformed youth justice system for persistent offenders, the extended boundaries within which social workers and

23   Ibid, at p 37.

probation officers will be working will provide an important site and space for good practice which promotes the positive aspects of reform such as prevention and rehabilitation. Practitioners will have to guard against a possible and unwelcome impact of the reforms, that is the unwarranted and disproportionate exercise of professional intervention in the legitimate autonomy of young people and their parents. The considerable powers envisaged by the proposals, particularly those concerning prevention and parental responsibility, have a quasi civil rights context that should not be ignored or underestimated.

4 CASE STUDIES

1.   Ricky Smith is 16 years old. He has been found guilty of robbery and possession of an offensive weapon, a lock knife. The facts of the case are as follows:

Two boys, one of whom was Ricky, followed a 48 year old Sri Lankan woman along a suburban street and assaulted her stealing a gold chain from around her neck. The chain was worth £500 and in the process of the robbery the woman was cut and bruised around her neck and chest. The two boys ran off but were chased by three building workers who had responded to the shouts of the woman. They challenged the two boys and Ricky pulled the knife. In the ensuing fight Ricky was knocked unconscious by one of the men. The police were called and Ricky was arrested. The other boy escaped and has not been traced.

Ricky was committed for trial to the Crown Court and pleaded not guilty. He was found guilty of both offences. The judge has asked for a pre-sentence report. You have been asked to prepare the report. Ricky is now willing to admit his part in the robbery but does not seem to be concerned about the seriousness of the offence or his position. Ricky is on unconditional bail.

The family history is one of a broken home where both Ricky and his mother were physically abused by his father before he left the home. Ricky's younger sister was killed in a road accident two years ago and he has been getting into trouble since then. He has two previous convictions; one for possession of an offensive weapon and one for theft. On the first offence he was conditionally discharged and on the second offence he was fined.

a) Draft a pre-sentence report concentrating on the seriousness of the offence and the range of sentences available to the court.

2. To bring the Ricky case down to a youth court hearing change the offence to assault and the facts to describe a fight outside the gates of the school where Ricky used to be a pupil. Ricky has gone to the school to take revenge on a younger boy who had 'insulted the memory of my sister'.

This is a good case study for role playing. Parts which can be scripted include Ricky, his mother, his lawyer to mitigate on his behalf, the social worker or probation officer who writes the report, the magistrates who make the decision having read the report, and the court clerk who gives the magistrates legal advice on the sentencing options open to them. The role play could take place in different settings and at different times, eg the interview between Ricky and social worker or probation officer; in the retiring room with the magistrates; and in court when mitigation is given and sentence passed.

3. You are a social worker representing the social services department on an inter-agency or cautioning panel which meets to discuss the cases of children and young people who have come to the notice of the police. In each case the panel decides whether to recommend that the child or young person concerned be prosecuted or receive a 'formal caution' or a 'caution plus'.

In each of the following cases indicate your recommendation and outline the reasons for it:

a) Tim is 11 and has been caught acting as a lookout for his older brother who was stealing a pedal bike from a garden shed. Both boys live with their parents in a large house in a prosperous area of town. Tim's father is a local vicar and is very concerned about any adverse publicity and is keen to do anything to help Tim.

b) Tom is Tim's brother. He has been caught stealing the bike. He is 16 and has been cautioned once before for a similar offence. Tom lives at home and his father's concerns include him as well as Tim.

c) Tracey is 14 and has been caught at the conclusion of a shoplifting 'spree' in the High Street. All the goods stolen were recovered except for a half bottle of vodka which she drank most of before she was caught. Her mother is a single parent living in a council flat and is angry with Tracey for 'being caught'. Tracey has never been in trouble before and her mother refused to come to the police station when she was arrested.

d)   Lambert is 16 and has been caught trying to sell a car radio which he stole from a BMW parked at the local tube station. Some £100 damage was done to the car. He was difficult at the police station and has refused to talk to you. The police are very concerned about such crimes which have increased considerably in the area in the last few months.

e)   Glanville has been arrested after having been found smoking a joint outside his school. He had a number of packets of cannabis in his bag and has told the police that he was going to give them to his friends as a present. Glanville is 14 and has never been in trouble with the police.

If and when cautioning is replaced by the new system of police reprimands and Final Warnings the case study can be amended to explore how both these provisions might be used. In particular the exercise could concentrate on any appropriate intervention and support to be provided by the Youth Offender Team as a part of the Final Warning.

4.   You have been invited by the Clerk to the Justices to talk to the magistrates at the next meeting of the youth court panel about the reforms of the youth justice system envisaged/specified by the Crime and Disorder Bill/Act. You have been told that they are delighted about being given greater powers.

What you are going to say to them?

5   ACTIVITIES

1.   There is no substitute for seeing the youth court working. It may be possible to gain access as part of a social services or probation placement subject to the approval of the court itself. Students on other placements may be able to get access to the youth court by seeking the permission of the Clerk to the Justices.

A letter of introduction from college or agency asking for permission and giving assurances about protecting the confidentiality of proceedings is normally enough to obtain the necessary authority. A visit to the youth court can be combined with the preparation of an observation report. Such a report should identify the proceedings observed and provide an outline of the jurisdiction of the court. Observations can also be made on the identity, functions and competence of all those involved in the proceedings. Brief summaries of the cases heard can be provided together with any criticisms of the proceedings themselves. Concluding comments might centre on the 'quality of justice' provided by the youth court.

2.   Design a leaflet for defendants and their parents explaining what goes on in criminal proceedings in the youth court.

3.   Find out whether there is an 'alternative to custody' scheme operating in your area and get some information on how it works.

4.   Where is the attendance centre for your area? Contact the centre and arrange to visit when it is working.

5.   What intermediate treatment schemes are operating in your area? How do they work?

6.   Talk to a community service officer and find out how community service is organised for youth offenders.

7.   What 'diversionary schemes or procedures' operate in your area? Are there any statistics available? Which agencies are involved?

8.   Contact the Children's Legal Centre and get a publications list and any free materials they provide.

9.   Become a member of NACRO. You will receive mailings of their briefing papers, report summaries, the NACRO News Digest, the annual report and their publications list. NACRO is one of the leading pressure groups in the criminal justice field and provides excellent information.

10.   Identify the membership and work of the youth justice team (young offender team) in your area.

11. Monitor the introduction of the reforms of the youth justice system envisaged in the White Paper and provided for in the Crime and Disorder Bill 1997.

12. Contact your local youth justice team and ask for copies of their published reports, initiatives, etc.

6 ADDRESSES

Children's Legal Centre
Essex University
Wivenhoe Park
Colchester
Essex CO4 3SQ.
Phone Advice Line: 01206 873820
Fax: 01206 874026
E-mail: CLC@essex.ac.uk
Admin phone number: 01206 872466

National Association for the Care and Resettlement of Offenders (NACRO)
Youth Crime Section
169 Clapham Road
London SW9 0PU.
Phone: 0171 582 6500
Fax: 0171 735 4666

National Association of Youth Justice
Membership Secretary
193 Markfield Road
Groby
Leicester LE6 0FT.

A whole range of useful materials can be accessed on the internet. The Penal Lexicon web page is at:

www.penlex.org.uk

The Home Office can be accessed through the internet. Their web page is at:

www.open.gov.uk/home_off

7 MATERIALS

Ashford, M and Chard, A, *Defending Young People in the criminal justice system*, (1997) Legal Action.

Asquith, S (ed), *Children and Young People in Conflict with the Law*, (1996) Jessica Kingsley Publishers.

Ball, C, McCormac, K and Stone, N, *Young offenders, law, policy and practice*, (1995) Sweet and Maxwell.

Gordon, W, Watkins, M and Cuddy, P, *Introduction to the Youth Court*, (1996) Waterside Press.

Raynor, P, Smith, D and Vanstone, M, *Effective Probation Practice*, (1994) Macmillan.

Smith, D, *Criminology for Social Work*, (1995) Macmillan.

Misspent Youth: Young People and Crime, (1996) Audit Commission.

National Standards for the Supervision of Offenders in the Community, (1995) Home Office, Department of Health and the Welsh Office.

New National and Local Focus on Youth Crime: A Consultation Paper, (1997) Home Office.

No More Excuses – A New Approach To Tackling Youth Crime in England and Wales, (1997) Home Office.

Tackling Delays in the Youth Justice System: A Consultation Paper, (1997) Home Office.

Tackling Youth Crime, (1997) Home Office.

CRIMINAL PROCEEDINGS AGAINST CHILDREN AND YOUNG PEOPLE -COURT STRUCTURE

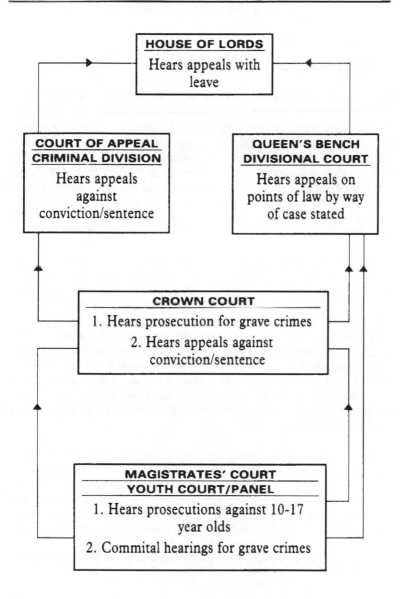

HOUSE OF LORDS
Hears appeals with leave

COURT OF APPEAL CRIMINAL DIVISION
Hears appeals against conviction/sentence

QUEEN'S BENCH DIVISIONAL COURT
Hears appeals on points of law by way of case stated

CROWN COURT
1. Hears prosecution for grave crimes
2. Hears appeals against conviction/sentence

MAGISTRATES' COURT YOUTH COURT/PANEL
1. Hears prosecutions against 10-17 year olds
2. Commital hearings for grave crimes

CHAPTER 10

Social security benefits

1 INTRODUCTION

1.1 SOCIAL WORK AND THE SOCIAL SECURITY SYSTEM

The importance of ensuring that service users are receiving all that they are entitled to by way of social security benefits cannot be over emphasised. Consequently benefit entitlement can be understood as an issue that links social work practice across the band of different groups of service users. For some, social security benefits will constitute their only source of income and though the level of benefits means that this income is often at subsistence level only, the importance of securing maximum entitlement is crucial.

A number of benefits are specifically designed for particular groups of claimants. Included in this category are benefits for claimants who are ill or have a disability, for elderly people and for single parents, and it is no coincidence that these groups of claimants represent a substantial proportion of social work service users. It is quite legitimate to speculate about the link between the status and character of social security claimants and social work service users and though such a discussion is beyond the boundaries of this book it is not difficult to assert that the lack of adequate financial resources available through the benefit system forces a number of claimants to seek social work support. At the very least research has established a clear link between disablement and poverty.[1]

If the importance of social security benefits to service users is accepted then it is necessary to identify how social work practice might relate to the social security system. Social workers have no statutory rights or duties in this area of work and so any involvement will be determined by individual and perhaps agency definitions of good practice. For local authority social workers much will depend

---

1 *The financial circumstances of disabled adults living in private households*, (1988) Office of Population and Censuses and Surveys, HMSO.

upon whether an individual practitioner's employing authority has a welfare rights team or adviser. For social workers in such a fortunate position the 'social security burden' is much reduced in the sense that specialist advisers can give advice and other help to individual practitioners and their service users. Nonetheless social workers will still need to know their way around the system so that service users can be given informed advice and assistance and so that complex and difficult problems can be recognised for what they are and referred on for specialist help.

For local authority social workers who do not have such a facility and particularly for those working in the voluntary sector or doing residential work, the problem is more acute. Decisions will need to be made about the extent to which social work practice involves 'social security practice'. Such a decision will depend on a number of factors including the availability of and access to, expert social security knowledge and skills through, for example, a law centre, citizens' advice bureau or other advice agency.

Some discussion of the extent to which social work practice might involve 'social security practice' will allow an identification of the skills and knowledge involved in this area of work and some assessment of how far social work can and should become involved. A number of questions can be posed:

- Should social workers merely offer basic social security information and advice to service users?

- Should help be provided in the actual claiming of benefits, eg by completing claim forms, accompanying service users to the Benefits Agency or the Employment Service; by contacting the department on behalf of the service user by letter or telephone?

- Should social workers be involved in appeals either as witness, accompanying friend or as advocate/representative?

Behind these questions are concerns about the relationship between social worker and service user; the social worker as advocate, as facilitator, as enabler. Probation officers are required to advise, assist and befriend offenders made subject to a probation order; what is the proper relationship between a social worker and a service user who is also a claimant; what knowledge and skills in relation to the social security system does a social worker require?

1.2 MATERIALS

The complexity of the social security system is legendary and a basic text on social work and the law can only provide an introduction to the system and the various benefits. Social workers will need to know this basic information so that they can make use of the specialist materials that are available, and it is recommended that a basic reference library is compiled and updated. Fortunately this is both easy and relatively inexpensive and can be accomplished by the purchase of claimants' guides; the three below are published as new editions around April each year. These guides are:

Disability Rights Handbook. Published annually by the Disability Alliance Educational and Research Association.

National Welfare Benefits Handbook. Published annually by the Child Poverty Action Group (CPAG).

Rights Guide to Non-Means Tested Benefits. Published annually by CPAG.

This chapter will deal only with benefits administered by central government departments. Housing benefit, which is administered by local government, is considered in the chapter on housing rights. Social security benefit rates are updated each year and any rates identified in this chapter are those that apply for the year April 1997 to April 1998.

2 THE LAW

Before identifying and describing the individual benefits it is important to understand some of the major concepts that are used as part of the language and culture of the social security system.

2.1 CONTRIBUTORY AND NON-CONTRIBUTORY BENEFITS

Much of the social security system is financed by the national insurance contributions paid by employers and employees. As well as providing some of the funds from which many benefits are paid, contributions are also used as a qualification for benefit entitlement. This insurance principle works on the basis that entitlement to some benefits, called contributory benefits, is partly dependent on the claimant having paid sufficient and appropriate contributions. Incapacity benefit is a contributory benefit, so that a claimant who is incapable of work will not be entitled to the benefit unless they have a sufficient and appropriate contribution record.

2.2 MEANS-TESTED AND NON-MEANS-TESTED BENEFITS

Another division that is frequently made in the social security system is that which distinguishes between means-tested benefits and non-means-tested benefits. Entitlement to a means-tested benefit depends, among other things, on an examination of the financial circumstances of the claimant, and possibly others in their family, and a decision that their means fall below a particular figure. Income support and family credit are means-tested benefits.

The financial resources of the claimant are irrelevant to the question of entitlement to non-means-tested benefits. Incapacity benefit is non-means tested.

2.3 BENEFITS WHICH ACT AS PASSPORTS TO OTHER BENEFITS

Entitlement to some benefits acts as a passport to entitlement to others. A claimant who is receiving income support is also entitled to free dental treatment and free prescriptions etc. Claimants receiving disability living allowance are entitled to disability premiums where they are receiving income support.

2.4 INDUSTRIAL AND NON-INDUSTRIAL BENEFITS

A number of benefits are available only to claimants who have a work related injury or who have contracted an industrial disease.

2.5 SOCIAL SECURITY LAW

Social security law is found in a series of Acts of Parliament and in numerous complex regulations made by the Secretary of State under powers given to him or her in the Acts. This statutory law is sometimes interpreted in appeal cases from one of the various 'social security tribunals' by specialist Social Security Commissioners and the courts; these decisions constitute precedents which are themselves legally binding on the tribunals and the adjudication officers who make decisions on benefit entitlement.

2.6   THE ADJUDICATION STRUCTURE

Benefit claims are decided upon by independent adjudication officers. The majority of decisions made by adjudication officers can be appealed against to a Social Security Appeal Tribunal (SSAT). It may be possible with leave, to appeal against the decision of a SSAT to the Social Security Commissioners. There is the possibility, again with leave, to appeal against the decision of the Commissioners to the Court of Appeal. Legal aid is not available for claimants to be represented before SSATs or the Commissioners.

Decisions concerning disability living allowance and disability working allowance are made by adjudication officers working in Disability Benefits Centres. Appeals are heard by Disability Appeal Tribunals.

A number of decisions, including those concerning contribution records, are made on behalf of the Secretary of State by authorised officers known as Secretary of State's Representatives; these decisions cannot be appealed against to a SSAT.

2.7   TIME LIMITS FOR CLAIMS

The Social Security (Claims and Benefits) Regulations 1987 have been recently amended to specify time limits for claiming individual benefits. These limits are subject to very limited extensions in circumstances specified by the Regulations. These amendments, which abolish the general ground of good cause for a late claim, mark a distinct toughening of the rules for claiming.

2.8   THE BENEFITS

This section will be divided into four:

i)   non-means tested benefits;

ii) means tested benefits;

iii) disability benefits;

iv) industrial injury benefits.

This section will provide a basic outline only of each benefit. Detailed information can be obtained from the appropriate claimant's guide.

2.8.1   Non-means tested benefits

Job seekers allowance (contributory benefit)

This benefit is paid to claimants who are unemployed or working for less than 16 hours per week, but who are available for work, are actively seeking work, and who have signed a job seekers agreement. The law specifies a number of circumstances in which the claimant can be sanctioned and lose entitlement to benefit. Sanctions for misconduct or voluntarily leaving employment without just cause may result in a sanction for up to 26 weeks.

Job seekers allowance (contributory benefit) is payable for up to six months. The weekly benefit will be reduced by any earnings apart from a £5 disregard. There are no dependency additions. The benefit is taxable and claimants must satisfy the appropriate contribution requirements.

The level of benefit paid means that most claimants who have a family will also have to claim income based job seekers allowance as a means tested 'top up' to bring their income up to the subsistence level represented by the income based job seekers allowance income personal allowances.

Short term sickness and disability benefits

Statutory sick pay (SSP) is paid to employees who are incapable of work because of some mental or physical incapacity. SSP is paid at a flat rate by employers, though a number of employees are excluded from entitlement because, for example, they are on a short term contract, or earn less than the threshold level (currently set at £62 a week). SSP is treated in the same way as wages or a salary and so is subject to deductions for tax and national insurance contributions. SSP is the minimum that must be paid to employees; they may also be entitled to sick pay under any occupational scheme provided by their employers. The method by which an employee must notify his or her employer of their sickness will be determined by the employer, hopefully by agreement, but is circumscribed by regulation.

Incapacity benefit is paid to those who are incapable of work because of their illness or disability. It is a contributory benefit paid to those who are not able to claim SSP either because the claimant is not employed, or is self-employed, or because entitlement to SSP has been exhausted. Incapacity for work is assessed either by the 'own occupation test' for those who have recently been in employment, or by the 'all work test' for those who have no recent connection with employment, or who have been incapable of work for 28 weeks. The own occupation test determines incapacity by reference to the claimant's ability to do work which they could reasonably be expected to do, normally their own occupation. The all work test uses a series of physical and mental criteria tests to determine a claimant's functional ability. Incapacity benefit is paid at short term and long term rates with adult and child dependency additions.

Non-means tested maternity benefits

Statutory maternity pay (SMP) is the equivalent of statutory sick pay for women during maternity leave and is paid by employers as a minimum entitlement to those women who are entitled. The maximum period for which SMP can be paid is 18 weeks though many women will not be entitled to SMP for the full period. SMP is paid at a flat rate and is subject to tax and deductions in respect of national insurance contributions.

Maternity allowance (MA) may be payable to women who are not entitled to SMP but who have given up employment during their pregnancy, changed jobs or are self-employed. MA is a contributory benefit paid for up to 18 weeks.

Child benefit

Child benefit is one of the most important benefits for claimants with families. It is a universal benefit in the sense that it is non-contributory, non-means tested and tax free and is paid to all families with children unless the child is in the care of a local authority and living away from home. Entitlement normally ceases when a child reaches 16 but is extended if the child continues in full time secondary education. Priority is given to a mother as the claimant.

Single parents are entitled to child benefit which is paid at a higher rate for the first child. The claimant must not be living together with the parent of the child, or with their spouse or living with a partner as husband and wife.

Where a person is looking after a child who is effectively orphaned and is entitled to child benefit in respect of that child they may also be entitled to *Guardian's Allowance*.

Widows' benefits

There are a number of non-means tested benefits to which a widow (a woman married to a man at the time of his death) may be entitled. Widow's payment, the widowed mother's allowance and the widow's pension are contributory benefits in the sense that entitlement will depend, among other matters, on the widow's late husband having fulfilled the required contribution conditions.

Retirement pensions

There are two main contributory retirement pensions; *category A pensions* which are paid on the basis of the claimant's own contribution record, and *category B pensions* which are paid to married women, widows and some widowers and are based on the contribution record of the claimant's spouse.

Retirement pensions are paid to those who have reached pensionable age (60 for women and 65 for men).

Category A pensions are paid to claimants on the basis of their own contribution records and there are a number of additions which may be added to the basic pension including a benefit to reflect graduated contributions paid between 1961 and 1975 and an additional pension based on any SERPS (state earnings related pension scheme) contributions.

Category B pensions are paid on the basis of the claimant's spouse's contributions and are paid to a married woman, a widow or a widower over pensionable age. Again category B pensions can be increased by additional payments including those in respect of graduated contributions and SERPS contributions.

State Earnings Related Pension Scheme (SERPS)

This scheme provides an earnings related pension for employees whose employers have not contracted out of the scheme. Where the employer has contracted out an additional occupational pension will be paid via the employer. Employees may choose to join a personal pension scheme as an alternative.

2.8.2   Means-tested benefits

This category of benefits is dominated by income based job seekers allowance, income support and the social fund. The social fund, a largely discretionary based benefit, is designed to provide for exceptional circumstances and expenses by a series of grants and loans. The discretionary basis of the scheme has been heavily criticised, but in reality recourse to the social fund may be necessary for a significant number of service users. Family credit provides a means tested benefit for low paid families and is best understood as a supplement to the weekly income of a family with children trying to live on low wages.

Family credit

Family credit is paid to couples or single parents with children who are in low paid work. There are a number of conditions which must be satisfied for entitlement to family credit:

- residence in Great Britain;

- the claimant or partner must usually work for more than 16 hours per week;

- the claimant or partner must be responsible for a child who is a member of their household;

- the family's capital must not exceed £8,000;

- weekly income must be below a certain level which will depend upon the size of the family and the age of the children.

Working out the amount of family credit is done on the basis of a complicated arithmetical formula involving a comparison between the family income (for family credit purposes) and the applicable amount. The applicable amount is set by the government and is increased each year; the current figure is £77.15. If the family income is below the applicable amount then the family credit entitlement will be the maximum for the particular family calculated by reference to a set of scale rates. If the family income is above the applicable amount then the family credit entitlement will be the maximum family credit amount reduced by 70% of the excess of income over the applicable amount. There are complex rules concerning the calculation of income.

Family credit is normally paid for 26 weeks and a change of circumstances during that period will not usually alter entitlement.

Income support

Income support is the benefit which has provided the safety net for the social security system. It is designed to provide a subsistence level of weekly income for those whose financial resources are not sufficient to meet their needs. The majority of claimants have historically been drawn from three categories: pensioners, single parent families and the long term unemployed.

The law of income support is contained in the Social Security Contributions and Benefits Act 1992 and the Social Security Administration Act 1992, and in a series of complex regulations contained in statutory instruments. The legislation is subject to interpretation by the Social Security Commissioners and very infrequently by the Court of Appeal or even the House of Lords.

Basic conditions for entitlement to income support:

* claimant must be in Great Britain;

* generally aged 18 or above (there is limited entitlement for 16–17 year olds);

* not in full time advanced education;

* claimant must not be working for 16 hours or more a week;

- if the claimant has a partner, s/he must not be working for 24 hours or more a week;

- must be available for work and actively seeking work;

- capital must not be in excess of £8,000;

- claimant must be in one of the categories of people eligible for income support (particularly those who are not required to be available for work or actively seeking work, eg those who are incapable of work).

For most claimants income support acts as a top up benefit in the sense that it fills the gap between the total of other benefits paid to the claimant together with any other income, and the weekly level of income which the government has fixed as being appropriate for a person in the claimant's circumstances. This latter figure, which is called the applicable amount, is supposed to provide for normal weekly needs and is made up of three elements: personal allowances, premiums for regular additional expenses, and housing costs. So income support can be understood as:

APPLICABLE AMOUNT – INCOME = INCOME SUPPORT PAID

The applicable amount is made up of personal allowances, premium payments and allowable housing costs. Personal allowances for the claimant and his or her dependants, are fixed by government each year and represent an official definition of the subsistence costs of living. They differ by reference to age and marital status.

Premiums are weekly additions to personal allowances and are paid to take account of the additional costs incurred because the claimant has children or is a single parent, or because the claimant or a dependant is a pensioner, or because of the disability of the claimant or another person in the household.

The housing costs of claimants who are paying rent will normally be met through the housing benefit scheme administered by local authorities. Claimants placed by local housing authorities in bed and breakfast accommodation will also have their housing costs paid through housing benefit. Special rules apply for those living in registered care homes and nursing homes. Claimants paying a mortgage may have the interest met through income support as a housing cost.

Income is a generic term that includes both capital and income. Capital is not defined by law but includes savings, lump sum payments and some property. There is sometimes difficulty in deciding whether an item is a capital asset and if so how to treat it for income support purposes. Some capital is taken wholly into account in the calculation of entitlement to income support, other items are partially disregarded in the calculation and others are wholly disregarded.

Claimants and their partners who have aggregated capital assets of over £8,000 are not entitled to income support. Capital of over £3,000 but under £8,000 is taken to produce a weekly income of £1 for every £250 of capital.

Income can take a number of forms including earnings, other benefit payments and maintenance. Earnings from part-time work will be taken into account in the calculation of income subject to a £5 or £15 disregard. A number of claimants, including those receiving premiums based on sickness and disability, may be entitled to a £15 disregard on their income.

Most benefits paid to income support claimants are counted as income though some, such as disability living allowance, are ignored in the calculation of income. Most maintenance payments are counted as income and are taken into account in the calculation of income. The rules in relation to income calculation for income support purposes are extremely complex and further reference can be made to the CPAG *National Welfare Benefits Handbook* for comprehensive information.

Aggregation and cohabitation

Social workers with service users who are claiming income support will come across a number of common problems which therefore warrant some consideration. A principle of aggregation operates within income support, by which the income and capital of the claimant is taken to include the resources of his or her spouse or cohabitee. There is a legal obligation on spouses to maintain each other and their children but no such obligation exists between cohabitees. A single mother who is claiming income support for herself and her child(ren) may have her benefit withdrawn if she enters into a relationship with a man which the Benefits Agency considers as living together as man and wife. In such circumstances the man may claim benefit for the whole family but if he is working 24 hours or more per week then neither he nor the woman is entitled to benefit. This situation is compounded by the fact that the woman has no right to be maintained by her new partner at a time when she has lost her independent right to benefit.

Maintenance and child support

The right of a spouse to be maintained can be enforced through the law but the difficulties of securing adequate maintenance through the courts are such that many women with children who have been deserted are forced to claim income support. When such a claim is made the Child Support Agency, established by the Child Support Act 1991, is responsible for assessing the level of child support to be paid by parents who are not discharging their legal obligation to maintain their children and for collecting and enforcing assessments.

Premiums

It is important for social workers to do all they can to ensure that service users are receiving any appropriate premiums to which they are entitled. Entitlement to the family premium, the lone parent premium and the pensioner premium should not be difficult to establish and entitlement to other premiums, though sometimes complex, is specified by regulation. Entitlement to the disability premium flows from receipt of other disability benefits such as disability living allowance, long term incapacity benefit and severe disability allowance, and also from being registered blind. There are other avenues of entitlement and it is important that social workers check that service users who are disabled are receiving their full entitlement to income support.

The general rule is that a claimant may receive only one premium though they may qualify for more than one. If there is multiple qualification the most valuable premium will be paid. This general rule applies to the disability premium, the pensioner premium, the higher pensioner premium, and the lone parent premium. The family premium will be paid in addition to any of these and the disabled child premium is paid in addition to any other premium.

Income based job seekers allowance

Income based job seekers allowance is the equivalent benefit to income support for claimants who are required to be available for work, actively seeking work, and to have signed a job seekers agreement. The benefit is means tested and taxable. Claimants and their partners must not have more than £8,000 aggregated capital and the claimant's partner is not working or is working less than 24 hours a week. It can be paid to provide a subsistence level of income and may be paid to top up contribution based job seekers allowance.

The social fund

The social fund, which was originally legislated for in the Social Security Act 1986, is divided into two quite separate parts. The statutory social fund provides legal entitlement to a maternity payment, to funeral expenses and cold weather payments. Claims are decided by an adjudication officer and appeals can be made to a SSAT. The discretionary social fund provides for claimants faced with exceptional expenses; this part of the social fund makes community care grants, budgeting loans and crisis loans on a discretionary basis only. There is no legal entitlement to such benefits so that claimants are forced to rely on the discretionary decision making of a social fund officer.

Social Fund Officers are required by the Social Security Contributions and Benefits Act 1992 to decide any claim or other social fund matter, in accordance with any general directions issued by the Secretary of State and in determining any such question shall take account of any general guidance issued by him. The directions are binding on social fund officers but they do not constitute a legal entitlement for claimants. They tell an officer what s/he may award and what cannot be awarded. Officer discretion is itself circumscribed by the cash limited budget of the social fund so that if the budget of an office has been exhausted no social fund payments will be made.

There are three types of discretionary payment which may be made by the fund.

Community care grants

These payments are made by way of grants and are designed to facilitate and support care in the community for an individual rather than institutional care. They can be paid so as to keep someone out of care or to help someone coming out of institutional care. Grants can also be made to help a family cope with an exceptional pressure or stress. Claimants for a community care grant must be on income support and there is a capital limit of £500 so that any capital above that amount must be used to meet the need.

Budgeting loans

These are loans from the social fund to income support claimants for special expenses which they are unable to meet from their normal weekly budget. Income support must have been in receipt for at least 26 weeks and the same £500 capital rule applies. The maximum loan is £1,000 and all loans are repaid by deductions from weekly income support.

Crisis loans

These are loans made to pay for costs arising from an emergency or disaster. Anyone may make an application provided they have no savings and no other way of meeting the need. The loan must be the only way to prevent serious risk to the health or safety of any member of the family.

The outlines of these three types of social fund payment tend to hide the difficulties associated with claiming them. In addition to the limited budgets for grants and loans the social fund directions frequently exclude categories of payment and categories of claimant from receiving grants and loans. These directions are binding on social fund officers and social workers advising service users about the possibility of a claim on the social fund should be aware of the directions relating to each of the three social fund payments. These directions, which are published in the *Social Fund Manual*, are reproduced in the *Disability Rights Handbook* and they are essential, if depressing, reading for any social worker dealing with the social fund.

Directions and guidance

Many of the directions tell social fund officers what they cannot do and this negative aspect of the social fund is often reinforced by the guidance which officers must take account of. The guidance states that:

> The overriding principle upon which the budgetary system is based is that the total cost of payments made by any local office in a financial year must not exceed its budget allocation for that financial year.

In order to facilitate the application of a fixed budget the guidance states a series of priorities for social fund payments so that a hierarchy of needs and claimants is established. Despite the fact that the guidance is not binding on social fund officers there is little doubt that they stick very closely to the priorities listed and that claimants whose needs have a relatively low priority are unlikely to be successful in their application for a grant or loan.

Challenging a social fund decision

Because the discretionary part of the social fund is not based on legal entitlement there are no rights of appeal to a SSAT. There is, however, a right to have a review of social fund decisions including those concerning the refusal of a loan or grant, the amount awarded and the award of a loan rather than a grant. It is also possible to seek a review of the decision concerning the repayment of a loan. A review is carried out by a social fund officer by reference to the law and all the circumstances of the case and will include a review of the way in which the decision was reached and whether the social fund officer exercised his or her discretion fairly. If the review does not go wholly in favour of the claimant then the claimant must be invited for an interview at which the decision will be explained and the claimant will be able to put his or her case. If the case is not decided in the claimant's favour after interview it is referred to a senior social fund officer for decision. This decision, which is given in writing, may be further reviewed by a social fund inspector.

2.8.3 Industrial injuries benefits

There is a specific set of benefits available to employed claimants who have suffered an industrial injury or contracted an industrial disease. In some cases the character of the benefit and the level at which it is paid compares favourably with the non-industrial equivalent.

General conditions

An industrial injury is a personal injury which has been caused by an accident which has arisen out of and in the course of employment. If the different elements of this definition are established the claimant may be entitled to one or more of the industrial injury benefits. An industrial disease is a disease which has been identified by law as having a clear occupational cause. A number of occupations are prescribed in relation to such diseases and in specified circumstances a claimant who is employed in a particular occupation and who is suffering from a disease prescribed for that occupation is accepted as suffering from an industrial disease and again may be entitled to one or more of the industrial injuries benefits.

The benefits

A short term, temporary incapacity for work caused by an industrial injury or disease is provided for under the statutory sick pay scheme.

Disablement benefit

This is paid where the claimant has suffered a long term disability resulting from loss of mental or physical faculty which has been assessed at 14% or more. The amount of the benefit depends on the extent of the disablement.

Two benefits are paid as increases to disablement benefit:

1. Constant attendance allowance which is the industrial equivalent to attendance allowance, is paid to claimants who are entitled to disablement benefit at the 100% rate and who require constant attendance because of their loss of faculty.

2. Exceptionally severe disablement allowance will be paid to claimants who are receiving more than the normal maximum constant attendance allowance.

2.8.4   Disability benefits

The availability of benefit income is important for many service users who are disabled or dealing with long term chronic illness.

Benefits for long term or permanent sickness or disability

Incapacity benefit

This benefit spans short and long term illness and disability. For claimants who develop a longer term or permanent incapacity for work their entitlement to statutory sick pay is likely to be superseded by an entitlement to the contributory incapacity benefit. Incapacity for work is established by the 'own occupation' test or the 'all work' test. The 'own occupation' test is used for those still in employment or who have recently had to give up employment because of their illness or disability. Essentially the test is whether the claimant is incapable of doing their own job. The more rigorous 'all work' test applies to claimants without recent employment and to claimants who have been subject to the 'own occupation' test for 28 weeks. This test involves an assessment of the claimant's functional ability against a number of physical and mental task criteria.

Severe disablement allowance
This benefit is the non-contributory equivalent of incapacity benefit. The claimant must have been incapable of work for at least 28 weeks and, except for those whose incapacity began before their twentieth birthday, be classed as 80% disabled. This level of disablement is automatically satisfied by receipt of attendance allowance, disability living allowance, or by being registered blind.

Disability living allowance
Disability living allowance is designed for people who need help with looking after themselves and for those who find it difficult to walk or get around. Disability living allowance therefore has two components – a care component and a mobility component; both have different disability tests and both have different levels of payment. The benefit is non-means tested, non contributory and is paid on top of income support and other social security benefits.

There are strict age tests· there is no lower age limit for the care component; the claimant must be aged 5 or over for the mobility component. Disability living allowance is payable for life but the claimant must have started to qualify for the benefit before his or her sixty-fifth birthday; and the claim must be made no later than the day before the claimant's sixty-sixth birthday.

Attendance allowance
This benefit, which is non-contributory and is not means tested, is the equivalent of disability living allowance care component for those whose need for the benefit develops after their sixty-fifth birthday.

Disability working allowance
This benefit which is tax free and non-contributory is paid on top of low wages or self employed earnings to people whose disabilities put them at a disadvantage in getting a job. The person with a disability must be working for more than 16 hours a week.

Invalid care allowance
This benefit is paid to the carer of someone who is receiving attendance allowance or disability living allowance. The care must be

'regular and substantial' and in effect is the equivalent of a full time job for the law deems caring for 35 hours a week to satisfy this requirement and disqualifies from entitlement anyone who is gainfully employed or in full time education. This is a non-contributory non-means tested benefit.

Disability premiums in income support

Many claimants with a disability rely upon the extra income provided by the disability premiums paid in addition to their basic income support. The disability premiums are paid in respect of someone who is under 60 and where the claimant satisfies the incapacity condition or the claimant or their partner passes the disability condition. (For those over 60 the disability premium is replaced by the higher pensioner premium.)

The incapacity condition requires the claimant to have had an incapacity for work for a 52 week qualifying period. The disability condition can be satisfied by the claimant or their partner being registered as blind, or receiving attendance allowance (or constant attendance allowance), disability living allowance, disability working allowance, long term incapacity benefit, mobility supplement or severe disablement allowance.

Severe disability premium can be awarded in addition to the disability premium or the higher pensioner premium. The claimant gets disability living allowance care component at the middle or higher rate, or attendance allowance, and no-one gets invalid care allowance for looking after you, and the claimant counts as living alone. For a claimant who is one of a couple qualification for the severe disability premium depends upon both the claimant and partner receiving the above benefits. Where both are being cared for by someone who is receiving invalid care allowance the premium will not be paid.

The character of disability benefits

There is little doubt that the complexity of the benefit system for people who have a disability disadvantages a number of claimants. Currently the system is based on a number of individual benefits each designed to provide for a specific need. Some are contributory benefits, most are non-contributory. Income support and its disability premiums are means tested; other disability benefits are non-means tested. Invalid care allowance is paid to a carer whilst attendance allowance or disabled living allowance is paid to the disabled person. Entitlement to some benefits acts as a passport to others so that a claimant for invalid care allowance must be caring for someone who is receiving attendance allowance, constant attendance allowance or disability living allowance care component at the middle or higher rate; entitlement to the income support disability premiums depends, among other factors, on receipt of a qualifying benefit which includes attendance allowance, disability living allowance and severe disablement allowance.

For many people who have a disability social security benefits provide their only source of income and it is argued by many commentators that the current system of disability benefits is not the best means of providing adequate financial support for this group of claimants. It must also be remembered that the benefit system provides only financial support, other forms of support are available through the community care system. Pressure groups working on behalf of people who have a disability have for some time been calling for a radical reform of the benefit system and specifically for the introduction of a unified and comprehensive disability benefit to be paid at a level which relates directly to a claimant's needs. These calls continue despite the introduction in 1992 of the disability living allowance and the disability working allowance.

3   SOCIAL WORK AND THE LAW: some issues for discussion

3.1   SOCIAL WORK AND THE SOCIAL FUND

There is no doubt that the introduction of income support and the social fund in 1988 has had a profound impact on the ability of many social work service users to make ends meet. Income support only provides a subsistence level of income and claimants faced with an extra item of expenditure, such as a new cooker, are forced to seek help from the social fund. The basis of a claim on the discretionary social fund is essentially a request for help; there is no legal entitlement. The nature of that help, if it is forthcoming, is likely to be in the form of a loan which must be repaid by deductions from weekly income support. If there is no money left in the budget or the claim is of a low priority then no loan will be made. If it is decided that the claimant cannot afford to pay the loan back then no loan will be made notwithstanding the degree of necessity for the item in question. In such circumstances it is not surprising that a number of service users turn to social services departments for help in circumstances that in the era of supplementary benefit and the single payments system, were obtainable by legal right from the Department of Social Security.

This tendency towards a shift of responsibility from state benefit to social services has been exacerbated by the introduction in 1993 of the care in the community provisions of the National Health Service and Community Care Act 1990, and by changes in the funding of residential care. For a number of commentators these shifts are seen as a quite deliberate policy decision by the previous government and there is no doubt that the implications of the social fund for local authority social services departments were envisaged by government. Guidance to social fund officers refers specifically to the need to create close links with other agencies, particularly with social services departments.

The social fund has been subject to substantial criticism from social services departments, and groups representing social workers see the social fund as an attempt to transfer responsibility for a large number of poorer families and individuals from the Department of Social Security to social services; from central government to local government. As a result many social workers have seen co-operation with the fund as no part of their business. Nonetheless the nature of the social fund and the position of many of those who are forced to seek help from it means that the availability of help in claiming or challenging a decision may be important. The British Association of Social Workers has argued for a policy of determined advocacy which is designed to ensure that individual claimants are properly equipped to deal with the social fund and thereby maximise their claim on the fund.

The Disability Alliance has identified the need for claimants to be fully informed:

> Different organisations may have some difference in emphasis, or in their philosophy, and may call their policy by different names, such as 'determined', or 'aggressive' advocacy, or the 'rights' approach. The central idea is that you (the claimant) must have the right to decide for yourself what course you wish to take. And to do that, you need fully informed advice and information about the social fund. Advisors who take this approach will not take on the role of social fund officers and so will not make judgements

or get drawn into discussions about relative priorities between their clients.[2]

The seventeenth edition of their Handbook provided some strategic advice to claimants:

- ask for all the help you need; an advisor should be ready to help you fill in the application form so that you can present your case in the most effective way;

- ask for a grant rather than a loan;

- if you are awarded a loan, try and negotiate the longest repayment period possible ...;

- check to see if your need is specifically excluded from help in the directions, or if your situation excludes you from help; if you are not sure, go ahead and ask for help in any case;

- if you are refused help, 'appeal' through the review procedure;

- if you still don't get help, seek further advice.

Many social workers are increasingly finding that the social fund fails to meet the needs of their service users and they are being forced to turn to charities for help. In turn the Charity Commissioners have issued a set of guidelines concerning the social fund to the trustees of charities. The essence of the guidelines is that whilst charities might properly supplement help from the social fund charitable funds should not replace such help. The Commissioners stress that those in need should look to the social fund first for grants and/or loans before approaching charities for help and that social fund officers should only refer a claimant onto a charity for help having first sought the advice of the charity. Charities should expect to help where grants cannot be made and the social fund directions list those things for which a loan or grant cannot be made. These include an educational or training need (including clothing and tools), the cost of respite care, medical, surgical, optical, aural or dental items or services and anything for which an application was made in the previous 26 weeks unless the circumstances have changed.

---

2   *The Disability Alliance ERA*, Advice About the Social Fund, Disability Rights Handbook (14th edn).

The nature of the discretionary social fund denies claimants any legal entitlement to a grant or loan. It also means that the decisions of social fund officers can only be reviewed, there is no right to appeal to an independent appeal body such as a Social Security Appeal Tribunal. Because the social fund is cash limited the size of the annual budget is fundamental to the ability of the fund to meet the needs of claimants. Each local office is allocated a budget for grants and a budget for loans, and there is, in theory, some ability to transfer funds between offices and to supplement an office budget from a small contingency fund. In relation to grants, funds that are under spent in any one year will only go to reducing the exchequer contribution for the next year. Social fund officers are not allowed to make payments which exceed the office budget and they must have regard to the size of the budget when deciding to make a loan or grant. In practice it seems that social fund officers are discouraged by budgetary limitations from making grants and loans. No application can be considered in isolation from its financial implications for the budget. Every grant or loan made reduces the budget for other grants and loans. Such a system encourages, indeed it is based on, parsimony with the result that claims, which social work and other voluntary agencies would understand as perfectly legitimate, are denied.

3.2 ENFORCING SOCIAL SECURITY RIGHTS

Entitlement to social security benefits (excluding the social fund) is based on the existence of legal rights provided for in statute and regulations. The decision of an adjudication officer can be appealed against to an independent Social Security Appeal Tribunal (SSAT). Unfortunately the positive character of these statements is somewhat undermined by the complexity of most social security law and the unavailability of legal aid for representation before a SSAT or the Social Security Commissioners. Many claimants are discouraged from appealing because of the intimidating nature of the appeal process and those that do exercise their rights of appeal are often not able to make the best use of a tribunal hearing.

There are a number of possible practical responses to this situation for a social worker with a service user who has had a claim denied or limited. It is to be hoped that social workers will have enough knowledge of the social security system to be able to spot a potential appeal and if necessary refer the service user to specialist advice and assistance. This may be available through a law centre or welfare rights agency or could be provided by a lawyer under the green form scheme (legal aid advice and assistance).

The legal aid scheme does not cover representation before Social Security Appeal Tribunals so that a service user will be left very much to their own knowledge and skills unless a representative can be provided by one of the welfare or rights agencies, or by Citizens' Advice Bureaux. Advocacy before tribunals by social workers on behalf of their clients was often very effective in establishing an exceptional need or the risk of serious harm or serious damage to health in an appeal involving supplementary benefit and single payments. These issues are now dealt with (or not) by the social fund and there is less scope for effective advocacy based on establishing such characteristics. Nonetheless the experienced and knowledgeable social worker can provide important help and support for a service user who is appearing in an income support appeal before a SSAT or a review with a social fund officer. The greater the social worker's knowledge and experience of the social security system the greater the help and support they can provide to service users seeking to establish their legal right to social security benefits or the legitimacy of their request for a social fund grant or loan.

These difficulties, which are considerable, will be exacerbated by reforms to the adjudication system contained in the Social Security Bill 1997. The provisions of this legislation include the abolition of adjudication officers with all decisions to be taken by officials on behalf of the Secretary of State; and the abolition of the Independent Tribunal Service which currently administers the system of independent tribunals. The work of the Service will be taken over by the Department of Social Security. The existence of a right of appeal to an independent tribunal is clearly under threat and there is little doubt that these administrative changes will undermine the ability of service users to enforce their rights to benefit income.

4 CASE STUDIES

The case studies in this section are designed to provide an introduction to working with a variety of benefit systems. As such they are relatively simple; however the methods needed are common to more complicated circumstances. It will be necessary to refer to current benefit rates, which are updated in April each year, and to one of the social security rights guides. Where appropriate an opportunity has been taken to include circumstances which require consideration of aspects of social work practice not concerned with social security benefits but which are of relevance for the claimants/service users portrayed in the problem.

1.   Erica, who is 25, is a single mother with two children aged four and eight; they live in local authority accommodation. She has no savings and relies entirely on state benefits for her income.

What is her entitlement to income-based benefits?

Explain how this figure was worked out.

2.   Lloyd and Loretta are married and have two children aged nine and fourteen. They live in local authority accommodation. Lloyd has been unemployed for two months and is receiving job seekers allowance. Loretta has a part-time job (twelve hours per week) earning £35 net per week. Lloyd was paid £4,500 in redundancy money when he became unemployed and this figure is in a building society account.

What is the family's entitlement to income based job seekers allowance?

Explain how this figure was worked out.

What benefits would the family be entitled to if Loretta were working full time earning £85 per week (net)?

3.   George and Ethel are both 72 and receive the basic state pension. They have no savings. They live in a local authority house. Ethel has very bad arthritis and is unable to get upstairs to the bathroom any more or to walk to the shops which are at the end of the road. Their cooker is not working and they cannot afford to get it repaired or to replace it.

What social security benefits are they entitled to?

4.   Bill and Mary have been married for ten years and have two children, Andrew, seven, and Michael, five. Andrew has severe learning difficulty; he has epilepsy and needs constant nursing and

care. Bill works as a lorry driver and earns £120 per week (net). Mary does not work.

What social security benefits are the family entitled to?

What benefits would the family be entitled to if Bill had been involved in an accident while he was driving his lorry and had been off work for ten weeks?

5.   Remi is a single parent living with her three children aged two, five and twelve. Raddi (the five year old) has a degenerative muscle disease, his mobility is very limited and he needs constant day time care and occasional help at night which Remi undertakes at home. The family has no income other than their entitlement to state benefits. Their housing costs are paid through the housing benefit scheme.

Establish the benefits to which the family are entitled by detailing the appropriate benefit and entitlement criteria.

Provide an approximate entitlement calculation.

6.   Alan and his wife Sonia live in their own home (not subject to a mortgage). Alan left his job three months ago when his chronic skin condition became so bad that he was no longer able to work. He also has angina and cannot walk more than a 100 yards without having severe chest pains. They have four children aged three, seven, eight and fifteen. Sonia used to work part time but has been made redundant by her employers. She left her job last Friday with a redundancy payment of £5,000.

Establish the benefits to which the family may be entitled by detailing the appropriate benefit and entitlement criteria.

5 ACTIVITIES

1.   It is important to build up a good selection of reference materials. The three major guides are the basic materials:

Disability Rights Handbook (Published by the Disability Alliance Educational and Research Association).

Rights Guide to Non-Means Tested Benefits (Published by the Child Poverty Action Group (CPAG)).

National Welfare Benefits Handbook (Published by CPAG).

Each of these guides is updated annually by the publication of a new edition in April or May. It is important to have the current edition.

Benefit rates are updated in April each year.

2.   To supplement these basic materials it is worth identifying specialist social security advice for particular groups of service users. As an example Age Concern publishes a number of fact sheets and briefing papers dealing with social security for older people.

See in particular:

Income Support and the Social Fund.

Income Related Benefits: income and capital.

Attendance Allowance and Disability Living Allowance.

3.   Publication lists can be obtained from Age Concern, The Disability Alliance, CPAG and from other groups concerned with social security issues.

4.   The Department of Employment and the Department of Social Security publish explanatory leaflets for all benefits. Many of these can be obtained free from post offices. For full publication lists write to the department concerned.

5.   There is a Benefit Enquiry Line for general advice. 0800 882200. There is also a forms completion service for disability related benefit claim packs: 0800 441 144.

6.   It is important to know of local advice centres and other agencies who can provide service users (and others) with help on social security matters. This information can be investigated and compiled in the form of a local directory which can be made available to service users and others.

The *Disability Rights Handbook* has an excellent section at the back of its guide which contains the names, addresses and phone numbers of pressure groups, law centres, advice centres, tribunal representation units and other agencies working in the social security field.

6 ADDRESSES

Age Concern England
Astral House
1268 London Road
London SW16 4ER.
Phone: 0181 679 8000

Benefits Agency Leaflets are available from:
The Stationery Office Ltd
The Causeway
Oldham Broadway Business Park
Chadderton
Oldham OL9 9XD.

Child Poverty Action Group
1-5 Bath Street
London EC1V 9PY.
Phone: 0171 253 3406
Fax: 0171 490 0561
E-mail: staff@cpag.demon.co.uk

Disability Alliance Educational and Research Association
Universal House
88-94 Wentworth Street
London E1 7SA.
Phone: 0171 247 8776
Fax: 0171 247 8765
Rights Advice Line: 0171 247 8763

Help the Aged
St James's Walk
London EC1R 0BE.
Phone: 0171 253 0253
Fax: 0171 306 0808
E-mail: HTA@dial.pitex.com
Web: www.helptheaged.org.uk

7   MATERIALS

Disability Rights Handbook (New edition each April), Disability Alliance Educational and Research Association.

National Welfare Benefits Handbook (New edition each April), Child Poverty Action Group.

Rights Guide to Non-Means Tested Benefits (New edition each April), Child Poverty Action Group.

Keeping up to date on social security matters is a major problem. The following are bulletins which are published regularly and aim to provide updated information:

Welfare Rights Bulletin, published bi-monthly by the Child Poverty Action Group.

Disability Rights Bulletin, published four times a year by the Disability Alliance.

Benefits Agency Leaflets:

Sick or disabled? FB28. Benefits Agency.

Social security benefit rates. NI 196. Benefits Agency.

Which benefit? FB2. Benefits Agency.

Mesher, J and Wood, P, *Income Related Benefits: The Legislation*, Sweet and Maxwell (Annual editions and supplements).

Bonner, D et al, *Non-Means Tested Benefits: The Legislation*, Sweet and Maxwell (Annual editions and supplements).

Ogus, A, Barendt, E and Wikeley, N, *The Law of Social Security*, (4th edn) Butterworths.

Chapter 11

Discrimination

1 INTRODUCTION

The principle of anti-discriminatory practice is central to all aspects of social work. Professional practitioners will confront discrimination in their work and many will have experience of discrimination in their personal lives. The Central Council for Education and Training in Social Work (CCETSW) has its own equal opportunities policy statement and though it cannot apply to local authority social service provision or to individual practitioners, because it is addressed to education and training, it encapsulates the spirit of a principle that should underpin all social work practice:

> ... the onus is on people to recognise and understand the need for anti-discriminatory practice; to recognise and tackle different forms of discrimination; to understand and promote people's rights, strengths and uniqueness; and to promote appropriate services.[1]

The recognition of the importance of anti-discriminatory practice should be informed by an understanding of what might be called 'discrimination law'. Consequently this chapter will provide an outline of the law as it relates to discrimination on the grounds of race, gender and disability. It should however be recognised that the principles of anti-discriminatory practice go beyond the categories of discrimination identified in the Sex Discrimination Act 1975, the Race Relations Act 1976, and the Disability Discrimination Act 1995. Examples can be found in the Children Act welfare checklist (section 1(3)) and in community care policy guidance (LAC 90/12). The National Standards for the Supervision of Offenders in the Community includes explicit anti-discriminatory standards that are far more comprehensive than the provisions of legislation:

---

1 Quoted in Michael Preston-Shoot, *Acting Fairly: Working Within The Law To Promote Equal Opportunities in Education and Training*, (1998) CCETSW.

PSRs[2] and proposals for community sentences must be free of discrimination on the ground of race, gender, age, disability, language ability, literacy, religion, sexual orientation or any other improper ground. All probation services and social services departments must have a stated *equal opportunities policy* and ensure that this is effectively implemented, monitored and reviewed. Effective action to prevent discrimination (anti-discriminatory practice) requires significantly more than a willingness to accept all offenders equally or to invest an equal amount of time and effort in different cases. The origin, nature and extent of differences in circumstances and need must be properly understood and actively addressed by all concerned – for example, by staff training, by monitoring and review and by making extra effort to understand and work most effectively with an offender from a different cultural background.[3]

In the area of racial discrimination many Afro-Caribbean and Asian social workers will come to their practice with personal experiences of life in a society which discriminates against them. White social workers will be working with Afro-Caribbean and Asian service users and must be sensitive to the differences in life experience and expectations that are determined in part by race and ethnicity.

A number of institutions and agencies working with service users including social services departments, the police, the probation service, the criminal justice system, and local government housing departments have been accused of incidents of racism. Indeed some commentators have remarked on the perception of black people that the criminal justice system is itself racist.[4] The Race Relations Act 1976 was, and remains an acknowledgement of racism in our society. The Act established the Commission for Racial Equality (CRE), which is responsible for improving race relations and taking action against racial discrimination. Despite the fact that the Act has been implemented for over twenty years many social workers and many service users continue to experience aspects of society as racist. The Policy Studies Institute in its third survey, *Black and White Britain*, published in 1984, reported that people who are Afro-Caribbean and Asian disproportionately live in bad housing, have low paid jobs, receive poor health care and inadequate education, are more heavily

---

2   Pre-sentence reports.
3   *National Standards for the Supervison of Offenders in the Community*, (1991) Home Office, Department of Health, and the Welsh Office.
4   *Black People's Experience of Criminal Justice*, (1991) National Association for the Care and Resettlement of Offenders.

policed and are over-represented in the prison population. Subsequent research and comment has done nothing to counteract the results of this survey. Indeed factsheets published by the CRE in 1997 confirm a similar picture.[5] The CRE continues to argue for a strengthening and extension of the Race Relations Act 1976 to improve its effectiveness in combating racism and its effects.

In another facet of the experience of racism, the nationality laws and the administration of the immigration service seem to those who experience them, and to many others, to be designed to discriminate against non-white immigrants and in particular against applicants from the Indian subcontinent.[6]

The law of race relations concerns itself with the incidence of discrimination and racial hatred in the population as a whole and as a result it contains no statutory duties or provisions which specifically determine social work practice other than section 71 which imposes a duty on local authorities to discharge their functions so as to eliminate unlawful racial discrimination; and promote equality of opportunity, and, good relations between persons of different racial groups. There is no equivalent to section 71 in the Sex Discrimination Act 1975 or the Disability Discrimination Act 1995. Other legislation imposes statutory duties which have a direct impact on social work practice. Section 22(5)(c) Children Act 1989, which specifies the duties of local authorities in relation to children being looked after by them, requires the local authority, when making any decision concerning such a child, to give due consideration to the child's religious persuasion, racial origin and cultural and linguistic background. Section 95 of the Criminal Justice Act 1991 refers to the need for all those involved with the administration of criminal justice to avoid discrimination; and such issues are now also covered in official guidance such as the National Standards for the Supervision of Offenders in the Community which specifies the need for anti-discriminatory practice. It is important to note that though the legislation referred to above is concerned with discrimination on the grounds of race, gender and disablement, the principle of anti-discriminatory practice goes beyond these categories to specify a principle that refers to all forms of discrimination on improper grounds.

5 Factsheets on racial attacks and harassment, immigration and citizenship, policing, employment, the criminal justice system, and other matters.
6 Gordon, P, *Fortress Europe? The meaning of 1992*, (1989).

2 THE LAW

2.1 STRUCTURE

2.1.1 Race and gender

The Sex Discrimination Act 1975 established the Equal Opportunities Commission and the Race Relations Act 1976 established the Commission for Racial Equality. They are charged with the objective of working toward the elimination of sexual and racial discrimination, promoting equality of opportunity and keeping the working of the equality laws under review. The 1976 Act also defined a criminal offence of incitement to racial hatred, with a variety of offences now being contained in the Public Order Act 1986.

The definitions of racial and sexual discrimination in the Acts cover both direct and indirect discrimination. These concepts are expressed in the following language which is taken from the context of racial discrimination: direct discrimination consists of *treating one person less favourably than another on grounds of colour, race, ethnic or natural origin, in the provision of goods, facilities and services, employment, housing, and advertising.* Indirect discrimination can be understood as *discrimination by the imposition of certain conditions which can be met by more people of one colour, race, ethnic or natural origin than another so long as it is unjustifiable.*

A person who has been discriminated against can take an individual civil action against the discriminator in the appropriate forum. In employment matters this will be an industrial tribunal; for discrimination in other circumstances a county court action is available. By definition complaints by an individual to an industrial tribunal or a civil action for damages are taken largely to secure compensation and prevent the continuation of discrimination against an individual. Where discrimination operates to disadvantage a large group of people such individual actions may not be an effective response unless taken as a test case.

The Commission for Racial Equality and the Equal Opportunities Commission both have investigative and enforcement powers which can be used against discriminators. The Commissions have powers under their respective Acts to conduct formal investigations and to issue non-discrimination notices. Such notices, which may be served where the Commissions think that their Acts are being broken, can be enforced if necessary through an application by the Commissions to the courts for an injunction.

Racial and sexual harassment is unlawful and may be the basis for an action in the industrial tribunal for harassment that relates to employment, or to the county court for other non-criminal or employment matters, such as the provision of goods and services. Harassment includes physical assault, verbal abuse and any other form of behaviour perceived as humiliating, offensive, distressing, intimidating or demeaning.

2.1.2 Disability discrimination

The Disability Discrimination Act 1995 attempts to counter discrimination against disabled people. The major provisions of the Act are concerned with discrimination in employment and the provision of, and access to, goods and services; there are other provisions concerning education and public transport. The Act defines disability as:

> ... a physical or mental impairment which has a substantial and long-term adverse effect on a person's ability to carry out normal day-to-day activities.[7]

Part II of the Act outlaws discrimination on the grounds of disability in the field of employment, though these provisions do not apply to employers with fewer than 20 employees. Discrimination occurs when a disabled person is treated less favourably than someone else and the treatment relates to that person's disability and that reason does not apply to the other person, and the treatment cannot be justified. The employment provisions of the Act cover recruitment and retention of employees, promotion and transfers, training and development, and the process of dismissal. Employers are also under a duty to make reasonable adjustments to their premises and to employment arrangements, if these substantially disadvantage a disabled employee, or prospective employee, when compared to a non-disabled person.

The Act makes it unlawful for people who provide goods, facilities or services (service providers) to discriminate against disabled people. It is irrelevant whether the service is free or paid for and the Act

7   Section 1(1). One of the consequences of using such a functional definition of disability is that not all disabled people will be covered by the provisons of the Act. An example might be a person with a physical impairment which has a substantial adverse effect on their ability to carry out normal day-to-day activities but is not long term, such as acute but short term asthma attack brought on by an allergic reaction.

includes local authorities and other social work service providers. Discrimination in this area occurs when a disabled person is treated less favourably than someone else and the treatment is for a reason relating to the person's disability and that reason does not apply to the other person, and this treatment cannot be justified. It will include refusing to serve a disabled person, offering a disabled person a lower standard of service, offering a disabled person less favourable terms, and failing to make alterations to a service or facility which makes it impossible, or unreasonably difficult, for a disabled person to use. Service providers may have to make reasonable alterations and adjustments to their service provision or premises to comply with these duties.

Legal actions alleging discrimination in the employment field are taken to the Industrial Tribunal, while those concerning goods, facilities and services are taken to the county court.

The Act established the National Disability Council to advise government on eliminating and reducing discrimination against disabled people, and on the operation of the Act, excluding the employment provisions. Advice on employment matters concerning disabled people comes from the National Council on Employment of People with Disabilities.

2.1.3   Local authority duties

Section 71 of the Race Relations Act requires local authorities:

> ... to make appropriate arrangements with a view to securing that their various functions are carried out with due regard to the need –
>
> a) to eliminate unlawful racial discrimination; and
>
> b) to promote equality of opportunity, and good relations, between persons of different racial groups.

2.1.4   The criminal law

The law in relation to the generic criminal offence of incitement to racial hatred is now contained in six offences specified by the Public Order Act 1986. The two major offences are established in sections 18 and 19. Under section 18 (use of words and gestures) a person is guilty of an offence if:

a) he uses threatening, abusive or insulting words or behaviour, or

b) he displays any written material which is threatening, abusive or insulting, and

c) either he intends thereby to stir up racial hatred, or

d) having regard to all the circumstances racial hatred is likely to be stirred up thereby, and he intended his words or behaviour or the written material to be, or was aware that they might be, threatening, abusive or insulting.

Under section 19 (publishing or distributing written material) a person is guilty of an offence if:

a) he publishes or distributes written material, and

b) the written material is threatening, abusive or insulting, and

c) either he intends thereby to stir up racial hatred or having regard to all the circumstances racial hatred is likely to be stirred up thereby.

Racial hatred is defined by section 17 to mean hatred against a group of persons in Great Britain defined by reference to colour, race, nationality (including citizenship) or ethnic or national origins.[8]

The other criminal offences cover stirring up racial hatred by the public performance of a play, through sound or visual recordings, broadcasting, and the possession of racially inflammatory material. The utility of the criminal law as a weapon against racial hatred is severely limited by the requirement that the Attorney-General consent to a criminal prosecution. Between 1965 and 1973 (under the old law) only seven prosecutions against fifteen people were brought. It seems that successive Attorneys-General have taken the view that such prosecutions do nothing to improve race relations and there is no evidence that under the 1986 Act this view has changed:

> One case involving incitement to racial hatred was referred to the Attorney General during 1994 for prosecution under the Public Order

---

8   For further discussion on this definition and generally on the racial hatred offences see Thornton, P, *Public Order Law*, Chapter 4, Financial Training.

Act 1986. Two consents for prosecution were given during the year, and three people were convicted.[9]

Other sections of the Public Order Act 1986 may be relevant for the prosecution of offences with an element of racism. Section 4 requires an intent to cause a person to believe that immediate unlawful violence will be used against him or another. Section 4A requires that there is an intent to cause harassment, alarm or distress and that a person caused harassment, alarm or distress. Section 5 deals with threatening, abusive or insulting words or behaviour likely to cause harassment, alarm or distress.

Section 4 provides that:

(1) A person is guilty of an offence if he –

(a) uses towards another person threatening, abusive or insulting words or behaviour, or

(b) distributes or displays to another person any writing, sign or other visible representation which is threatening, abusive or insulting,

with intent to cause that person to believe that immediate unlawful violence will be used against him or another person, or to provoke the immediate use of unlawful violence by that person or another, or whereby that person is likely to believe that such violence will be used or it is likely that such violence will be provoked.

Section 4A, a new section introduced by the Criminal Justice and Public Order Act, provides that:

(1) A person is guilty of an offence if, with intent to cause a person harassment, alarm or distress, he –

(a) uses threatening, abusive or insulting words or behaviour, or disorderly behaviour, or

(b) displays any writing, sign or other visible representation which is threatening, abusive or insulting,

thereby causing that or another person harassment, alarm or distress.

9   *Criminal Justice in England and Wales*, Factsheet, (1997) CRE.

Section 5 deals with the causing of harassment, alarm or distress but does not require intent or proof that the victim suffered the consequences, both of which are required by the new section 4A. An offence under the new section 4A is therefore more serious and can attract a custodial sentence of up to 6 months.

Section 5 provides that:

(1) A person is guilty of an offence if he –

(a) uses threatening, abusive or insulting words or behaviour, or disorderly behaviour, or

(b) displays any writing, sign or other visible representation which is threatening, abusive or insulting,

within the hearing or sight of a person likely to be caused harassment, alarm or distress thereby.

The protections offered by the Public Order Act 1986 have been supplemented by the provisions of the Protection from Harassment Act 1997. The Act was designed to deal primarily with stalking, but also applies to racial harassment. Section 2 provides that it is an offence to pursue a course of conduct which amounts to harassment. The course of conduct must involve conduct on at least two occasions. Section 4 deals with conduct which causes a fear of violence. Both offences can attract a custodial sentence, with a maximum of 5 years for a section 4 offence.

Section 95 of the Criminal Justice Act 1991 requires the Secretary of State to publish each year information to enable people working in the administration of criminal justice to avoid discriminating against any persons on the ground of race or sex or any other improper ground.

It is a well established principle of sentencing that those convicted of racially motivated crimes should be punished more severely; racism aggravates the seriousness of the offence.[10]

10   *R v Ribbans, Duggan and Ridley* (1995) 16 Cr App Rep (S) 698.

3 DISCRIMINATION LAW AND SOCIAL WORK: some issues for discussion

3.1 THE LIMITS AND ENFORCEMENT OF DISCRIMINATION LAW

Anti-discriminatory practice is a fundamental element of good social work. For example the principles of such practice feature prominently in CCETSW's regulations on training, and statements requiring adherence appear in guidance concerning social work practice with children and families, in mental health work and criminal justice work.[11]

The welfare check list in the Children Act requires courts, and by implication practitioners, to take account of the child's background and characteristics. Where a local authority is looking after, or proposing to look after a child, it must give due consideration to the child's religious persuasion, racial origin and cultural and linguistic background, when it makes any decision with respect to the child. It is clear that such issues should figure prominently where the welfare of the child is a matter for consideration by practitioners, such as where a report is being prepared by the guardian ad litem or the court welfare officer.

The Introduction to the Code of Practice to the Mental Health Act 1983 identifies a number of broad principles for practice with people who are being assessed for possible admission under the Act, or to whom the Act applies. They include the principle that such people should receive respect for and consideration of their individual qualities and diverse backgrounds – social, cultural, ethnic and religious.

Practice within the criminal justice system should take place within the anti-discriminatory principle of section 95 of the Criminal Justice Act 1991 and similar principles articulated in the National Standards for the Supervision of Offenders in the Community.[12]

This chapter has identified the statutory structure of anti-discrimination law as it relates to race, gender and disability. Consequently,

---

11 See also *Anti-racist Social Work*, CCETSW; part of the Northern Curriculum Development Project.
12 See above, p 346.

though other forms of discrimination, such as on the grounds of age, are identified in 'social work' guidance and national standards, they are not the subject of legal prohibition, and as such are not unlawful. The nature and administration of immigration and nationality law is discriminatory;[13] discrimination against people on the grounds of their HIV status alone is not unlawful,[14] and other than in Northern Ireland, their is no law which renders religious discrimination unlawful unless it also amounts to racial discrimination. It appears that in many respects the law lags behind the principle of anti-discriminatory practice which is well established in many professions including social work.

Mention should also be made of the Welsh Language Act 1993 which provides that all public bodies in Wales must have a Welsh language policy approved by the Welsh Language Board, and which is also responsible for promoting and facilitating the use of the Welsh language. However the Act does not apply to the private and voluntary sectors and does not give individuals the right to speak Welsh when dealing with public bodies.

If then the content of anti-discrimination law is less than comprehensive, what is the position concerning enforcement?[15] Both the Commission for Racial Equality and the Equal Opportunities Commission have powers to hold formal investigations and to issue non-discrimination notices. Such notices can be enforced by an application by the appropriate Commission to the High Court for an injunction. Legal actions by individuals can be assisted by the Commissions who can also provide mediation services.

There is some concern that the courts are unsympathetic to legal actions by the Commissions, at least to the extent that the principles enshrined in the legislation are interpreted restrictively in the light of the due process rights of the alleged discriminator. Where actions are taken by individuals either in the Industrial Tribunals or the county courts' awards of compensation are often unable to radically challenge established institutional discrimination.

---

13   *Immigration and Citizenship*, Factsheet, (1997) CRE.
14   While asymptomatic a person with HIV will not come within the definition of disability in the Disability Discrimination Act.
15   See *Enforcing the Race Relations Act, A Code of Practice for the CRE*, (1995) CRE.

Though legal aid may be available for an action in the county courts this is not the case for representation before the Industrial Tribunal. This omission is particularly serious because the procedure in these tribunals is adversarial and employers are often legally represented:

> Even where the law does provide a framework for combating discrimination in employment and service provision, and a means of redress, the approach individualises peoples problems rather than challenges in any fundamental way the social attitudes and structural inequalities in which discrimination is rooted. The law does not effectively tackle the roots of discrimination. Rather, it focuses on the manifestations of discrimination, but this is not unproblematic. Enforcement is difficult. There are restrictions on group actions, each aggrieved individual having to press their own case rather than being joined to action already initiated by others in a similar position. Cost, the weakness of the available penalties and the track record of courts in understanding the needs and experiences of people from minority groups, together with the difficulty of proving discrimination, will deter some individuals from seeking redress. Using the tribunal system is not without its hazards for future employment prospects and, furthermore, compensates the victim without any guarantee of changing the workplace in which discrimination occurred. Again, difficulties of proof, together with the requirement to relive painful experiences when giving evidence, and the low success rate, act as deterrents.[16]

The enforcement of the Disability Discrimination Act 1995 is even more problematic. The negative comments concerning the enforcement of individual rights under the race and sex discrimination legislation apply equally to disability discrimination legislation. In addition there is currently no possibility of Commission led enforcement because the National Disability Council has no such powers and is not able to investigate complaints of discrimination against individual disabled people. The government has now acknowledged this lack of enforcement powers and is proposing to establish a Disability Rights Commission as part of its 'commitment to comprehensive and enforceable civil rights for disabled people'.[17]

Race relations and sex discrimination legislation was enacted over 20 years ago and progress towards the elimination of discrimination

---

16   Preston-Shoot, M, *Acting Fairly: Working Within The Law To Promote Equal Opportunities in Education And Training*, (1998) CCETSW.
17   *Triple Whammy for Disability Rights*, Department For Education and Employment Press Release 304/97, October 1997.

in our society on the grounds of race and gender has been slow. The legacy of individual legal actions taken in industrial tribunals and through the appeal process in the domestic legal system appears to have had little impact against established discriminatory practices. However, if and when sex discrimination cases are taken to Europe for an action in the European Court of Justice they are often decided in ways that promote the principle of equal opportunity and equal treatment. A good example was the case of *Marshall v South West Health Authority* [1986] QB 401 which declared differences in the retirement ages of men and women to be illegal. The impact of the European law on domestic English law particularly in the field of discrim-ination on the grounds of gender and sexuality should not be underestimated.

It is too early to assess the impact of the Disability Discrimination Act 1995 though any optimism should be tempered by the current lack of institutional enforcement powers bought about by the refusal of the last government to give the National Disability Council equivalent powers to those of the CRE and EOC. In this sense disability discrimination legislation is even weaker than its race and gender counterparts.

It is possible to offer some more positive comment within the prospect of the incorporation of the European Convention on Human Rights into domestic English law. Currently English law only affords its citizens those rights which are enacted for within Acts of Parliament. As a result there are rights about discrimination which are concerned with race, gender and disability. There are no such rights concerning discrimination on the grounds of age or religion. The incorporation of the Convention will establish a principle of non-discrimination which should extend beyond the groups covered by existing legislation.

It should also be recognised that anti-discrimination legislation has both instrumental as well as symbolic importance. Criticism of the current state of the law in this chapter has centred on the instru-mental impact of legislation. An assessment of the symbolic impact of legislation after 20 plus years of implementation is far more difficult. Though there has undoubtedly been some progress in the area of equal opportunities, particularly in relation to gender, research in the field of race relations suggests that there is little cause for optimism. For example commentators in the field of criminal justice continue to find evidence of racism. In *Race and Sentencing: A Study in the Crown Court*, Dr Roger Hood found that black males were 17% more likely to receive a prison sentence than their white counterparts. The research also found significant racial disparities in the use of non-custodial sentences so that black offenders were more likely to receive community penalties higher up the tariff than white offenders.[18]

Researching for the Royal Commission on Criminal Justice, Marion Fitzgerald concluded:

> The research available addresses many of the concerns which have been raised by the ethnic minorities about their experience of criminal justice. It does not do so definitively, however, and many gaps remain. Yet Hood adds weight to the evidence already accumulated which strongly suggests that, even where differences in social and legal factors are taken into account, there are ethnic differences in outcomes which can only be explained in terms of discrimination.[19]

Anti-discriminatory social work practice will inevitably confront discrimination, not least because many service users will have experienced the impact of discrimination on the basis of their race, their gender and/or their disability. It is possible that the positive impact of anti-discriminatory practice may be limited by a code of anti-discrimination legislation which is characterised by its relative 'softness'. Even where the Commission for Racial Equality and the Equal Opportunities Commission have enforcement powers the exercise of these powers is often short term and reactive rather than long term and transformational.

3.2 RACIAL VIOLENCE AND HARASSMENT

The government has recently issued two consultation papers which are concerned with, among other things, racial violence and the provision of remedies for the victims of racial harassment.[20] Based upon police figures which show a rise in the number of racial incidents from 4,383 in 1988 to 12,222 in April 1995–March 1996, the government is proposing the introduction of new statutory racial crime offences and the introduction of anti-social behaviour orders. These

---

18 Clarendon Press, 1992.
19 *Ethnic Minorities and the Criminal Justice System*, (1993) HMSO.
20 *Community Safety Order: A Consultation Paper*, Home Office, September 1997; *Racial Violence and Harassment: A Consultation Document*, Home Office, September 1997.

provisions will extend increased provision already introduced through the implementation of the Protection from Harassment Act 1997.

The new statutory offences would mirror offences under the Offences Against the Person Act 1861, the Public Order Act 1986 and the Protection from Harassment Act 1997, but would provide for more severe maximum sentences where a racial motivation was established. It is already well established by the guideline case of *R v Ribbans, Duggan and Ridley* (1995)[21] that racially motivated crime should attract a heavier sentence. As part of its initiative the government propose to legislate for this principle in the Crime and Disorder Bill 1997. Clause 22 provides a definition of racially aggravated offences and Clauses 23–25 provide for increased sentences for racially aggravated offences under the Offences Against the Person Act 1861, the Public Order Act 1986 and the Protection from Harassment Act 1997.

In its proposals for an anti-social behaviour order the government has identified harassment as a ground for an application to the courts for such an order by the police or local authority. The order would be issued against particular individuals and would require them to comply with the requirements of the order. Breach of the order would be a criminal offence. These proposals are incorporated in Clause 1 of the Crime and Disorder Bill 1997.

These proposals are part of what the government calls 'an overall package to tackle racial crime'. They are to be welcomed as a response to the documented increase in racial crime and racially motivated harassment. They will offer increased protection to ethnic communities; however such improvements will sit uncomfortably with a criminal justice system which continues to evidence discrimination against the same communities.[22]

4 CASE STUDIES

This chapter provides only a brief introduction to discrimination law and as a result the case studies do not address the complexity of the law as it may be encountered. (Practitioners and service users involved in such disputes should be advised to seek specialist legal

---

21   (1995) 16 Cr App Rep (S) 698.
22   *Criminal Justice in England and Wales*, Factsheet, CRE (1997).

help, possibly through the offices of the Commission for Racial Equality or the Equal Opportunities Commission.) Consequently these case studies provide no more than a starting point for a discussion of some of the issues raised in this chapter.

1.   Hassan is unemployed and sees an advert in the paper for a job as a packer. He rings the phone number and when he gives them his name he is told that the job is filled. He knows that the company needs lots of packers and so he gets his friend Alan to ring. Alan is asked to attend for an interview and is offered a job.

What can Hassan do?

2.   Michael and Chantelle are a black couple who have recently moved onto a local authority housing estate. Ever since they moved into the house their neighbours have been rude and abusive toward them. Recently this abuse has become racist and their garden fence has also been daubed with obscene and racist slogans.

Chantelle is frightened and wants to know how she can stop this harassment.

(Consideration might also be given to housing law; eg can the local authority re-house Michael and Chantelle; in the event that the perpetrators are also local authority tenants, could they be evicted. If Michael and Chantelle left the accommodation would they be intentionally homeless for the purpose of the duties owed to them by the housing authority?)

3.   Sharmina is a staff nurse in the local hospital. She is very well qualified and has been on a number of training courses. Her annual assessments are always good and she is well thought of in her hospital. She has applied for promotion on a number of occasions but has never been shortlisted or interviewed. A number of more junior nurses have recently been promoted over her and Sharmina has noticed that they are all men and that they are all white. When she asked the personnel officer why she wasn't considered she was told that she wasn't sufficiently well qualified or experienced for promotion.

How would you advise Sharmina?

4.   Hanif has been arrested on a theft charge. While he was being questioned at the police station he was racially insulted by two police officers. He was kept in custody overnight and when he appeared

in court the next morning he asked the magistrates whether he could see the duty solicitor. The chairman of the bench refused and when Hanif asked for bail the chairman said 'oh no; not for your sort'.

You are the probation officer on court duty and you saw what went on in the court. You speak to Hanif in the cells who tells you about his experiences in the police station. What are you going to do?

5.   Robinson, who was born in Barbados but came to Britain at the age of three, has just graduated with a very good English degree. He wants to be a journalist and he sees an advert in his local paper for trainee journalists. The advert asks for graduates in English but also specifies that applicants must be 'native born English speakers'.

Robinson applies for an interview and states on his form that he was born in Barbados. He receives a letter three weeks later which tells him that the post has been filled.

What can he do?

6.   Robert is blind and applies for a job as a computer keyboard operator. He is well qualified and has appropriate experience. The employer rejects his application in a letter which tells Robert that his blindness disqualifies him from such a job.

Is this unlawful discrimination under the Disability Discrimination Act 1995? If so, what remedies are available to Robert?

7.   Marcia is a wheelchair user and receives community care services in her own right and as a carer for her disabled mother. She is provided with transport so that she can visit a physiotherapist. She receives a letter from the authority telling her that as this transport is more expensive for wheelchair users she is to be charged £3 for each journey. Non-wheelchair users are to be charged £2 for identical transport services.

Advise Marcia.

8.   A deaf local authority tenant visits the housing authority offices with an interpreter in the hope of seeing a housing adviser. He has not made an appointment but housing advisers often see 'pop ins'. However on this occasion no adviser is willing to see the tenant because the interview will take longer because of the need for the

interpreter. Consequently they would not be able to see other tenants with appointments.

Is this a breach of the Disability Discrimination Act 1995?

5 ACTIVITIES

1. Get hold of publications lists from the Commission for Racial Equality, the Equal Opportunities Commission and the National Disability Council. This will assist in the compilation of an appropriate set of materials and references.

2. Publications lists are also available from many pressure groups working to reduce and eradicate discrimination.

3. Try to establish how particular social work agencies and providers are dealing with the anti-discrimination dimension of their work. What systems are in place to promote anti-discriminatory practice in the provision of social work services and within the agency itself?

4. A service user needs advice concerning discrimination on the grounds of race, gender or disability. Where can they go for specialist help? Identify the agencies who can help.

5. Do the local police have a community relations section? Find out what sort of work they are involved in.

6. For information and advice on all aspects of immigration and nationality contact the Joint Council for the Welfare of Immigrants (see addresses section).

7. Get hold of the list of local Community Relations Councils from the CRE and get in touch with your local council.

6 ADDRESSES

Advisory, Conciliation and Arbitration Service
Clifton House
83-117 Euston Road

London NW1 2RB.
Phone: 0171 396 5100
Fax: 0171 396 5159
Web: www.acas.org.uk

Commission for Racial Equality
Elliot House
10/12 Allington Street
London SW1E 5EH.
Phone: 0171 828 7022
Fax: 0171 630 7605

The Commission has regional offices in Birmingham (phone 0121 632 4544), Manchester (phone 0161 831 7782), Leicester (phone 0116 2423700), Leeds (phone 0113 243 4413), and Cardiff (phone 01222 388977).

Equal Opportunities Commission
Overseas House, Quay Street
Manchester M3 3HN.
Phone: 0161 833 9244
Fax: 0161 835 1657

Institute of Race Relations
2/6 Leeke Street
London WC1X 9HS.
Phone: 0171 837 0041
Fax: 0171 278 0623
Web: www.homebeat.co.uk

Liberty
21 Tabard Street
London SE1 4LA.
Phone: 0171 403 3888
Fax: 0171 407 5354
E-mail: liberty@GN.atc.org

Joint Council for the Welfare of Immigrants
115 Old Street
London EC1 9JR.
Phone: 0171 251 8706

National Disability Council
6th Floor Adelphi

1-11 John Adam Street
London WC2N 6HT.

Runnymede Trust
133 Aldergate Street
London EC1A 4JA.
Phone: 0171 600 9666
Fax: 0171 600 8529
E-mail: runl@btinternet.com

7 MATERIALS

Casserley, C, *The Disability Discrimination Act, one year on*, Legal Action, December 1997.

Clarke, L, *Discrimination*, (1994) Institute of Personnel Management.

Dominelli, L, *Anti-Racist Social Work*, 2nd edn (1997) Macmillan.

Doyle, B, *Disability Discrimination – Law and Practice*, (1997) Jordans.

Gooding, C, *Blackstone's Guide to the Disability Discrimination Act 1995*, (1996) Blackstone.

Gooding, C, *Disability Discrimination Act 1995*, Legal Action, January and February 1997.

Malone, M, *Discrimination Law*, (1993) Kogan Page.

Macdonald, S, *All Equal Under the Act?* (1991) Race Equality Unit, National Institute of Social Work.

Palmer, C, Moon, G with Cox, S, *Discrimination at Work*, (1997) Legal Action Group.

Thompson, N, *Anti-discriminatory practice*, 2nd edn (1997) Macmillan.

Black People's Experience of Criminal Justice, (1991) NACRO.

Disability Discrimination Act Information Pack (DL50) containing a range of information leaflets. (Available free from the department of Social Security, phone 0345 622 633.)

Equal Opportunities Commission Code of Practice, *Equal Opportunities Policies, Procedures and Practices in Employment*, (1985) HMSO.

Gender and the Criminal Justice System, (1992) Home Office.

Race and the Criminal Justice System, (1992) Home Office.

Racial Discrimination: A Guide to the Race Relations Act 1976, Home Office, HMSO.

Series of factsheets published by the CRE (1997):

• Criminal Justice in England and Wales

• Employment and Unemployment

• Ethnic Minority Women

• Immigration and Citizenship

• Policing and Race in England and Wales

• Racial Attacks and Harassment

• Refugees and Asylum Seekers

CHAPTER 12

Housing rights

(Mary Holmes, Principal Lecturer in the School of Law, Kingston University.)

1 INTRODUCTION

Problems with housing affect a large number of social work service users and though housing law is a specialist area of legal practice an understanding of the basic principles and provisions will help social workers in their efforts to see that the housing rights of service users are protected and enforced where necessary.

Though social workers have no statutory rights or duties in the housing field their involvement with housing problems on behalf of service users is often considerable and for the purposes of this chapter can be identified as including the following issues:

- allocation of local authority housing;

- homelessness;

- security of tenure; squatters;

- harassment and eviction; anti-social behaviour;

- repairs to dwellings;

- housing benefit.

1.1 ALLOCATION OF LOCAL AUTHORITY HOUSING

Under the Housing Act 1996 the focus of allocation of social housing changed. All those with housing needs have been put on the same footing and allocation procedures standardised to ensure consistency of preference to applicants. When the Act was passed homelessness was no longer to be the short cut to permanent local authority housing; homelessness was perceived as a short term problem to be remedied by short term solutions – no homeless family would qualify for long term local authority housing. However, amendments introduced in late 1997 have extended the allocation scheme to include the homeless to whom the local authority now also owes a duty to secure accommodation.

1.2 HOMELESSNESS

Nevertheless homelessness is still a considerable problem and local authorities have statutory duties under the Housing Act 1996 and the Children Act 1989 to provide, in particular circumstances, accommodation for people who are homeless. This duty is undertaken by housing authorities and a number of local authorities have specialist social workers based in homeless persons units. Social work case loads may include families who are homeless and living in bed and breakfast accommodation; such service users may need social work support and it may be that the problems faced by families with children living in such circumstances warrant help and support under Part III and Schedule 2 of the Children Act 1989.

1.3 SECURITY OF TENURE AND PREVENTING HARASSMENT AND UNLAWFUL EVICTIONS

For a number of service users security of tenure is an important aspect of their housing rights. Again this is a specialist area of housing law expertise but the ability to recognise a problem and provide elementary, but informed, advice and support is a valuable practice skill. This is also the case in helping service users protect themselves from a landlord who is harassing them or attempting to evict them unlawfully.

1.4 REPAIRS

The condition of much of both public and private rented housing accommodation is poor and tenants often need help in encouraging and persuading landlords to meet their obligations in respect of repairs. The social worker who has a basic understanding of the relevant legal rights of tenants in this area will be able to identify when the law can be used to secure appropriate housing rights and be able, if necessary, to refer a service user to specialist legal help.

1.5 HOUSING BENEFIT

Entitlement to housing benefit is of crucial importance to large numbers of service users. In the same way that social security entitlement is an area of specialist expertise so also is housing benefit entitlement and social workers should have an understanding of the principles of the system.

1.6 THE SOCIAL WORK ROLE

The role of the social worker in relation to 'housing rights' will be determined by a number of factors which include the nature of their employment (eg social services, voluntary sector, residential work, probation officer), the availability, or otherwise, of specialist housing rights advice and expertise, the willingness of local authorities to comply with their legal duties in the field of housing rights and, importantly, their own ability in terms of housing rights knowledge and skills. As a minimum social workers should have a basic understanding of the provisions and principles in the field of housing rights so that they are able to 'identify a problem', ensure that a service user does not act to their own detriment and refer them on to specialist help where that is necessary, whilst all the time being able to offer informed basic advice and support.

2 THE LAW

2.1 ALLOCATION

Under Part VI of the Housing Act 1996 a new framework for allocation of housing has been created which must be adhered to by local authorities in their allocation of 'secure' or 'introductory' tenancies. This framework will not apply to transfers of existing tenancies but does apply to the selection of new tenants or nominations by the local authority to social landlords (eg housing associations) for new tenancies. This part of the Act is supported by a Code of Guidance which contains advice as to how the local authority might exercise its powers.[1] The Code does not, however, have the force of law but local authorities must have regard to it in coming to any allocation or homelessness decision.

2.1.1   Housing register and qualifying persons

Local authorities must maintain a 'housing register' of 'qualifying persons', similar to the old waiting list, and must make most allocations of housing from this register. Regulations identify classes of persons who must appear on the housing register, eg those over 18 years who are in priority need and unintentionally homeless (see **2.2.4** below.) In addition a local authority has considerable discretion as to who is a qualifying person but it must exclude certain 'people from abroad'[2] including all asylum seekers, until they have received a favourable decision as to their status, and all intentionally homeless applicants. The Code of Guidance suggests that, although a minimum age limit may normally be considered appropriate, the needs of the vulnerable young single person, such as some care leavers, should be borne in mind. A local authority might also wish to exclude certain categories of applicant such as those with a history of anti-social behaviour or tenants with a record of rent arrears. An applicant has the right to see a copy of their entry on the register.

2.1.2   Allocation in accordance with scheme

A local authority must have a scheme for allocation (section 167(2)) which gives reasonable preference to:

* people occupying insanitary or overcrowded housing or otherwise living in unsatisfactory housing conditions;

* people occupying accommodation which is temporary or occupied on insecure terms;

* families with dependent children;

1   A new Code of Guidance will be published in early 1998 to take account of the changes in the law relating to allocation and homelessness since the Act came into force.
2   Assessing an applicant's immigration status is a complex task; amendments have already been made to the relevant regulations on status which will be reflected in the new Code of Guidance.

- households consisting of or including someone who is expecting a child;

- households consisting of or including someone with a particular need for settled accommodation on medical or welfare grounds;

- households whose social or economic circumstances are such that they have difficulty in securing settled accommodation;

- homeless applicants owed a duty to be accommodated under sections 193 and 195(2) of the 1996 Act (see **2.2.6** below);

- people who were homeless and are owed a continuing duty to be accommodated after an initial two year period under section 194 of the 1996 Act; and

- people who have been provided with advice and assistance in order to secure suitable accommodation.[3]

The local authority is free to decide on the structure of its scheme, which it must publish. The Code indicates that there should be flexible, as opposed to formulaic, operation of the scheme and that each authority should have arrangements for determining priority and assessing severity of need which may be by points, date order or quota based. The local authority is also required to secure additional preference for individuals who cannot reasonably be expected to find accommodation for themselves in the future. The Code of Guidance describes this provision as being aimed at the particularly vulnerable, for example, as a result of old age, physical or mental illness and/or because of a learning or physical disability. Applicants with community care needs could clearly fall into this category.[4]

2.1.3   Challenges to decisions about status and priority.

Anyone who is considered by the local authority not to be a qualifying person or who is removed from the register, must be notified in writing, giving the reasons and explaining that the person has a right

---

3   The last three categories were added in regulations which came into force in November 1997 as the new government's response to the exclusion of the homeless from 'reasonable preference' in the original provisions.
4   See joint guidance from Dept Health/Dept Environment on *Housing and Community Care: Establishing a Strategic Framework*.

to a review of the decision within 21 days. There is no further right of appeal from a review (as there is with homelessness decisions); any further challenge would need to be by way of judicial review.

There is no provision at all for internal review of priority given to applicants. Complaint to the authority through local councillors is an obvious route. If maladministration is suspected the Local Government Ombudsman is the appropriate recipient of complaints and, finally, an applicant who cannot get satisfaction elsewhere may have to resort to an application for judicial review.

2.2   HOMELESSNESS

The Housing (Homeless Persons) Act 1977 placed important duties on local government housing authorities in respect of people who are homeless. These duties are now contained in Part VII of the Housing Act 1996 and, whereas they do not amount to a right to a home for people who are homeless, they do provide a route for some people to accommodation, although under the 1996 Act this may not be permanent accommodation. The law again gives local authorities a significant amount of discretion in the way they exercise their duties and this part of the Act is also supported by the Code of Guidance, indicating to local authorities how the provisions of the Act in relation to homelessness should be put into practice. In addition the Code contains references to the duties of social workers towards the vulnerable and those who are at risk of homelessness. Most local authorities, especially in the big cities, are very short of housing stock; some authorities are sympathetic to people who are homeless whilst others are conspicuous in their determination to avoid all but their basic duties under the Act. Section 179 of the Act imposes a new duty upon every local housing authority to ensure that advice and information about homelessness and its prevention is available to anyone free of charge; this duty applies even in respect of those who may be otherwise disqualified from assistance under the homelessness provisions.

It is perhaps easiest to see the provisions of Part VII of the 1996 Housing Act as establishing a number of conditions which need to be fulfilled by the person who is homeless in their application for accommodation:

•   Is the applicant homeless or threatened with homelessness?

- Is the applicant eligible?

- Is the applicant in priority need?

- Is the applicant unintentionally homeless?

- Does the applicant have a local connection elsewhere?

The duty of the local authority will vary depending on the answers to these questions.

2.2.1 Is the applicant homeless or threatened with homelessness?

Sections 175–177 specify situations in which people will be considered as being homeless or being threatened with homelessness:

- there is no accommodation available which they are legally entitled to occupy, including any accommodation in another country;

- they have accommodation but cannot secure entry to it, eg because of illegal eviction;

- they have accommodation but it is moveable, eg a caravan or houseboat, and they have nowhere to put it;

- they have accommodation but it does not provide for the family unit, which is split up because they have nowhere to live together, or for any other person who might reasonably be expected to live there, such as a carer;

- they have accommodation but it is not reasonable for them to stay in it because there is a danger of domestic violence if they live there;

- they have accommodation but it is not reasonable for them to stay in it, eg because of overcrowding or the standard of the accommodation (this criterion is relative in the sense that the accommodation is subject to comparison with prevailing accommodation conditions in the area);

- they are living in emergency or crisis accommodation, eg a refuge.

Being threatened with homelessness is defined as having accommodation but likely to be homeless within 28 days.

If the housing authority has reason to believe that an applicant is a person who is homeless or threatened with homelessness they must make enquiries to satisfy themselves that s/he is 'eligible' and whether any other of the homelessness conditions is satisfied. So the first step is to get the housing authority to accept (after their enquiries if necessary) that the applicant for accommodation is a person who is homeless or threatened with homelessness. The Code of Guidance requires that the homelessness unit liaises with other bodies in establishing the homelessness status of an applicant where there is an apparent care, health or support need.

2.2.2   Is the applicant 'eligible' for housing assistance?

Section 185 removes from consideration for housing under these provisions anyone who is 'ineligible', ie anyone whose immigration status prevents them from claiming benefit, who has failed the DSS 'habitual residence' test or who is an asylum seeker who is excluded from claiming DSS benefits because they failed to claim asylum immediately on arrival in this country.

2.2.3   Is there a priority need?

Section 189 defines four categories of people with a priority need:

- a person with dependent children living with them or who might reasonably be expected to live with them;

- a person who is homeless through flood, fire or disaster;

- a person, and anyone who might reasonably be expected to live with them, who is especially vulnerable because of age, mental illness or disability, physical disability or other special reasons;

- a woman who is pregnant or the woman with whom the person is living or might reasonably be expected to live is pregnant.

Two categories of priority need are of particular interest to social work:

a)   The applicant with children is treated as a 'family' even though the children may be being looked after by a local authority or have gone to live elsewhere when the family was made homeless. By treating such an applicant as a 'family' a priority need is established so that accommodation should be provided for the applicant and children to live together as a family. This is intended to prevent homelessness being the cause of a family breaking up and the children being accommodated by a local authority on a long term basis. It is not possible, however, for a dependent child to apply to the housing authority in its own right. If a child is homeless and a member of a family, the housing authority only has duties toward the family – the child's personal housing needs must be dealt with by way of application under Part III of the Children Act. However, just as a housing authority can, under section 213 of the Housing Act 1996, request the assistance of social services to discharge their functions under the Act, so can social services ask for a housing authority's assistance. In *R v Northavon District Council, ex p Smith*, the House of Lords[5] made it clear that although housing and social service authorities were expected to co-operate, a housing authority need only comply with a request for assistance from social services consistent with their own statutory functions. In the final analysis children remained the responsibility of social services which could not 'get round' adverse findings of the housing authority by the back door.

b)   A number of social work service users may be considered as 'vulnerable' so that they have a priority need under the terms of the Act. The definition of 'vulnerable' is clearly important and the Code of Guidance identifies people with a mental illness or learning disability or physical disability, the chronically sick, including those with HIV and AIDS as vulnerable. Housing authorities are also advised by the Code to consider as vulnerable those who are above the normal retirement age and those who are approaching retirement age and are particularly frail or in poor health. Some housing authorities are prepared to accept women without children who have been assaulted by their partner as vulnerable and young people, particularly those leaving institutional care, who are perceived to be susceptible to risks associated with drugs or alcohol abuse, sexual abuse, prostitution or violence as vulnerable. Vulnerability, however, must be established; it should not be assumed automatically because of disability etc. Social workers clearly have some scope for per-

5   [1994] 3 All ER 313.

suading housing authorities that a service user is vulnerable and thereby enabling them to be accepted as having a priority need. A disabled person must, however, be capable of accepting or rejecting an offer of accommodation to qualify as an applicant for housing.

Where there is apparent homelessness, eligibility and priority need, the local authority has an interim duty to accommodate while it makes further enquiries.

2.2.4   Is the applicant intentionally homeless?

Section 191 defines intentional homelessness in terms of the applicant deliberately doing or failing to do something the result of which is that they have ceased to occupy accommodation which is available for their occupation and which it would have been reasonable for them to continue to occupy. Failure to take up suitable accommodation will also be considered as intentional homelessness, as can failure to take advantage of a council's duty to help where an applicant has been assessed as unintentionally homeless. Any collusion between a landlord and a tenant for the tenant to be evicted in order to get rehoused by the local authority will also be considered intentional homelessness.

It is up to the housing authority to establish the intentionality of an applicant's homelessness and they may take past events into account in reaching their decision. For example, being evicted from settled accommodation because of a wilful refusal to pay rent would amount to intentional homelessness but being evicted because of non-payment of rent due to circumstances beyond the control of the tenant, such as redundancy, may not amount to intentional homelessness. Decisions on intentionality must take all relevant matters into account and they must be reasonable. It is not surprising, therefore, that there has been a considerable amount of case law on what amounts to intentional homelessness.

2.2.5   Does the applicant have a local connection?

By section 198 housing authorities can avoid their statutory responsibilities to make accommodation available where they accept that the applicant has satisfied the other four conditions, has no local connection with the district to which he has applied BUT does have a local connection with another local authority in England, Wales or Scotland. This transfer of responsibility can also arise where someone who could reasonably be expected to live with the applicant has a local connection elsewhere. Note that it is not necessary for the applicant to have a local connection with the district to which he has applied in order to be housed, only that the responsibility for housing can be transferred *if* there is a local connection with another local authority area. The local connection provision will not apply to an applicant who fears domestic violence if returned to another area. The local authority to whom the applicant is referred (the notified authority) is bound by the decision of the referring authority as to the housing obligation, even if the notified authority has previously rejected the applicant as intentionally homeless.

2.2.6 What is the applicant entitled to?

a) Where an applicant has satisfied the four conditions of i) being homeless, ii) being eligible, iii) having a priority need and iv) not being intentionally homeless, the local authority have a duty either

- if satisfied that other suitable accommodation is available in their district, to provide such advice and assistance as to enable him to secure such accommodation (section 197), or

- to secure him accommodation (section 193) for a minimum of two years, after which the authority must satisfy themselves that the person remains entitled under the legislation (section 194),

unless the local authority decides to refer the application to another local authority on the grounds of local connection. The power to refer a homeless applicant who satisfies all the criteria for assistance to suitable accommodation in the private rented sector is new. Accommodation will only be suitable where the local authority is satisfied that it will be available for at least two years.[6] It is likely, therefore, that the local authority will need to identify a particular landlord and an address, terms of the tenancy and details of rent.

b) Where an applicant has satisfied the local authority (as a result of their enquiries) that they are threatened with homelessness, are

---

6   Amendment introduced in regulations in October 1997.

eligible for assistance and have priority need the local authority have a duty to secure that accommodation does not cease to be available for occupation.

c)   Applicants who are homeless and have a priority need *but* who are also intentionally homeless are only entitled under the Act to advice and help with finding accommodation and temporary accommodation sufficient to give them time to make their own arrangements, after which no further duty is owed.

d)   Anyone who is homeless but not in priority need, such as a healthy single person, under retirement age and with no children, is only entitled to receive advice and assistance which may be nothing more than a list of cheap hotels or hostels. Some local authorities are more helpful and others even offer accommodation despite having no obligation to do so.

e)   It is possible that 'ineligible' people may be able to receive some basic assistance from a local authority under its general duty under section 179 or under the social service powers contained in section 21 of the National Assistance Act 1948.

2.2.7   Notification and reviews of decisions

Section 184 requires that the local authority notifies applicants, in writing, of their decisions and, if the decision is adverse, reasons must be given. The notification must also inform applicants of the right to request a review which must be made within 21 days of notification of a decision.

The review procedure is a new statutory requirement. Reviews may be requested concerning decisions on the applicant's eligibility, the local authority's duty, a local connection referral, suitability and availability of accommodation offers. The applicant should be notified of the review decision within eight weeks and should be informed of his right of appeal to the county court on a point of law.

Local authorities have no duty to provide accommodation pending a review or an appeal, although they may choose to do so.

2.2.8 Challenging housing authority decisions about homelessness

Although Part VII of the Housing Act 1996 imposes duties on local auth-orities in relation to the homeless, authorities have considerable discretion as to how those duties are interpreted and administered. As a result the ability of an applicant to challenge the decisions made by the authority is crucial. A major omission of previous Housing Acts was the absence of any rights of appeal for the applicant so that challenges to authority decisions mostly had to be made through an application for judicial review. This defect has to some extent been remedied by the review procedure and the right of appeal to the county court on a point of law only (as opposed to a finding of fact). It is envisaged, however, that judicial review may still be necessary to challenge local authority decisions where the applicant wants to show that the local authority did not exercise its discretion properly.

2.3 SECURITY OF TENURE

For a large number of people living in rented accommodation the security, or otherwise, of their tenure in that accommodation is often a matter of considerable concern. Security of tenure is an issue which goes to the heart of housing law and its complexity is such that only a very basic outline can be provided in a book of this nature. Service users who are unsure of their housing tenure rights or who receive a notice to quit their accommodation or who think they face eviction should seek specialist advice as soon as possible.

2.3.1 Tenancies and licences

The vast majority of those who are living in accommodation as a tenant have established rights of tenure and can only be lawfully evicted by a court order. Licensees have only a permission to occupy accommodation and, therefore, have no security of tenure although a court order will be required to obtain the eviction of most licensees. It is important, therefore, to be able to identify whether someone is occupying accommodation as a tenant or as a licensee. It is not necessary to have an agreement in writing for it to be legally binding but it may be more difficult to prove what was agreed between the landlord and tenant if it is not in writing. The title given to any 'accommodation agreement' is not conclusive as to its true nature and the indications that an agreement constitutes a tenancy are the payment of rent and the right of exclusive possession.

2.3.2 Private tenants

The law relating to tenancies was changed in the 1988 Housing Act and again in the 1996 Housing Act so that the date that the tenant moved into the accommodation has become critical:

a) Where the tenant moved in *before 15.1.89* and:

- they have exclusive possession of at least one room;

- there is no resident landlord;

- no meals or substantial services are provided by the landlord;

then there is likely to be a *fully protected tenancy (a regulated tenancy)* with the result that:

- the landlord must establish grounds for possession set out in the Rent Act 1977;

- the tenant cannot be evicted without a court order;

- the tenant may apply for a fair rent to be established.

A number of tenancies which began *before 15.1.89* are not fully protected by the Rent Act 1977. These include tenancies where:

- the rateable value is very high;

- where the rent is very low;

- the rent includes a payment for 'board';

- where the rent includes payment for a substantial amount of personal services for the tenant;

- the letting is to a student by an educational institution;

- there is a holiday letting;

- where the landlord is resident;

- accommodation is shared with the landlord.

Tenants in similar situations who moved in *on or after 15.1.89* may be:

- occupiers with basic protection (sometimes known as un-protected or non-assured tenants) who cannot be evicted without four weeks' notice in writing after which the landlord must apply for a court order, or

- excluded occupiers who can be evicted at the end of a fixed term or after reasonable notice from the landlord.

b) Where the tenant moved in *on or after 15.1.89* and *before 28.2.97* and:

- the tenant has exclusive possession of at least one room;

- there is no resident landlord;

then the tenancy will be covered by the Housing Act 1988 and must be either an *assured tenancy* or an *assured shorthold tenancy*.

i) *Assured tenancy:*

- possession will only be possible through a court order;

- the tenant will pay a market rent.

After 28.2.97 all newly created assured tenancies will automatically be assured shorthold tenancies unless the landlord has notified the tenant otherwise (eg where the landlord is a housing association) or there was a previous tenancy of a different nature with the landlord.

ii) *Assured shorthold tenancy created before 28.2.97:*

- the tenant's right to remain in the property will be determined by the length of the tenancy agreement which must have been notified to the tenant in advance (minimum of six months);

- possession will be granted by a court order;

- the tenant will pay a market rent.

After 28.2.97 it is not necessary for an assured shorthold tenancy to be a fixed term but a landlord must give two months' notice to the tenant to quit the property and a court will not be able to order a tenant to leave until at least six months from the start of the tenancy.

2.3.3   Housing association tenants

a)   Tenants who moved in *prior to 15.1.89* have a *secure tenancy* with the result that:

- they can only be evicted by a court order on proof of grounds justifying eviction;

- a fair rent will be registered;

- the tenant will enjoy a number of rights known as the 'Tenant's Charter', including the right to buy (except where the association is a charitable housing association), the right to take in lodgers and the right, in certain circumstances, to carry out repairs.

b)   Tenants who moved in *on or after 15.1.89* will have an *assured tenancy* with the result that:

- eviction will only be possible through a court order;

- there is no entitlement to a fair rent;

- there is no right to buy.

c) Tenants who moved in *on or after 28.2.97* are still likely to have an assured tenancy, by way of housing association powers to opt for such tenancies, but a tenant housed under the homelessness provisions will only have an assured shorthold tenancy.

2.3.4   Local authority tenants

Most local authority tenants have a *secure tenancy* with the result that:

- eviction will only be possible through a court order;

- the rent will be fixed by the local authority;

- the tenant will enjoy the rights of the 'Tenant's Charter' including the right to buy.

However there are some significant exceptions, some of whom may also have contact with social services, and who include:

- those who have been given temporary accommodation because of homelessness;

- those who have a new 'introductory tenancy'– possibly because of past history of anti-social behaviour (these tenancies will last for twelve months, after which they can become secure tenancies);

- residents in council hostels.

Tenants who think that their security is in any way threatened, eg by receipt of a notice to quit, must get immediate specialist advice. A list of housing aid centres and law centres, who will be able to provide the necessary help appears in the Housing Rights Guide published by Shelter (see the addresses and materials sections at the end of the chapter).

2.4 PROTECTION FROM EVICTION

The eviction of tenants by a landlord without the necessary legal powers is a crime. Harassment is committed by landlords who try to get tenants out directly or indirectly by threats or violence or by withdrawing services such as water and gas. Both harassment and unlawful eviction are criminal offences under the Protection from Eviction Act 1977 (as amended) and may also be the basis for a civil action. Once civil proceedings have begun a tenant may be able to obtain an interim injunction preventing the landlord continuing the harassment or stopping any attempt to evict the tenant. This interim injunction may be confirmed as permanent at a full hearing and a tenant who has been harassed or illegally evicted may be entitled to substantial damages. A criminal prosecution for illegal eviction or harassment may be brought by a local authority tenancy relations officer. A successful prosecution can result in a fine and the court can make a criminal compensation award to the victim.

Some categories of occupiers, where the occupancy began *on or after 15.1.89*, are only entitled to notice before eviction and are not otherwise protected:

- those who share living accommodation with the landlord or his family;

- those who were originally squatters but who now have a temporary tenancy or licence;

- those living in holiday lettings;

- licensees in hostels run by the council;

- anyone living rent free.

2.5 LICENSEES

The majority of licensees, except those listed above, come within the provisions of the Protection from Eviction Act 1977 with the result that a landlord wishing to evict them must serve a written notice and obtain a court order before evicting them.

2.6 SQUATTERS

A squatter is someone who enters and occupies premises without the permission of the owner. In law squatters are trespassers and can be evicted very easily. Squatters risk criminal prosecution if they break into property in order to occupy it or if they use gas or electricity without making proper arrangements with the relevant utility company.

Squatters will normally occupy property that has been unoccupied for some time. However, if the premises were occupied as a residence immediately before squatters moved in, the displaced residential occupiers can require squatters to leave. Refusal could amount to a criminal offence.

Owners who intend to live in the property themselves – protected intending occupiers – can require squatters to leave premises upon receipt by the squatters of a sworn statement to this effect. Failure to leave may lead to prosecution. People offered tenancies of premises owned by public sector landlords, but occupied by squatters, must supply a certificate of intended occupation from the public sector landlord in order to require the squatters to leave.

Squatters who have been in occupation for more than 28 days can be evicted by the owners after obtaining a possession order from the court. This procedure can take less than a week. Squatters who have been in a property for less than 28 days can be served a notice of possession by the owner, who can then obtain an interim possession order giving the squatters only 24 hours to leave the property or risk arrest. Owners who try to evict squatters by using force may themselves commit criminal offences.

2.7 ANTI-SOCIAL BEHAVIOUR AND NOISE

Recent statutory provisions provide local authorities with new powers to combat neighbour nuisance.

a) The Noise Act 1996 enables local authorities, who wish to adopt its provisions, to take swift action to prevent the misery that can be caused to residents by noisy neighbours.

b) The Housing Act 1996, sections 152–158, enable the local authority to apply to the court for an injunction to prevent anti-social behaviour. The purpose of the injunction is to enable local authorities to combat nuisance caused by young people, often in gangs, on local authority estates, threatening or using violence and thereby causing significant risk of harm to residents. Anti-social behaviour includes conduct likely to cause a nuisance to someone living in local authority accommodation or using premises for immoral or illegal purposes. Persistent disobedience runs the risk of arrest.

c) The Protection from Harassment Act 1997 provides civil and criminal remedies for a variety of anti-social behaviour including racial harassment and neighbour disputes.

2.8 HOUSING REPAIRS

The condition of many rented flats and houses is very poor, sometimes to the extent that it affects the health of those living in such accommodation. Responsibilities concerning the fabric and repair of rented accommodation are regulated by statute and by the terms of the lease under which the property is occupied. The legal aspect of housing repairs is again very complex and specialist help should be sought. The environmental health department of a local authority may take on the task of enforcing repairs on behalf of private tenants. Independent advice will be available from law centres, housing aid centres, housing advice centres and citizens' advice bureaux.

2.8.1 Statutory responsibilities of landlords:

Section 11 of the Landlord and Tenant Act 1985

Where a tenancy, which is not for a fixed term of more than seven years, has been granted after 24.10.61, section 11 of the Landlord and Tenant Act 1985 implies into that tenancy agreement an obligation on the landlord to keep in repair the structure and exterior of the accommodation, basins, sinks, baths and other sanitary installations in the dwelling and installations for heating water and space heating.

Tenants can enforce these duties against a landlord who has not done the repairs, after reasonable notice, by an action in the county court for an order that the repairs are done and for appropriate damages. Tenants can also ask the local authority environmental health department to inspect the property and take action against the landlord.

Section 4 of the Defective Premises Act 1972

A landlord has responsibility for any damage to property or injury to any person caused by defects in the property which he knows about or which he should have known about. This applies not only to tenants but also to members of their household, visitors and licensees. It is possible to take action in the county court against the landlord for damages and compensation for the damages and/or injury.

2.8.2 Landlords' obligations at common law

If a landlord is negligent in respect of the performance of his duties he could be sued for damages. In one case a local authority was found negligent in failing to get rid of cockroaches from a flat in a block that it owned because, although they treated the flat, they failed to treat the common parts (ducts and other spaces) and the flat became reinfested.[7]

---

7   *Sharpe v Manchester Metropolitan District Council* (1977) 5 HLR 71.

The court may be prepared to imply a term into a tenancy agreement (contract) in order to make sense of it. For example, where a wheelchair bound tenant was forced to use a rear access path, over which she had only a right of way, as the only means that she had of entry to her home, an obligation to maintain that path was implied by a court on the part of the local authority landlord or she would not be able to get into her own home.[8]

2.8.3 Local authority responsibilities

Local authority environmental health officers have wide powers under the Housing Act 1985 and the Environmental Protection Act 1990 to enforce the principle that private tenants should not be forced to live in accommodation that is likely to affect the health and safety of tenants or that is unfit for human habitation.

a) The Environmental Protection Act 1990 (section 80) provides that where a local authority is satisfied that there is a statutory nuisance it must serve an abatement notice on the person responsible. In relation to premises a statutory nuisance is defined as 'any premises in such a state as to be prejudicial to health or a nuisance' (section 79). Shelter's *Housing Rights Guide* identifies examples: dampness, leaking roof, broken banisters, rotten floorboards, piles of rubbish, dangerous wiring, falling slates and rotten window frames. The abatement notice will specify the necessary repairs and a time within which they must be completed. If the order is not complied with the local authority may apply to the magistrates' court for an order against the landlord which may be enforced by a fine and compensation order where appropriate. In the event of continuing default the necessary repairs can be undertaken by the local authority with the cost recovered from the landlord. Expedited orders are available under the Act where urgent repairs are needed. Criticism of these powers centres on i) the delay which is often involved; ii) the reluctance of some authorities to take action; and iii) the fact that the Act may tackle only the manifestation of a problem which may return in time.

Tenants can take a landlord to court themselves under section 82 of the Act where the level of disrepair constitutes a statutory nuisance.

---

8 *King v South Northamptonshire District Council* [1992] 1 EGLR 53.

b)   The Housing Act 1985 provides local authorities with wide powers to deal with disrepair, in particular housing which may be describe as 'unfit for human habitation'. Fitness is defined by reference to structural stability, freedom from serious disrepair, freedom from dampness which may be prejudicial to the health of occupants, adequate lighting, heating and ventilation, adequate piped wholesome water, facilities for the preparation and cooking of food, including a sink with hot and cold water, a suitably located water-closet for the exclusive use of occupants, a suitably located fixed shower or bath and wash-hand basin all with hot and cold water and for the exclusive use of the occupants and an effective system for drainage of foul, waste and surface water. The fitness standard for flats is the same with the addition that if the building in which the flat is situated is 'unfit' that may affect the flat. The fitness standard for houses in multiple occupation (HMO) includes adequate means of escape from fire and other adequate fire pre-cautions. Guidance from the Department of the Environment suggests that the standard should be applied by considering the dwelling rather than its occupants, though a house should be suitable for all types of occupants, who might reasonably be expected to occupy it, including, as appropriate elderly and children. There are matters which are not included in the criteria for fitness, for example, lack of gas or electricity, modern wiring or insulation or freedom from infestation from vermin or bugs.

If a property is found to be unfit then the authority has to consider the most satisfactory course of action, ie whether this should be repair, demolition or closing. In determining the most satisfactory course the local authority must take into account a wide range of issues including the cost, the social implications, alternative courses of action, local character and life of the community, views of those involved and the effect of any action in relation to the area affected. Where the local authority considers that repair is the most satis-factory course of action it must serve a repair notice on person having control of the property, with copies to other interested parties, requiring works of repair or improvement to be begun and completed within a specified time. An appeal against the notice can be made within 21 days, otherwise the specified works must be carried out.

If the property is not unfit, but in substantial disrepair or in bad enough condition to interfere with the comfort of the tenant, then the authority can serve a notice on the landlord under section 190 of the Housing Act 1985 giving details of the repairs needed and a time in which the work must be completed. *In either case* if the landlord fails to do the work the local authority can do the work themselves and claim the cost from the landlord.

If it is not possible to repair the property then the accommodation must no longer be used for human habitation;[9] it must be closed and the occupier must be rehoused.[10] The owner can, however, make a proposal to reconstruct the premises; if this done to the local authority's satisfaction the closing/demolition order may be revoked. The tenant will not have to be reinstated in the property, having already been rehoused, and the landlord is able to sell with vacant possession. Landlords who fail to remedy substantial disrepair either wilfully or through neglect can, thereby, benefit from having a cleared site or vacant possession. The tenant who does not want to be rehoused will need to be persistent in requiring the local authority to enforce its duties under the repair provisions before a house falls into such substantial disrepair that a closing or demolition order is the only satisfactory course of action.

c) Local authority tenants have essentially the same rights in relation to repairs as private tenants under the Landlord and Tenant Act 1985 and section 82 of the Environmental Protection Act 1990. However, because local authorities cannot serve 'repair notices' on themselves, tenants cannot use legislation which would, in effect, require environmental health officers to serve notices on their own authority. This excludes the provisions of the Housing Act 1985 and section 80 of the Environmental Protection Act 1990 discussed above, although an informal system of notification exists under which environmental health officers called in by council tenants will notify housing departments of repairs which would otherwise have led to notices being issued under the Act against a private landlord. Local authority tenants have had some success using section 82 of the Environmental Protection Act against local authorities to secure improvements in their housing conditions.

Local authority tenants also have the right to do minor repairs themselves and to seek reimbursement from the authority. Housing association tenants have all the same rights in respect of repairs as private tenants. They also have a right to repair and to seek payment from the association.

9   Housing Act 1985, s 264 (as amended).
10   Land Compensation Act 1973, s 39.

d)   Local authorities have the discretion to give special grants to owner-occupiers, tenants and landlords for renovation, improvement and repairs in order to improve sub-standard accommodation.[11] The availability of such grants has been extended in some circumstances to the occupiers of mobile homes and houseboats.

2.9   HOUSING BENEFIT

2.9.1   Principles

Housing benefit is a means tested benefit which provides help with rent for those with low incomes. It is administered by local authorities. The law concerning housing benefit is contained in the Social Security Contributions and Benefits Act 1992 and in regulations made under the Act, principally the Housing Benefit (General) Regulations 1987 (as amended.) The housing benefit scheme is extremely complex and advice should be sought to determine the exact position of any particular claimant.

2.9.2   Eligibility

Those entitled to housing benefit will include:

* private tenants

* local authority tenants

* lodgers, boarders, licensees

* occupants of houseboats, caravans, mobile homes, almshouses

Those not entitled will include:

* owner-occupiers

* most asylum seekers and those failing the habitual residence test

11   The Housing Grants, Construction and Regeneration Act 1996.

- people living with close relatives

- most full-time students

Housing benefit is made up of distinct elements: a rent rebate for council tenants and a rent allowance for housing association and private tenants.

2.9.3 Challenging a housing benefit decision

Applications for housing benefit are made to the claimant's local authority and the decision on a claim must be notified to the claimant in writing. A full statement detailing how a particular housing benefit decision has been reached must be provided by the authority on request. Claimants can require the authority to review their housing benefit decision and on completion of the reconsideration a written decision with reasons must be provided. The claimant has the right to a second review, or 'appeal', to be heard by a review board made up of local authority councillors acting independently of the authority.

2.10 COUNCIL TAX BENEFIT

Council Tax is payable by most occupiers of dwellings, whether tenants, owners or licensees. It is set by and paid to local authorities and varies from one area to another. It is based on an assumed valuation of property from year to year and all properties are put into one of eight bands (A–H), with A being the lowest. The higher the band, the greater the council tax.

Council Tax Benefit is available to those on low incomes and there are reductions for disability (to the valuation band below the one allocated to that property) claimable by the person liable to pay the Council Tax if a disabled person resides in the home and the home has specially adapted facilities for the disabled person. Council Tax is assessed on the assumption that two adults live in each property, discounts are available where the person liable to pay council tax lives on their own.

Eligibility for Council Tax Benefit depends on assessment of income and capital and is based on weekly net liability for Council Tax after deductions for disability and discounts.

3 HOUSING LAW AND SOCIAL WORK: some issues for discussion

3.1 OTHER ASPECTS OF HOUSING FOR PARTICULAR SERVICE USERS

Though housing is an issue in which social workers do not have direct statutory powers or duties there are nevertheless areas of practice which are circumscribed by statutory duties which involve housing matters. Even without reference to specialised housing or homelessness legislation many social workers working with service users who are ill, have a physical disability or learning difficulty, will find significant aspects of their practice concerned with housing. Thus any attempt to provide a definition of 'housing rights' for social work would have to include the access of clients to Part III accommodation and the availability of alterations and adaptations to service users' homes provided for by the Chronically Sick and Disabled Persons Act 1970. The community care provisions of the National Health Service and Community Care Act 1990 relating to assessment and care service provision and the availability of disabled facilities grants under the Housing Grants, Construction and Regeneration Act 1996 may also be relevant.

Section 21 of the National Assistance Act 1948 allows, and where the Secretary of State so directs requires, local authorities to arrange for the provision of (Part III) residential accommodation for 'persons who by reason of age, illness, disability or any other circumstances are in need of care and attention which is not otherwise available to them'.

Section 29 of the National Assistance Act 1948 establishes an enabling power for local authorities to promote the welfare of people who are disabled. Pursuant to that power the Chronically Sick and Disabled Persons Act 1970 provides by section 2(1)(e) for 'the provision of assistance for that person in arranging for the carrying out of any works of adaptation in his home or the provision of any additional facilities designed to secure his greater safety, comfort or convenience'.

It should also be remembered that the Social Fund provides community care grants and it may be possible to persuade a social fund officer that a grant should be paid to a service user on income support for furniture, minor structural repairs and maintenance costs, redecoration and refurbishment and other similar expenses where such a grant is connected with establishing that person in the community or preventing them having to enter institutional care.

3.2 ENFORCING 'HOUSING RIGHTS'

It should be clear that any discussion of 'housing rights' is a particularly broad one and in this book it also includes material covered in other chapters. Talking in terms of 'rights' is problematic in a number of respects. Housing law is complex and it is unlikely that many service users will be able to enforce their 'housing rights' without specialist advice and assistance. Few social workers will have such an expertise and it is likely therefore that service users will have to be referred to one of the (fortunately) many specialist housing aid or housing advice centres. Such expertise is also available from law centres and from a number of solicitors who specialise in housing law, although advice and assistance from a solicitor will have to be paid for. Such advice *may* be available under the legal aid scheme.

Social workers may find themselves acting as crisis managers for people who are homeless and as an advocate and negotiator with the housing authority on behalf of such service users. Their responsibilities may not end with the provision of accommodation. Those defined as having a priority need in relation to accommodation are also likely to have 'social work' needs. As an example families with young children forced to live in bed and breakfast accommodation will require whatever support and help can be offered under Part III and Schedule 2 of the Children Act 1989 so as to support and promote the care and upbringing of the children by their family.

People with a mental disorder who are homeless will often require social work support, for their vulnerability exists in respect of both housing and social work needs. Local authorities may have duties to such people under sections 21 and 29 of the National Assistance Act 1948, section 2 of the Chronically Sick and Disabled Persons Act 1970 and the National Health Service and Community Care Act 1990 but enforcement is problematic, if not impossible, and the financial resources for community care are inadequate. So, although the housing needs of such service users may be 'satisfied' in the sense that the vulnerable should be entitled to some accommodation under the homelessness legislation, appropriate accommodation and other support is often not available, with the result that their 'social work' needs are not provided for.

4 CASE STUDIES

These case studies are primarily concerned with housing rights though they raise a number of other issues concerning social work practice. Responses can be limited to the housing issues but a broader consideration of how social work might respond to the circumstances faced by these potential or existing service users will provide a more comprehensive and realistic discussion.

1.   Sharon is 19 and is living with her mother and stepfather in a small house. She does not get on with them and has violent arguments with her stepfather who hits her. She is pregnant and wants a flat of her own.

She has approached the social services department for help.

What help can be offered to her?

Is she entitled to accommodation from the housing authority?

2.   Hassan has been living in a bedsit in a house belonging to his landlord Derek for a year. Derek lives in a flat on the bottom floor of the house. The house is in a serious state of disrepair; the roof leaks, there is condensation everywhere and the wiring is dangerous. Hassan told Derek about the problems some months ago but nothing has been done. Last week he told Derek that he was going to complain to the council about the state of the house and his bedsit. Derek was abusive and yesterday Hassan received a letter from Derek which included the following threat:

> *If you don't get out of the house by the end of the week my brother will lock you out. He has a nasty temper.*

You have been working with Hassan; he wants to know what his position is concerning the threat, his security of tenure and the repairs to his bedsit.

3.   Rena and Vassili are a married couple. Rena is pregnant. Before they got married they both lived in single rooms in bedsit accommodation. Vassili left his room after a row with his landlord over the rent. He moved in with Rena, but her room was so cramped that they left and moved in with her parents in the neighbouring town. They do not get on with her parents and would like to move into

council accommodation in Hackney, the part of East London Vassili was brought up in as a child.

Advise them on the best course of action regarding their accommodation and explain their legal rights (if any) to obtain accommodation in Hackney.

4.   Alf has been a voluntary patient at a psychiatric hospital for the last five years. He was discharged three weeks ago when the hospital was closed. Though accommodation had been arranged for him he has been living rough since he left hospital. He says he went to have a look at the place but didn't like the look of it. He is clearly very depressed and withdrawn and his physical health is not good. He has a very bad cough and his clothes are dirty and damp.

Alf has been picked up by the police as he was taking a milk bottle from a front step. The police have rung the social services department and asked you, as the duty social worker, to 'take him on or we will have to charge him!'

What can you do?

5.   Suzy is 17 and has been living in London for a month since she arrived from Glasgow. She has been referred to you by the police after they raided a squat in a drugs raid. Suzy, who is very depressed and upset, tells you that she has been living in the squat and raising money by working as a prostitute and occasionally selling drugs for someone else who also lived in the squat. It transpires that she left home in Glasgow when she had a violent row with her boyfriend with whom she was sharing a bedsit.

Advise her on her entitlement, if any, to housing assistance.

5   ACTIVITIES

1.   Social workers should be aware of the policies and services provided by their local authority for people who are homeless. This information may be readily available to social workers but may require social work students to investigate the situation.

2.   It is interesting to identify how the channel of communication between social services departments and housing authorities works.

How, for example, does a social worker deal with a service user who has local authority accommodation which is in need of urgent repair? What do you do if the repairs are not done?

3. Does the housing authority have a homeless persons unit? Are there any social workers attached to it? If so, how are cases and clients divided between them and social services?

4. It is important to know where independent specialist advice and assistance is available. Is there a law centre in your area? Which local solicitors will do housing rights work under the legal aid scheme ? Is there a housing advice/aid centre in your area?

5. Build up a set of good reference materials including the Housing Booklets published by the Department of the Environment.

6. Get an up to date edition of the *Housing Rights Guide* which is published annually by Shelter.

7. Get hold of a copy of the *Department of Social Security Guide to Housing Benefit* from their leaflets section (address in chapter on social security).

8. Become familiar with the way in which your local authority handles enquiries and problems concerning housing benefit. If a claimant wants to have a review of the decision or take an appeal is there anyone who can give appropriate advice and assistance?

9. Become aware of sources of housing information on the internet.

6 ADDRESSES

National Homeless Alliance (Housing Campaign for Single People)
5-15 Cromer Street
London WC1H 8LS.
Phone: 0171 833 2071
Fax: 0171 278 6685
E-mail: NHA@home_all.org.uk

Child Poverty Action Group Ltd
1-5 Bath Street

London EC1V 9PY.
Phone: 0171 253 3406
Fax: 0171 490 0561
E-mail: staff@cpag.demon.co.uk

Department of the Environment
Eland House
Bressenden Place
London SW1E 5DU.
Phone: 0171 276 0900
Web: www.open.gov.uk.doe/doehome.

Housing Corporation (information for housing association tenants)
Tel: 0171 393 2228.

Shelter (National Campaign for the Homeless
88 Old Street
London EC1V 9HU.
Phone: 0171 505 2000
Fax: 0171 505 2000
E-mail: roof@compuserve.com
website: www.shelter.org.uk
(Shelter has useful links on its website to other sources of information.)

Shelter Wales
57 Walter Road
Swansea SA1 5PZ.
Phone: 01792 469400
Fax: 01792 460050

7 MATERIALS

Arden, A, *Manual of Housing Law*, 6th edn, (1997) Sweet and Maxwell.

Arden, A and Hunter, C, *Homelessness and Allocations*, 5th edn, (1997) Legal Action Group.

Luba, J and Knafler, S, *Repairs: Tenants Rights*, 3rd edn, (1997) Legal Action Group.

Moorhouse, P, Tait, G and Ballantyne, J, *Rights Guide for Home Owners*, 11th edn, (1996) Shelter.

Zebedee, J and Ward, M, *Guide to Housing Benefit and Council Tax Benefit*, 5th edn, (1997–98) Shelter and Chartered Institute of Housing.

Department of the Environment Housing Booklets:

The Council Tenant's Charter, 95 HCA 006.

A Better Deal for Tenants – Your new right to compensation for improvements, 94 HCA 448.

A Better Deal for Tenants – Your new right to repair, 94 HCA 386.

A Guide to Access to Personal Files (Housing) Regulations 1989, 94 HCA 274.

Assured and Assured Shorthold Tenancies – a guide for tenants, 97 HC 228 A.

Repairs, 95 HCA 074.

'He wants me out'. Protection against Harassment and Illegal Eviction, 92 HUG 218.

Notice that you must leave, 92 HUG 220.

Want to rent a room?, 92 HUG 169.

Letting rooms in your home, 93 HUG 219.

Housing Renovation Grants, 96 HC 202 C.

Home Repairs Assistance, 96 HC 202 A.

Disabled Facilities Grants, 96 HC 202 B.

Mobile Homes – Guide for Residents and Site Owners, 93 HUG 386.

Bothered by Noise? What you can do about it, 94 EP 184.

Guide to Housing Benefit, Department of Social Security.

Housing Rights Guide (published annually), Shelter.

Housing Wallcharts published by Shelter on Homelessness and Allocation, Housing Benefit, Council Tax and Homeowners.

Shelter Housing Rights Guides:

No.1 *Homeless? Read this.*

No.2 *Repairs – tenants' rights.*

No.3 *Stopping the bailiffs.*

No.4 *Private tenants's rights.*

No.5 *Finding a place to live.*

No.6 *Mortgage arrears.*

No.7 *Housing benefit.*

No.8 *Housing association tenancies.*

No.9 *Council tenants' rights.*

No.10 *Leaseholders' rights.*

No.11 *Young people.*

No.12 *Rents.*

No.13 *Mobile homes.*

No.14 *Occupiers with limited rights.*

Index

Abuse
  child. See CHILD ABUSE
  elder abuse, 175-176
Accommodation
  adaptations to, 155-156
  local authority, provided by. See
    LOCAL AUTHORITIES
  secure, 43-44
Activities
  Children Act 1989, 73-74
  community care, 182-183
  criminal justice system, 270-271
  disability, children with, 106-107
  discrimination, 362
  family breakdown, 135-136
  housing, 394-395
  legal system, 26-27
  mental health, 235
  social security benefits, 341-343
  youth justice, 311-313
Actus reus
  requirement of, 17
Addresses
  Children Act 1989, 75-76
  community care, 183-185
  criminal justice system, 271-272
  disability, children with, 107-108
  discrimination, 362-364
  family breakdown, 136-138
  housing, 395-396
  legal system, 27-28
  mental health, 236-237
  social security benefits, 343
  youth justice, 313
Admission of patient. See MENTAL
  HEALTH
Adoption
  Children Act 1989, provisions of,
    33
Advice
  legal advice and assistance, 22

Age Concern
  work of, 140
Allocation of housing. See HOUSING
Ancillary proceedings
  divorce, 113-115
Anti-social behaviour
  local authority, powers of, 384
Appeal
  child support appeal tribunal, to,
    119
  Court of Appeal. See COURT OF
    APPEAL
  youth offender, by, 296
Arrest
  non-molestation order, powers
    attached to, 125
  occupation order, powers attached
    to, 127
Assessment
  carer of disabled child, of, 83-84
  carers, needs of, 150-151
  child assessment order, 56
  community care services, 149-150,
    162-165
  disabled children, services for, 83-84
  disabled persons, services for, 148-
    149
  mental health. See MENTAL
    HEALTH
Assistance
  family assistance order, 48, 122
Assistance by way of representation
  (ABWOR)
  availability of, 22-23
Attendance allowance
  availability of, 333
Attendance centre order
  availability of, 252
  youth justice, 291-292
Attorney, power of
  continuing, 228

Attorney, power of–*contd*
  enduring power of attorney, 153
  mental incapacity, in case of, 153
Bail
  approved bail hostels, management
    of, 259-260
  child as suspect, 279-281
  grant of, 242-243
  young person as suspect, 279-281
Benefits. *See* SOCIAL SECURITY
  BENEFITS
Binding precedent
  system of, 15-16
Breach of statutory duty
  community care, relating to, 161
Breakdown of family. *See* FAMILY
  BREAKDOWN
Care in community. *See*
  COMMUNITY CARE
Care order
  availability of, 48-49
  contact for child in care, 52-53
  court based work, involvement of
    social worker in, 4
  discharge of, 54
  divorce proceedings, 116-117
  exclusion requirement, 127
  family, working in partnership
    with, 60-61
  figures for, 64
  grounds for grant of, 49-50
  interim order, 51-52
  legal effect of, 52
  who may apply, 49
Care proceedings
  significant challenges for social
    work practitioners, 69
Carers
  assessment of needs of, 150-151
  disabled child, of, assessment of,
    83-84
Case studies
  Children Act 1989, 70-73
  community care, 179-182
  criminal justice system, 268-270
  disability, children with, 105-106
  discrimination, 359-362
  family breakdown, 133-135
  housing, 393-394
  mental health, 230-234
  social security benefits, 339-341
  youth justice, 309-311
Cautioning
  youth offenders, 296-299

Central Council for Education and
  Training in Social Work
  (CCETSW)
  equal opportunities policy, 345
Central government
  civil disputes involving, 19
Chancery Division
  specialist jurisdiction, 21
Child abuse
  emergency protection order,
    discharge of, 58
    duration of, 58
    effect of, 58
    excluding alleged abuser, 59
    figures for, 64
    grounds on which granted, 57-
      58
  excluding alleged abuser, 59
  inquiries of late 1980s, 30
Child assessment order
  nature of, 56
Child benefit
  availability of, 322-323
Child care law
  Children Act 1989. *See*
    CHILDREN ACT 1989
  children's rights and children's
    welfare, tensions between, 31
  contact for child in care, 52-53, 68
  interaction between lawyers and
    social workers, 7-8
  practice, 29-31
  reform of, 31-32
Child protection
  abuse. *See* CHILD ABUSE
  area committees, 62
  conferences, 62-63
  failure to intervene in family life, 30
  issues for discussion, 61-63
  official guidance, 16-17
  reviews, 63
  risk, child at,
    court orders,
      child assessment order, 56
      emergency protection order,
        discharge of, 58
        duration of, 58
        effect of, 58
        excluding alleged abuser,
          59
        grounds on which
          granted, 57-58
        figures for, 64
        generally, 56

Child protection–*contd*
  risk, child at–*contd*
    duty to investigate, 55-56
    generally, 55
    police powers, 59-60
Child support
  introduction of, 118-119
  maintenance and, 328
Child Support Agency
  application to, 118
Child support appeal tribunal
  appeal to, 119
Children
  child in need, meaning, 37-38
  contact between family and, 41-42
  contact order, 116
  disability, with,
    accommodation, 85
    activities, 106-107
    addresses, 107-108
    assessment, 83-84
    case studies, 105-106
    Children Act 1989, 82-85
    Chronically Sick and Disabled
      Persons Act 1970, 85-87
    disability living allowance, 95-97
    disabled facilities grants, 92
    Disabled Persons (Services,
      Consultation and
      Representation) Act
      1986, 87
    education Act 1996, 88-91
    generally, 79-80
    health care, 93-94
    housing and homelessness, 91-92
    income support, 97
    invalid care allowance, 97
    issues for discussion, 97-105
    job seekers (income based)
      benefit, 97
    law, generally, 81-82
    materials, 108-109
    meaning, 82
    mental health services, 92-93
    principles for practice, 80-81
    quality of service delivery, 104-
      105
    services,
      Commissioner for Local
        Administration, 101-
        102
      complaints procedures, 99-
        100
      judicial review, 102-103

Children–*contd*
  disability, with–*contd*
    services–*contd*
      provision of, 84-85
      quality of service delivery,
        104-105
      remedies, 99
      resources, 98-99
      rights to, 98-103
      tribunals, 100-101
    severe disablement allowance, 97
    social security benefits, 94-97
    special educational needs, 88-91
  local authority services for, 37-39
  non-molestation order, application
    for, 125
  rehabilitation, principle of, 41-42
  residence order, 116
  special educational needs, with,
    88-91
Children Act 1989
  activities, 73-74
  addresses, 75-76
  adoption, 33
  applications under, 63-64
  care order,
    availability of, 48-49
    contact for child in care, 52-53
    discharge of, 54
    figures for, 64
    grounds for grant of, 49-50
    interim order, 51-52
    legal effect of, 52
    who may apply, 49
  case studies, 70-73
  child at risk, protection of,
    court order,
      child assessment order, 56
      emergency protection order,
        discharge of, 58
        duration of, 58
        effect of, 58
        excluding alleged abuser,
        59
      figures for, 64
      grounds on which
        granted, 57-58
      generally, 56
    duty to investigate, 55-56
    emergency protection order,
      discharge of, 58
      duration of, 58
      effect of, 58
      excluding alleged abuser, 59

Children Act 1989–*contd*
  child at risk, protection of–*contd*
    emergency protection order–*contd*
      figures for, 64
      grounds on which granted, 57-58
      generally, 55
      police powers, 59-60
    children's rights and children's welfare, tensions between, 31
  complaints procedure, 42-43
  court welfare officer, role of, 66
  courts,
    child care jurisdictions, 36-37
    investigation ordered by, 54-55
    structure of, 78
  disability, children with,
    accommodation, 85
    assessment, 83-84
    generally, 82-83
    meaning, 82
    services, 84-85
  education supervision order, 54
  emergence of, 31-32
  family assistance orders, 48, 122
  family breakdown, implications for, 120-122
  family proceedings,
    family assistance orders, 48
    generally, 37
    parental responsibility, 44-45
    section 8 orders,
      availability of, 47-48
      contact order, 45-46
      generally, 45
      prohibited steps order, 46
      residence order, 46
      specific issue order, 47
  generally, 29, 33–34
  Gillick case, effect of, 30-31
  guardian ad litem, role of, 64-65
  guidance, 33
  implementation, 29
  investigation ordered by court, 54-55
  links between politics, policy and law, 11
  local authority,
    accommodation provided by,
      children being looked after, duties relating to, 41

Children Act 1989–*contd*
  local authority–*contd*
    accommodation provided by–*contd*
      generally, 39-40
      objections to, 40
      removal from, 40
      secure, 43-44
    contact between children and family, 41-42
    rehabilitation, principle of, 41-42
    secure accommodation, 43-44
    services for children and families, 37-39
  materials, 76-77
  parental responsibility, concept of, 36
  principles of, 34-36
  principles underpinning, 2
  regulations, 33
  representing child, 64-65
  secondary legislation under, 12
  secure accommodation, 43-44
  structure of, 32-33
  supervision order,
    administration, 53
    availability of, 48-49
    discharge of, 54
    education, 54
    grounds for grant of, 49-50
    interim order, 51-52
    who may apply, 49
  welfare,
    checklist, 35-36
    principle(s), 34-35
  working together under, 60-61
  youth justice, 33
Civil law
  civil courts, 21
  civil disputes, 19
  common law distinguished from, 15
  language of civil justice system, 19, 21
Civil legal aid
  means test, 23
  merits test, 23
Civil rights
  patient, of, 200
Clients
  lawyers, relationship with, 3-4
Codes of guidance
  nature of, 14

Cohabitation
  income support, claim for, 327-
    328
Combination order
  availability of, 252
  probation service, work of, 258-
    259
  youth justice, 293
Commission for Racial Equality
  (CRE)
  establishment of, 346
  investigative and enforcement
    powers, 348
Commissioner for Local
  Administration
  community care, complaint
    relating to, 158-159
  disabled children, services for,
    101-102
Common law
  civil law distinguished from, 15
  housing repairs, landlord's
    obligations relating to, 385-
    386
  lawyers, position of, 2
  pragmatic character of, 2
Community care
  accommodation, adaptations to,
    155-156
  activities, 182-183
  adaptations to accommodation,
    155-156
  addresses, 183-185
  assessment, needs and resources,
    162-165
  assessment of services, 149-150
  care and after-care for sick, 147
  carers, 150-151
  case studies, 179-182
  complaints,
    default powers, 157
    generally, 156-157
    local authority monitoring
      officer, to, 158
    local government ombudsman,
      to, 158-159
  direct payments, 151
  disability. See DISABILITY
  domiciliary care services, 147
  enforcing rights to services, 165-167
  expectant mothers, services for, 147
  generally, 140-141
  home helps, 147

Community care–*contd*
  identification of service users, 145-
    146
  judicial review, applications for,
    159-161
  laundry services, 147
  legal structure, 143-144
  legislative structure, 145-151
  local authority monitoring officer,
    complaint to, 158
  local government ombudsman,
    complaint to, 158-159
  materials, 185-186
  mental disorder, people with, 206-
    211, 212-215
  mental health. See MENTAL
    HEALTH
  nursing mothers, services for, 147
  old people, promotion of welfare
    of, 146
  organisation, 141-143
  pressure groups, work of, 140-141
  reform, 141-143, 177-179
  remedies,
    breach of statutory duty, 161
    complaints, 156-157
    default powers, 157
    judicial review, applications
      for, 159-161
    local authority monitoring
      officer, complaint to, 158
    local government ombudsman,
      complaint to, 158-159
    statutory duty, breach of, 161
  residential care, 167-170
  social security benefits, 155
  vulnerable service users,
    elder abuse, 175-176
    generally, 170-172
    law for work with, 172-177
    mental health law, 176-177
    personal welfare, 173-175
Community sentences
  attendance centre order, 252
  combination order, 252
  community service, 251
  curfew orders, 252
  enforcement, 253
  pre-sentence reports, 252-253
  probation, 251
  revoking, 253
Community service order
  availability of, 251

Community service order–*contd*
  probation service, work of, 258
  youth justice, 292
Companies
  civil disputes involving, 19
Compensation order
  sentence in adult court, 250-251
Complaints
  Children Act 1989, procedure
    under, 42-43
  disabled children, services for, 99-
    100
  local authority monitoring officer,
    to, 158
  local government ombudsman, to,
    158-159
  procedures, 156-157
Conferences
  child protection, 62-63
Contact
  child in care, for, 52-53, 68
  children and family, between, 41-42
  divorce, orders relating to, 116
Contact order
  basic legal principle, 45-46
  divorce, relating to, 116
  number of applications, 64
Council tax benefit
  entitlement to, 390-391
County courts
  binding precedent, system of, 15
Court of Appeal
  civil division, 21
  criminal division, 21
  formulation of legal rules, 15
  influence of judiciary, 15
  jurisdiction, 21
Court of Protection
  jurisdiction, 153-154, 205-206
  new, 228
Court welfare officer
  role of, 66
Court welfare service
  probation officers, work of,
    mediation, 119-120
  reports, 119
Courts
  child care jurisdictions, 36-37
  Children Act proceedings,
    structure for, 78
  children in care, tension with local
    authorities relating to, 66-68
  civil, 21

Courts–*contd*
  court based social work,
    care order, application for, 4
    education supervision order,
      application for, 4
    emergency protection order,
      application for, 4
    generally, 4
    guardian ad litem, role of, 4
    National Assistance Act 1948,
      application under, 4
    pre-sentence report,
      preparation of, 4
  Court of Appeal. *See* COURT OF
    APPEAL
  criminal, 17, 19
  guardian ad litem, appointment of,
    65
  hostile environment, perceived as, 1
  House of Lords. *See* HOUSE OF
    LORDS
  investigation ordered by, 54-55
  local authorities and, tension
    relating to children in care,
    66-68
  social work practitioner's
    involvement in court based
    work, 4
  youth. *See* YOUTH COURT
Crime
  criminal justice system and, 17
Criminal justice system
  activities, 270-271
  actors of, 17
  addresses, 271-272
  approved probation and bail
    hostels, management of,
    259-260
  bail, 242-243
  case studies, 268-270
  categories of criminal offences,
    either way offences, 241-242
    generally, 241
    indictable offences, 242
    summary offences, 241
  combination orders, 252, 258-259
  community service orders, 251, 258
  crime and, 17
  criminal courts, 17, 19
  Criminal Justice Act 1991,
    principles underpinning, 2
  criminal offences,
    categories of, 241-242

Criminal justice system–*contd*
criminal offences–*contd*
either way offences, 241-242
indictable offences, 242
racially motivated crimes, 350-353
summary offences, 241
criminal trial,
Crown Court, 246
magistrates' court, 244-245
pre-trial procedure, 244
Crown Court, 246
either way offences, 241-242
indictable offences, 242
language of, 17
links between politics, policy and
law, 11
magistrates' court, 244-245
management of approved
probation and bail hostels,
259-260
materials, 272-273
mental disorder, people with,
assessment, remands for, 198-199
detention, 198
generally, 197-198
insanity, 199-200
questioning, 198
remands for assessment and
treatment, 198-199
sentencing, 199
suspects, 198
treatment, remands for, 198-199
unfitness to plead, 199-200
pre-sentence reports, 252-253,
260-262
pre-trial procedure, 244
principles of criminal justice and
criminal law, 240-241
probation orders, 257-258
probation service, criminal justice
work of,
approved probation and bail
hostels, management of,
259-260
combination orders, 258-259
community service orders, 258
generally, 255-257
management of approved
probation and bail
hostels, 259-260
probation orders, 257-258

Criminal justice system–*contd*
probation service, criminal justice
work of–*contd*
supervision before and after
release from custody,
260
supervision orders, 259
race and criminal justice, 265-267
racial violence, 267-268
racially motivated crimes, 350-353
reform of, 239-240, 262-265
sentences and sentencing,
adult criminal courts, in, 246-249
community sentences,
attendance centre order,
252
combination order, 252
community service, 251
curfew orders, 252
enforcement, 253
pre-sentence reports, 252-253
probation, 251
revoking, 253
custodial sentences, 253-255
discharges,
absolute, 249
conditional, 249
financial penalties,
compensation orders, 250-251
fines, 249-250
social work involvement in, 239
summary offences, 241
supervision,
before and after release from
custody, 260
orders, 259
trial. *See* criminal trial, *above*
youth justice. *See* YOUTH JUSTICE
Criminal law
crime and, 17
Criminal legal aid
application for, 23
criteria for granting, 23-24
means test, 23
Crown Court
binding precedent, system of, 15
criminal prosecutions, 17, 19
procedure in, 246
youth justice, 295

Crown Prosecution Service (CPS)
   criminal justice system,
      administration of, 17
Curfew orders
   availability of, 252
   youth justice, 293-294
Custodial sentences
   requirements relating to, 253-255
   youth justice,
      Crown Court, 295
      generally, 294-295
      youth court, 295
Custody
   child remanded to, 279-281
   young person remanded to, 279-281

Detention
   mental disorder, people with, 198
Development
   meaning, 50
Direct payments
   community care service users, to,
      151
Directions
   nature of, 12
Disability
   adaptations to accommodation,
      155-156
   assessment for services, 148-149
   benefits. See SOCIAL SECURITY
      BENEFITS
   children with,
      accommodation, 85
      activities, 106-107
      addresses, 107-108
      assessment, 83-84
      case studies, 105-106
      Children Act 1989, 82-85
      Chronically Sick and Disabled
         Persons Act 1970, 85-87
      disability living allowance, 95-97
      disabled facilities grants, 92
      Disabled Persons (Services,
         Consultation and
         Representation) Act
         1986, 87
      Education Act 1996, 88-91
      generally, 79-80
      health care, 93-94
      housing and homelessness, 91-92
      income support, 97
      invalid care allowance, 97
      issues for discussion, 97-105

Disability–*contd*
   children with–*contd*
      job seekers (income based)
         benefit, 97
      law, generally, 81-82
      materials, 108-109
      mental health services, 92-93
      principles for practice, 80-81
      quality of service delivery, 104-
         105
      services,
         Commissioner for Local
            Administration, 101-
            102
         complaints procedure, 99-
            100
         judicial review, 102-103
         provision of, 84-85
         quality of service delivery,
            104-105
         remedies, 99
         resources, 98-99
         rights to, 98-103
         tribunals, 100-101
      severe disablement allowance,
         97
      social security benefits, 94-97
      special educational needs, 88-91
   council tax benefit, 390-391
   information about local authority
      services, 146-147
   learning. See MENTAL HEALTH
   mental health. See MENTAL
      HEALTH
   premium, entitlement to, 328
   services, assessment for, 148-149
Disability Alliance
   work of, 140
Disability living allowance
   availability of, 333
   care component, 96
   disabled child, for, 95-97
   mobility component, 96-97
   rates, 95-96
Disability working allowance
   availability of, 333
   child support, 118
Disablement benefit
   payment of, 332
Discrimination
   activities, 362
   addresses, 362-364
   black patients, 211-212

Discrimination–*contd*
  case studies, 359-362
  criminal justice, race and, 265-267
  criminal law, 350-353
  disability, 349-350
  enforcement of law, 354-358
  gender, 348-349
  generally, 345-347
  harassment, 267-268, 358-359
  issues for discrimination, 354-359
  limits and enforcement of law,
    354-358
  local authority duties, 350
  materials, 364-365
  minority ethnic patients, 211-212
  race and gender, 348-349
  racial violence, 267-268, 358-359
  sex, 348-349
Disputes
  civil, 19
  tribunals, functions of, 21
Divorce
  ancillary proceedings, 113-115
  discussion of issues, 128-129
  facility of, 112
  finance, 115-116
  grounds, 112-113
  mediation, importance of, 129-132
  orders,
    care, 116-117
    contact, 116
    finance, 115-116
    property, 115
    residence, 116
    supervision, 116-117
  petition stage, 113
  property, 115
  reform of law, 128-129
Domestic violence
  civil law procedure, disadvantages
    of, 122-123
  criminal assault, as, 122
  discussion of issues, 132-133
  exclusion requirements, 127
  Family Law Act 1996, Part IV,
    123-127
  generally, 122-123
  harassment, protection from, 127-
    128
  law and social work practice, 132-
    133
  non-molestation orders, 123-125
  occupation orders, 125-127

Domestic violence–*contd*
  social workers, powers and duties
    of, 123
Duty solicitor schemes
  free legal advice available through,
    24

Education
  special educational needs, 88-91
Education supervision order
  court based work, involvement of
    social worker in, 4
  nature of, 54
Either way offences
  nature of, 241-242
Elderly people. *See* OLD PEOPLE
Emergency
  Mental Health Act 1983, under.
    See MENTAL HEALTH
Emergency protection order
  court based work, involvement of
    social worker in, 4
  discharge of, 58
  duration of, 58
  effect of, 58
  excluding alleged abuser, 59
  exclusion requirements, 127
  figures for, 64
  grounds on which granted, 57-58
Enduring power of attorney
  mental incapacity, in case of, 153
Enforcement
  community care services, rights to,
    165-167
  community sentences, of, 253
  discrimination law, 354-358
  housing benefits, of, 392-393
  social security rights, of, 338-339
Equal Opportunities Commission
  investigative and enforcement
    powers, 348
European Convention on Human
    Rights
  incorporation of, 15
  influence of judiciary, 15
Eviction
  licensees, of, 383
  protection from, 367, 382-383

Family
  assistance order, 48, 122
  breakdown. *See* FAMILY
    BREAKDOWN

Family–*contd*
  contact between children and, 41-42
  local authority services for, 37-39
  rehabilitation, principle of, 41-42
  working in partnership with,
    care orders, 60-61
    issues for discussion, 60-61
Family breakdown
  activities, 135-136
  addresses, 136-138
  case studies, 133-135
  Children Act 1989, implications
    of, 120-122
  content of chapter, 111-112
  court welfare service, work of
    probation officers in,
    mediation, 119-120
    reports, 119
  discussion of issues, 128-133
  divorce. *See* DIVORCE
  domestic violence. *See* DOMESTIC
    VIOLENCE
  examples of social work
    involvement, 110-111
  family assistance order, 122
  generally, 110-111
  magistrates' court, matrimonial
    jurisdiction of, 117-119
  materials, 138-139
  mediation,
    court welfare service, work of
      probation officers in,
      119-120
    divorce process, importance in,
      129-132
Family credit
  child support, 118
  payment of, 324-325
Family Division
  specialist jurisdiction, 21
Family premium
  entitlement to, 328
Family proceedings
  Children Act 1989, under, 37
  family assistance order, 48
  parental responsibility, 44-45
  section 8 orders,
    availability of, 47-48
    contact order, 45-46
    generally, 45
    prohibited steps order, 46
    residence order, 46
    specific issue order, 47

Family proceedings court
  social work in and for, 69-70
Finance
  direct payments, 151
  divorce, orders on, 115-116
  mental disorder, affairs of person
    with, 222-224
Fines
  sentence in adult court, 249-250

Grants
  disabled facilities, 92
Green form scheme
  preliminary advice and assistance,
    provision of, 22
Guardian ad litem
  court based work, involvement of
    social worker in, 4
  role of, 64-65
Guardianship
  Mental Health Act 1983, under,
    151-152, 196-197
Guidance
  Children Act 1989, under, 33
  circular, issued by, 14
  codes of, 14
  local authorities, 13
  nature of, 12-14
  official, 16-17
  policy or formal, distinguished
    from practical or general,
    13

Harassment
  prevention of, 367
  protection from, 127-128
  racial violence, 267-268, 358-359
  unlawful eviction, 367, 382-383
Harm
  meaning, 50, 229
Health
  disability, children with, 93-94
  meaning, 50
  mental. *See* MENTAL HEALTH
High Court
  binding precedent, system of, 15
  civil disputes heard in, 21
  divisions of, 21
Home helps
  social services authorities,
    provision by, 147
Home Office
  guidance issued by circular, 14

Homelessness. *See* HOUSING
House of Lords
  formulation of legal rules, 15
  influence of judiciary, 15
  jurisdiction, 21
Housing
  activities, 394-395
  addresses, 395-396
  allocation of local authority
      housing,
    generally, 366-367, 368-369
    housing register and qualifying
        persons, 369
    priority, challenges to decisions
        about, 370-371
    qualifying persons, 369
    scheme for, 369-370
    status, challenges to decisions
        about, 370-371
  anti-social behaviour, 384
  benefit. *See* HOUSING BENEFIT
  case studies, 393-394
  council tax benefit, 390-391
  disability, children with, 91-92
  disabled facilities grants, 92
  eligibility for assistance, 373
  enforcement of rights, 392-393
  eviction, protection from, 367,
      382-383
  generally, 366
  homelessness,
    applicant considered as
        homeless, 372-373
    applicant eligible for housing
        assistance, 373
    challenging housing authority
        decisions about, 378
    conditions satisfied by
        applicant, 376-377
    entitlement of applicant, 376-377
    generally, 367, 371-372
    intentional, 375
    local connection, 375-376
    notification of decisions, 377
    priority need, 373-375
    review of decisions, 377
    threatened with, 372-373
  intentional homelessness, 375
  licensees,
    eviction, protection from, 383
    security of tenure, 378
  local connection, applicant with,
      375-376

Housing–*contd*
  materials, 396-398
  matrimonial home. *See*
      MATRIMONIAL HOME
  noise, local authority powers
      relating to, 384
  particular service users, 391-392
  repairs,
    common law, landlords'
        obligations at, 385-386
    generally, 368, 384-385
    landlords,
      common law, obligations at,
          385-386
      statutory responsibilities of,
          385
    local authority responsibilities,
        386-389
    statutory responsibilities of
        landlords, 385
  security of tenure,
    generally, 367, 378
    housing association tenants, 381
    licences, 378
    local authority tenants, 381-382
    private tenants, 379-381
    tenancies, 378
  social work role, 368
  squatters, 383-384
  threatened homelessness, 372-373
  unlawful eviction, 367, 382-383
  vulnerable service users, 374-375
Housing association tenants
  security of tenure, 381
Housing benefit
  challenging decision, 390
  eligibility, 389-390
  entitlement to, 368
  principles, 389

Ill-treatment
  meaning, 50
Illness
  care and after-care of ill, 147
  domiciliary care services for
      prevention of, 147
Incapacity benefit
  availability of, 322, 332-333
Income support
  aggregation, principle of, 327-328
  basic conditions for entitlement to,
      325-327
  child support and, 118

Income support–*contd*
claimants, 325
cohabitation, 327-328
disability premiums in, 97, 334
interpretation of legislation, 325
Indictable offences
nature of, 242
Individuals
civil disputes involving, 19
Industrial injuries benefits
availability of, 331
disablement benefit, 332
general conditions, 331-332
nature of benefits, 332
Information
services provided for service users,
on, 146-147
Interim order
care, 51-52
excluding alleged abuser, 59
exclusion requirements, 127
supervision, 51-52
Invalid care allowance
availability of, 97, 333-334
Investigation
court, ordered by, 54-55

Job seekers allowance
contributory benefit, 321
income based,
child support, 118
disabled child, relating to, 97
requirements relating to, 328-
329
Judicial review
community care, application
relating to, 159-161
disabled children, services for,
102-103
Judiciary
criminal justice system,
administration of, 17
decision making powers of, 1
influence of, 15-16
judicial law making, 14-15
Juries
criminal justice system,
administration of, 17

Landlords. *See* HOUSING
Language
civil justice system, of, 19, 21
criminal justice system, of, 17

Laundry services
social services authorities,
provision by, 147
Law
principles underpinning, 2-3
Law centres
functions of, 24
Lawyers
clients, relationship with, 3-4
common lawyers, as, 2
service users, attitude towards, 1
social workers, relationship with,
5-9
Learning disability. *See* MENTAL
HEALTH
Legal aid
assistance by way of representation
(ABWOR), 22-23
child as suspect, 281
civil, 23
criminal, 23-24
elements of scheme, 22
green form scheme, 22
legal advice and assistance, 22
Review of Civil Justice and Legal
Aid (1997), 26
young person as suspect, 281
Legal services
duty solicitor schemes, 24
law centres, 24
legal aid. *See* LEGAL AID
provision of, 22
service users, for, 25-26
Legal system
activities, 26-27
addresses, 27-28
binding precedent, system of, 15-
16
civil justice system,
civil courts, 21
civil disputes, 19
language of, 19, 21
content of chapter, 10-11
Court of Appeal. *See* COURT OF
APPEAL
criminal. *See* CRIMINAL JUSTICE
SYSTEM
directions, 12
generally, 10
guidance, 12-14
House of Lords. *See* HOUSE OF
LORDS
judicial law making, 14-15

Legal system–*contd*
  judiciary, influence of, 15-16
  legal aid. *See* LEGAL AID
  legal services, provision of, 22
  materials, 28
  official guidance, 16-17
  Parliament's legislative procedures,
    11-12
  secondary legislation, 12
  service users, legal services for, 25-
    26
  social work practice within, 1-5
  tribunals, 21
  youth justice. *See* YOUTH
    JUSTICE
Legal values and practice
  social work values and practice,
    tensions with, 5
Legislation
  date of implementation, 11-12
  judicial law making, 14-15
  Parliament's procedures, 11-12
  secondary, 12
Licences. *See* HOUSING
Local authorities
  accommodation provided by,
    child remanded to, 279-281
    children being looked after,
      duties relating to, 41
    disabled child, requirements of,
      85
    generally, 39-40
    objections to, 40
    removal from, 40
    secure, 43-44
    young person remanded to,
      279-281
  allocation of housing. *See*
    HOUSING
  anti-social behaviour, powers
    relating to, 384
  Children Act complaints
    procedure, 42-43
  children in care, tension with
    courts relating to, 66-68
  contact between children and
    family, 41-42
  council tax benefit, 390-391
  direct payments to community care
    service users, 151
  directions, 12
  discrimination, duties relating to,
    350

Local authorities–*contd*
  family, working in partnership
    with,
    care orders, 60-61
    issues for discussion, 60-61
  guidance, 13
  housing. *See* HOUSING
  information about services, 146-147
  law centre movement, funding of,
    24
  monitoring officer, complaint to,
    158
  noise, powers relating to, 384
  rehabilitation, principle of, 41-42
  repairs. *See* HOUSING
  secure accommodation, 43-44
  services for children and family,
    37-39
  tenants. *See* HOUSING
Local authority monitoring officer
  complaint to, 158
Local government
  civil disputes involving, 19
  ombudsman. *See*
    COMMISSIONER FOR
    LOCAL
    ADMINISTRATION
Lord Chancellor
  proposals of, 26
Lord Chancellor's Department
  law centre movement, funding of, 24
Lord Chief Justice
  responsibilities of, 21

MENCAP
  work of, 141
Magistrates' court
  criminal trial, 244-245
  matrimonial jurisdiction, 117-119
Magistrates' courts
  assistance by way of representation
    (ABWOR), 23
  binding precedent, system of, 15
  criminal justice system,
    administration of, 17
  criminal prosecutions, 17, 19
  decision making powers, 1
Maintenance
  child support, 118-119, 328
Management
  approved probation and bail
    hostels, of, 259-260
  property, of. *See* PROPERTY

Marriage
    magistrates' court, matrimonial
        jurisdiction of, 117-119
Master of Rolls
    responsibilities of, 21
Materials
    Children Act 1989, 76-77
    community care, 185-186
    criminal justice system, 272-273
    disability, children with, 108-109
    discrimination, 364-365
    family breakdown, 138-139
    housing, 396-398
    legal system, 28
    mental health, 237-238
    social security benefits, 344
    youth justice, 314
Maternity
    non-means tested benefits,
        maternity allowance (MA), 322
        statutory maternity pay (SMP),
        322
    services for expectant and nursing
        mothers, 147
Matrimonial home
    exclusion requirements, 127
    occupation orders, 125-127
Means test
    civil legal aid, relating to, 23
    criminal legal aid, relating to, 23
Mediation
    court welfare service, probation
        officers in, 119-120
    discussion of issues, 129-132
    divorce process, importance in,
        129-132
Medical treatment. *See* MENTAL
    HEALTH
Mens rea
    requirement of, 17
Mental disorder. *See* MENTAL
    HEALTH
Mental health
    Act of 1983, 189-191
    activities, 235
    addresses, 236-237
    admission,
        application for,
            assessment, 192
            generally, 192-193
        assessment, for, 195
        emergency, in, 193-194
        treatment, for, 195-196

Mental health–*contd*
    after-care services for patients, 148
    approved social worker, work of,
        191-196
    assessment,
        admission for, 195
        application for admission, 192
        remands for, 198-199
    care in community, 206-211, 212-
        215
    case studies, 230-234
    community, patients in, 150
    continuing powers of attorney,
        228
    Court of Protection,
        jurisdiction, 205-206
        new, 228
    discharge from hospital,
        generally, 203
        mental health review tribunals,
        203-204
    emergency,
        admission in, 193-194
        powers, 197
    financial affairs, 222-224
    generally, 187
    guardianship, 151-152, 196-197
    health care matters, 220-222
    hospital, discharge from,
        generally, 203
        Mental Health Review
        Tribunals, 203-204
    learning disability. *See* mental
        disorder, *below*
    management of property and
        affairs,
        attorney, power of, 153
        Court of Protection, 153-154
        enduring power of attorney,
        153
        generally, 152-153
        Public Trust Office, 153-154
    materials, 237-238
    medical treatment. *See* treatment,
        below
    mental disorder,
        admission,
            application for,
                 assessment, 192
                generally, 192-193
            assessment, for, 195
            emergency, in, 193-195
            treatment, for, 195-196

Mental health–*contd*
mental disorder–*contd*
approved social worker, work
of, 191-196
assessment,
admission for, 195
application for admission,
192
remands for, 198-199
black patients, 211-212
care in community, 206-211,
212-215
civil rights of patient, 200
Court of Protection, 205-206
criminal justice system,
detention, 198
generally, 197-198
insanity, 199-200
questioning, 198
remands for assessment and
treatment, 198-199
sentencing mentally dis-
ordered offenders,
199
suspects, 198
treatment, remands for,
198-199
unfitness to plead, 199-200
discharge from hospital,
generally, 203
mental health review
tribunals, 203-204
emergency,
admission in, 193-194
powers, 197
generally, 187-188
guardianship, 196-197
Mental Health Act 1983, 189-
191
Mental Health Act
Commission, 205
mental impairment, meaning,
189
minority ethnic patients, 211-
212
psychiatric and social services,
organisation of, 215-
218
psychopathic disorder,
meaning, 189
reform of law, 215-218
severe mental impairment,
meaning, 189

Mental health–*contd*
mental disorder–*contd*
treatment,
admission for, 195-196
generally, 201-202
remands for, 198-199
voluntary patients, 191
Mental Health Act Commission,
205
mental impairment,
meaning, 189
severe, meaning, 189
mental incapacity,
best interests, incapacity and,
226-227
continuing powers of attorney,
228
current legal structure, 220-225
definitions, 218-220
financial affairs, 222-224
general authority to act
reasonably, 227
generally, 218, 229-230
harm, meaning, 229
health care matters, 220-222
medical treatment, 220-222
new Court of Protection, 228
personal care, 220-222
personal welfare, 224-225
property affairs, 222-224
public law protection for
vulnerable people at
risk, 228-229
reform of law, 225-229
vulnerable people,
harm, meaning, 229
meaning, 228
public law protection, 228-
229
mentally disordered offenders,
after-care services for, 148
personal care, 220-222
property affairs, 222-224
psychopathic disorder, meaning,
189
sentencing mentally disordered
offenders, 199
severe mental impairment,
meaning, 189
treatment,
admission for, 195-196
current legal structure, 220-222
remands for, 198-199

Mental health–*contd*
  voluntary patients, 191
  vulnerable service users, 176-177
Mental health review tribunal
  assistance by way of representation
    (ABWOR), 23
  discharge from hospital, 203–204
Mental incapacity. *See* MENTAL
    HEALTH
Merits test
  civil legal aid, relating to, 23
Monitoring
  local authority monitoring officer,
    complaint to, 158

National Assistance Act 1948
  magistrates' court, application to, 4
National Council on Employment of
    People with Disabilities
  functions of, 350
National Disability Council
  functions of, 350
Noise
  local authority, powers of, 384
Non-molestation orders
  application for, 124-125
  arrest, power of, 125
  associated person, meaning, 124-
    125
  children, application by, 125
  ex parte, 124
  molestation, meaning, 123

Occupation order
  arrest, powers of, 127
  court's power to make, 125-127
Offences
  criminal. *See* CRIMINAL JUSTICE
    SYSTEM
  either way, 241-242
  indictable, 242
  racially motivated, 350-353
  summary, 241
Old people
  elder abuse, 175-176
  welfare, promotion of, 146
Orders
  care. *See* CARE ORDER
  child assessment, 56
  contact. *See* CONTACT ORDER
  emergency protection. *See*
    EMERGENCY
    PROTECTION ORDER

Orders–*contd*
  finance, 115-116
  interim, 51-52
  non-molestation, 123-125
  occupation, 125-127
  property, 115
  residence. *See* RESIDENCE
    ORDER
  section 8. *See* SECTION 8
    ORDERS
  specific issue. *See* SPECIFIC ISSUE
    ORDER
  supervision. *See* SUPERVISION
    ORDER

Parental responsibility
  acquisition of, 44-45
  allocation of, 44-45
  concept of, 36
  continuing responsibility, as, 45
  meaning, 36
  statistics, 64
Parliament
  legislative procedures, 11-12
Parole Board
  assistance by way of representation
    (ABWOR), 23
Partnership
  local authority and family,
    between, 60-61
  principle of, 60
Pensions
  retirement, 323-324
  State Earnings Related Pension
    Scheme (SERPS), 324
Petition
  divorce, 113
Place of safety order
  mental incapacity, person with,
    224
  number of applications, 64
Police
  child at risk, powers relating to,
    59-60
  criminal justice system,
    administration of, 17
  duty solicitor schemes, 24
Pre-sentence report
  criminal justice system, 260-262,
    252-253
  youth justice, 284-285, 294
Premiums
  entitlement to, 328

Private tenants
  security of tenure, 379-381
Probation officers
  mediation, 119-120
  reports, 119
Probation order
  additional requirements included
    in, 251
  conditions for making, 251, 257-
    258
  objectives of, 258
  youth justice, 292-293
Probation service
  criminal justice system,
    administration of, 17
  criminal justice work of,
    combination orders, 258-259
    community service orders, 258
    generally, 255-257
    management of approved
      probation and bail
      hostels, 259-260
    probation orders, 257-258
    supervision before and after
      release from custody,
      260
    supervision orders, 259
  management of approved
    probation and bail hostels,
    259-260
Prohibited steps order
  figures for, 64
  nature of, 46
Property
  divorce, orders on, 115
  management for those unable to
    do so themselves,
    attorney, power of, 153
    Court of Protection, 153-154
    enduring power of attorney, 153
    generally, 152-153
    Public Trust Office, 153-154
    mental disorder, affairs of person
      with, 222-224
  See also HOUSING
Protection of child. See CHILD
  PROTECTION
Psychopathic disorder
  meaning, 189
Public bodies
  civil disputes involving, 19
Public order
  racially motivated crimes, 350-353

PublicTrust Office
  powers of, 153-154

Queen's Bench Division
  specialist jurisdiction, 21
Questioning
  mental disorder, people with, 198

Racial discrimination. See
  DISCRIMINATION
Racial hatred
  meaning, 351
Racial violence
  government proposals, 267-268,
    358-359
Reform
  child care law, 31-32
  community care, 141-143, 177-
    179
  criminal justice system, 239-240,
    262-265
  divorce law, 128-129
  mental health law, 215-218, 225-
    229
  separation, law of, 128-129
  youth justice system, 301-309
Regulations
  Children Act 1989, under, 33
Rehabilitation
  children and family, between, 41-
    42
Relationship breakdown. See FAMILY
  BREAKDOWN
Remedies
  community care service users, for,
    breach of statutory duty, 161
    complaints, 156-157
    default powers, 157
    judicial review, applications
      for, 159-161
    local authority monitoring
      officer, complaint to,
      158
    local government ombudsman,
      complaint to, 158-159
    statutory duty, breach of, 161
  disabled children, services for, 99
Repairs. See HOUSING
Report
  court welfare service, probation
    officers in, 119
  pre-sentence. See PRE-SENTENCE
    REPORT

Residence order
divorce, relating to, 116
figures for, 64
nature of, 46
Residential care homes
code of guidance, 170
inspection of, 168-169
positive role of, 167-168
registration of, 168
regulation of, 169
small, 169
Wagner Report, 167-168
Resources
community care services, 162-165
disabled children, services for, 98-99
Retirement pensions
payment of, 323-324
Reviews
child protection, 63
Royal Association for Disability and
Rehabilitation (RADAR)
work of, 141

Secondary legislation
nature of, 12
Secretary of State
default powers, 157
Section 8 orders
availability of, 47-48
contact order,
basic legal principle, 45-46
number of applications, 64
generally, 45
prohibited steps order, 46
residence order, 46
specific issue order, 47
Secure accommodation
child accommodated by local
authority in, 43-44
Secure training orders
persistent young offenders, 295-296
Security of tenure. *See* HOUSING
Sentencing
absolute discharges, 249
community sentences,
attendance centre order, 252
combination order, 252
community service, 251
curfew orders, 252
enforcement, 253
pre-sentence reports, 252-253
probation, 251

Sentencing–*contd*
community sentences–*contd*
revoking, 253
youth justice,
attendance centre orders,
291-292
combination order, 293
community service orders,
292
curfew order (not yet in
force), 293-294
generally, 289
National Standards, 294
probation, 292-293
reports, 294
supervision orders, 289-291
conditional discharges, 249
criminal courts,
community sentences,
attendance centre order,
252
combination order, 252
community service, 251
curfew orders, 252
enforcement, 253
pre-sentence reports, 252-253
probation, 251
revoking, 253
custodial sentences, 253-255
discharges,
absolute, 249
conditional, 249
financial penalties,
compensation orders, 250-251
fines, 249-250
maximum powers of, 19
principles in, 246-249
custodial sentences, 253-255, 294-295
financial penalties,
compensation orders, 250-251,
288-289
fines, 249-250, 288
mentally disordered offenders, 199
youth offenders,
binding over, 287
community sentences,
attendance centre orders,
291-292
combination order, 293
community service orders,
292

Sentencing–*contd*
  youth offenders–*contd*
    community sentences–contd
      curfew order (not yet in
        force), 293-294
      generally, 289
      National Standards, 294
      probation, 292-293
      reports, 294
      supervision orders, 289-
        291
    compensation order, 288-289
    custody,
      Crown Court, 295
      generally, 294-295
      youth court, 295
    discharges, 288
    fines, 288
    generally, 285-287
    range of sentences, 288-296
    secure training orders (not yet
      in force), 295-296
Separation
  discussion of issues, 128-129
  reforming law of, 128-129
Service users
  community care. *See*
    COMMUNITY CARE
  housing. *See* HOUSING
  identification of, 145-146
  lawyers' attitude towards, 1
  legal services for, 25-26
  social workers, relationship with,
    3-4
  vulnerable. *See* VULNERABLE
    SERVICE USERS
Services
  children with disability, provision
    for,
      Commissioner for Local
        Administration, 101-102
      complaints procedures, 99-100
      judicial review, 102-103
      provision of, 84-85
      quality of service delivery, 104-
        105
      remedies, 99
      resources, 98-99
      rights to, 98-103
      tribunals, 100-101
    mental health, 92-93
Severe disablement allowance
  availability of, 97, 333

Severe mental impairment
  meaning, 189
Sickness benefits. *See* SOCIAL
    SECURITY BENEFITS
Significant
  meaning, 50
Social fund
  budgeting loans, 155, 330
  challenging decision, 331
  community care grants, 155, 329-
    330
  crisis loans, 155, 330
  directions, 330-331
  generally, 329
  guidance, 330-331
  issues for discussion, 335-338
Social security benefits
  adjudication structure, 320
  benefits acting as passports to
    other benefits, 319
  budgeting loans, 155, 330
  community care grants, 155, 329-
    330
  community care service users, 155
  contributory benefits, 318-319
  crisis loans, 155, 330
  disability, children with,
    disability living allowance, 95-
      97
    generally, 94-95
    income support, 97
    invalid care allowance, 97
    job seekers (income based)
      benefit, 97
    severe disablement allowance,
      97
  disability benefits,
    attendance allowance, 333
    availability of, 332
    character of, 334-335
    disability living allowance, 95-
      97, 333
    disability premiums in income
      support, 334
    disability working allowance,
      333
    incapacity benefit, 332-333
    income support, disability
      premiums in, 334
    invalid care allowance, 333-
      334
    severe disablement allowance,
      333

Social security benefits–*contd*
  enforcing rights, 338-339
  generally, 320-321
  housing benefit. *See* HOUSING
    BENEFIT
  income support. *See* INCOME
    SUPPORT
  industrial injuries benefits,
    disablement benefit, 332
    general conditions, 331-332
    generally, 319, 331
  invalid care allowance, 97
  job seekers allowance,
    contributory benefit, 321
    income based, 97, 328-329
  materials, 318
  means-tested benefits,
    budgeting loans, 330
    community care grants, 329-330
    crisis loans, 330
    family credit, 324-325
    generally, 319, 324
    income based job seekers
      allowance, 328-329
    income support, 325-328
    maintenance and child support,
      328
    premiums, 328
    social fund, 329-331
  non-contributory benefits, 318-319
  non-means-tested benefits,
    child benefit, 322-323
    generally, 319
    incapacity benefit, 322
    job seekers allowance
      (contributory benefit),
      321
    maternity allowance, 322
    maternity benefits, 322
    retirement pensions, 323-324
    short term sickness and
      disability benefits, 321-
      322
    State Earnings Related Pension
      Scheme (SERPS), 324
    statutory maternity pay, 322
    statutory sick pay, 321-322
    widows' benefits, 323
  severe disablement allowance, 97
  social fund. *See* SOCIAL FUND
  social security law, 319-320
  social security system, 316-317
  time limits for claims, 320

Social services departments
  disabled children, provision of
    integrated services for, 80-81
Social work
  practice within English law and
    legal system, 1-5
  values and practice, tensions with
    legal values and practice, 5
Social workers
  court based social work,
    care order, application for, 4
    education supervision order,
      application for, 4
    emergency protection order,
      application for, 4
    guardian ad litem, role of, 4
    involvement in, 4
    National Assistance Act 1948,
      application under, 4
    pre-sentence report,
      preparation of, 4
  involvement in court based work, 4
  lawyers, relationship with, 5-9
  professional ease with law, 1-2
  service users, relationship with, 3-4
Solicitors
  duty solicitor schemes, 24
  regional directories, 25
Special educational needs
  children with, 88-91
  tribunals, 101
Specific issue order
  nature of, 47
Squatters
  occupation of property, 383-384
Statistics
  Children Act 1989, applications
    under, 64
Statutory sick pay (SSP)
  availability of, 321-322
Summary offences
  nature of, 241
Supervision order
  administration, 53
  availability of, 48-49
  discharge of, 54
  divorce proceedings, 116-117
  education, 4, 54
  grounds for grant of, 49-50, 53
  interim order, 51-52
  probation service, work of, 259
  who may apply, 49
  youth justice, 289-291

Suspect
child as,
bail, 279-282
custody, remand to, 279-281
generally, 278-279
legal aid, 281
local authority
accommodation, remand
to, 279-281
mental disorder, person with, 198
young person as,
bail, 279-281
custody, remand to, 279-281
generally, 278-279
legal aid, 281
local authority
accommodation, remand
to, 279-281

Tenants. See HOUSING
Treatment. See MENTAL HEALTH
Trial
criminal. See CRIMINAL JUSTICE
SYSTEM
Tribunals
child support appeal tribunal, 119
disabled children, services for,
100-101
functions of, 21
mental health review tribunals,
203-204
special educational needs, 101

Violence
domestic. See DOMESTIC
VIOLENCE
racial, 267-268
Vulnerable service users
community care law, 172-173
elder abuse, 175-176
generally, 170-172
harm, meaning, 229
mental health law, 176-177
personal welfare, 173-175
public law protection, 228-229
recognition of rights and interests
of, 171
vulnerability, meaning, 170-171
vulnerable person, meaning, 228
Welfare
children, of,
checklist, 35-36
principle(s), 34-35

Welfare–contd
old people, of, 146
vulnerable service users, of, 173-
175
Welfare service. See COURT
WELFARE SERVICE
Widows' benefits
payment of, 323

Young person
interaction between lawyers and
social workers, 6
Youth court
attendance at, 283
custody by, 295
jurisdiction of, 282-283, 299-300
magistrates, 283
pre-sentence reports, 284-285
proceedings, 283-284
structure, 315
Youth justice
activities, 311-313
addresses, 313
appeals, 296
case studies, 309-311
cautioning of youth offenders,
296-299
Children Act 1989, under, 33
court structure, 315
court. See YOUTH COURT
law, generally, 277
materials, 314
model for, 275-276
politics of, 275
principles of Criminal Justice Act
1991, 277
reform of system, 301-309
sentencing youth offenders,
appeals, 296
binding over, 287
community sentences,
attendance centre orders,
291-292
combination order, 293
community service orders,
292
curfew order (not yet in
force), 293-294
generally, 289
National Standards, 294
probation, 292-293
reports, 294
supervision orders, 289-291

Youth justice–*contd*
  sentencing youth offenders–*contd*
    compensation order, 288-289
    custody,
      Crown Court, 295
      generally, 294-295
      youth court, 295
    discharges, 288
    fines, 288
    generally, 285-287
    range of sentences, 288-296
    secure training orders (not yet
      in force), 295-296

Youth justice–*contd*
  social work involvement in, 274-
    275
  suspect, child or young person as,
    bail, 279-281
    custody, remand to, 279-281
    generally, 278-279
    legal aid, 281
    local authority
      accommodation, remand
      to, 279-281
  youth court. *See* YOUTH COURT